The Host Gaze in Global Tourism

... in the land of mediocrity knowledge is a handicap ...
... and the bully has proven nothing but his support for mediocrity.

The Host Gaze in Global Tourism

Edited by

Omar Moufakkir

*Groupe Sup de Co La Rochelle,
La Rochelle Business School of Tourism, France*

and

Yvette Reisinger

James Cook University, Singapore

www.cabi.org

CABI is a trading name of CAB International

CABI
Nosworthy Way
Wallingford
Oxfordshire OX10 8DE
UK

CABI
38 Chauncey Street
Suite 1002
Boston, MA 02111
USA

Tel: +44 (0)1491 832111
Fax: +44 (0)1491 833508
E-mail: info@cabi.org
Website: www.cabi.org

Tel: +1 800 552 3083 (toll free)
Tel: +1(0) 617 395 4051
E-mail: cabi-nao@cabi.org

A catalogue record for this book is available from the British Library, London, UK.

Library of Congress Cataloging-in-Publication Data
The host gaze in global tourism / edited by Omar Moufakkir and Yvette Reisinger.
  p. cm.
 Includes bibliographical references and index.
  ISBN 978-1-78064-021-1 (hardback)
 1. Tourism--Psychological aspects. 2. Culture and tourism. 3. Culture and globalization. I. Moufakkir, Omar. II. Reisinger, Yvette.

 G155.A1H665 2013
 338.4'791--dc23

2012026678

ISBN-13: 978 1 78064 021 1

Commissioning editor: Claire Parfitt
Editorial assistant: Emma McCann
Production editor: Simon Hill

Typeset by AMA DataSet, Preston, UK.
Printed and bound in the UK by the MPG Books Group

Contents

Editors and Contributors

Editors

Professor **Omar Moufakkir** is director of the Tourism Management Institute, Groupe Sup de Co La Rochelle, La Rochelle, France. He was educated in Morocco, France, the Netherlands and the USA, where he earned a PhD in park, recreation and tourism resources at Michigan State University. He has published about gaming development, and more recently on tourism and peace. His research interests centre around the impact of immigration-integration on travel propensity and destination choice. He is the founder of the International Center for Peace through Tourism Research, and editor of *The Journal of Tourism and Peace Research*, an open access journal (www.icptr.com). Omar serves on the advisory board of *Tourist Studies*, and is on the editorial board of the *Journal of Heritage Tourism*. He is also policy adviser to the European Network of Places of Peace, and a founding member of the Network of Expert Researchers on Arab Tourism. omar.moufakkir@gmail.com.

Yvette Reisinger is an adjunct professor of business at James Cook University, Singapore. She has a PhD in tourism marketing from Victoria University, Australia. Her research mainly focuses on cultural influences on tourist behaviour, and communication and destination marketing. She is the author of three books and 140 papers on cross-cultural behaviour in international tourism. She received research awards for her work on cultural differences among Asian tourist markets. She has a wide spectrum of professional and personal experience spanning across Australia, Europe, the USA and Asia. yvette.reisinger@gmail.com.

Contributors

Jo Ankor is a research associate in the Department of Tourism, Flinders University, South Australia. As research associate, Jo continues to explore cross-disciplinary research in travel, creative practice, philosophy, cultural studies and tourism. She has a particular interest in research methodologies that allow expression of the complex experiences of travel. drjoankor@gmail.com.

Alexis Celeste Bunten is a senior researcher for the FrameWorks Institute and the project ethnographer for Intellectual Property Issues in Cultural Heritage (IPinCH) at Simon Fraser University. With degrees in art history and anthropology, Dr Bunten's areas of expertise include the heritage industry, cultural production, interpretation, cross-cultural communication, community development and the anthropology of work. abunten@gmail.com.

Bonnie Canziani is an associate professor in hospitality and tourism at the University of North Carolina Greensboro. She focuses on research in cultural issues in hospitality and tourism, services management, and evaluation and assessment. bmcanzia@uncg.edu.

Noga Collins-Kreiner is a senior lecturer (PhD), in the Department of Geography and Environmental Studies at the University of Haifa, Israel, and a member of the Center for Tourism, Pilgrimage and Recreation Research at the University of Haifa, Israel. Her main research interests are: religious tourism, pilgrimage and tourism development and management. she is also a resource editor of the *Annals of Tourism Research* and has published many papers on the topic of tourism, and especially religious tourism and pilgrimage. nogach@geo.haifa.ac.il.

Jennifer Francioni is a graduate student at the University of North Carolina Greensboro in the area of travel and tourism. She was formerly associated with the North Carolina Division of Tourism, Film and Sports Development.

Alon Gelbman is a senior lecturer in the Department of Tourism and Hotel Management at Kinneret College on the Sea of Galilee, Israel. He is a cultural geographer and his research interests include international tourism and geopolitical borders, tourism and peace, urban/rural tourism, host–guest relationships and wellness tourism. His research papers have been published in leading scientific journals. He has participated in more than 20 international scientific conferences and visited more than 50 different countries around the globe. Dr Gelbman is also an associate editor of *The Journal of Tourism and Peace Research* and a reviewer for various scientific journals in the field of tourism. alongelbman@013.net.

Ulrike Gretzel is an associate professor of marketing at the University of Wollongong, Australia. She received her PhD in communication from the University of Illinois in Urbana-Champaign, USA. Her research focuses on understanding emotional and sensory components of tourism experiences and the use and design of intelligent systems in tourism. ugretzel@uow.edu.au.

Keith Hollinshead is a transdisciplinary/adisciplinary commentator on representations of culture, nature and heritage, researching the 'visioning' of the world through tourism. Having worked in Wales, the USA and (mainly) Australia, he inspects the symbolic repertoires of organizations/interest groups using tourism for psychic/political advantage. With particular interests in Indigenous cosmologies, he explores the long-time inheritances of populations that are versioned through tourism. A distinguished professor of the International Tourism Studies Association (Peking University: China), and former vice president (international tourism) of the International Sociological Association, Keith functions as critical reviews editor for *Tourism Analysis* and *Tourism, Culture and Communication*. Currently, his research explores world-making authority and the fantasmatics of peoples, places, pasts. He is professor of public culture – the University of Bedfordshire (UK). khdeva@ptopenworld.com.

Petri Hottola is a professor of cultural geography in the Department of Geography, University of Oulu, Finland. He has previously been a professor of tourism and intercultural studies in the Finnish University Network for Tourism Studies (FUNTS), University of Eastern Finland. He is also a member of the Association for Tourism and Leisure Education (ATLAS) executive board, the ATLAS Independent Travel Research Group and the

International Geographical Union (IGU) Commission on the Geography of Tourism, Leisure and Global Change. petri.hottola@oulu.fi.

Chunxiao Hou is a post-disciplinary thinker on national and cultural representations of the world, notably of media and special interest persuasions. Born in Xinjiang (north-west China), Dr Hou is well experienced in the civilities of Xian and Beijing, and regularly explores how 'China' is understood/misunderstood 'abroad'. Obtaining an MSc in environmental tourism in the UK, Dr Hou has stayed in Europe to inspect the inscriptive power of performative fields like tourism. She has an abiding interest in East–West relationships, and in 'soft power' articulations of peoples and places. Currently, Chunxiao is an independent researcher connected to the University of Bedfordshire (UK), and examines the gaps in understanding between the longstanding philosophical orientations of Asia and those of Europe and North America.

Metin Kozak is a professor of tourism in the School of Tourism and Hospitality Management, Mugla University, Mugla, Turkey. He holds both Master's and PhD degrees in tourism management. His research focuses on consumer behaviour, benchmarking, destination management and marketing, and Mediterranean tourism. He acts as the co-editor of *Anatolia: An International Journal of Tourism and Hospitality Research*. M.Kozak@ superonline.com.

Vannsy Kuon was a lecturer at the Royal University of Phnom Penh, Cambodia. He has acquired experience in tourism and tourism studies before joining the University of Bedfordshire, where he is undertaking a PhD in tourism. He is examining the representation of the cultural gene bank of Cambodia, where tourism is of vital importance to the nation's economic, social and political life. As part of his research agenda, Vannsy is particularly exploring the axialities and the agency of tourism in the discursive formation, projection and articulation of the present-day Cambodia. vannsykuon@yahoo.com.

Yoon Jung Lee is a lecturer at Kyonggi University, Korea. She earned her doctorate in tourism from Texas A&M University and holds a Master's degree in political science from the State University of New York at Stony Brook. Her research focuses on religious tourism, host–tourist interaction, volunteer tourism and cultural adaptation. mesalina78@ gmail.com.

Ian A. Morrison is a lecturer in the Department of Sociology, Trent University (Toronto, Canada) and the contemporary studies programme, Wilfrid Laurier University (Toronto, Canada). His research involves investigation of the constitution of self and other in discourses of citizenship, religion and nationality. morrison.iananthony@gmail.com.

Michael O'Regan completed a two-year research Master's degree in business studies at the University of Limerick, Ireland in 1997. He has worked alongside the National Tourism Development Authority of Ireland; Gulliver – Ireland's Information and Reservation Service; and as marketing executive for Wicklow County Tourism, Ireland before starting a PhD programme at the Centre for Tourism Policy Studies (CENTOPS), School of Service Management, University of Brighton, UK, which he completed in 2011. He is currently a senior lecturer in tourism at Dongbei University of Finance and Economics (Dalian, PR China). His current research interests include tourist-, urban-, historic-, future-, slow-, cultural- and backpacker mobilities, which follow on from his PhD, which was entitled 'Backpacker mobilities: the practice and performance of travellerscapes in a global world'. michael.oregan@gmail.com.

Helen Pattison was recently awarded her doctorate on 'Becoming a "host" in Gambian tourism spaces' from Lancaster University, UK. Her research interests centre on the politics of non-Western host identity, agency and power and the use of visual methodology and methods. Helen is currently a research assistant at Northumbria University, Newcastle-Upon-Tyne, UK. pattison.h@gmail.com.

Philip Pearce is the foundation professor of tourism, James Cook University, Australia. He is fundamentally interested in the behaviour and experience of tourists. philip.pearce@jcu.edu.au.

Amy Savener is a doctoral student and instructor in the Department of Geography at Indiana University, USA studying cultural tourism. She has a Master's degree in planning from the University of Cincinnati, USA. Her thesis was a tourism feasibility plan for Barahona, Dominican Republic, when the international airport was under construction. amymgray@umail.iu.edu.

Thomas Ugelvik is a post-doctoral research fellow in the Department of Criminology and Sociology of Law at the University of Oslo. His main research interest is in prisons and other places of incarceration, and he is currently working on an ethnographic study of state power with a particular focus on immigration detention. His research interests also include crime and globalization, crime and the media, and crime and gender. thomas.ugelvik@jus.uio.no.

Esmé Visser is a cultural anthropologist who graduated from the University of Groningen (the Netherlands) in 2008 with a Master's degree in eastern European studies and a thesis on holiday behaviour of Russian tourists.

Stephen Wearing is an associate professor in the School of Leisure, Sport and Tourism, University of Technology Sydney, Australia. Stephen's research falls into the social sciences areas with a specialization in the social and cultural dimensions and impacts on self-identity and community development through global travel. He has authored seminal contributions to the critical tourism, leisure and ecotourism fields, which have provided path-blazing links within and between these areas of study. stephen.wearing@uts.edu.au.

Mao-Ying Wu is a PhD candidate in tourism at James Cook University, Australia. She is interested in tourism community studies and research methodologies. maoying.wu@gmail.com.

Introduction: Gazemaking: Le Regard – Do You Hear Me?

Omar Moufakkir and Yvette Reisinger

Introduction

This book is based on the notion that analysis similar to that of the tourist gaze (Urry, 1990, 2002) can be applied to the host gaze. We can use our understanding of the gaze to make sense of the wider society. In Urry's words, to consider how host communities construct their gaze upon tourists is a 'good way of getting at just what is happening in the "normal society"' (Urry, 2002, p. 2). We gaze at what we encounter, and this gaze is socially and culturally organized (Foucault, [1963] 1973). The concept of Foucault's medical gaze can help us to grasp tiny anomalies in our globalized world. For the purpose of this book, the gaze of the medic can help us to gaze systematically upon the gazes of the host. The host gaze involves looking at the host–guest encounter with interest and curiosity. There is the gaze of the gazer and the gaze of the gazee or the object of the initial gaze. Both gazes are subject to change with changing economic, demographic, social, political, cultural and other societal phenomena (MacCannell, 2001; Urry, 2002). Just as the tourist gaze is dynamic (Urry, 2002), the host gaze is also changing, depending on who is the tourist and who is the host (Moufakkir, 2011). Just as there is no single tourist gaze, the host gaze must also vary by society, social group

and historical period. Host gazes are constructed through cultural similarities and dissimilarities (Moufakkir, 2011). Surely, there must be different gazes from the same gazer upon different gazees. Thus, to speak of a 'general gaze' (Foucault, [1963] 1973, p. 156) would be not only confusing but also misleading.

The purpose of this volume is to cover at least a few aspects of the host gaze: How is the host gaze constructed and reinforced? How has it changed and developed? How does the host gaze vary? What are its consequences for the tourists who are its object? What are the aspects of the host gaze that distinguish it from the tourist gaze and from conventional gazes encountered in everyday life? What determines the host gaze? Are there any pre-existing cultural images of the host gaze? How do hosts gaze upon or view different tourists? How do different nations construct their host gazes? What are the differences in the host gaze across regions and nations? What are the sociocultural and economic aspects of the host gazes? What are the elements of the host gaze in the changing global economy of the tourism industry? How do the tourism development and its particular industries/sectors influence the host gaze? What helps in constructing and developing our gaze as hosts? How is the host gaze constructed and reinforced? What are the consequences of this gaze for the places that are its object and tourists who are its subject? These and questions similar to those concerning the tourist gaze have partially been addressed in this volume.

It is thus hoped that this compilation of host gaze cases and theoretical perspectives will stir up a new wave of host gaze studies. Such an endeavour can lead us to move on from the 'conventional gaze' (MacCannell, 2001; Urry, 2002) or the obvious in host–guest encounters (Moufakkir, 2011) towards a decortication and deconstruction of the gaze in tourism. A critical analysis can shed more light not only on 'gazemaking' in tourism but also on the making of the world.

The gaze

> One of the characteristics of Foucault's language is his repeated use of certain key words. Many of these present no difficulty to the translator. Others, however, have no normal equivalent... I have used the unusual 'gaze' for the common 'regard'. (Foucault, [1963] 1973, A.S. Sheridan, translator's note, p. vii.)

It is common for those who speak French to use 'voir' and 'regarder' interchangeably for the English words 'to look' or 'to see'. However, there is a degree of confusion but also a sense of consciousness about the proper use of both terms. For example, a Google search for 'difference entre voir et regarder' (difference between voir and regarder) resulted in 13,200,000 entries. The richness of the found synonyms attests to the difficulty of defining the term 'le regard' and the complexity of using it. Le regard has about 27 synonyms. Generally, dictionaries agree on defining the English gaze as an intentional and steady look at something that excites admiration, curiosity or interest.

Definitions of the gaze do not capture its complexity. For a proper understanding of the gaze, its utility and usage, one has to, naturally, immerse oneself in Foucault's *The Birth of the Clinic*. His gaze takes place in the clinic, a place where the medic looks at the solid and visible body of the patient

with insistence and penetration. Since the patient's illness is articulated on the body, a passive gaze, he says, only reduces illness to what is visible. Yet, what is visible is only the symptoms of what is invisible to the eye. Foucault explains:

> the strange character of the medical gaze; it is caught up in an endless reciprocity. It is directed upon that which is visible in the disease – but on the basis of the patient, who hides this visible element even as he shows it; consequently, in order to know, he must recognize, while already being in possession of the knowledge that will lend support to this recognition. And as it moves forward, this gaze is really retreating, since it reaches the truth of the disease only by allowing it to win the struggle and to fulfil, in all its phenomena, its true nature. (Foucault, [1963] 1973, p. 9.)

The nature of a disease is manifested in its apparent symptoms; its true nature, however, is hidden in the invisible, which is there to be dug out and brought to the surface to decipher for a better diagnosis. It is this depth of perceptual exploration that makes the gaze an agent of epidermic discovery. This discovery of the "invisible visibility" (p. 204) represents the triumph of the gaze. A revealing and transparent gaze conducting the autopsy to uncover the hidden content of the disease denudes the disease by removing the layers of opacity that lead to confusion around its diagnosis. While Foucault talks about the patient in a clinic, social theorists have adopted the analogy of the clinical gaze to explain other societal phenomena. Ours is encounters in tourism, analogous to a medical examination of host gaze encounters through the gaze. Like the gaze of the medic, ours is that of the tourism academic, which has been cast upon tourism environments with a particular interest in understanding why host communities gaze. The analogy between the clinic and the tourism environment lends a closer look at tourist–guest encounters, similar to that of the medic. After all, our prognoses could even be helpful in curing certain gaze pathologies, preventing some from taking root, and developing, prescribing and promoting cures for a healthier tourism.

This book is about host–guest encounters in tourism; 'it is about the act of seeing, the gaze' (Foucault, [1963] 1973), gazers gazing at the gaze of the host community gazing at tourists. It is about anatomy of the host gaze. This anatomy discloses the gaze of the host, making it open to the academic, the host and the tourist. In other words, the host gaze opens up the space of host–guest encounters to the gaze of the tourism academic, who can see beyond the symptoms of the gaze – the constructed gaze of the gazer and gazee, and analyse the gaze of the gazer host in order to hear what that particular gaze is about. The clinical gaze recognizes that signs and symptoms are of different orders. The tourism academic gaze recognizes that as there are multiple tourism environments, tourism histories, types of tourists and host communities, there are, too, multiple perceptions and subsequently different gazes. This book presents case studies on the host gaze from Thailand, Panama, Turkey, Israel, Gambia, Tibet and the Netherlands. This limitation underscores the complexity of host gaze studies and their popularity.

Host gaze studies

Studies of the host gaze in tourism have just begun to describe tourism encounters that have for a long time remained at the threshold of the visible and expressible in host–guest relations. As the medical gaze needs to become attentive to the construction of the gaze, so must the academic gaze. The purpose of this volume is to bring depth to perceptual explorations that have resulted from resident attitude surveys. Host gaze studies have been confused with residents' attitudes surveys, where locals' perceptions are quantified, and simplistically (though not simplified) examined. Not to say that such analyses of resident opinions have no merit, but by analogy to Foucaults' gaze, perception studies tend to reduce the reality of the gaze to what is visible; yet we know that what is visible is not the whole truth, for, as Foucault explains: 'The eye becomes the depository and source of clarity; it has the power to bring a truth to light that it receives only to the extent that it has brought it to light; as it opens, the eye first opens the truth' (Foucault, [1963] 1973, p. xiii).

Furthermore, the gaze in tourism has been criticized on many fronts (Holloway *et al.*, 2011). It has been, for example, critiqued as being gendered (MacCannell and MacCannell, 2001), limited to the visual (Chambers, 2007) or myopic (Moufakkir, 2011). Academics who have specifically written about the host gaze in tourism (e.g. Chan, 2006; Maoz, 2006; Moufakkir, 2011) agree about the limited literature on the host gaze compared with that of the tourist gaze. That is, despite a few attempts to deconstruct the host gaze *a la Foucault*, the host gaze in tourism remains covered by resident's attitudes surveys; whereas a gaze study *a la Foucault* must go beyond the hows to uncover the whys of attitudes and perceptions. Taking the example of Foucault's Pomme and Bayle, the host gaze starts where perceptions surveys stop:

> Between Pomme, who carried the old myths of nervous pathology to their ultimate form, and Bayle, who described the encephalic lesions of general paralysis for an era from which we have not yet emerged, the difference is both tiny and total. For us, it is total, because each of Bayle's words, with its qualitative precision, directs our gaze into a world of constant visibility, while Pomme, lacking any perceptual base, speaks to us in the language of fantasy. But by what fundamental experience can we establish such an obvious difference below the level of our certainties, in that region from which they emerge? How can we be sure that an eighteenth-century doctor did not see what he saw, but that it needed several decades before the fantastic figures were dissipated to reveal, in the space they vacated, the shapes of lungs as they really are? (Foucault, [1963] 1973, p. xi.)

Analogically, gaze studies need not be preoccupied with the surface of the gaze, a gaze that is 'passive' and 'reductive' (Foucault, [1963] 1973). The medical gaze, Foucault asserts needs to become attentive to the construction of the gaze. Bayle made the gaze legible to the gazer and object of the gaze through his 'meticulous', 'constant', 'anatomical', 'penetrating' and 'revealing gaze' (Foucault, [1963] 1973), an invitation that has also challenged the contributing authors of this book. Many phenomena, even when deciphered, still remain at the threshold of the visible and expressible in host–guest encounters.

By gazing at the gaze of the gazer upon the gazee, new theories must arise for several reasons. First, most of the social and cultural theories of tourism have been developed from the experiences of Western tourists and consequently some may not be directly applicable to non-Western tourists, such as the Asian, the African or the Middle Eastern. Second, most theories of tourism encounters are based on the Anglo-American experience and mostly focus on the interplay between the culture of the host in a developing country and that of the guest from a developed country. Third, an examination of tourism literature shows little cross-cultural research. Fourth, much of the existing host–guest literature is outdated. Fifth, information about the host gaze is negligible compared with that on the tourist gaze. Hence, there is no doubt that more ground is needed to cover for the host gaze to match our understanding of the tourist gaze. Our presumption here, which also underlines the importance of this book, is that our understanding of the host gaze will also *reinforce* our understanding of the tourist gaze.

Content Previews

The opening chapter by Hollingshead and Kuon focuses on the foundational concept of the tourist gaze. This foundation offers the reader a concentrated overview of the complexity not only of Foucault's philosophical world, but also the complexity of borrowing from this world to inform our understanding of the host gaze. In the chapter, the gaze is taken to be the institutionalized form of power. Thus, the chapter

explains that under Foucauldian light, the gaze is not so much an act of seeing, but an act of knowing. In order to help practitioners and researchers in tourism management/tourism studies gain a richer understanding of Foucault's concept of the gaze, the chapter provides a glossarial depiction of what ten key Foucauldian constructions on the governmentality of things (such as 'discourse', 'panopticism' and 'self-regulation') actually mean, and a table is provided that gives examples of what the discourse of institutions/organizations/agencies conceivably constitutes in range and commonality.

In Chapter 2, Canziani and Francioni examine host perspectives of the tourist gaze from the viewpoint of occupational and resident roles in the destination. Role-taking and role behavioural compliance are seen as a form of internalization of the tourist gaze that can lead to emotional outcomes, host defensive tactics and shifts in host self-concept.

In Chapter 3, Morrison argues that through developing an understanding of the perceptions and experiences of the Thai host in the tourist space, the Thai–tourist encounter, in general, and the recent measures to govern visitors and the image of Thailand, in particular, should be seen as embedded in particular relations of alterity.

In Chapter 4, Reisinger, Kozak and Visser examine the Turkish hoteliers' gaze at Russian tourists visiting the south coast of Turkey. The gaze of the owners, managers and employees of all-inclusive resorts and hotels in the holiday districts of Antalya is analysed. The reasons for the specific host gaze are explained by focusing on cultural identity of Russian tourists and cultural underpinning of their behaviour. The chapter shows how cultural misperceptions and misunderstandings between hosts and tourists can upset the hosts and create a negative gaze. The chapter concludes by discussing the implications and relating to the cultural relativism theory.

In Chapter 5, Savener explains that the history of the Kuna people of Panamá is constituted of resistance to outsiders – and that tradition continues today with tourists.

Although the Kuna are known worldwide for their hand-sewn mola panels, they remain an elusive mystery to the tourists who come to their islands.

In Chapter 6, Gelbman and Collins-Kreiner discuss how tour guides in Israel gaze upon the groups of Christian pilgrims that they lead in light of their familiarity and cumulative experience with them. The Holy Land has always been a main destination for Christian pilgrims from around the world, and also today religious tourism remains the main market segment of tourism to Israel. The gaze is a way people view the world, and when it is focused, it may include both visual and non-visual elements. Their findings contribute to the current literature by understanding the host gaze: how tour guides view different types of Christian pilgrims, their behaviour and their worldview.

In Chapter 7, Pattison highlights the conceptual value of approaching and understanding host gazes through engaging with alternative, non-Western discourses and knowledge communities. Her case study of a community-based tourism initiative in Gambia demonstrates how respondent-led photography captures host gazes as hosts reflect upon representations and meanings of self, community and tourism.

Chapter 8 by Bunten deconstructs elements of the host gaze within the context of Indigenous tourism, demonstrating its utility as an analytic tool. The host gaze can be a valuable mechanism that helps hosts to better accommodate guests, resist stereotyping, define themselves and enjoy the positive aspects of working in tourism.

In Chapter 9, Wu and Pearce explore how young Tibetans view the future of the tourism sector in the context of Lhasa. It pursues three notable themes – a non-Western setting, a location with a rapid evolution of tourism and a focus on the future – to continue the exploration of the gaze concept.

In Chapter 10, Lee and Gretzel's case focuses on Thai and Cambodian locals' gazes as perceived by US and South Korean short-term mission travellers. The authors try to understand differences in perceptions. The findings suggest a diverse set of

cultural values needs to be considered in this context and illustrate the complexities emerging from encounters with Christian and non-Christian hosts.

In Chapter 11, O'Regan looks at the reflexive practice of hospitality exchange, enabled by the site, couchsurfing.com, an apparatus that enables individuals to seek new solidarities, encounters, relations and feelings, through and with others. By asking who are guests and hosts in the age of mobility, networks and flow, the chapter argues that the standardized classification and binary model of host–guest blurs once transformative changes are individually realized through and with human and non-human others. The framework of the chapter offers a theoretical approach that moves beyond presumed oppositions between host and guest.

In Chapter 12, Ankor and Wearing consider the development of the concept of 'gaze' in Western cultural and critical theory. They then examine the *flâneur* as a gazer and introduce the concept of the choraster, as the relationship of visitor and host in the space of the 'other' and self. The notion of gaze is thus expanded from one of disassociation to emphasize a more engaged set of experiences that can reflect the imagined-real of both the traveller space and the host community. It draws on philosophy for an understanding of the response to gaze in the touristic encounter and leads to a framework able to deal with the complexity of contemporary tourism experiences. This chapter contributes to an understanding of tourism that is subject-centred, dynamic and capable of dealing with the host's role in developing tourist cultures. It contributes to the building of theory that enables the gaze to be constructed from the diverse and unpredictable interactions that occur and make up the encounter – the space, the host community's values and the tourist's experience.

In Chapter 13, Ugelvik compares two different kinds of professional gazes: that of the hotel bellman and that of the prison officer. By using the two as each other's analytical mirrors, he hopes to give novel insights on both sides. Although different in many respects, the author argues that the two have in common a bifocal gaze partly focused on the needs of others and partly on the potential problems and dangers these others represent.

In Chapter 14, Moufakkir builds upon MacCannell's second gaze to propose a third gaze: a gaze that offers a deeper look into the gaze, and this time goes truly beyond the visible to reach the invisible in the unconscious of the host gaze. The third gaze is ingrained in psychoanalysis and psychoanalytical concepts and theories advanced by Freud and Lacan. Similar to Foucault's gaze of the medic, this gaze is the gaze of the tourism academic upon the gaze of the tourism gaze. The third gaze is defined as the gaze of the gazer upon the gaze of the gazer gazing upon the object of the gaze. The intention of this gaze tries to understand the *whys* of the host gaze from a psychoanalytical perspective.

In Chapter 15, Hottola discusses the host gaze as a gaze that is culturally and stereotypically maintained and perpetuated in tourism encounters. In his documentation of Western women tourists in India and Sri Lanka, he offers us a deeper understanding on the origins of the male host gaze, a gaze that is rooted in the Indian culture and its gender relations, power, rules, attitudes, behaviour and expectations. Maintaining that morality is situational, he also offers perspectives on how women travellers interpret, understand and negotiate this 'sexualized' host gaze. This chapter adds to the understanding of the gendered aspects of the host gaze, the nature of real-and-imagined spaces of intercultural situations and the global production of sociotypic perceptions on ethnicity and culture.

In Chapter 16, Hollinshead and Hou have subjected the gaze to scrutiny, offering the reader a comprehensive analysis of the gaze, the Foucauldian gaze and the gaze in tourism. Building on Hollinshead's previous work on the gaze and Chapter 1 in this book, the authors locate the gazes of the preceding chapters in Hollinshead's dimensions of the tourism gaze, and relate the coverage of the contributors to the ten Foucauldian concepts presented in Chapter 1. In doing this, the authors lead us through the past, present and future of tourism gaze studies.

References

Ames, B.N. and Gold, I. Jr (1990) Nature's chemicals: comparative toxicology. *Proceedings of the National Academy of Sciences USA* 87, 7782–7786.

Anon. (1988) *Official Methods of Analyses, 11th edn.* The World Bank, Washington, DC, pp. 1–15.

Cao, G.R. (1988) *Experimentally induced yellow-wood intoxication in sheep.* MSc thesis, The University of Queensland, Brisbane, Australia.

Skinner, D.Z., Budde, A.D. and Notteghem, J.L. (1992) Molecular karyotype analysis of fungi. In: Bennett, J. and Lasure, L. (eds) *More Gene Manipulations in Fungi.* Academic Press, Orlando, Florida, pp. 86–103.

Chambers, D. (2007) An agenda for cutting edge research in tourism. In Tribe, J. and Airey, D. (eds) *Developments in Tourism Research.* Elsevier Science Ltd, London, pp. 233–245.

Chan, Y.W. (2006) Coming of age of the Chinese tourists: the emergence of non-Western tourism and host–guest interactions in Vietnam's border tourism, *Tourist Studies* 6(3), 187–213.

Foucault, M. [1963] (1973) *The Birth of the Clinic.* Translated by A.S. Sheridan. Presses Universitaires de France, New York.

MacCannell, D. (2001) Tourist agency, *Tourist Studies* 1(1), 23–37.

Maoz, D. (2006) The mutual gaze, *Annals of Tourism Research* 23(1), 221–239.

Moufakkir, O. (2011) The role of cultural distance in mediating the host gaze, *Tourist Studies* 11(1), 73–89.

Urry, J. (1990) *The Tourist Gaze: Leisure and Travel in Contemporary Societies.* Sage, London.

Urry, J. (2002) *The Tourist Gaze.* Sage Publications, London.

1 The Scopic Drive of Tourism: Foucault and Eye Dialectics

Keith Hollinshead and Vannsy Kuon

Introduction

This first chapter focuses upon the foundational concept (for the book) of the tourist gaze, identifying it as a recent parallel within Tourism Management/Tourism Studies with the French litero-philosophical term *le regard*, as utilized by Foucault in his examinations of the manner in which humans (and human 'things') are divided and governed in and under the complex relations of contestation and resistance in institutional life. In this chapter, and within what Foucault considered to be a society of normalization, the gaze is taken to be the institutionalized form of power or (to Foucault) the power/knowledge edifice through which specific subjects are ruled and regulated or governmentalized. Thus, the chapter explains that under Foucauldian light, the gaze is not so much an act of seeing, but an act (in talk (discourse) and in deed (praxis)) of knowing – indeed, of institutional/interest group/social pre-knowing. In order to help practitioners and researchers in Tourism Management and Tourism Studies gain a richer understanding of how Foucault's concept of the gaze (be it the clinical gaze, the gaze over madness, the magisterial gaze – and here (after his death) the tourist gaze), the chapter provides a glossarial depiction of what ten key Foucauldian constructions on the governmentality of

things (such as 'discourse', 'panopticism' and 'self-regulation') actually mean, and a table is provided that gives examples of what the discourse of institutions, organizations and agencies (that inherit, operate or engage the tourist gaze) conceivably constitute in range and commonality. But the chapter offers no unsullied exaltation of the conceptual genius of Foucault, and a second table is provided that warns readers about a number of lead problematics (or difficulties) that various schools of critical thought have with the ordinary application of Foucauldian inspections of power and knowledge (or with the eye dialectics by and through which institutional circuits of domination and exploitation are exercised).

Preamble to the Foucauldian Gaze: Matters of Seeing, Knowing and Pre-Knowing

In a book devoted to studies of the host gaze and the tourist gaze in action, it is crucial that the social science term 'the gaze' is first explained and clarified. This is the function of this first chapter in *The Host Gaze in Global Tourism*. Fundamentally, there are two commonplace usages of the term 'the gaze' to describe the generative activity of and around cultural entities. While one

derives largely from the radical film critiques of the 1970s, which were pivotally
inspired by Freud's thinking on *scopophilia*
(i.e. the pleasure received in observing
screen images) and by Lacan's insight into
those reflected objects with or from which
individuals construct their *perfect/united
identities* (Mulvey, 1989), the other use centres upon Foucault's scrutiny of institutional relations of power. This chapter, and
indeed this book, is focused upon the latter,
that is upon Foucauldian analyses of the
way the world is seen and thereby related to
and governed by the institution of 'Tourism
Management' (read, in context hereafter, the
institution of 'Industrial Tourism', the institution of 'Tourism Studies', the institution
of 'Tourism/Travel Research', the institution of 'Western Tourism', the institutions
of 'Whatever'). And, in order to draw pronounced or clarifying attention to these
contextual forces of institutional governmentality, such organizations will be given
capital letters in both this first chapter on
eye dialectics (by Hollinshead and Kuon)
and later in the book's closing chapter on
agents of normalcy (by the same two contributors).

Under Foucauldian thought (emanating
from Michel Foucault (1926–1984)), social
science researchers who inspect the institutional gaze at work or in force tend to examine the *panopticist* ways in which the world
is regulated, where panopticism is a form of
visionary (and productive, but potentially
malevolent power named after *panoptes*, the
all-seeing Argus of the ancient Greek myths
(Serres, 1989)). Thus, those who examine the
existence of a suspected or conceivable gaze
tend to look for the manner through and by
which an institution 'sees' the world around
and about it, or rather relates to and thereby
disciplines (seeks to discipline) things. Panopticism is thereby taken to be a type of
power (or rather, of power/knowledge in
strict Foucauldian terms) that is exercised at
a given time and place by that institution's
'apparatus', that is, by its 'whole set of instruments, techniques, procedures, levels of
application, [and] targets' (Foucault. *Discipline and Punish*, as selected in Rabinow,
1984, p. 206). Thus, panopticist inquiry

(research into *a* or *the institutional gaze*)
tends to constitute an anatomy of power, or
rather a study of the technology of power or
knowledge of a body or organization that has
come to operate with a specialized authority
(or governance or governmentalizing influence) on and over a particular field of activity, responsibility or play. Foucauldian
inspections of a or the gaze in action therefore are inclined to search for the sorts of
vision (for which, read understandings) that
specialised authorities, bodies or organizations work with and through in regular organized and reinforcive ways via their internal
(and importantly, their internalized (disciplinary) mechanisms of power (power/
knowledge, again)). Those who pry into a or
the gaze at work thereby generally search for
those forms of consciousness by and through
which a particular institution or entity does
and does not work in its own allocated, designated or claimed area of responsibility in
and across society. That area of responsibility, that area of 'life', that area of governance
is said to be juridically subject to *the disciplinary authority* (i.e. power (or power/
knowledge)) of that panoptic apparatus that
is ordinarily in action. And that power/
knowledge is seen to work as a regulating
power or a codified power particularly
through the exercise of its infinitely minute
web of panoptic techniques (Foucault, *Discipline and Punish*, Rabinow, 1984, p. 213), as
they establish universalizing norms for the
'world' (within that specialized area of institutional governance). Hence, one who sus-
pects the presence of a distinct or an actual
governmentalizing gaze, then tends to
inspect for the force of a juridical system at
play in that field (i.e. that force-field),
whereby that subjectification takes place
through the detailed or petty manner in
which the order of things is identified, characterized, classified around these norms.
Consequently, that specialized field (i.e. that
area of disciplinary or juridical activity)
becomes a realm or sphere of accorded or
designated 'specialized responsibility'
where individuals (or individual things,
places or entities) are hierarchically ordered.
Some such things in that force-field will be
duly qualified and validated in some fashion

by that gaze-in-action, and other things will be disqualified and invalidated in some fashion at the same time.

Those who tend to work under Foucauldian light (inspecting panoptic modalities of power (power/ knowledge)) in action are inclined to find that the normalizing work of panopticist vision and authority is coercive towards particular forms of consciousness/ understanding/awareness, and silences, suppresses or subjugates other 'knowledges'. Thus, for each institution, or each area of *juridical responsibility*, for each force-field, there can be a dark side to this specialized governmentality in operation. The disciplinary systems of the classification of the world, and the mundane everyday exercise of the specialized and detailed micropower at work, are not inherently or essentially egalitarian, nor are they inherently or essentially symmetrical. In the given force-field, some consciousnesses and awareness become 'healthy' or 'dominant', while others are chastised and become 'outlawed' or 'denied'.

Put another way, those who conduct Foucauldian inspections of the gaze in action, commonly look for the consciousnesses about the world which are carried within what the institution says (i.e. via its discourse) and does (i.e. via its praxis). That discourse and that praxis in tandem are conduits for the way in which the world is not only perceived but judged. Thus, Foucault was not so much interested in 'sight', *per se*, but in the held knowledges, the held dominances and the held subjugations that course through the enactments of the gaze. In this sense, the gaze is not a matter of sight, *ipso facto*, it is a matter of seeing, of not seeing, and thereby of regulating: in this anti-ocular sense, it is a matter of *knowing* rather than *seeing* (Brooker, 2003); and it is probably more richly and faithfully understood as a matter of *pre-knowing* than even of knowing (Hollinshead, 1993). Constantly, one who enquires into the agency or authority of a gaze in action might scrutinize for those things that are classified and rendered by that normalized pre-knowing institutional activity: they tend to inspect for those things that are objectified adventitiously and treated as being 'wonderful' or 'sovereign',

and for those things that are objectified less favourably as casualties in that governmentalized (micro-managed) act of pre-knowing. Thus, analysis of a suspected gaze is generally built up in particular settings (or under the sway of organizations, specialist regimes or governing agencies) via the gathering of 'evidence' or from the functioning discourse and praxis (rather than the discourse alone) of that target force-field. It is not so much a quest to find what is visible in and under the generation of that suspected *panoptic surveillance*, but what is invisible there – that is, what are the hitherto undersuspected or underexamined understandings or the formulated/preformulated consciousnesses that are seemingly regularly deployed there.

Consequently, when located in the realm of Tourism Management or in the spectrum of Tourism Studies, inspections of a or the gaze necessarily compose – in Foucauldian hue – an examination of not so much the way thoughtlines about the world's peoples, places and pasts are organized, but the way they have been pre-organized over time to course through the governing public bodies of tourism, and/or through the techno-corporate empires of the private-for-profit sector, and/or through the other sanctioning interest groups of the third sector (the private-not-for-profit) sphere. As Foucault intoned, the world at the Renaissance was understood (centuries ago) as a kind of volume that God had written out where 'everything (nature, people's behaviour, buildings) could be interpreted in terms of a divine code which had to be deciphered' (Danaher *et al.*, 2000, p. 19). But today, as Foucault also intoned, the modern age is an era of institutionally authorized knowledge (power/knowledge at work) where instead specific and specialized bodies have carried out that governing scriptwork. Following Nietzsche (which Foucault was prone to do), the Foucauldian research agenda is one that not only researches 'the meaning of things', but the struggles, the battles and the violences that have yielded it (Danaher *et al.*, 2000, p. 27), notably where the protagonists involved were not necessarily aware of or were scarcely alert to the fact that these struggles over 'knowledge' or the battles over 'meaning' were actually taking place. Thereby, in examining the conceivable exercise of power in, of, and through *the force-field of tourism* – or rather, the force-fields (multiple and infinitous) of tourism – which consciousnesses have been rendered 'dominant' or 'distinguished' and which have been rendered 'outlaw' or 'obsolete' through the quotidian industrialized workings of a or the apparatus of tourism? In this regard, the Foucauldian gaze is akin to the philosophical vision of Plato: such vision is not so much the vision of the operating 'eye', *ipso facto*, it is the vision of 'the inner eye of the mind' (see Jay, 1994, p. 27). An individual sees through one's eyes, not with them. Such is what Merleau-Ponty called *the madness of vision* (see de Certeau, 1982). And it would be most unusual if the institutional realm of Tourism and Travel – indeed the institutional realms (plural) of Tourism and Travel – do not have their many 'madnesses' of vision. Ergo, this book on local, national and international tourism might clearly be about *the eye dialectics* (after Sloterdijk, 1987, p. 145) of tourism, but it is also inevitably about the 'madnesses' of celebration and ceremony in terms of the understanding held by some populations and about the 'madnesses' of violence and vicissitude in terms of the understandings cherished by other populations. If Foucault wrote in his most discriminating and challenging way in his mid-1960s work *Les Mots Et Les Choses* (Foucault, 1966) about 'The Order of Things', this work by Moufakkir and Reisinger (almost 50 years later) is about 'The Things Ordered By and through Tourism'. The following chapters will thus contribute to our own early 21st century knowledge about the misty 'madnesses' and idiosyncratic inanities we indulge in *and* concretize *and* materialize as we ogle (and thereby pre-ogle) the world.

Introduction to the Glossary on Governmentality: the Unimpeded Empire of 'The Gaze'

The Foucauldian concept of 'the gaze' is quite commonly misinterpreted. In Rajchman's (1988, p. 96) view, Foucault fundamentally endeavoured to search for 'what is unthought in our seeing and to open [it up to] as yet unseen ways of seeing': to that end, the normalizing or governmentalizing gaze is an epistemic phenomenon (i.e. it is one belonging to a particular historical period or setting of time-and-place that is constructed linguistically (meaning historically/institutionally/socially) just as much as it is visually. Indeed, late in his life, Foucault began to regret his choice of the term 'the gaze' (le regard) because people were prone to assuming 'it' comprised a singular and unified entity rather than being 'an enunciative modality' (that is to say, a subject-making understanding that emerges, or rather, that is made manifest in and through the work of 'discourse' and 'praxis') (see Jay, 1994, p. 392).

If such a slippery Foucauldian concept as *the gaze* and a number of related Foucauldian neologisms are to serve as the bedrock syntax for this book, it is important that some effort is taken to corral those lubricated concepts and explain them for the benefit of those readers who are not used to continental philosophy. Accordingly, attention is now turned in this chapter to provision of ten concepts that Foucault regularly used to explain what was visible and could be discussed within institutions via 'the unimpeded empire of the gaze' (Foucault, 1975, p. 39). The chosen concepts are drawn from an extensive but unpublished glossary of 70 Foucauldian terms produced by one of the authors (Hollinshead) in Texas in 1998. They are:

- Agents-of-normalcy;
- Carceral society;
- Discourse;
- Dominance;
- Gaze (the clinical);
- Panopticism;
- Micropower;
- Historical meaning;
- Scopic drive;
- Self-regulation.

For each of the above ten concepts, a general explanation of the Foucauldian meaning is first provided, and then a brief attempt is made to situate that particular concept in the field of Tourism/Tourism Management/ Tourism Studies. In a manuscript recently prepared for the journal *Tourism Analysis*, an effort was made by Hollinshead (unpublished) to define a further 12 Foucauldian terms for a special issue on destination management. This dozen consisted of:

- Apparatus;
- Capillary action;
- Disciplinary mechanism;
- Discursive knowledge;
- Eye-of-authority;
- Governmentality;
- *Homo docilis*;
- Juridical space;
- *Rapport à soi*;
- Regime-of-truth;

- Specular bias;
- Truth statements.

Before the glossary itself is provided, two strong caveats ought to be given regarding Foucault's syntax on and about the gaze. First, those who inspect Foucauldian ideas perhaps tend to do so mostly enough the medium of *discourse*. Thus, it is useful to provide not just the offered definition of what 'discourse' is in the glossary itself, but to also provide elucidation as to the sorts of sayable things that might constitute it in any 'institutional talk' setting. Table 1.1 has thus been compiled to reveal what discourse, itself, might be in Tourism/Tourism Management/Tourism Studies contexts, and six commonplace types of discourse

Table 1.1. Stabilized and regulated 'talk' in tourism: a comparison of the discourse in/of 'tourism' with that of/about 'madness'.

Key:

- ● Discursive statements (in Foucault) of/about madness
- ➔ *Like (Foucauldian) discursive statements in/of tourism*

- ● Statements about madness THAT give us [general] knowledge concerning madness
- ➔ *Statements in tourism or in Tourism Management/Tourism Studies that give us knowledge about the general benefits/advantages of tourism itself*

- ● The rules that prescribe what is 'sayable' or 'thinkable' about madness
- ➔ *Statements in tourism that prescribe what is 'sayable' or 'thinkable' about the supposed celebratory or visitable qualities of city A (or province B, or country C)*

- ● Subjects that personify the discourses of madness, that is, of the 'mad man'
- ➔ *Subjects that seemingly capture or actualize the held discourse of a must-visit special 'population', 'place' or 'past' – such as (perhaps) the longstanding tradition of the Beefeaters (at the Tower of London), the restorative qualities of the waters of Lourdes (France) or the unmatched brilliance of the Mayan civilization (Central America)*

- ● The processes by which discourses of madness acquire authority and truth at a given historical moment
- ➔ *The processes by which discourses of national literary greatness acquire governmental backing (and, thereby authority and truth) in, for instance, the PR China today (in contrast to the time of 'the People's Revolution')*

- ● The practices within institutions that deal with madness
- ➔ *The practices within local/regional tourist boards that have a geographical or administrative responsibility for a specific designated area or territory*

- ● The idea that different discourses about madness will appear at later historical moments producing new knowledge and a new discursive formation
- ➔ *The idea that different discourses (about, for instance, the importance of tourism or regarding the standards of host-destination services) will appear at later historical moments (as, perhaps, new insights into sustainability or stewardship) thereby producing (helping to produce) new knowledge and a new discursive formation*

Source: ●The six listed discourses of/about madness (in the work of Foucault) are taken from Barker (2004, p. 54).

are provided for the field (for Foucault never specifically wrote about 'tourism') in contrast with Barker's heuristic list for 'Madness' (which Foucault did indeed write about, at length).

The second caveat concerns a number of difficulties that are often loaded up against the work of Foucault on the gaze – or more properly stated, on his longstanding oevre or power/knowledge/institutionality/ governmentality. As Brown (1998) has cogently stated, the real value in and of Foucault's regime of work rests upon what it actually opens up for social scientists from political scientists to philosophers, and from anthropologists to historians. Foucault is best regarded as a catalyst who can help generate a host of new approaches by which a given 'subject' or a suspected 'entity' may be examined, but he is not a formulaic methodologist (Hollinshead, 1993) who can or who ought to be faithfully followed in the field at each juncture or on the ground at each ontological/epistemological point. Foucault is thus something of a poor prescriptivist, as the problematics of Table 1.2 suggest.

Table 1.2 is drawn from *The Later Foucault*, a collation of 11 critiques put together by Moss (1998) in the effort to examine why and how Foucault's work on, for instance, governmentality, genealogy and the gaze has been of such central significance in so many social science fields, and why and how his opus delivers 'a provocative challenge to orthodox, habitual forms of belief

Table 1.2. Problematics with Foucault's power/knowledge dyad: difficulties involved in the net value of Foucault's work on the operation of 'power'.

- ☐ Common criticisms of the overall applicability of Foucault's ideas on governmentality, according to Moss *et al.*(1998)

- ☐ *The absence of individual freedom in Foucault?*
  Foucault's account of the functioning of power glosses over the important role of subjects (human, political or administrative) in wielding it, or in responding to it (Moss, 1998, p. 2)

- ☐ *The neglect of wider global effects in Foucault?*
  Foucault's emphasis on the microphysics of power ignores the more general 'global' strategies of power which may be in/are in operation (Moss, 1998, p. 2)

- ☐ *The narrowness of contextuality in Foucault?*
  Foucault's critique of power/knowledge (particularly in his later work on 'genealogy') leaves no room for an or any alternative set of narrative assumptions in the given setting (Moss, 1998, p. 6)

- ☐ *The inherent despair embedded in Foucault?*
  Foucault's work on power/knowledge offers no alternative ideal – that is, no conception either of human being or of human society freed from the bonds of power (Patton, 1998, p. 64)

- ☐ *The inherent nihilism freighted with Foucault?*
  Foucault refuses to talk about or delineate what is 'good' or even 'bad', merely being inclined to identify what is 'dangerous' in and of every discourse or 'strategy' (Brown, 1998, p. 34)

- ☐ *The absence of regard for others in Foucault?*
  Foucault's strong recommendations about the need for individuals to create themselves 'as a work of art' may be all well and good in and of itself, but it is not necessarily synonymous with the need to care for or show responsibility for others (Smart, 1998, p. 85)

- ☐ *The commonplace obscurity in Foucault?*
  Foucault's responses to questions (especially to expressly 'political' interrogations) are frequently vague, oblique, deflective or simply bland (Brown, 1998, p. 33)

- ☐ *The failure to generate panoramic and variegated summary assessments of/about 'power'?*
  Foucault's work on an 'institutional'/'governmentalized' power/knowledge is heavily particularistic and offers no umbrella claims about 'power' – that is, it yields no formal schemes of general validity about the functioning of 'power' (Allen, 1998).

and practice' (Moss, 1998, back cover). While the book is not a one-sided condemnatory assault on Foucault's writings on *power, agency* and *subjectivity*, neither is it a tame eulogy, being seasonably balanced in its assessment of the contribution of Foucauldian thought to questions of freedom, authority and ethical thought. In this light, Table 1.2 has been drawn up to capture some of the more troublesome aspects that tag along with the deployment of Foucauldian conceptualities. While Foucault's critical philosophical *cum* critical historical approaches can be (and have been) used in a litany of fields to maintain watch over the claimed domain of ruling reason – and notably over the raging 20th century and 21st century 'modern rationality which demands that everything and everyone be "managed"' (Moss, 1998, p. 9) – a number of strong warnings about the on-the-ground applicability of Foucauldian ideas may be gleaned from scrutiny of *The Later Foucault*. As presented in Table 1.2, these forewarnings counsel social scientists (who seek new angles to inspect power in action) that Foucault's own work (especially his genealogical commentaries) often relies upon the very same assumptions about knowledge-production that it seeks to criticize (Moss, 1998, p. 6). Other lead problematics over efforts to deploy Foucauldian conceptions in the field/on the ground (as captured in Table 1.2) include:

1. Protests from humanists that his work heralds no possibility of and for meaningful individual freedom. They often claim that even though Foucault is (at face value) 'a staunch enemy of humanism and its values, he [still] nevertheless appears to appeal to traditional humanist values to give his work normative force' (Moss, 1998, p. 10 (drawing from Fraser, 1989));
2. Complaints from critical activists that his work is not only nihilistic in tone but despairing (as Foucault himself admitted), merely being capable of generating forms of pessimistic activism (Brown, 1998, p. 34);
3. Remonstrations from ethicists that Foucault's analyses of power/knowledge do not actually generate any worthwhile 'criteria

for judgement' by which some regimes of governance can be deemed to be 'oppressive' and others applauded as being 'progressive' (Patton, 1998, p. 64). They argue that Foucault's work is excessively orientated to 'the self' and that any responsibility to 'others' is almost indifferent, always secondary to his preoccupation with individualality (Smart, 1998, pp. 89–90);
4. Affirmations from Marxists and Neo-Marxists (amongst others) that Foucauldian thought patently disregarded economic realities, and indeed offers no alternative ideal save 'a bleak political horizon on which the subject will always be an effect of power relations, and on which there is no possibility of escape from domination of one sort or another' (Patton, 1998, p. 65).

So there we have it. On the plus side, Foucault's work is a brilliant subversive challenge to all disciplines in the social sciences and the humanities, forcing each domain, each institution, each interest group to reconsider the assumptive practices through which it acts, and the unquestioned manner in which it perhaps prescribes universal essences in or for objects and things. In this vein, Foucault is hailed as a supreme examiner of the degree to which institutions and individuals of all sorts are ever really free to think and act (Danaher *et al.*, 2000, pp. 1–29). On the minus side, however, Foucault's work is merely seen to be an anarchistic commentary in the dullest of Nietzschean hue, an almost lawless scholarship where political regardedness is subsumed by the nothingness of aesthetics, and where the inherent struggle of a 'war of all against all is dystopian and unacceptable' (Sawicki, 1998, p. 95, drawing from Hartsock, 1990).

Let those who work in Tourism Management/Tourism Studies make up their own minds as they consider engagement with Foucauldian ideas on *the gaze* (or on genealogy and/or governmentality). As they may seek to add to – or to replace! – existing knowledge about the conceivable essentialization, normalization or naturalization of peoples, places, pasts and presents in and through tourism, they might find the ten conceptualizations of the following glossary (from *agents-of-normalcy* to *self-regulation*) to be very useful creative visualizations about not only who is doing what to whom, where, when, how and why, but who is thinking what about which in the projection/reprojection/deprojection of place and space.

Yet, that selfsame investigator or practitioner in Tourism Management/Tourism Studies should heed the warnings of watchdog humanists, watchdog critical activists, watchdog ethicists and watchdog Marxists/Neo-Marxists (and all) and guard against an over-inhalation of what Connolly (1998, p. 110) has styled *Fou-connism*. The political and historicist and aesthetic 'conceptual bounce' that may be won from in-the-field ruminations about, for example, the tourist gaze exercise of *micropower* at work within the scopic drive of these institutions that conceivably help constitute *a carceral society* may be prodigious, but it will be regarded by many other observing pundits of politics and/or analysts of agency as no more than a mere spectral or spiritual gape on the governance of things – a hasty and phantom rubbernecking towards real institution life.

Thus, there is much merit in taking critical stock of Foucault's inspections of the political economy of truth that conceivably circulates to, within and from institutions, but the practitioner or researcher who unduly breathes in (and thereby totalizes) his or her interrogation of the disciplinary authority of power/knowledge may fast become prey to an overindulged kind of *Foucaultianism* (after Connolly, 1998, p. 110). Too much subversive Foucauldian conceptuality – like too much ice-cream on any single day on holiday – cannot be a wholly wholesome thing!

Glossary of Foucauldian Terms Used in this Chapter

Agents of normalcy

Generally, Foucault wrote with an adamantine distrust of institutions (Merquior,

1985, p. 155) and of the acts of normalization they tended to indulge in, much of it (to him) not consciously enacted by individuals working for or with the said agency. To Foucault, such individuals tended to serve as agents – of – normalcy, quietly normalizing or naturalizing this and that through their everyday discourse (talk; see *discourse* below) and their praxis (deeds). And power was not so much 'possessed' by those agents of normalcy, but was rather transmitted within and across the agency through them (Morris and Patton, 1979, p. 59). In this fashion, established agents of normalcy served as normative overseers as they variously carried out their mundane or everyday acts of surveillance and regulation as, for instance, 'teacher–judges', as 'doctor–judges', as 'educator–judges' or as 'social worker–judges' in the respective field of concern (Merquior, 1985, p. 96). Throughout his academic and advocacy career, Foucault was concerned about the quotidian exercise of totalitarian forms of power through the large and (most importantly) the petty actions of such institutionally embedded agents of 'the normal', 'the appropriate' and 'the proper' (Miller, 1993, p. 281).

Thus in Tourism Studies, is there anyone currently examining who is mainstreaming (for instance) which particular constructions of 'ecotourism' or 'sustainable tourism', or are there any Tourism Management/Tourism Studies researchers otherwise inspecting who precisely is working in everyday petty ways to commodify the travel myths of Shangri-La, Eden and/or Nirvana? In the early 1990s, Hollinshead (1993, p. 3) explored the production of governing interpretations about the heritage of Texas, not only in terms of the role of administrators of that state's heritage as they conceivably worked as *tourism–judges* serving as vehicles of governing authority regulating particular places and narratives. In this work, Hollinshead also inspected *the non-agency* life of certain myths, legends and storylines that had their own normalizing/naturalizing 'careers' not necessarily limited by the work of a or any formal state administrative 'agency'.

Carceral society

To Foucault, modern societies act as a prison that regulates the life of individuals through the discipline of institutions, agencies and collective bodies, and that regulation of individuals is particularly coercive when carried out through highly professionalized orders of supervising/supervisory officials (Miller, 1993, p. 212). In such institutional, agentive or collective spaces, people are imprisoned – according to Foucault (Morris and Patton, 1979, p. 117) – within a network of power relations that acts not so much as a matter of mere ideological preference, but as a heavily inscribed and deeper Nietzschean matter of 'blood and cruelty' (Nietzsche, 1969, p. 61). To Foucault, these heavy and incremental matters of regulatory coercion began to quickly and unsuspectingly consolidate in the West from the late 18th century, via the newly imposed surveillances of the police, of statistical record keeping and of property management, etc. (Horrocks and Jevtic, 1997, p. 115). Under such increasingly common forms of administrative oversight and professional discipline in the West, more and more forms of everyday behaviour became 'codified' in one sense and 'intimidated' in another, and all manner of individual lifecourse activity became normalized. Hence, to Foucault, carceral society developed as a society normalized through the various approved supervisory or managerial gazes (see *gaze – clinical*, below). According to Foucault, individuals became rule-bound and subjugated in many disparate areas of life in the West – and conceivably, increases in knowledge-making through the expanded projections of tourism in the 20th century has been but a later example of the normalisation of or the fixing of understandings about peoples, places, and pasts.

And then in tourism, is there anyone currently preparing to take the work regime of Shames and Glover (1989) on the ethnocentrisms and eurocentrisms of international Hospitality Management into broader spheres of Tourism Management? Do indeed the set service standards of the tourism industry, the set marketing practices and the set human resource development strategies indeed incarcerate the staff of tourism operations, the local hosts and the visiting guests in particular places? What goes: whose hands, budgets and orientations are nowadays 'tied up' carcerally where, and how? Under extreme Foucauldian thought, 'there is no way around or outside of the power/knowledge of discourse [see 'discourse', below]; [there is no way of escaping its effects, but also no way of being except as one of its effects" (Rapport and Overing, 2000, p. 293). It will be interesting to note if there is any evidence or interpretation presented in the succeeding chapters of this book that reveals or suggests there are groups, communities or populations in particular destinations or in specific locales who find it extraordinarily difficult to exist in the 21st century outside of the industrially scripted power/knowledge of the dominant projections of tourism in their region. In another light, no doubt many Tourism Studies researchers will feel that (in terms of their own publication experiences) they themselves are incarcerated under the over-close restrictions and disciplinary normalizations (Rabinow, 1984, p. 237) of the peer review systems in vogue at certain lead journals!

Discourse

In his ongoing studies of the *governmentality* of things, Foucault constantly sought to unearth the rule structures that guided the circulation of truth across institutions or across given societies: he sought to reveal how those 'structures of knowledge' came into being, and what they privileged or mainstreamed compared with what they disenfranchised or chastised (Davidson, 1997, p. 11). As such, Foucault was not so much interested in the formal possibilities of knowledge as a discrete and constant 'linguistic system', but rather as an accumulated discourse – or set of statements – which came over time to claim the status of knowledge in the given institutional milieu, and which from time to time transformed things (Davidson, 1997, p. 11) through the *power/ knowledge dyad* Foucault's analysis of the discourse – that is, the talk and text – of agencies, organizations and populations constitutes a new political style of the examination of discourse, which probes discourse not as a fixed, pre-existent 'grammar', but as a strategic field of understanding where contesting forces were perpetually at battle (Davidson, 1997, pp. 4–5). In this light, Foucauldian discourse ought not to be seen as that set of signs which refer to real phenomena in and of the world, but rather as practices of war that form and project afresh the objects of which that agency, organization or population wishes to speak (Horrocks and Jevtic, 1997, p. 64) and thereby recognize. Hence the objects of Foucauldian discourse are not fixed objects or universally rooted experiences, and different discourses do not necessary relate conversationally to the same 'objects', but rather to others discourse (Horrocks and Jevtic, 1997, p. 88). Hence powerful discourse should be regarded not so much as precious documents, *ipso facto*, under Foucauldian critique, but as tall monuments: in this regard, what counts is not their historical validity over time, but their self-testimony (Horrocks and Jevtic, 1997, p. 87) under a particular episteme or within a particular institutional context. Hence in Foucauldian history, and in Foucauldian contemporary analysis, one does not tend to look for the capacity of an author to use a given discourse, but more commonly for the ways in which that discourse itself constrains or empowers the author and his or her *utterances*. In Tourism Management/ Tourism Studies, Jaworski and Pritchard made a useful attempt to link empirical outlooks on tourism with theoretical perspectives on discourse (Jaworski and Pritchard, 2005), but the pivotal Foucauldian concepts like 'the gaze', 'governmentality', 'power/ knowledge' and even 'Foucault' are not included in the work's index; notably absent from consideration amongst the works, are chapters on (variously) destination development, tourist experience and performance authority. The twin fields of Tourism Management/Tourism Studies still need to cultivate investigations of institutional discourse at work, and of power/

knowledge in action: such are the ideas and the statements in and of 'tourism' that allow certain peoples, places or pasts/presents to be made sense of and (in Foucauldian terms) be 'seen' (Danaher *et al.*, 2000, pp. X, 33, 37). To Foucault, himself, such studies would pose the limits and forms of 'the sayable', 'the conserved', 'the memorized', 'the activated' and 'the appropriated' (Foucault, 1991a, pp. 59–60).

Dominance

To Foucault, power is a constituent element of modes of production and functions as the power/knowledge of the given system of government, sequestration or production (Morris and Patton, 1979, p. 61), and every agent of power in those agencies, organizations or fields of oversight becomes an agent in and of the construction of knowledge (Morris and Patton, 1979, p. 63). The cardinal task of the investigator of the discourse and praxis of institutions (see *discourse*, above) is to locate the petty talk and the small quotidian deeds where those modes of production have become dominant (Foucault in Foucault and Chomsky, 1997, p. 130).

Through the everyday exercise of such talk and deeds, society is regulated and people are normalized in banal fashion: as 'the social straitjacket' (after Nietzsche) of the elaborate customs, mores, laws and other minutiae is imposed on and across the said society in and of the West, individuals within the shadow, purview or oversight of the particular instrumentality are made 'calculable', 'regular' and 'necessary' – and individuals who work in and for that said agency are also so tamed (Miller, 1993, p. 215). Such ongoing taming renders some individuals or groups dominant, over time, as their interests, habits and histories more neatly match the discursive knowledge being quietly and often under-suspectingly mainstreamed, and other populations are subjugated, chastised and silenced as the realities they uphold do not so comfortably reflect the dominant truths being produced and peddled. Yet to Foucault, such power (or rather power/knowledge) is never absolutely on one side of things (Morris and Patton, 1979, p. 60). The talk and the text (and therefore the mainstreaming truth production) is never totally controlled from one outlook: power is never monolithic (Morris and Patton, 1979, p. 60), to Foucault. As the power/knowledge in currency turns humans into subjects, no held truth is ever completely and perpetually dominant, and from time to time different forms of dominant productive power/knowledge replace each other (Simons, 1995, p. 3). Thus dominance is always a field of tension between competing poles of 'truth' rather than an absolute effectivity. That truth production is constituted by a whole assemblage of complex threads – of instincts, drives, tendencies and actions (Rabinow, 1984, p. 220).

In Tourism Management/Tourism Studies, an endeavour to inspect by Foucauldian lines of dominance would therefore seek to investigate whether the particular instrumentality or board or organization had begun to act as what Foucauldian specialists might call an 'austere' or a 'complete' institution, thereby steadfast and secure in its time and context within and through its silently organized 'field of objectivity' (Rabinow, 1984, p. 224). The Tourism Management/Tourism Studies researcher would then seek to enquire whether that instrumentality, board or organization had begun to (or continued to!) work with what might be impersonal and largely unconscious systems of significance as 'its' preferred visions of place and space were signified via the resultant arrangements and depersonalized network of images (Kearney, 1988). Thus, the Foucauldian researcher in Tourism Management/Tourism Studies tends to pay less attention to the individual speaker or actor in the discursive context – the latter is 'dissolved' or 'decentred' (Rapport and Overing, 2000, p. 120) – but more attention to (perhaps) a found hierarchy of 'subject positions'. Where such is found to exist (everywhere?), the uncovered 'dominance' in the tourism and travel settings inspected would be seen to be both a symbolic process of linguistic expression and a social practice of speaking and acting. Such dominant discourse and such dominant praxis are regarded as *a* or *the conscience collective* through which the world is classified. The particular realm of tourism or spectrum of travel is classified via these dominant/subordinate subject positions, and those who work in tourism or who 'live' in those settings are said or felt to inevitably find themselves proscribed by these particular versions of the world – that is, by these interested, partisan and power-loaded visions (Rapport and Overing, 2000, p. 121). In this manner, Foucauldian analysis of 'tourism' probes for the dominant discourses, practices and gazes that inhabit the institutions of tourism and travel and habituate the mind there. In tourism and travel (as in any field), human beings are 'bodies' totally marked and stamped by history (Thomas, 1994, p. 5) as those discourses, those practices, those gazes enlarge and change, and jockey against each other.

Gaze (the clinical)

The 'gaze' of a group, collective or institution is the direction, force and will (or *will-to-power*) of that group's vision as orchestrated by its *scopic drive* (see below) on and over the world (Merquior, 1985). Hence, the gaze of that collective or institution is the Foucauldian *will-to-truth* – after Nietzsche – which results from the panoptic exercise (after Bentham) (see *Panopticism*, below) of that scopic drive over time as a power of universal surveillance over those aspects or areas of the world which that group, collective or institution seeks to discipline (Foucault, 1980, pp. 146–165). Under the gaze, or otherwise under the panoptic vision of institutions, subjects that are held under regular oversight never quite know when they are being observed, and so they are inclined to regulate themselves over time. But the observers within that institution also normalize and police themselves as they carry out those everyday acts of surveillance over their incarcerated subjects (see *carceral society*, above). As the years progress, the gaze therefore becomes a productive network that disciplines all manner of people's behaviour as it runs through the given social body. It is the constant petty and mundane surveillance of things via that institution's gaze that gradually produces knowledge, transmits truth and bestows rights there (Morris and Patton, 1979, p. 66)). Consonantly, it is Foucault's view that within social bodies, 'power' is not so much something possessed by an individual, it is rather 'a capillary force' that is distributed through that institution's gaze, and which acts via disciplined and normalized panoptic human agency (Morris and Patton, 1979, p. 131). Many of Foucault's insights into the scopic drive of collective groups stem from his studies of health clinics:

> the clinic was probably the first attempt to order a science on the exercise and decisions of the gaze... [and, later,] the medical gaze was also organized in a new way. First, it was no longer the gaze of any observer, but that of a doctor supported and justified by an institution. (Foucault, 1976, p. 89)

Had Foucault himself inspected tourism operations and travel settings, he would no doubt have been drawn to analysing whether there were indeed any equivalent *clinical gazes* (read operating gazes) at work there as an eye of power or an eye of authority. And, in this light, contemporary Tourism Management/Tourism Studies researchers should remember that 'the gaze' of an institution ought not be understood so much as a literal way of seeing things, but as a particular social and intellectual regime that produces discourse and praxis (and thereby *classified understanding*) about them (Brooker, 2003, p. 108). Indeed 'the gaze' is part and parcel of Foucault's conceptual armoury in his own contribution to 'anti-ocular' French thought (Foucault, 1975). Just as Foucault's famous work on the gaze in the *Birth of the Clinic* was not much about the act of 'seeing', *per se*, but about 'space, language, and death' (Foucault, 1975), so this Moufakkir and Reisinger study of the host gaze(s), the tourist gaze(s) and the tourism gaze(s) is also a work about 'space, language and death' if it is to be faithful to its Foucauldian conceptuality. In the same

light, Duke's penetrative study of the constructed Minoan and other pasts in Crete (his *Tourist Gaze/Cretans Glance* work on heritage tourism in the Mediterranean (Duke, 2007)) could also be said to be a book about 'space, language and death' and not just about 'sight' *per se*. For instance, the back cover of Duke's six-chapter work indeed details it expansively to be a volume that addresses 'heritage and tourism and their relationships to local community, economic development, regional ecology, heritage conservation and preservation, and related indigenous, regional, and national and political and cultural issues'. It is not hard to find 'the space', 'the language' and 'the death' in that critique of such a deep-seated bundle of operational gazes (Duke, 2007, back cover), even if Duke like Urry (1990) before him – another borrower of the Foucauldian concept of *the gaze* – offers readers no careful open critique or contextual translation of *the gaze* (or of *le regard*) itself.

Historical meaning

Foucault has frequently been labelled a structuralist along with other French post-existentialist philosophers, Barthes, Lacan and (particularly) Lévi-Strauss. But Foucault was unimpressed with the monolithic character of structuralism: its search for universal underlying rules and permanent structures into which individuals are born proved to be too inflexible for him (Horrocks and Jevtic, 1997, p. 90). Foucault was not so interested in the formal possibilities of language, or myth in society, but rather how important meanings and value had changed over time – hence Foucault's 'archaeology' of understanding (Horrocks and Jevtic, 1997, p. 90). And later, Foucault was more interested in the way these meanings, values or truths had been tactically rather than functionally used within given historical periods – hence Foucault's 'genealogy' of understanding (Dean, 2010, pp. 3–4, 52–61). And rather than stressing the functional/structural purpose of aspects of culture or of domains of society, Foucault tended to write of and about *the historical meaning of things in the present* from an oppositional rather strictly pro-social and pro-public point of view. Yet, in his treatment of history and in his historical analysis of the present and the future, Foucault is no evocator of promise, no augur of the propitious – to Simons, he was instead a prophet of entrapment in the West 'who induces despair by indicating that there is no way out of our subjection ... [thereby] suggesting that we can only replace one domination with another' (Simons, 1995, p. 3). Foucault tempered this dark view of future society, however, by calling affirmatively for individuals to adopt more aesthetic and liberal modes of living where they would and should be able to escape from the limitations imposed by the suzerainty of the historical truths regulating them and otherwise from the emergent *power/knowledge* (see below) of the era. Accordingly, he tended to hover uneasily between being the prophet of entrapment and the advocate for gorgeous, inventive and artful living (Simons, 1995, p. 3), a tension that no doubt occurred because of the degree to which society was still regulated by the fictive power of scientific and administrative truth of all kinds (Miller, 1993, p. 152), and still governmentalized (for *governmentality*, see Dean, 2010, p. 3; pp. 24–30) by and through the unchecked authority of specific intellectuals who had risen up under modernity to occupy 'savant/expert' positions in society of real importance, but from which the rest of society had little watchdog protection (Morris and Patton, 1979, pp. 43–44).

In Foucault's view, the control of certain specific intellectuals over received historical meaning, and thereby also over evolved contemporary discourse and praxis, gave those specific intellectuals certain abilities (*puissances*) to favour life or to destroy it definitively (Morris and Patton, 1979, p. 44). To Foucault, truth is not only a thing of the world; it is so frequently the evolved or transmitted prerogative of the specific intellectuals of our contemporary social, cultural and administrative domains. So, by extension, who are the specific intellectuals

of Tourism Management/Tourism Studies? What external, public and political responsibilities do they admit or acknowledge? How can broad society guard itself against their specific volitions (see *will to power* and *will to truth*, of Nietzschean understanding)? Who is watching and monitoring the *dispositif* (i.e. the apparatus) of tourism management and development? Under Foucault's genealogical critique (after Nietzsche; Danaher *et al.*, 2000, pp. 24–28) the work of interest groups, institutions and instrumentalities filters, selects, prioritizes and excludes 'other interpretations' of and about things (Robinson and Groves, 1999, p. 166). Such is the power of all interest groups, institutions and instrumentalities to legitimize that past and the present via the historical meanings that they have quietly and under-suspectingly internalized: there can be nothing in and of tourism that can render it alien to the normalizing agency of 'held truths' duly 'received' from the past. Tourism, too, will have its own histories of the present – that is, its own various competing truths about what was important and what now is important about peoples and places. While all knowledge that is sayable and doable, and material can be changed (under Foucauldian lines of inspection), no knowledge in tourism (or anywhere) can ever be neutral: 'no knowledge is' (Macdonnell, 1982, p. 80).

Micropower

In *Discipline and Punish*, Foucault took a particularly strong Nietzschean stance on knowledge and maintained that it is an invention of the will, produced in fragile fashion as a by-product of the interest and influence of corporeal powers (Miller, 1993, p. 214). To Foucault, the self is the important vehicle that helps produce and transmit that knowledge within the concrete system of belonging which that will-to-power and those corporeal powers help constitute (Miller, 1993, p. 140) – such are matters of *truth production*. Consonantly, the self has an immediate role to play in the production and circulation of knowledge without the need for force or authority, because knowledge is generated purely and simply through the everyday 'talk' (and 'deeds') of the individual (Miller, 1993, p. 140): no individual may escape that mundane imperative – it is the everyday micropower by which knowledge is generated and circulated (via *truth statements* and through *will to power*; Danaher *et al.*, 2000, p. 107). Drawing from Baudelaire, Foucault sees this productive micropower as an element of the heroism of the prosaic and workaday institutional life (Horrocks and Jevtic, 1997, p. 143), by which the self is activated in service of the *will to truth* (Robinson and Groves, 1999, p. 86) of the particular field of relations. In attempting to clarify these Foucauldian perspectives on the micro-power of knowledge-invention and truth-production, Deleuze suggests that it may be healthier not to envisage any single *dispositif* or state apparatus of power within any field, but instead a diffuse and heterogeneous multiplicity of micro-*dispositifs* that help circulate and transmit the knowledge and/or truths in question (Deleuze, 1997, p. 184). To Deleuze, these Foucauldian micro-dispositifs work neither through repression nor ideology, but are the absolute mechanism by which the self/each self engages in the constant prompting and triggering of the held *institutional truth*. Since the activation of the micro-power is therefore tiny and widespread, these individuals permit the institution to see without necessarily being seen (Deleuze, 1997, p. 184) — see *panopticism*, below. The sum total of these everyday petty actions is an *opaque power* network wherever strong discourse merges with strong self-normalized practice (Hollinshead, 1993, p. 284). Hence micro-power aggregates through its local, constant, productive and all-pervasive character to become the capillary force (see *capillary circulation*, above) of opaque power — a *biopower* (McHoul and Grace, 1995, pp. 77–87), which invades or is absorbed into people's bodies rather than into their head, or rather than into their heads alone (Habermas [on Foucault], 1987, p. 283).

And so, who in Tourism Management/ Tourism Studies is investigating the possible/ probable disciplinary consequences of the micro-power of the industry or of vested public or not-for-profit interests active in tourism and travel? Who in the field is investigating whether a biopower is present across sectors of the industry that regulate the ways in which culture, heritage and the environment are conceivably harnessed to suit the needs of the industry or of groups or communities who seek to legitimate this or that? Who is inquiring into what Foucault terms the imaginary geopolitics (Foucault, 1980, pp. 70–71) of the particular carceral domains (see *carceral society*, above) of tourism? Hollinshead (1993, pp. 797–800) has studied how administrators of statist forms of identity and heritage have 'written' Texas, and shaped the ways in which the viewable and visitable places and spaces of the Lone Star State ought to be celebrated. But the field needs much more longitudinal inquiry of this type into the non-neutral iconographic scripting of tourism.

Panopticism

Foucault's neologism 'panopticism' was derived from Jeremy Benthan's (1791) book *Panopticon* in which the English jurist and reformer recommended the design and construction of a circular gaol in which all prisoners could be continually supervised from a tall and centrally located watchtower – hence the title of the book, as derived from the Greek *panoptes* for 'all-seeing' (Miller, 1993, pp. 219–220). Thus, Foucault's panopticism is that process where everything is visible under the institutional *eye-of-power* (see *scopic drive*, below): it is the everyday and ceaseless gaze (see *gaze (the clinical)*, above) through which the surveillance of a given population (or of all people) is conducted, and by which a particular dominant influence is maintained and through which an endless normalization of things is enacted (Harland, 1987, p. 164). Foucault's discovered panoptic vision is, therefore, an all-pervasive oversight, an omnipresent disciplinary power (see *disciplinary instruments* and *disciplinary procedures* in McHoul and Grace,

1995, p. 71) to which individuals are sub-jected and by which individuals learn to subject and regulate themselves (Habermas [on Foucault], 1987, p. 252). It is the disci-plinary drive of modern bourgeois society (Merquior, 1985, pp. 91–92) that anony-mously regulates people (Rabinow, 1984, p. 19), and renders them submissive to supervision (Miller, 1993, p. 219), thereby capable of being marked and classified (Fou-cault, 1980, p. 71). Yet panopticism is not something that is just issued by central, head office or national capital points of control, for its real effectiveness lies in the degree to which its supervisory and self-supervisory practices become generalized over a popula-tion under the gaze: in accordance with Fou-cauldian conceptuality, the panoptic system produces dispersed panopticism (Foucault, 1980, p. 72). Hence panoptic power ought not be seen as a unique and privileged instru-ment of central authority, but rather as that sort of ambiguous *opaque power* which is transmitted via fine channels of *capillary cir-culation* (Foucault, 1980, p. 72): 'systems of domination and circuits of exploitation cer-tainly interact, intersect, and support each other [under panopticism], but they do not coincide' (Foucault, 1980, p. 72).

Now, while it is the sustained thesis of Foucault that panopticism thrives in the barracks, in the schools, in the hospitals and in the prisons of the Western world, may one also assume it is pervasively pres-ent at the tourism sites and settings of the world – and also in the administrative 'pal-aces' where the themes, programmes and packages for tourist visitation are conceived and projected? While those who investigate who is doing what to whom, where and when through tourism will not be expected to literally look for Benthamite circular gaols or all-seeing concrete watchtowers, it would be propitious in many locations for Tourism Management/Tourism Studies research teams to inspect for panoptic forms of authoritarian governmentality. In tour-ism, or for other industries and fields, such forms of authoritarian governmentality might 'generate [decisions] through [an] intensive and generalised use of sovereign instruments of repression' (Dean, 2010,

pp. 155–173). Thereby Tourism Studies research teams that suspect the presence of a dominant authoritarian or other normal-ization at work might fruitfully explore which outlooks on the world have thereby been fostered and which ways of being and becoming have been coterminously disal-lowed. And how aware of the force-field of these governmentalities were the individu-als who operated the technology and found disciplinary instruments and disciplinary procedures (Rabinow, 1984, p. 206)? And where those whose being and becoming had conceivably been suppressed by such pan-optic technology, how aware in fact were those subjected groups, communities or peoples of their own docility (i.e. their own docile role in their self-surveillance or self-regulation (Rabinow, 1984, p. 207)?

Scopic drive

In French litero-philosophy – and particu-larly under Foucauldian lines of institu-tional analysis – the scopic drive of an organization, community or epoch is the proclivity and conviction of that body or that era's outlook as is generally actualized through its 'gaze' (see *gaze* (*the clinical*), above) over the locale or the entire world. Hence, the scopic drive of that organization or that community is the exercise of the Nietzschean *will to truth* that results from the Benthamite panoptic (see *panopticism*, above; Rabinow, 1984, pp. 206–213) deploy-ment of that gaze over that governing field of relations which the institution wishes to take care of, regulate or discipline. There-fore, the scopic drive is a normalizing power of local or universal *surveillance* that acts as an *eye-of-authority/eye-of-power* over the domain which that organization or community seeks to serve, to control or to punish. When the scopic drive is well enmeshed within the panoptic agency of that body's ongoing work regime, it is nota-bly penetrating since those who are held under that surveillance never quite know when they are ever being overseen. And when the power of 'punishment' is strongly articulated, they accordingly tend to regulate themselves over time. And that very act of surveillance also is inclined to reinforce a commitment to the imperatives of the scopic drive amongst those *who carry out* those everyday acts of surveillance and normalization – they, too, are accordingly self-disciplined (Foucault, 1980, pp. 146–165). Clearly, the scopic drive of institutions is a 'game' or a site of constant struggle for the definition of reality and for the establishment of the 'correct' vision based on those consensual or empowered 'truths' – and may be said to be a *game of truth*. While a given scopic drive may become highly 'productive' and 'performative' over time (Morris and Patton, 1979, p. 36), its existence (to Foucault) is always inherently precarious (Merquior, 1985, p. 77). Such is the never-total and never-absolute Foucauldian *specular bias* of institutions.

Had Foucault ventured into studies of tourism and of the declarative authority of policy makers, practitioners and players in the public culture, the public heritage and the public nature domains of tourism and travel, he would clearly not just have been interested in how the gazes of industrial or public tourism were institutionalized and overseen, but also in what they 'consubstantially produced' or help produce (Foucault, 1980, p. 159). Foucault always tended to stress that the scopic drive of organizations was constantly being transformed as other or new disciplinary forces rose and as fresh, transcending disciplinary mechanisms appeared on the given scene. Thus, following Foucault's entreaties on the scopic drive of bodies, research teams in tourism and travel may want to be highly circumspect about their analyses of power mechanisms: they ought (after Foucault, 1980, p. 163–164) to resist the possible built-in tendency to always show the 'power' (i.e. the power/knowledge) being exercised as being singularly victorious 'there'. What mattered to Foucault were the constantly changing productive forces that were at play in the particular institutional domain, and the contesting relations of production that seemingly rose and fell there (Foucault, 1991b, pp. 103). And given the global reach of international tourism and its fecundity in the many matters of 'social', 'cultural', 'political', 'psychic', 'environmental', 'economic' and 'other' circumstances, one might expect that research teams in international tourism will inevitably find the scopic drive of tourism interest groups, institutions and instrumentalities to be particularly subject to many sorts of open and organic dynamic processes (see Dean, 2010, pp. 118–121 on bio-politics). Or, will the last (i.e. summary) chapter of this book reveal instead that the bio-politics of tourism (and even of international tourism) is still a contained game of truth production – a limited but ubiquitous game of governmentality?

Self-regulation

One of the major 'projects' in and of Foucault's historico-philosophical writing is his advocacy for *the public self*, whereby he encouraged the keen and regular practice of techniques of the self, which he termed *practique de soi*, and *rapport à soi* (Rapport and Overing, 2000, p. 298). In recognizing the need to regularly engage in such honest matters of self-rapport, Foucault was much influenced by Plato's dialogue entitled *Alcibiades* in which Alcibiades engages in various 'public' debates with the seemingly honourable Socrates (Horrocks and Jevtic, 1997, p. 153): in these public debates, it becomes plain to Alcibiades that if he is to decently want to take care/responsibility for others, he must first be at one with himself.

Foucault's interest in the ongoing care of the self was also enhanced during a late 1970s visit to Japan where he involved himself heavily in Zen thought (Horrocks and Jevtic, 1997, p. 136), and where he realized that to be effective and directive in one's communications and contributions, one must be and become – not necessarily the same thing in terms of Foucault's logic of transcendental experience – *one's own project* throughout one's life.

Perhaps such thoughts on the fit between self-rapport and civic duties is best witnessed in Foucaults third (and sadly, last) volume of his *History of Sexuality* (entitled 'The Care of the Self'), where he paid deep attention to the self-regulatory practices of Hellenic and Roman times (Foucault, 1984). In this work and in related interviews Foucault sought to engender a new 'ethics' or 'stylistics' of existence whereby 'power' was not about honouring duties to others or to the state, but was attained through the constant effort to govern the self through thought, reason and controlled action (Horrocks and Jevtic, 1997, p. 157). To Foucault, there would always be matters (such as the very right to be different) that should be left unregulated by society (Miller, 1993, p. 32). In order to decently govern, the individual must be able to self-regulate themselves, and thereby learn not only how to exercise free will, but how to set new limits for one's own experiences and conduct (Miller, 1993, p. 317).

What individual practitioners in Tourism Management or individual researchers in Tourism Studies may wish to explore, therefore – if they value Foucault's insights on *pratique de soi* and *rapport à soi* – is the ways in which they themselves have conceivably become subjects constituted in and through the multi-seated and iterative processes of work in international tourism, in travel development, in cultural tourism research, etc. Thus, without needing to build up causal models of understanding – for Foucault never sought such absolute forms of theoretical insight (Lurry, 2008, p. 578) – how is the individual indeed linked to, associated with and influenced by the micro-practices of the institutions they work for or otherwise come into contact with? To some extent, Caton (2008) has already begun to explore such relational matters in tourism, explicitly in terms of the degree to which (for instance) educational travel brokers 'are willing to put up with [particular styles of site mediation]' (Caton, 2008, p. 144): her work is perhaps inherently a reflexive journey into such banal and cumulative forms of self-regulation. Hopefully, Caton can expand her research agenda on the technologies of self-subjectification over the coming decade(s) into other areas of Tourism Studies scholarship.

References

Allen, B. (1998) Foucault and modern political philosophy. In: Moss, J. (eds) *The Later Foucault: Politics and Philosophy*. Sage, London, pp. 164–198.

Barker, C. (2004) *The Sage Dictionary of Cultural Studies*. Sage, London.

Brooker, P. (2003) *A Glossary of Cultural Theory*. Hodden Arnold, London.

Brown, W. (1998) Genealogical politics. In: Moss, J. (ed.) *The Later Foucault: Politics and Philosophy*. Sage, London, pp. 33–49.

Caton, K. (2008) Encountering the others through study abroad. PhD thesis, The University of Illinois, Illinois, USA.

Connolly, W. (1998) Beyond good and evil: the ethical sensitivity of Michel Foucault. In: Moss, J. (ed.) *The Later Foucault: Politics and Philosophy*. Sage, London, pp. 108–128.

De Certeau, M. (1982) La folie de la vision. *Espirit*, 66.

Danaher, G., Schirato, T. and Webb, J. (2000) *Understanding Foucault*. Sage, London.

Davidson, A.I. (1997) *Foucault and His Interlocutors*. University of Chicago Press, Chicago, IL.

Dean, M. (2010) *Governmentality: Power and Rule in Modern Society*. Sage, Los Angeles, CA.

Deleuze, G. (1997) Desire and pleasure. In: Davidson, A.I. (ed.) *Foucault and His Interlocutors*. University of Chicago Press, Chicago, IL, pp. 183–194.

Duke, P. (2007) *The Tourist Gaze, the Cretans Glance: Archaeology and Tourism on a Greek Island*. Left Coast Press, Walnut Creek, CA.

Foucault, M. (1966) *L'homme est-il mort?* [Interview] Arts et Loisirs. 15th June 1966.

Foucault, M. (1975) *The Birth of the Clinic: the Archaeology of Medical Perception*. Vintage, New York.

Foucault, M. (1976) *The Birth of the Clinic*. Tavistock, London.

Foucault, M. (1977) *Discipline and Punish*. Pantheon Books, New York.

Foucault, M. (1980) *Power/Knowledge: Selected Interviews and Other Writings 1972–77*. Edited by Gordon, C., translated by Marshall, L., Mepham, J. and Soper, K. Pantheon Books, New York.

Foucault, M. (1984) *The History of Sexuality: Vol. I – an Introduction*. Translated by Hurley, R. Vintage, New York.

Foucault, M. (1991a) Politics and the study of discourse. In: Burchell, G., Gordon, C. and Miller, P. (eds) *The Foucault Effect: Studies in Governmentality*. University of Chicago Press, Chicago, IL, pp. 53–72.

Foucault, M. (1991b) Governmentality. In: Burchell, G., Gordon, C. and Miller, P. (eds) *The Foucault Effect: Studies in Governmentality*. University of Chicago Press, Chicago, IL, pp. 87–104.

Foucault, M. and Chomsky, N. (1997) Human nature: justice versus power. In: Davidson, A.I. (ed.) *Foucault and His Interlocutors*. University of Chicago Press, Chicago, IL, pp. 107–145.

Fraser, N. (1989) Foucault on modern power: empirical insights and normative confusions. In: Fraser, N. (ed.) *Unruly Practices*. University of Minnesota Press, Minneapolis, MN.

Habermas, J. (1987) *The Philosophical Discourse of Modernity*. Translated by Lawrence, F. M.I.T. Press, Cambridge, MA.

Harland, R. (1987) *Superstructuralism: the Philosophy of Structuralism and Post-Structuralism*. Methuen, London.

Hartsock, N. (1990) Foucault on power: a theory for women. In: Nichalson, L. (ed.) *Feminism/Postmodernism*. Routledge, New York, pp. 157–175.

Hollinshead, K. (1993) The truth about Texas: a naturalistic study of the construction of heritage. PhD thesis, Texas A&M University, College Station, TX.

Horrocks, C. and Jevtic, Z. (1997) *Foucault for Beginners*. Icon Books, Cambridge.

Jaworski, A. and Pritchard, A. (2005) *Discourse, Communication and Tourism*. Channel View Publications, Clevedon.

Jay, M. (1994) *Downcast Eyes: the Denigration of Vision in Twentieth Century French Thought*. University of California Press, Berkeley, CA.

Kearney, R. (1988) *The Wake of Imagination: Ideas of Creating in Western Culture*. Hutchinson, London.

Lurry, C. (2008) Cultural technologies. In: Bennett, T. and Frow, J. (eds) *The Sage Handbook of Cultural Analysis*. Sage, Los Angeles, CA, pp. 570–586.

Macdonnell, D. (1982) *Theories of Discourse*. Basil Blackwell, Oxford.

McHoul, A. and Grace, W. (1995) *A Foucault Primer: Discourse, Power, and Subject*. University College, London.

Merquior, J.G. (1985) *Foucault*. Fontana Press, London.

Miller, J. (1993) *The Passion of Michel Foucault*. Doubleday, New York.

Morris, M. and Patton, P. (1979) *Michel Foucault: Power, Truth, Strategy*. Feral Publications, Sydney.

Moss, J. (1998) Introduction: the later Foucault. In: Moss, J. (ed.) *The Later Foucault: Politics and Philosophy*. Sage, London, pp. 1–17.

Mulvey, L. (1989) *Visual and Other Pleasures*. Macmillan, London.

Nietzsche, F. (1969) *On the Genealogy of Morals*. Edited by Kaufman, W. Random House (Vintage Books), New York.

Patton, P. (1998) Foucault's subject of power. In: Moss, J. (ed.) *The Later Foucault: Politics and Philosophy*. Sage, London, pp. 76–77.

Rabinow, P. (1984) *The Foucault Reader*. Pantheon Books, New York.

Rajchman, J. (1988) Foucault's art of seeing. *October*, 44, pp. 88–117.

Rapport, N. and Overing, J. (2000) *Social and Cultural Anthropology: The Key Concepts*. Routledge, London.

Robinson, D. and Groves, J. (1999) *Introducing Philosophy*. Icon Books, Cambridge.

Sawicki, J. (1998) Feminism, Foucault and 'subjects' of power and freedom. In: Moss, J. (ed.) *The Later Foucault: Politics and Philosophy*. Sage, London, pp. 93–108.

Serres, M. (1989) Panoptic theory. In: Kavanagh, T.M. (ed.) *The Limits of Theory*. Stanford, CA,

Shames, G.W. and Glover, G.W. (1989) *World Class Service*. International Press, Yarmouth, ME, pp. 25–50.

Simons, J. (1995) *Foucault and the Political*. Routledge, London.

Sloterdijk, P. (1988) *Critique of Cynical Reason*. Translated by Eldred, M. University of Minnesota Press Minneapolis, MN.

Smart, B. (1998) Foucault, Levinas, and the subject of responsibility. In: Moss, J. (ed.) *The Later Foucault: Politics and Philosophy*. Sage, London, pp. 78–92.

Thomas, N. (1994) *Colonialism's Culture: Anthropology, Travel and Government*. Princeton University Press, Princeton, NJ.

Urry, J. (1990) *The Tourist Gaze: Leisure and Travel in Contemporary Societies*. Sage, London.

2 Gaze and Self: Host Internalization of the Tourist Gaze

Bonnie Canziani and Jennifer Francioni

Introduction

The present chapter reviews the literature on socio-cultural impacts of tourism from a theoretical perspective of role and identity. Particular emphasis is placed on host perspectives of the tourist gaze from the vantage point of occupational and resident roles in the destination. The definition of host herein constitutes any person who is recognized as a resident of the destination or a member of destination enterprises serving tourists, and may include persons whose origins are different from the tourist destination. The authors interpret tourism role-taking and role behavioural compliance as a form of internalization of the tourist gaze that can lead to emotional outcomes, host defensive tactics and shifts in host self-concept. This chapter contributes to the theoretical evolution of the *tourist gaze* beyond Urry's (1990) treatment of the topic and expands conceptual understanding of the gaze as a prevailing force on the destination by offering a set of theoretical propositions for future study.

Within the literature, the gaze concept has evolved beyond the notion of a one-sided tourist gaze. Maoz (2006) implies the likelihood of a mutual gaze between host and guest, but portrays both guests and hosts as faceless members of barely tolerated, imagined geographies. Alternatively,

Ateljevic (2000) views the mutuality of gazes as the negotiated production of interacting host and tourist agents. The expansion of the theoretical definition of the gaze to one of mutuality has been supported by work that shows hosts meeting tourists with a predetermined gaze of their own (Steiner and Reisinger, 2004; Uriely, 2005; Osagie and Buzinde, 2011). Note that the authors do not adopt an *a priori* assumption of 'we–they' dichotomies between tourists and hosts; rather the focus lies on the interactions between hosts and tourists as sources of social influence on behaviour and on host self-perception.

Across the literature, host gazes seem to be described in three distinct ways: the *classifying gaze*, where hosts as human observers or consumer behaviourists view tourists in order to label and categorize them into cognitive schemata, the *stakeholder gaze*, where host community members are looking at the effects of tourists and tourism on the destination, and the *internalized gaze*, where hosts incorporate elements of the tourist gaze into their own behaviour and into subsequent perceptions of self. The authors will explore more fully this third type of self-revealing and self-protecting host gaze to better understand the personal consequences of hosts gazing at themselves under the influence of others in the tourist destination.

The Internalized Gaze of the Host

Internalization of the tourist gaze commences when hosts become cognizant of norms and behaviours that emerge to accommodate the demands of the tourism enterprise. Authors interested in the power embedded in tourist gazes, for example, Wearing et al. (2010), suggest that the tourist gaze, like Foucault's (1973) clinical gaze, obliges a host community to view itself from the perspective of its visitors and to respond by meeting the demands of its visitors in order to sustain a viable position in the world economic or social order. Both Foucault (1973) and Bourdieu (1984) stress the notion of power in their analyses of observers and the objects of observation. When the observer is more powerful than the observed, as in the case of 'rich tourists with hard currency', the result can be the servant production of tourism 'art' to the frivolous dictates of the tourist 'patron'. In like manner, the tourist gaze corresponds to an internalized host gaze that guides host response to tourists and host reflection upon the self.

While there are multiple sociological and psychological theories that might help explain individual responses in the face of tourist scrutiny, role theory will be the primary theoretical framework used in this chapter. Furthermore, while much of the tourism literature has addressed the social impacts of tourism and tourist gaze on host populations from a societal or collective point of view (Brunt and Courtney, 1999; Lindberg et al., 2001; Besculides et al., 2002), this chapter offers theoretical propositions on the potential impacts of the tourist gaze on individuals.

of resident opinion have specified the continued importance of preserving the welfare of the host community through the promotion of shared objectives and sustainability values (e.g. Moyle et al., 2010). Tourism scholars in areas such as stakeholder studies (Robson and Robson, 1996; Easterling, 2005), community-based tourism (e.g. Kayat, 2008) and sustainable tourism (e.g. Choi and Murray, 2010) have contributed valuable insights into the perceived and real impacts of tourists on host quality of life and well-being.

However, focus on the host vis-a-vis the community has largely ignored influences of the tourist gaze on individual self-image. More investigation is still needed into how the host's definition of self might be influenced by the tourist gaze and how hosts manage their self images during host–tourist encounters. The current authors are particularly interested in finding theoretical explanations for increased distancing from tourists (e.g. Bunten, 2008; Moyle et al., 2010) and resident mobilization and resistance to tourist interference with their residential roles (e.g. Tucker, 1997; Joseph and Kavoori, 2001; Chhabra, 2010). Another area of interest is the significance of host reflection on occupational and resident roles in the destination. In the remaining sections of this chapter, role theory will be the primary window through which host internalization of the tourist gaze will be viewed. Role theory provides a backdrop from which host internalization of the tourist gaze can be conceptualized at the level of the individual subject and suggests ways in which hosts define and locate themselves within host–tourist encounters and relationships in the destination.

Host Response: from the Collective to the Individual

Previous study of socio-cultural impacts of tourism has centred on the aggregated response of the host community to tourism and its impacts (Gursoy and Rutherford, 2004; Andereck et al., 2005). Such analyses

Relevant Concepts of Role Theory

Biddle (1986) asserts that role carries significant theoretical relevance for research on human behaviour. Role theorists continually refer to role-contained expectations for behaviour in social situations; such beliefs were found in early 20th-century philosophy and social science, for example, *degrees of domination* and *freedom* and *multiple statuses of the self* described by Georg Simmel (Rossides, 1998, pp. 171–180) and *role-taking* and *reflexiveness* concepts introduced by George Herbert Mead (Aboulafia, 1986).The degree to which a role is salient in a person's mind when responding to situations is seen to be a factor in determining the degree to which behaviour will be affected by the role (Ashforth and Johnson, 2001).

Role has been empirically linked with constructs of self; Stryker (2007) and Burke and Reitzes (1981) demonstrate that an individual has multiple role identities that together form a sense of self and potentially shape behaviours in specific settings. Two primary definitions of self are relevant to this discussion: self-concept and identity. Self-concept has been interpreted as a cognitive rendering that originates within the individual, while identity is more broadly socially constructed and tends to mark the self within the societal domain through examinations of similarity and differences to others (Baumeister, 1998). The self-concept can switch among various spontaneous selves at the surface level, while deeper beliefs about one's identity do not change as readily; McGuire *et al.* (1978) found that those selves that were salient during an interaction were triggered by one's perception of uniqueness or role in a social situation, for example, a boy in a group of girls. In order to limit the scope of the present theoretical analysis to matters of individual host cognition and response, self-concept rather than identity, will be the influenced 'object' of the tourist gaze.

Role theory has received its share of criticism due to legitimate concerns. In her review of role theory, Jackson (1998) determines that role theorists promote social stereotypes through static characterizations of role positions and role behaviours. She notes that some role theoretical analyses of human behaviour exhibit overconfidence in predicting role behaviours. Despite these shortcomings, role concepts seem to have sufficient stability across the research community and provide an excellent framework

from which to examine host responses to the tourist gaze, with the understanding that the tourist gaze is viewed herein as a *constraint on* rather than as a *predictor of* host behaviour.

Cognitive role theory, inasmuch as it centres attention on individuals' mindfulness of their roles and behaviours, seems particularly fruitful as an avenue of inquiry regarding host internalization of the tourist gaze. In his review of cognitive role theory, Biddle (1986) states that:

> Attention has been given to social conditions that give rise to [role] expectations, to techniques for measuring expectations, and to the impact of expectations on social conduct...[and] the ways in which a person perceives the expectations of others and with the effects of those perceptions on behaviour. (Biddle, 1986, p. 74)

Several assumptions aligned with cognitive role theory need to be specified prior to advancing a theoretical conceptualization of the host internalization of the tourist gaze, as follow:

- *Role* is defined as scripts and/or expectations for behaviour that explain characteristic responses to situations and events.
- A person's choice to act (or not) or choice of action (or non-action) may be cognitively associated with a role through the cognitive acknowledgement of rules governing behaviour in that role.
- Choices may be associated with one role or with multiple roles at the same time.
- Choice may be influenced by other people directly or by recognition of greater societal forces, for example, cultural norms or economic needs that constrain or support specific options.
- Human cognition is viewed as a critical element in role theoretical analysis, since choices may be paired with both cognitive intentions and reflections.

While only a limited number of studies have used role concepts to explain social behaviour in tourism contexts (e.g. Holloway,

1981; Cohen, 1985; Gibson and Yiannakis, 2002; Uriely, 2005; Duim, 2007; Warden *et al.*, 2007), the tourism literature is replete with examples of roles that hosts might undertake in a destination: *tour guides* (e.g. Holloway, 1981; Cohen, 1985; Fine and Speer, 1985), *artisans* (e.g. Graburn, 1984; Cone, 1995; Grünewald, 2002) and *cultural performers* (e.g. Jordan, 1980; Goldberg, 1983; Wang, 2007; Condevaux, 2009). One need not, however, be a member of a highly organized tourism business to be subject to the tourist gaze. Evidence shows that tourism casts a wide net. Hosts in occupational and entrepreneurial roles outside the mainstream tourism attractions are also influenced by tourist feedback and remuneration for services rendered (Smith, 1988).

A majority of host roles surfacing in tourism studies do correspond to occupational positions related to tourism, either directly, as in a tour guide, or tangentially, as in a retail shop owner. Yet some roles may be more reflective of a resident role where hosts are implicated in social encounters as co-consumers in a business serving tourists or as bystanders in a public venue visited by tourists. It would seem that the abundance of occupational and resident role examples in the literature justifies the present focus on these two roles in the following role theoretical analysis.

Role Theoretical Analysis of Host Response to Tourism

Figure 2.1 depicts an overarching model of how the tourist gaze is believed to impact the self concepts of hosts by encoding expectations for behaviour within occupational and resident roles. In a process of commoditization, the tourist gaze institutionalizes role behaviours that best correlate with tourist needs and expectations and assigns positive value to these selected role behaviours (Canziani, 2011). Most probably, the influence of the tourist gaze is exercised through either the formal institutionalization of role scripts or the tourist's repetitive reinforcement of casual host behaviours. The tourist does not operate alone to reinforce host behaviours (e.g Cornelissen, 2005; Palmer, 2007). Third-party standards, government, media, organizational or professional, may dictate how a role is to be enacted As per the previously stated assumptions of cognitive role theory, the host, when confronted with expectations and valuations from others regarding potential behavioural performances, may respond in a variety of ways, for example, implementing expected behaviours, manipulating behavioural expectations and/or manifesting affective displays of emotion and buffering tactics, as well as cognitive impacts on self-concept.

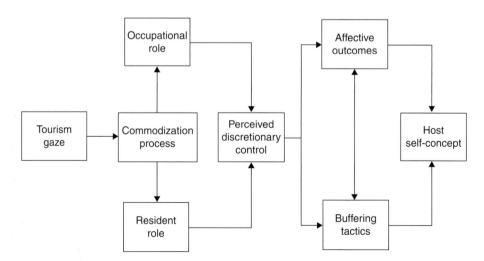

Fig. 2.1. Model of host internalization of the tourist gaze.

In order to substantiate the suggested model in Fig. 2.1, we turn to the literature in search of evidence of characteristic behaviours enacted by hosts in the presence of tourists. The case of tourist gaze influence on host behaviours and self-concept will become clearer through an analysis of two types of expected performances (hospitable behaviours and cultural behaviours) often associated with occupational and resident roles in destinations.

Occupational and resident roles

A primary mechanism by which the tourist gaze introduces role expectations into a destination is through the employment of hosts in occupations that involve contact with tourists. The host may be seen to undertake any of a number of functions in the conduct of tourism in a destination: tour guide, restaurant worker, hotel housekeeper, museum docent, sex worker, spectacle performer, souvenir seller, event planner, diving instructor, bed and breakfast owner. Although job titles may govern wildly fluctuating tasks, for the most part, jobs that involve interpersonal encounters with tourists carry at least a skeletal set of tourist expectations for persons in those positions.

Occupational roles do not have to be 'tourism' specific, but merely jobs where tourist/host encounters may arise. Clearly, since hosts in tourism-specific occupational roles have increased potential contact with tourists, they also have significant potential to encounter the tourist gaze and be impacted by it. In his review of the literature on tourism work, Blanton (1981, pp. 119–120) finds evidence of the following: tourism jobs replicate colonial relationships and obligate hosts to display pseudo or commoditized cultures; workers are the first to encounter stereotypes and misconception about history and culture; tourism work is demeaning, low in status, and tends to routinize and commercialize interpersonal relationships. These various factors strongly suggest that occupational roles might be particularly sensitive to the tourist gaze.

Hosts take on the resident role when preoccupied with the use of community services and spaces to which they feel entitled as locals. The authors believe that people in general are able to discriminate between these two social roles they occupy, at least when discussing these roles in relation to encounters with tourists. It should be noted that the role of resident is not as clear-cut in terms of being regularly exposed to the tourist gaze through personal contact with tourists. When the number of tourists goes up, the destination moves steadily towards the erection of more and more barriers to keep tourists at bay, leading to bubble designs (Jaakson, 2004; Carrier and Macleod, 2005), increased policing and security staffing, and a vast reduction of the likelihood of direct interaction with members of the host society. Tourism can also restrict the geographical mobility of locals, by barring non-tourism related traffic from accessing transportation routes and tourist spaces (Quinn, 2007). Nonetheless, residents do live and work in the neighbourhoods frequented by tourists, and do at times patronize retail, transit and recreation services tourists visit as well. On occasions when tourists and residents meet as co-consumers of local space, the tourist gaze can attempt to operate on the resident in ways similar to its projected influence on occupational workers.

Hospitable Behaviour as Role Performance

One expectation pertinent to both occupational and resident roles is the *expression of hospitableness* (Brotherton, 1999) to the tourist. Tourists' expectations for specific signs of hospitableness and related deference behaviours can influence both occupational and resident role performance. The display of hospitable behaviours to strangers has been a principle both in business and in personal homes that has governed relationships between hosts and travellers since the early ages (Aramberri, 2001). Hospitable behaviours are often guided by a belief that one should do what it takes to ensure the comfort of a guest. Most major hospitality and tourism companies have converted this ethic of hospitableness into a doctrine that is both pervasive across corporate training programmes and viewed as instrumental in generating increased revenues and employee tips.

Institutionalizing what might have been viewed by rights as a common courtesy of individuals to other individuals presumably exerts greater control over the actual behaviours performed by hosts in tourism encounters. Expectations for overt signs of hospitableness vary across occupational roles. Roles that are governed by explicit organizational service standards may encourage hosts to exhibit hospitable and deference behaviours in more visible and prescribed ways. Disney University provides an example of training where cast members (what Disney calls its employees) are trained on how to talk, point, act, look (appearance) and much more (Byrman, 1999).

In the occupational role, hospitableness converted into commercialized hospitality becomes a professional code that is posted on walls, laminated on cards carried by organizational employees and generally disassociated from the person occupying the worker role. Socialization of hosts is supported by tourist or organizational feedback about role performance that occurs in host interactions with the tourist. For example, customer satisfaction surveys may be used to develop quantitative measures of selected hospitality dimensions and employees may be rewarded on the basis of their customer feedback scores.

In the case of the resident role, tourists and third-party stakeholders may also expect hospitable behaviour from the population at large. Answering tourist questions and guiding tourists in the right direction may be part of a day's work for occupation holders serving tourists, but not necessarily the preferred daily grind for a local. Interestingly, government agencies have sought to socialize their communities to be more sympathetic to the needs of tourists, as in a Parisian scheme whereby the city authorities created Paris Tourist Day (Sage, 2007)

and circulated pamphlets to citizens and to tourists in an attempt to engender greater empathy between the two groups. Since residents do not always see immediate benefits in the form of direct tourism receipts from their behaviours toward tourists, it is hard to predict the extent to which institutionalized forms of hospitality behaviour will become embedded successfully in resident roles in destinations. Quinn (2007), reporting on attitudes of Venetian residents toward tourists, shares the following:

> [Venetians] do not want to be photographed chatting to their neighbours, or delayed carrying home their shopping.... For some this sort of behaviour was viewed as inappropriate and was interpreted to mean 'there's a lack of respect for those who live here'. (Quinn, 2007, p. 469)

While on occasion residents may display genuine hospitableness by aiding a lost tourist, they may exhibit increased irritation if this type of request occurs with more and more frequency due to surges in tourist arrivals in the shared space. And if the tourist communicates expectations of hospitality that move the resident/tourist encounter into the playing field of tourism transaction rather than spontaneous social etiquette, the resident feels a sense of obligation and resentment.

Cultural Role Performance

In addition to having expectations for hospitableness from hosts, tourists expect hosts to act like tourists think locals should act. More formally, cultural role performances are defined as expecting hosts in either occupational or resident roles to authenticate the cultural representation carried mentally by the tourist. Such expectations can be as simple as expecting hosts to have strong local accents or to know the best local eateries. It may be that attempts to commoditize culture are viewed by hosts with more disfavour than are commercialized hospitality and customer service systems; however, both are intentionally designed to satisfy consumers by approaching host behaviours from an instrumentalist point of view.

As in the case of hospitality behaviours, cultural behaviours enacted within mainstream tourism attractions tend to adhere to institutionalized standards. The occupational role thus delivers culture as it would food and beverage, objectified and priced to sell. Often cultural standards are institutionalized through the creation of theatrical productions, offering a sanitized version of cultural rituals and rites (Jordan, 1980; Goldberg, 1983; Condevaux, 2009). Yet the most random souvenir hawker or hander on may over time develop a strong sense of what behaviours help him sell the most due to tourist reinforcement of speech, dress and other performed cultural nuances (Wang, 2007).

From an ethical stance Rekom and Go (2006) suggest that social constructions of culture are the entitlement of members of a host community. They support this position in their application of social identity theory to tourism where they allude to a social group's right to distinguish itself from other groups in the social environment. Nonetheless, in the tourism setting, host cultural behaviours are commoditized, in the same way that Bourdieu's (1984, pp. 316–317) figure of patron determines what a 'patronized' artist's creation is worth.

Evidence abounds of cultural attractions that are focused on a quick run-through of the site with strategically placed stops for the taking of snapshots with 'authentically' dressed host characters. According to Garrod (2009), tourist photography more than likely supports the image constructed by the tourist gaze rather than facilitating host control over development of the cultural image in the minds of tourists. Tourists expect to see cultural performances that have been propagated by media representations and tourist designs, as well as by continued word of mouth socialization efforts among tourists themselves. Tourists take on a more dominant role in the valuation of cultural performances as they share their pre-constructed expectations with other tourists (Glover, 2008). With multi-stop designs, the time period of the tourist's stay is too brief to facilitate awareness of individual hosts (Hottola,

2004). When time is short, tourists cannot be expected to question the veracity of contrived host behaviours because they have not seen any alternative cultural explanations through interaction with the host community.

The conversion of cultural aspects of host behaviour to 'theatrical cultural performance' is not a response limited to hosts involved in occupational roles. Cohen et al. (1992) found that the tourist gaze also commoditizes cultural aspects of the resident role through feedback in practical terms such as inviting residents who 'look the part' to stand for photos or by rewarding 'authentic' displays with greater positive commentary as tourists observe the appearance and behaviours of locals on site.

Having seen that both resident and occupational roles experience the tourist gaze in the form of role expectations for hospitableness and cultural behaviours, we now turn to the issue of host response to the tourist gaze. It is expected that hosts will experience emotional responses to role situations in which they feel constrained by the expectations of others and that impacts on host self concept occur as hosts seek to manage emotions arising from these role situations.

Legitimate Authority and Sanctions

Evidence from Burke (2006) suggests that subjects conform to role expectations when they either (i) perceive legitimate authority on the part of others making requests; or (ii) anticipate sanctions for non-compliance. It is reasonable to assume that *hosts in occupational roles* comply with expectations in order to receive benefits and avoid sanctions. To the degree that tourists or employers are perceived as possessing either legitimate authority over the host or the ability to exercise sanctions, it is expected that hosts will exhibit desired role behaviours.

On the other hand, the *resident role* carries fewer sanctions for non-compliance with tourist expectations for hospitality. It is likely that people acting as residents perceive the authority of the tourist gaze to be a lot less legitimate than do workers who are dependent on tourism proceeds. However, government or community sanctions or incentives might come into play in some destinations. Propositions 1 and 2 summarize the importance of authority and sanctions to the influence of the tourist gaze on role performances.

- Proposition 1: The tourist gaze will influence host behaviour in occupational and resident roles by using perceived legitimate authority to institutionalize behavioural standards and by communicating sanctions for non-compliance.
- Proposition 2: Legitimate authority tied to tourist expectations and perceived threat of sanctions will be perceived as greater by hosts in occupational encounters with tourists than by hosts in resident encounters with tourists.

Emotional Responses to Tourist Expectations

One of the by-products of institutionalizing expectations for host behaviours is that host expressions of personal intent and proclivity towards being genuinely hospitable (or culturally authentic on his/her terms) are diminished and potentially disregarded in lieu of an organizational fostering of emotional labour. The concept of emotional labour was first theorized by Hochschild (1983) as 'the management of feeling to create a publicly observable facial and bodily display'. Characteristics of this phenomenon are '(a) emotional labour occurs in face-to-face or voice-to-voice interactions with customers; (b) emotions are displayed to influence other people's emotions, attitudes, and behaviours; and (c) the display of emotions has to follow certain rules' (Wong and Wang, 2009, p. 250). The emotion of the employee is controlled by the employer or the organization itself, in a process described as 'the commoditization of emotion' (Hochschild, 1979, 1983; Kim and Han, 2009). Subjects perceiving diminished discretionary control over their choice of behaviours experience nega-

tive emotional outcomes and over time can experience emotional exhaustion.

In most cases of emotional labour, workers are supposed to demonstrate the positive display rules that are expected by customers and employers. On the inside these workers may be feeling anger or frustration at the behavioural constraints placed on them yet at the same time may be experiencing a desire to receive positive affirmation about behaviours. Anticipation of receiving performance feedback is laden with the desire to be given positive validation of one's self-concept (Sedikides, 1993). According to evidence from Stets (2005) and Turner and Stets (2005), a person's emotional state is impacted by feedback on how congruent his or her behaviours are with the identified standards of behaviour dictated by the assumed role, whereby higher levels of congruence lead to more positive emotions in the role actor. Additionally, when the authority of the person giving feedback is perceived as legitimate, the person receiving the feedback will view it as more credible. Subjects examined in role-based studies show a marked tendency to self-verify on a continuous basis and to align their self-perceptions with feedback about role performance from credited or powerful sources (Burke, 2006). Propositions 3 and 4 focus attention on host discretionary control and emotional response.

- Proposition 3: As the tourist gaze increasingly institutionalizes host role behaviours through the use of legitimate authority and credible sanctions, hosts will experience decreased locus of control in encounters with tourists.
- Proposition 4: As hosts experience decreased discretionary control over role behaviours, they will experience increased negative emotions associated with those roles, absent the existence of relevant buffering tactics.

Emotional Buffering Tactics

Short of choosing to ignore tourist requests and organizational demands altogether and bearing the brunt of sanctions that accrue, hosts may resort to emotional buffering tactics to reduce the impact of the tourist gaze on their emotional state. Given that role theory links compliance with role expectations to external authority and sanctions, it is anticipated that hosts will seek to deploy tactics that alter either perceived authority/sanctions of the external agent or alter the felt impact of compliance on the self-concept. Either of these two tactics might result in an outcome where total compliance with role expectations becomes unnecessary or negative emotions attached to the role might be reduced or avoided.

Questions of authority and sanctions in instrumentalist relationships between host and tourist are critical issues since power imbalances create the expectation of deference as well as the expectation of specific role behaviours such as staged behaviour such as smiles, eye contact or stylized greetings. The exchange of benefits for role behaviours may justify specific hospitality and cultural performances on the part of the host, but the acceptability of humbling of the host by requiring overt deference to the tourist will be personally and culturally determined.

Cultures will have varying tactics to preserve face or esteem and ultimately self-concept. The authors do expect that in cultures where power distance (Hofstede, 1991) is low between authority figures and subordinates, a likely response to expectations of deference would involve examining one's own sources of power and influence to counter the tourist gaze.

- Proposition 5: As hosts experience increased negative emotions due to loss of discretionary control over role behaviours, they will seek to buffer their emotions through tactics that reduce the need for deference behaviours to tourists.

Professionalization of behaviours in occupational roles

In the case of occupational roles where behaviours are tightly constrained, hosts may seek to reduce their dependence, either materially or emotionally, on feedback from the tourist or influential other, for example, supervisors or employers. One remedy to counter the authority of the tourist gaze is for the host to display visible signs of professionalization of the role. The display of professionalized behaviours and communication of professional credentials permits the host to reassert control within the role, by moving encounters from a focus on control over the behaviours, that is, constraint and deference embedded in the role, to perceived standing of the individual, that is, role status.

Consequently, as professionalization of a role increases, the need for demeanours of deference may lessen. In some cultures, occupational roles that require greater levels of skill or educational credentials, for example, wine sommelier or diving instructor, will require fewer overt signs of deference to the client since the focus is on the expertise of the host rather than on the host as server. Feelings of professionalism in the role and respect accorded to skill can ameliorate the negative emotions of having to perform those behaviours on demand. It must be recognized, however, that occupational roles vary widely in their inherent opportunities for professionalization, and cultural frameworks vary widely in their assignment of respect to societal actors; thus, it is doubtful that this tactic of professionalization is universally applicable across all destinations.

A corollary tactic that might be more generally applicable across destinations and that achieves similar aims would be emphasizing bureaucratic aspects of roles that establish host power over the tourist, such as control over access to facilities, for example, museum guards, airport security agents or over destination resources, such as visa agencies. Such a tactic might be further exploited by hosts to ease negative emotions by reasserting control over behavioural choice.

Depersonalization as a buffering tactic

Given that role expectations for hospitality and cultural performances constitute a form of emotional labour, research also suggests that a possible response to continuous negative emotions ensuing from encounters under the tourist gaze would be depersonalization on the part of the host whereby the host detaches emotionally from the encounter and cognitively from the role. Quite possibly the 'commodified persona' that Bunten (2008) identifies among her tour guide subjects involves some degree of depersonalization. Hosts may be entirely committed to the role, but they do not personally embrace positive feedback because they have distanced themselves from the role. This reaction could occur equally in hosts in occupational roles and in residential roles. Depersonalization can have added negative emotional outcomes for hosts who highly value personalized interactions with others, compounding their deteriorated emotional state.

In addition, research on burnout and the erosion of work engagement (Schaufeli et al., 2008) empirically links high levels of emotional exhaustion with increased depersonalization. In the tourism context, depersonalization becomes a barrier between hosts and tourists (Karatepe and Uludag, 2008) and can lead employees to disregard tourist expectations for performance (Humborstad et al., 2008). Moreover, during the process of depersonalization, the role in question may be increasingly detached from the host personal self-concept unless other sources of positive emotions surface from host–tourist encounters to reinstate the role as meaningful to the self. Feedback, even positive feedback, belongs to the role and not to the self; thus the self-concept is reduced to exclude the role and remains unnourished by interaction with tourists.

- Proposition 6: As the host experiences increased negative emotions associated with the loss of discretionary control over role behaviours, hosts will experience increased levels of depersonalization in encounters with tourists.
- Proposition 7: When hosts experience increased emotional exhaustion and depersonalization in their roles, they will diminish the role's significance to their self-concept.

One additional observation can be made regarding buffering tactics in occupational roles. One option is that hosts seek to repersonalize the encounter while diminishing the authority structures that empower the tourist gaze to dictate role behaviours 'on the job'. Hosts can engage in extra-occupational relationships with tourists outside the job setting or can connect with tourists within their resident role outside the confines of the occupational institutionalized role behaviours. This extra-occupational technique is focused on creating unity between host and tourist, co-producing a new environment in which both host and tourist are fully participating. Hosts may seek to establish connections with tourists through storytelling, language tutoring, artistic collaborations, cultural teaching and medicinal and spiritual healing in order to demonstrate subject mastery that will strengthen the self image in the presence of the tourist.

Such tactics involve hosts using their mastery of their own cultural knowledge and skill in serving a real need of the tourist, increasing the tourist's dependence on the host as a local expert and/or friend rather than as a service professional. It is possible that the effects of depersonalization of occupational roles on the host can be offset through positive same host resident role–tourist encounters as long as the resident role is the more salient one to both actors, permitting the performance of the act to be one of personal interaction rather than enforced resident role hospitality or cultural performances.

Conclusion

This chapter has presented a theoretical model blending the literature on role theory and role-based identity with research on the tourist gaze. A review of the literature has shown that the tourist gaze has been refined to assimilate mutuality of gazes between tourist and host. This empowering of the host is a critical supposition for the present discussion in that much of the commoditization literature portrays hosts as objectified

and socialized into supply-side performances due to the instrumentalist sanction-
heavy tourist gaze.

Role theory is presented in this chapter
as a conceptual tool that may facilitate the
study of the host internalization of the tourist gaze. *Role* is rich in its wealth of implications regarding host awareness of tourism as
a goal, as a performance and as a force. People are seen to have roles across the many
facets of human life, for example, family
member, church goer, worker, citizen, envi-
ronmentalist, resident of a town. Comprehension of the plurality of roles associated
with destination-contextualized human
behaviour permits hosts to engage in guided
self-inspection of roles they engage in, for
example, occupational and resident roles.
Host consideration of role expectations
infers contemplation of the suitability of
behaviours culminating in choice: acquies-
cence, compromise or refusal to act in
accordance with scripts.

While other social roles, such as gender, occupied by the host may elicit alter-
nate expectations for behaviour, in the
present model, the impacts of the tourist
gaze on host self-concept are mediated by
occupational and resident roles enacted by
the host. Both occupational and resident
roles have the potential for direct interaction with tourists, implying therefore the
emergence of issues of power, interdependence and the potential for personal intimacy or impersonal distance, as well as for
threats to personal self-esteem and security.
Inasmuch as the host self-concept is entangled with occupational and resident roles,
the tourist gaze manifesting within tourist–
host encounters has the potential to impact
the individual host.

A theoretical model of the influence of
the tourist gaze on host self-concept has
been presented whereby the tourist gaze has
been conceptualized as a force that operates
through the institutionalization of role
behaviours that benefit tourists. Hosts are
exhorted to comply with tourist expectations through the imposition of legitimate
authority and sanctions that operate differentially across occupations and between
occupational and resident roles. Theoretical

propositions have been offered that support
further investigation into issues raised in
the chapter. Understanding of the model
has been facilitated by an exploration of
tourist expectations for hospitableness and
cultural behaviours often associated with
occupational and resident roles in tourist
destinations.

With respect to the limitations of this
model of host internalization of the tourist
gaze, it was necessary to narrowly interpret
the influence of the tourist gaze as occurring
through the process of commoditization of
host behaviours. It is recognized that other
forces, for example, globalization, accultur-
ation, nationalism, environmentalism,
impact hosts in tourist destinations. Membership in social groups defined by other
social labels, such as gender, age and ethnicity, were not foci in this discussion due
to limitations of time and space. Based on a
comprehensive review of socio-cultural
impacts of tourism, the tourist gaze in the
context of occupational and resident roles
was deemed an appropriate entry point
offering unique contributions to the field.
The tourist gaze is a compelling external
contingency that requires the host to self-
regulate and reflect within these two roles
and related situations. Since the selection of
expectations for hospitable and cultural
behaviours was neither arbitrary nor scien-
tifically rigorous, being topics of particular
interest to the authors and the field, it is
noted that study of other role expectations,
for example, financial acumen or foreign
language skills, may lead to significant
modifications of the posited relationships
among the tourist gaze, host role and host
self-concept.

To reflect on role is to reflect on rule;
thus cognitive role theory is consistent with
an ethical stance whereby hosts may be
active, rather than passive, in their cognitive
grasp of the gaze and their own affective and
behavioural responses to tourism. Cognitive
role theory invites a healing perspective in
that hosts may be encouraged to recognize
that role performances in tourism, as in any
other social domain, carry all the considerable affective baggage of resentment, guilt,
disappointment or relief associated with

human decisions. Only in the presence of this clarity regarding host affective response to role performances conducted before the tourist gaze, can a healing posture be adopted by hosts themselves.

Consideration of issues around emotional labour and burnout research has shown that hosts may be struggling to keep emotions at bay during interactions with tourists. As a social system that is increasingly impacted by forces of commoditization, tourism can affect levels of emotional exhaustion and impact the self-concept of hosts engaged in roles that are subject to the tourist gaze. Emotional buffering tactics have been described that include professionalization and depersonalization. Both professionalization and depersonalization potentially permit the host who complies with tourist expectations to reduce the negative emotions associated with the reduction of discretionary control over role behaviours.

Certainly, some of the issues or emotional buffering tactics may not be applicable across all destinations due to cultural differences. This requires further discussion. One area for future cross-cultural research is to study the ways in which tourists carry expectations for behaviour from their own country and introduce these beliefs into the host population via comments on expectations and feedback on role performances of hosts. Also of interest would be a cross-cultural comparison to determine the primary tactics, for example, professionalization of an occupation through skill development and certification or manipulation of bureaucratic rules, used to moderate the impact of tourist expectations for deference behaviours from workers and residents. Cultural research related to comparative power distances and sources of power would be useful in this arena. In terms of depersonalization in role performances, the issue of cultural and individual propensity for interpersonal distance, physical or emotional, versus intimacy would be one that might be fruitful when comparing host responses across cultures.

References

Aboulafia, M. (1986) *The Mediating Self: Mead, Sartre, and Self-Determination*. Yale University Press. New Haven, CT.

Andereck, K., Valentine, K., Knopf, R. and Vogt, C. (2005) Residents' perceptions of community tourism impacts. *Annals of Tourism Research* 32(4), 1056–1076.

Aramberri, J. (2001) The host should get lost: paradigms in the tourism theory. *Annals of Tourism Research* 28(3), 738–761.

Ashforth, B.E. and Johnson, S.A. (2001) Which hat to wear? The relative salience of multiple identities in organizational contexts. In: Hogg, M.A. and Terry, D.J. (eds) *Social Identity Processes in Organizational Contexts*. Psychology Press, Philadelphia, PA, pp. 31–48.

Ateljevic, I. (2000) Circuits of tourism: stepping beyond the 'production/consumption' dichotomy. *Tourism Geographies* 2(4), 369–388.

Baumeister, R.F. (1998) The self. In: Gilbert, D.T., Fiske, S.T. and Lindzey, G. (eds) *Handbook of Social Psychology*. McGraw-Hill, New York, pp. 680–740.

Besculides, A., Lee, M. and McCormick P. (2002) Residents' perceptions of the cultural benefits of tourism. *Annals of Tourism Research* 29(2), 303–319.

Biddle, B. (1986) Recent development in role theory. *Annual Review of Sociology* 12(1), 67–92.

Blanton, D. (1981) Tourism training in developing countries. The social and cultural dimension. *Annals of Tourism Research* 8(1), 116–133.

Bourdieu, P. (1984) *The Field of Cultural Production: Essays on Art and Literature*. Columbia University Press, New York.

Brotherton, B. (1999) Towards a definitive view of the nature of hospitality and hospitality management. *International Journal of Contemporary Hospitality Management* 11(4), 165–173.

Brunt, P. and Courtney, P. (1999) Host perceptions of sociocultural impacts. *Annals of Tourism Research* 26(3), 493–515.

Bunten, A.C. (2008) Sharing culture or selling out? *American Ethnologist* 35(3), 380.

Burke, P.J. and Reitzes, D. C. (1981) The link between identity and role performance. *Social Psychology Quarterly* 44(2), 83–92.

Burke, P.J. (2006) Identity change. *Social Psychology Quarterly* 69(1), 81–96.

Byrman, A. (1999). The Disneyization of cociety. *Sociological Review* 47(1), 25–49.

Canziani, B.F. (2011) Commoditisation effects on cultural identity: a process model. *International Journal of Tourism Anthropology* 1(2), 108–124.

Carrier, J.G. and Macleod, D.V.L. (2005) Bursting the bubble: the socio-cultural context of ecotourism. *Journal of the Royal Anthropological Institute* 11(2), 315–334.

Chhabra, D. (2010) How they see us: perceived effects of tourist gaze on the old order Amish. *Journal of Travel Research* 49(1), 93–105.

Choi, H.C. and Murray, I. (2010) Resident attitudes toward sustainable community tourism. *Journal of Sustainable Tourism* 18(4), 575–594.

Cohen, E. (1985) Tourist guide: the origins, structure and dynamics of a role. *Annals of Tourism Research* 12(1), 5–29.

Cohen, E., Nir, Y. and Almagor, U. (1992) Stranger-local interaction in photography. *Annals of Tourism Research* 19(2), 213–233.

Condevaux, A. (2009) Maori culture on stage: authenticity and identity in tourist interactions. *Anthropological Forum* 19(2), 143–161.

Cone, C.A. (1995) Crafting selves: the lives of two Mayan women. *Annals of Tourism Research* 22(2), 314–327.

Cornelissen, S. (2005) Producing and imaging 'place' and 'people': the political economy of South African international tourist representation. *Review of International Political Economy* 12(4), 674–699.

Duim, R. van der (2007) Tourismscapes an actor-network perspective. *Annals of Tourism Research* 34(4), 961–976.

Easterling, D. (2005) Residents and tourism. *Journal of Travel and Tourism Marketing* 18(4), 49–64.

Fine, E. and Speer, J. (1985) Tour guide performances as sight sacralization. *Annals of Tourism Research* 12(1), 73–95.

Foucault, M. (1973) *The Birth of the Clinic: The Archaeology of Medical Perception*. Vintage, New York.

Garrod, B. (2009) Understanding the relationship between tourism destination imagery and tourist photography. *Journal of Travel Research* 47(3), 346–358.

Gibson, H. and Yiannakis, A. (2002) Tourist roles: needs and the lifecourse. *Annals of Tourism Research* 29(2), 358–383.

Glover, N. (2008) Co-produced histories: mapping the uses and narratives of history in the tourist age. Public *Historian* 30(1), 105–124.

Goldberg, A. (1983) Identity and experience in Haitian voodoo shows. *Annals of Tourism Research* 10(4), 470–495.

Graburn, N. (1984) The evolution of tourist arts. *Annals of Tourism Research* 11(3), 393–419.

Grünewald, R. de A. (2002) Tourism and cultural revival. *Annals of Tourism Research* 29(4), 1004.

Gursoy, D. and Rutherford, D.G. (2004) Host attitudes toward tourism, an improved structural model. *Annals of Tourism Research* 31(3), 495–516.

Hochschild, A.R. (1979) Emotion work, feeling rules, and social structure. *American Journal of Sociology* 85(3), 551–575.

Hochschild, A.R. (1983) *The Managed Heart: Commercialization of Human Feeling*. University of California Press, Berkeley, CA

Hofstede, G. (1991) *Cultures and Organizations: Software of the Mind*. McGraw-Hill, London.

Holloway, J.C. (1981) The guided tour: a sociological approach. *Annals of Tourism Research* 8(3), 377–402.

Hottola, P. (2004) Culture confusion: intercultural adaptation in tourism. *Annals of Tourism Research* 31(2), 447.

Humborstad, S.I.W., Humborstad, B. and Whitfield, R. (2008) Burnout and service employees' willingness to deliver quality service. Journal of Human Resources in Hospitality and Tourism 7(1), 45–64.

Jaakson, R. (2004) Beyond the tourist bubble?: Cruise ship passengers in port. *Annals of Tourism Research* 31(1), 44.

Jackson, J. (1998) Contemporary criticisms of role theory. *Journal of Occupational Science*, 5(2), 49–55.

Jordan, J. (1980) The summer people and the natives: some effects of tourism in a Vermont vacation village. *Annals of Tourism Research* 7(1), 34–55.

Joseph, C.A. and Kavoori, A.P. (2001) Mediated resistance: tourism and the host community. *Annals of Tourism Research* 28(4), 998–1009.

Karatepe, O.M. and Uludag, O. (2008) Role stress, burnout and their effects on frontline hotel employees' job performance: evidence from northern Cyprus. *International Journal of Tourism Research* 10(2), 111–126.

Kayat, K. (2008) Stakeholders' perspectives toward a community-based rural tourism development. *European Journal of Tourism Research* 1(2), 94–111.

Kim, M.J. and Han, S.Y. (2009) Relationship between emotional labor consequences and employees' coping strategy. *Asia Pacific Journal of Tourism Research* 14(3), 225–239.

Lindberg, K., Andersson, T.D. and Dellaert, B.G.C. (2001) Tourism development: assessing social gains and losses. *Annals of Tourism Research* 28(4), 1010–1030.

Maoz, D. (2006) *The mutual gaze*. Annals of Tourism Research 33(1), 221–239.

McGuire, W.J., McGuire, C.V., Child P. and Fujioka, T. (1978) Ethnicity in the spontaneous self-concept as a function of one's ethnic distinctiveness in the social environment. Journal of Personality and Social Psychology 36(5), 511–520.

Moyle, B., Glen Croy, W. and Weiler, B. (2010) Community perceptions of tourism: Bruny and Magnetic Islands, Australia. *Asia Pacific Journal of Tourism Research* 15(3), 353–366.

Osagie, I. and Buzinde, C.N. (2011) Culture and postcolonial resistance: Antigua in Kincaid's a small place. Annals of Tourism Research 38(1), 210–230.

Palmer, N. (2007). Ethnic equality, national identity and selective cultural representation in tourism promotion: Kyrgyzstan, Central Asia. *Journal of Sustainable Tourism* 15(6), 645–662.

Quinn, B. (2007) Performing tourism Venetian residents in focus. *Annals of Tourism Research* 34(2), 458–476.

Rekom, J. van and Go, F.M. (2006) Cultural identities in a globalizing world: conditions for sustainability of intercultural tourism. In: Burns, P. and Novelli, M. (eds) *Tourism and Social Identities: Global Frameworks and Local Realities.* Elsevier, Oxford, pp. 79–90.

Robson, J. and Robson, I. (1996) From shareholders to stakeholders: critical issues for tourism marketers. Tourism Management 17(7), 533–540.

Rossides, Daniel W. (1998) *Social Theory: Its Origins, History, and Contemporary Relevance.* Dix Hills, General Hall.

Sage, A. (2007) French asked to be polite to tourists for 24 hours. *The Australian*, http://www.news.com.au/world/french-asked-to-be-polite-to-tourists-for-24-hours/story-e6frfkyi-1111113921929 (accessed 29 July 2011).

Schaufeli, W.B., Leiter, M.P. and Maslach, C. (2008) Burnout: 35 years of research and practice. *Career Development International* 14(3), 204–220.

Sedikides, C. (1993) assessment, enhancement, and verification determinants of the self-evaluation process. *Journal of Personality and Social Psychology* 65(2), 317–338.

Smith, S.L.J. (1988) Defining tourism: a supply-side view. *Annals of Tourism Research* 15, 179–190.

Steiner, C. and Reisinger, Y. (2004) Enriching the tourist and host intercultural experience by reconceptualising communication. *Journal of Tourism and Cultural Change* 2(2), 118–137.

Stets, J.E. (2005) Examining emotions in identity theory. *Social Psychology Quarterly* 68(1), 39–56.

Stryker, S. (2007) Identity theory and personality theory: mutual relevance. *Journal of Personality* 75(6), 1083–1102.

Tucker, H. (1997) The ideal village: interactions through tourism in Central Anatolia. In: Abram, S., Waldren, J. and Macleod, D. (eds) *Tourists and Tourism: Identifying With People and Places.* Berg, Oxford, pp. 107–128.

Turner, J.H. and Stets, J.E. (2005) *The Sociology of Emotions.* Cambridge University Press, Cambridge.

Uriely, N. (2005) The tourist experience: conceptual developments. *Annals of Tourism Research* 32(1), 199–216.

Urry, J. (1990) *The Tourist Gaze.* Sage, London.

Wang, Y. (2007) Customized authenticity begins at home. *Annals of Tourism Research* 34(3), 789–804.

Warden, C., Huang, S.C.T. and Chen, J. (2007) Restaurant service failure recoveries: role expectations in a chinese cultural setting. *Journal of Hospitality Marketing and Management* 16(1), 159–180.

Wearing, S.L., Wearing, M. and McDonald, M. (2010) Understanding local power and interactional processes in sustainable tourism: exploring village-tour operator relations on the Kokoda Track, Papua New Guinea. *Journal of Sustainable Tourism* 18(1), 61–76.

Wong, J.Y. and Wang, C.H. (2009) Emotional labor of the tour leaders: an exploratory study. *Tourism Management*, 30(2), 249–259.

3 The Thai Host Gaze: Alterity and the Governance of Visitors in Thailand

Ian A. Morrison

Introduction

Thailand has long been a destination for Western and non-Western travellers, missionaries, explorers, journalists, mercenaries, diplomats and traders. It was only, however, in the second half of the last century that it became a site of mass tourism. Between 1957 and 2003, the number of visitors to Thailand increased from 44,000 to more than 10 million per year (Saispradist, 2005, p. 12). Given the importance of the tourism industry for both the economy and the national image, it is not surprising that it has often been a site of interest and intervention for the Thai state. During the past decade, successive governments have engaged in a series of complementary interventions with the stated goal of improving the tourist industry in Thailand. It is possible to place these interventions under two closely related headings. The first concerns the governance of visitors to Thailand. These interventions involve the constitution of categories of desirable and undesirable visitors, and the institution of policies and practices that aim to attract desirable visitors and restrict the presence of undesirable visitors. The second aims to govern the image of Thailand. These interventions involve the constitution of desirable and undesirable images of Thailand, and the

institution of policies and practices that aim to promote a desirable image and undermine undesirable images. In short, the recent interventions by the Thai state in the realm of tourism policy have aimed to promote particular figures of the tourist and the Thai host, and to inhibit others. Stated otherwise, these interventions are attempts to govern both who gazes and the image that appears within their gaze.

Initially, it may appear that a thorough understanding of the Thai government's recent interventions in tourism policy can be developed by referring to the abundant literature concerning the tourist's experience of otherness. In relation to this literature, the policies of the Thai state would appear as attempts to refine the 'staged authenticity' of the 'tourist space' (MacCannell, 1973, 1976), or to alter and manage the 'tourist gaze' (Crawshaw and Urry, 1997; Urry, 2002). Undoubtedly, the policies of the Thai state aim to alter tourists' perceptions of Thailand and the Thai people. Focusing solely on the perceptions and experience of the tourists, however, allows for only a partial comprehension of the recent transformations in Thai tourism policies and practices. While such analysis can explain the effects of these interventions in terms of transformations in the way that Thailand is experienced and perceived by visitors, it does not adequately account for the role of the subjective experience of the host in determining the direction of the tourism policy. Therefore, it is necessary to supplement analysis of the tourist gaze with that of the host gaze. Through understanding the perceptions and experiences of the host, it becomes possible to develop alternative accounts of the Thai–tourist encounter, in general, and the recent government interventions into tourism policy, in particular.

This chapter offers such an alternative account, asserting that, in addition to being driven by economic rationale, the recent measures to govern visitors and the image of Thailand should also be seen as embedded in particular relations of alterity. The chapter first analyses the recent efforts of the Thai state to govern visitors, arguing that they involve attempts to minimize and control the presence of strangers. Second, it examines the Thai state's attempts to govern the image of Thailand, contending that the Thai reticence to the stranger is related to the capacity of this figure to disturb this carefully managed image.

The Tourist Gaze

In his seminal work, *The Tourist Gaze* (1990, 2002), John Urry deploys elements of a Foucauldian perspective in order to investigate historical practices of tourism. According to Urry, a significant aspect of being a tourist, and the encounters with otherness that constitute tourism, involve visually taking in or gazing upon objects, people and places. The tourist gaze that Urry describes is not the objective, unsituated 'view from nowhere'. Rather, it 'is as socially organized and systematized' as the gaze of the medical professional, as described by Foucault (Urry, 2002, p. 1). Just as particular historical discourses of health, madness and criminality allowed the psychiatrist or medic described by Foucault to comprehend, categorize and judge those under his gaze, the perceptions of tourists depend on, and are made possible by, the particular historical discourses

within which they are embedded. As tourists themselves are historical subjects, located in different social and historical contexts, the tourist gaze will vary depending on the particular historical discourse in which they emerge as subjects. Consequently, as Urry (2002, p. 1) asserts, 'there is no single tourist gaze as such'. The tourist's experience and perception of otherness varies according to society, social group and historical period.

Moreover, Urry demonstrates that the perceptions and expectations of tourists are institutionally supported, organized and authorized by a series of historically variable experts. These experts include academics, photographers, travel writers and broadcasters, travel agents, tour operators and bureaucrats. As such, 'different gazes are "authorised" by different discourses' (Crawshaw and Urry, 1997, p. 176). In his historical analysis, Urry describes several such discourses – a discourse of sanctity guiding the experience of pilgrims, in which travel was to provide religious experience; a discourse of education corresponding to the classical European Grand Tour, in which travel was an opportunity for neutral observation and the attainment of knowledge; the discourse of the sublime of the romantic Grand Tour, in which travel was undertaken in order to encounter beauty and authenticity; discourses of health related to the travel to spa towns, in which travel was meant to aid in the restoration of the tourist's well-being; and the discourse of play, which relates to liminal or post-tourism (Crawshaw and Urry, 1997, pp. 176–177; Urry, 2002, pp. 4–15). Each discursive formation involves particular experts and institutions that condition the experience and perception of the tourist.

Of particular importance to this and other academic investigations of tourism is Foucault's understanding of visibility and the power of the authoritative gaze. Foucault describes that with the development of the modern *episteme,* sense-data, particularly the sensory perceptions of the individual subject – rather than a priori knowledge – came to be seen as the locus of truth. It was only through the observation of visible phenomena – 'the sovereign power of the empirical gaze' – that one could determine the underlining structures of the world, which were hidden from our senses (Foucault, [1963] 1976, p. xiii; [1966] 2002). With this development, institutional authority was conferred upon those experts who had developed the tools and capacities for proper observation and interpretation of data. Moreover, it produced a relationship between observer and that which is observed, which is inherently one of objectification (Foucault, [1963] 1976, p. xiv). The object of observation, whether a physical phenomenon or an individual, appears in the gaze of the expert as an object in need of classification. The patient under the gaze of incipient psychiatry was an object whose characteristics were to be carefully observed and interpreted, so that he or she could be properly classified as a maniac, a melancholic, a hysteric, a hypochondriac or any number of other variations of insanity.

Following Adler (1989), Urry (2002, p. 147; Crawshaw, 1997, p. 178) argues that an important transformation in the discourse of travel accompanied this rise of empiricism. The conception of travel dominant in the era of the classical Grand European Tour, one of travel as a scholastic pursuit, was replaced by the notion of travel as an opportunity for eye-witness observation (Urry, 2002, p. 147). In other words, the focus of travel was no longer to hear from others but to see for oneself. Moreover, with the growing professionalization of the sciences, a distinction developed between travel and the scientific expedition. Consequently, the gaze of the traveller came to be associated with connoisseurship – a contemplative taking in, and collecting of surroundings and experiences (Adler, 1989, p. 22; Urry, 2002, p. 147). In other words, the experience of the traveller increasingly became one of sight-seeing. Particular sites – cities, towns, buildings, monuments, landscapes, works of art – came to be promoted in guidebooks and other literature as essential to the touristic experience. As such, travel became a means of enjoying otherness in particular prescribed ways.

An important aspect of the connoisseurship of tourism is the issue of representation. A great deal of academic literature concerning the experience of tourists has focused on how otherness is presented to tourists. Urry and others have noted the influential role of tourism professionals in designating that which is said to be representative of a particular culture, region or people. Central to these investigations of representations of otherness has been the question of authenticity. Representations of the host culture are said to be carefully contrived and controlled, in order to ensure that they are enjoyable and easily replicable. As Philip Duke (2007, p. 15) suggests, exposure to the host culture must be conducted in such a way as to ensure that 'a balance is always maintained between the exotic and the familiar' so that the tourist is 'temporarily confronted with something that is not so exotic as to make them feel uncomfortable, and not so different as to be unknowable'. It is in reference to these carefully managed representations that Boorstin (1964) developed the notion of the pseudo-event. He suggests that the tourist, isolated from the real world of the local population, is presented with an image that they gullibly take for an authentic representation of the host culture. As such, he suggests that what the tourist gazes upon is not the reality of otherness, but an illusion corresponding to the representations of otherness provided to them by professional experts.

Other studies, however, have disputed this portrayal of the tourist as simplistic and unrepresentative of the variety of tourists and touristic experiences. Erik Cohen (1979), for instance, argues that certain types of tourists, who he labels experiential, experimental and existential tourists, are not content to simply consume the image and experiences provided to them by conventional tourist services. Instead, they wish to have more authentic experiences and connections with the host people and culture. Edward Bruner (2005, p. 72) suggests that many tourists are able to employ a 'questioning gaze' in order to ascertain the level of authenticity of what is presented to them as host culture. Along with Cohen

(1988, p. 383), he further asserts that most tourists are fully aware that what they are presented with involves elements of both reality and illusion, yet still find the experience enjoyable. Dean MacCannell (1973) differentiates these 'front stage' representations of host culture from the authentic 'back-stage' experiences that many travellers seek. Yet he maintains that even these are examples of what he labels staged authenticity – attempts by the host or tourist professionals to profit from the tourist's desire to authentically experience the host culture.

As Crawshaw and Urry (1997, p. 178) argue, these encounters are marked by the visibility of the Other within the gaze of the tourist. Likening tourism practices to the surveillance of prisoners, they assert that within the tourist encounter it is the visitor who is conferred the authority to distinguish between authentic and inauthentic representations, and desirable and undesirable experiences. In other words, 'visitors are thought to possess all-seeing eyes which are able to identify real, authentic local people and local customs' (Crawshaw and Urry, 1997, p.178). It is within and through particular discourses of travel and otherness that the tourist and the tourism professional are able – in terms of possessing both the tools and the authority – to make such distinctions.

While this depiction of the encounter between tourist and host focuses solely on attempting to describe the manner in which the encounter is experienced by the tourist, it also points to the need to supplement such an analysis with that of the perceptions and experiences of the host. It is possible to locate elements of such analysis in discussions of the reaction of hosts to the seemingly all-seeing tourist gaze. Likening the tourist gaze to Foucault's discussion of the effect of the panopticon, Crawshaw (1994) suggests that locals may feel that they are always being gazed upon. In order to avoid this intrusion, they may attempt to take measures to reduce their visibility, such as limiting the tourist season or making certain areas out of bounds to visitors. Similarly, MacCannell (1976) depicts the development of staged authenticity as a

means for the host to profit from, as well as manage, the attempts of the all-seeing tourist eye to penetrate the back stage of the tourism space.

Alterity, Security and the Host Gaze

While importantly acknowledging the experiences of the host, these analyses of the tourist–host encounter do not address the manner in which the host's perception of the tourist is – like the tourist's perception of the host – the product of particular discourses of travel and otherness. In other words, what is overlooked is an analysis of the host gaze. The reactions to the presence of tourists described by Crawshaw and MacCannell occur within particular historical and social contexts and result from specific perceptions of encounters. At a fundamental level, these reactions are embedded in particular relations of alterity. As Engin Isin (2002) has demonstrated, the constitution of group identity does not involve merely the demarcation of those who are Other. Rather, it always emerges historically through various strategies and technologies of affiliation, identification, dissociation and misrecognition, which create a series of others. Thus, it is not only the academic observer or the travel professional who distinguishes between varieties of tourists. In the tourist space the host does not encounter the other as such, but rather a specific discursively determined category of tourist. Moreover, just as the tourist gaze varies depending on the social group, so too will the host gaze differ based on social and historical context, and their location within various discourses. Therefore, there exist a multiplicity of host gazes.

Among the most prominent and apparent of the gazes in the tourist space is that of the host state. In recent years, a body of literature has developed within the field of critical migration studies arguing that migration is increasingly portrayed, and dealt with, as an issue of security. This literature, inspired by Foucault's conceptions of power, discourse and governance, suggests that a discourse of migration has emerged and become dominant, within which migration is engaged with as an issue of security, a problem 'endangering a collective way of life that defines a community of people' (Huysmans, 2006, p. 46). According to Foucault, security, as technology of bio-power, is distinct from disciplinary and juridico-legal mechanisms of power. Unlike these other mechanisms of power, the object of concern for security is not the group or the individual, but the survival of the population – which is not merely an aggregate of individuals (Foucault, 2009, pp. 4–6). As such, what is of concern is not the eradication of particular behaviours or phenomena, but their maintenance within 'a bandwidth of the acceptable that must not be exceeded' (Foucault, 2009, p. 6). Thus, Foucault (2009, pp. 4–6) suggests that, in the Age of Security, what is of interest is the determination of the normal, the acceptable and the average, which in turn permits analysis and management of risk. In other words, in order to safeguard the survival of the population, mechanisms of security engage in an ongoing assessment of risk, and calculation of costs and benefits.

To illustrate the relationship between Foucault's concept of security, and its relation to discourses of migration (including tourism), it is useful to briefly attend to his discussion of security and governance. Foucault (2009, pp. 18–20, 64) suggests that towns pose a particular challenge for governance. As the location of markets, they require circulation. However, they are also often a site of revolt. Thus, some restriction of circulation is required to maintain order. In the town, consequently, circulation cannot be eliminated, as it is necessary for commerce. Nor, due to its inherent risks, can it be permitted to occur without restrictions. Consequently, it must be managed. The mechanism of security is a response to this problem of circulation. It involves 'organizing circulation, eliminating its dangerous elements, making a division between good and bad circulation, and maximizing the good circulation by diminishing the bad' (2009, p. 18). The objective is to optimize, rather than restrict, circulation, through 'maximizing the

positive element, for which one provides the best possible circulation, and ... minimizing what is risky and inconvenient' (2009, p. 19).

As Czajka and Gardner (2011) have recently argued, while the securitization of migration does often involve a portrayal of migration as a potential existential threat, the response of states has not been to nullify this risk through eliminating the phenomenon of migration. Rather, they have sought to manage the risks of migration through the implementation of various security mechanisms. Contemporary migration policies concern the maximization of desirable and minimization of undesirable circulations. In other words, the securitization of migration involves the determination of desirable and undesirable forms of migration, and the formulation of policies aimed to maximize the benefits associated with the former and minimize the risks associated with the later. Migration policies, through the institution of targeted incentives and obstacles, seek to attract particular migrants and restrict or manage the presence of others.

While generally overlooked in analyses of the securitization of migration, the mechanism of security is evident in the tourism policies of most states. With few exceptions, states, while acknowledging the social, cultural, environmental and even political risks associated with tourism, particularly mass tourism, have not implemented policies prohibiting visitors. Rather, they have implemented various policies and practices that aim to optimize the impact of tourism. Planners, immigration officials, the security apparatus and other figures have been conferred the authority to gaze upon, categorize, assess the desirability of and manage the presence of visitors and potential visitors. It is important to reiterate that, understood in the sense delineated above, securitization is not only a mechanism of negation. In relation to tourism, the securitization of migration does not only concern restricting the presence of the undesirable. It also entails attracting the desirable. The management of tourism, therefore, involves its optimization through the attraction of desirable visitors and the dissuasion of undesirable visitors.

Tourism and the Thai State

Since the early decades of the 20th century, the Thai state has taken active measures to promote Thailand as a destination for international tourism. The first of these measures involved the production and distribution of materials publicizing Thailand to potential American travellers. This was followed, in 1924, by the establishment of the first commercial airline travel between Europe and Thailand (Leksakundilok, 2004, p. 63), and the commissioning of the first guidebook for tourists – *Guide to Bangkok and Siam* – by the Authority of the Royal State Railways (Leksakundilok, 2004, p. 63; Saispradist, 2005, p. 12). Consistent with the characteristics of international tourism at the time, Western tourists visiting Thailand prior to the second half of the 20th century were numerically very limited, consisting almost exclusively of the very wealthy, who had both the financial means and leisure time to travel to far-off lands. Thus, although the Thai government took an active role in promoting tourism during this period, it remained a relatively limited phenomenon of only minor importance to the Thai economy. The few policies and programmes related to tourism in place concerned merely attracting and accommodating a small and relatively homogenous group of foreign travellers.

With the entrance of Thailand into the South-East Asia Treaty Organization (SEATO) and the commencement of the Vietnam War, the nature of tourism in the country was radically transformed in several crucial ways. First, this period marked the beginning of mass tourism in Thailand. By 1970, Thailand was receiving 628,671 foreign tourists per year, a number that would grow to over five million by 1990 (Leksakundilok, 2004, p. 69). The increased number of visitors reflected the broader phenomenon of the opening of possibilities for foreign travel to members of the post-Second World War Western middle class – what is often referred to as the democratization of travel. With decreased travel costs, and increases in income and leisure time, international travel was made possible for wider

segments of the population. Thus, the increased number of visitors to Thailand during this period can be characterized by both an expansion of tourism and a pluralization of the figure of the tourist.

This rapid increase in the number of foreign visitors resulted in tourism quickly becoming a vital sector of the Thai economy. Beginning with the severe economic recession of the late 1970s, tourism increasingly became an important source of foreign exchange earnings. Since 1982, income from tourism has been the largest source of foreign currency in the Thai economy (Leksakundilok 2004, pp. 65, 69; Saispradist, 2005, p. 12). The importance of the tourist industry to the Thai economy was further reinforced in the wake of the September 1997 collapse of the economies of the Asian Tigers, with tourism suddenly becoming not only the most important source, but one of the only sources of foreign currency.

Corresponding to the increased importance of tourism for the Thai economy was a rise in the involvement of the state in the tourist industry. In 1976, the Tourism Organization of Thailand (TOT) established the First National Tourism Plan. This was the first attempt by the Thai state to plot a comprehensive course for the development of a sustainable tourism sector in Thailand. The plan included growth targets, programmes to establish links between tourism and other sectors of the Thai economy, projects to improve the transportation infrastructure and marketing strategies. Significantly, it also marked an awareness of the potential threat to Thai culture and identity, and consequently, the need to 'endeavour to achieve the aforementioned objectives while maintaining a socio-cultural and historical identity' (Leksakundilok, 2004, p. 65).

In the years since the unveiling of the 1976 National Tourism Plan, numerous national, regional and provincial plans have been developed. Most of these plans have sought to integrate tourism and local development. Increasingly, though, the TOT and its successor, the Tourism Authority of Thailand (TAT), have had to manage tensions between the desire to attract foreign capital and criticism of the negative social, cultural and environmental impacts of mass tourism. By the early 1990s, protests by academics, planners, non-governal organizations (NGOs) and locals pushed the Thai government to place a greater focus on sustainable tourism and increasing the 'quality' of Thailand as a tourist destination (Leksakundilok, 2004, p. 65; Saispradist, 2005, pp. 12–14; Nuttavuthisit, 2007). A series of initiatives – from a National Ecotourism Policy (1998), to the 'community-tourism' aspects of the 1995 One Tambon, One Product (OTOP) policy for local economic development – have been developed to attend to these issues. However, as Anucha Leksakundilok (2004, p. 67) suggests, they have served chiefly to supplement, rather than transform the nature of the Thai tourism industry.

It is important to reiterate that securitization is not only a mechanism of negation. In relation to tourism, the securitization of migration does not only concern the restriction or elimination of undesirable visitors and activities. It also involves attracting desirable visitors and promoting tourist activities that are seen as beneficial for the host state. Planners, immigration officials, the security apparatus and other figures have been conferred the authority to gaze upon, categorize, assess the desirability of and manage the presence of visitors and potential visitors in order to optimize the impact of tourism for the host state. The management of tourism, therefore, involves its optimization through the attraction of desirable visitors and the dissuasion of undesirable visitors, as well as the promotion of desirable activities and the discouragement of undesirable activities.

Visa Policy and the Governance of Visitors to Thailand

Perhaps the most evident of such security measures is that of visa policy. In the case of Thailand, the distinction of desirable from undesirable visitors – and gradations of desirability – are evident in the distinction between visitors who require a visa to enter the country as visitors, those who may apply for a 'visa on arrival' permitting them to remain in Thailand for up to 15 days, and those who automatically receive 'visa exemptions' allowing them a stay in the Kingdom for 30 days. Perhaps not surprisingly, with few exceptions, these categories tend to correspond to the levels of wealth and development of particular states. The most desirable visitors appear to be those from Australia, Israel, Japan, Western Europe, North America and wealthier Gulf, South American and East Asian states, and the least desirable tend to be those from Africa and Central Asia, who must obtain a visa prior to arrival in Thailand. Among the most common rationale given for categorization is the likelihood that the visitor is seeking to enter Thailand for employment or residency, rather than to enjoy a short holiday. Not only are travellers from wealthier states seen as a greater source of tourism income, they also appear more likely to return to their home state after a short stay. In contrast, visitors from poorer states are seen as more likely to remain in Thailand and engage in undocumented work.

Beyond governing the admission of potential visitors, visa policies also permit states to regulate the length of stay and the parameters for re-entry for visitors. In doing so, they are able to further govern the characteristics of the visitor and the tourist experience. Recent Thai policies and governmental practices have sought to limit the duration of visits. First, consular officials have been instructed to be more restrictive in granting tourist visas to individuals who have previously been granted visas, as well as with visas permitting multiple entries. Second, recent policies have sought to restrict the phenomenon of visa runs, a practice popular with visitors wishing to remain in Thailand for extended periods. As visitors granted entry for 30 days are only permitted to apply to extend their stay for an additional seven days, the practice of the visa run was developed to aid those seeking to stay for longer periods of time. This practice involves visitors travelling to the border of a neighbouring state and immediately seeking re-entry into Thailand.

For many years visitors were able to prolong their stay in Thailand indefinitely by making monthly visa runs. As long as the visitor briefly left Thailand prior to the expiry of the 30-day stay granted to them upon each entry, there was no limit to the duration of their visit.

In 2008, the Thai government began implementing a series of policies seeking to restrict the phenomenon of visa runs. First, limitations were placed on the number of re-entries that a visitor was permitted. Visitors could no longer indefinitely extend their stay through making periodic visa runs. Second, the duration of stay was limited to 15 days (rather than the previous 30 days) for those entering Thailand through a land border checkpoint. According to the most recent variation of these regulations, effective since June 2009, visitors are permitted a maximum of four re-entries over the period of a year. Not only do these policies make the prospect of an extended stay in Thailand less appealing to visitors, as they require frequent visa runs, they also place a clear limitation on the duration of stay.

From these policies and practices, it is possible to discern some elements of the image of the desirable and undesirable visitor to Thailand. The desirable visitor is the national of a wealthy country who wishes to stay in Thailand for a pre-determined, short period of time. In other words, the desirable tourist is the mainstream tourist – one who wishes to make use of their leisure time to take a brief holiday in a foreign destination. In contrast, the undesirable tourist is the visitor whose stay is not as circumscribed. In contrast to the wanderer or the traditional tourist, who comes today and goes tomorrow, the undesirable visitor appears similar to Simmel's sociological figure of the stranger, and, therefore, may be one 'who comes today and stays tomorrow' (Simmel, [1908] 1950, p. 402). The undesirable visitor is the outsider whose presence threatens to linger indefinitely.

While the potential reasons for the undesirability of this figure will be discussed later, what is important to note at this point is that it is within the host gaze,

and specifically the gaze of the host state, that this figure appears as undesirable. Just as the tourist gaze permits the tourist to categorize subjects, objects and phenomena as desirable and undesirable, authentic and inauthentic, the host gaze allows for the categorization of potential visitors by degree of desirability. Rather than being faced with the visitor as such, the host state encounters various discursively constituted categories of otherness with corresponding levels of risk that must be managed.

The Governance of the Image of Thailand

In addition to the governance of the presence of particular categories of visitors, recent government interventions into Thai tourism policy have also sought to carefully manage the image of Thailand. As previously mentioned, a central insight of the literature concerning the tourist gaze is the acknowledgement of the influential role of tourism professionals in designating that which is said to be representative of a particular culture, region or people. Writers, academics, travel agents, photographers, tour guides and bureaucrats produce and authorize particular images of a tourist destination. In doing so, they influence both the traveller's expectations – through providing an image through which meaning can be attached to experience – and the experiences themselves – by directing the traveller towards, and presenting them with, particular activities and phenomena.

Since the advent of tourism in Thailand, the Thai government has launched various marketing campaigns aimed at attracting visitors. In 2001, the Thai government, with the help of two prominent business schools, undertook the Branding Thailand Project. The project aimed to understand international perceptions of Thailand, and to determine how to better market Thailand in the global marketplace (Nuttavuthisit, 2007, p. 22). Part of the Branding Thailand Project involved surveying individuals in 30 countries in order to ascertain their perceptions of Thailand. Among the questions that participants were asked to respond to were those involving word association such as: 'What are the first words that come to mind when thinking about Thailand?' While the responses to these questions presented an image of Thailand with many positive elements, they also revealed a strong negative association of Thailand with prostitution and sex tourism (Nuttavuthisit, 2007, p. 22). Moreover, responses to further questions asking for suggestions to improve the Thai tourism industry regularly stated the need to eliminate or better control the sex-trade industry. Respondents – including both those who had visited Thailand and those who had not – suggested that Thailand's association with sex tourism had seriously damaged its reputation as a tourist destination.

Since the early 1960s, sex tourism has been a significant element of the Thai tourist industry. As a member of SEATO, Thailand provided a base for American military interventions in Vietnam, Cambodia and Laos, as well as a destination for American GIs on rest and relaxation leave. The presence of the GIs, particularly in beach resorts such as Pattaya, led to a rapid expansion of the sex work industry in Thailand. Such was the growth of prostitution in Thailand that between 1957 and 1964 the number of sex workers in the country increased from approximately 20,000 to 400,000 (Hall, 2002, p. 274). Accompanying this growth was a process that has been referred to as 'Pattayazation' (Cohen, 1996, p. 23). This term refers to the branding, during the 1960s and early 1970s, of Thailand and particular locations within Thailand, as centres of sexual hedonism and the development of tourist-oriented prostitution (Leksakundilok, 2004, p. 62).

Until the end of the 1980s, the Thai government openly advocated and promoted sex tourism as a means of attracting foreign capital and creating job opportunities for women from the economically marginalized areas of east and north-east Thailand (Hall, 2002, p. 274). In 1989, in response to growing concerns regarding the effect of the growing AIDS epidemic on the tourism industry, this began to change in some ways. First, the Thai Public Health Ministry, which had previously sought to deny the extent of the epidemic within the sex work industry, embarked upon a campaign to curb the spread of AIDS. This campaign involved measures such as the distribution of condoms to visitors, public education, and the testing of sex workers and selected visitors (Hall, 2002, p. 275). Second, attempts were made to counteract the image of Thailand as a centre of sex tourism and AIDS. To do so, the government began to publicize the measures that were being taken to stop the spread of AIDS, downplay the extent of the epidemic and, despite the opposition of some involved in the sex tourism industry, attempted to publicize alternative images of Thailand to attract new forms of tourism (Hall, 2002, p. 275; Nuttavuthisit, 2007, p. 23).

As Hall (2002, p. 275) has noted, while some of the motivation behind these measures may have been a moral concern with sex work, the exploitation of women and children, and the impact of AIDS on the Thai population, this did not seem to be the sole or even primary concern of the Thai authorities. Rather, impression management seemed of vital concern. The measures undertaken by the Thai government did not aim to eliminate sex tourism but to better manage the sex tourism industry and its impact on the tourism industry as a whole. Moreover, they involved a reworking of categories and gradations of desirability for visitors. The risks of sex tourism for the tourist industry as a whole, and therefore the desirability of a tourism industry driven by the sex tourist had been altered. Consequently, new mechanisms were required, not to eliminate sex tourism, but to maximize its benefits and minimize its costs.

As the surveys conducted as part of the Branding Thailand Project make evident, however, the measures mentioned above failed to diminish the association of Thailand with sex tourism. One of the significant findings of the project was the important role played by other travellers in the development of a visitor's impression of Thailand. As Nuttavuthisit (2007, p. 24) suggests, 'people do not like to associate with others that they find unacceptable or undesirable and sex tourists create a negative impact on the country's image'. Consequently, despite attempts by the Thai tourism industry to portray an image of Thailand unrelated to sex tourism, the presence of undesirable others – in the form of the sex tourist – has served to undermine these attempts. In order to offset this negative image, the Thai government has attempted to attract alternative categories of tourists to that of the single male, including women and families. For instance, in 1992 the TAT organized a Women Visit Thailand campaign to encourage more female tourism (Hall, 2002, p. 276).

A significant aspect of the Thai state's attempts to construct an alternative image of Thailand as a tourist destination has involved 'rebranding' Thailand (Nuttavuthisit, 2007). Since 1997, the 'Amazing Thailand' campaign, which portrays Thailand as unique, remarkable, exotic and exciting, has been the main marketing tool of the Tourism Authority. In the past decade, this campaign has been augmented by several others, each emphasizing a particular image of Thailand and seeking to attract a particular category of tourist. First, in the wake of the attacks in New York in September 2001, the Thai government instituted the 'Be My Guest' campaign, aimed at portraying Thailand as a safe and welcoming destination, as well as placing more emphasis on the domestic tourist market. Second, in 2004, the focus of the TAT shifted to transforming Thailand into what it labelled a 'Quality Destination' (Saispradsit, 2005, p. 13). The emphasis of this project, and the associated 'Unseen Thailand' and 'Unseen Treasures' campaigns, was to attract a greater number of 'higher-end' international and domestic tourists, and to direct them to specific activities and destinations. In creating the image of Thailand as a 'Quality Destination', the TAT hoped to attract those taking part in package tours or other visitors wishing to enjoy a resort holiday.

Not only are there significant financial incentives in attracting this category of tour-

ist, it is also significantly less difficult to manage the impressions these visitors have of the host culture and people. As mentioned earlier, within the tourist space, there is a great deal of energy expended by the host in the task of impression management. Representations of the host culture are carefully contrived and controlled in order to be easily enjoyable and replicable, and so that they portray and remain consistent with the host's desired image. The stakes of impression management are further increased when, as MacCannell (1976) suggests, the image presented to the tourist also serves as a screen, obscuring the attempts of the all-seeing tourist eye to penetrate the back stage of the tourism space.

The Stranger's Gaze

The resort is the ideal location for impression management. Contacts with the host population and culture occur almost exclusively in the region of the front stage. There are only minor risks that cracks in this image will permit elements of the back stage to appear. Effective impression management only requires that the spectacle of difference does not contradict predetermined expectations. The location of the resort also allows for visitors to be easily insulated from exposure to undesirable phenomena, such as poverty or sex tourism. Consequently, the visitors that the 'Quality Destination' campaign has sought to attract high financial rewards while minimizing risks related to impression management. The promotion of Thailand as a 'Quality Destination' and the attraction of high-end tourists do not involve or require the elimination of sex tourism. Rather, it can be seen as an attempt to refashion the tourist industry in such a way that the presence of sex tourism and other undesirable phenomena do not contaminate the positive image of Thailand as a tourist destination.

In addition to their financial resources, therefore, the resort-bound tourist is desired by the host state due to the fact that his or her perceptions can be governed with relative ease and minimal risk. As these visitors tend to stay for only short periods of time and have minimal contact with the host population and other categories of visitor, their presence is less unsettling than that of those guests – the wanderer, the flâneur, the drifter or the previously mentioned figure of the stranger – whose stay in, and experiences of, Thailand are less easily circumscribed. Not only are these figures of the traveller troubling due to the often extended and unpredictable nature of their stays, but their experiences are also often not limited to that of the front stage. Whether, like the flâneur, they seek out the dark shadows of the back stage, or merely happen upon such experiences, they pose a significant risk to the carefully managed host image. The prolonged duration of their stay, and their unwillingness to abide by a constructed itinerary, makes restricting their exposure to alternative representations of the host culture and people more difficult. In other words, there is a greater possibility that these categories of visitor may see what they are not supposed to. With the presence of these figures, the space of the back stage – where the host is no longer required to attend to the projection and maintenance of a particular representation – is diminished both in terms of size and security. Thus, the front stage – that area where the gaze of the tourist is expected – expands, and the all-seeing tourist gaze seems increasingly capable of penetrating all areas of life. As such, the presence of these visitors makes the task of impression management one that is fraught with anxiety.

Of these figures, the stranger poses the greatest threat to disturbing the carefully managed host image. The stranger, like these other figures, is troubling, in part because of his lingering presence. However, the duration of the presence of the stranger is even more uncertain than that of the other figures of the long-term visitor. While the drifter, the wanderer and the flâneur may stay for extended periods of time, their presence is not permanent. At some, perhaps undetermined point in the future, they will leave. Like Simmel's description of the wanderer, each of these figures 'comes today and goes tomorrow'. In contrast, the stranger is the 'person who comes today and stays tomorrow' (Simmel, [1908] 1950, p. 402). Yet this staying is never certain. The stranger remains always the potential wanderer characterized by both attachment and detachment, wandering and belonging (Isin, 2002, p. 30). Accordingly, the relation between the stranger and the host group is marked by both closeness and distance. As Simmel ([1908] 1950, p. 404) describes, the stranger, as a 'fundamentally mobile person, comes in contact, at one time or another, with every individual, but is not organically connected ... with any single one'. Therefore, unlike the tourist as wanderer, flâneur or drifter, who are clearly outsiders, the stranger persists in a zone of estrangement. He is neither near nor far, attached or detached, involved or indifferent, outsider or full member of the group.

It is this social position that makes the figure of the stranger, and the tourist as potential stranger, appear particularly disturbing within the host gaze. First, it grants the stranger the capacity to develop objective knowledge of the group. As Simmel suggests, the objectivity of the stranger is not born of passivity and detachment, but of a synthesis of distance and nearness, and indifference and involvement, which permits a perspective that is at once knowledgeable of the group, yet free from the commitments and assumptions that could prejudice the perceptions of the full member of the group (Simmel, [1908] 1950, pp. 404–405). The stranger, due to his relative distance from the group, is privy to knowledge about the group that would be inaccessible to others. Often, this is as a consequence of receiving 'the most surprising openness – confidences which have the character of a confessional and which would be carefully withheld from a more closely related person' (Simmel, [1908] 1950, p. 404). The stranger's position in relation to the group, therefore, permits him what Simmel refers to as a 'freedom ... which allows [him] to experience and treat his close relationships as though from a bird's eye view' (Simmel, [1908] 1950, p. 405). The structural position of the stranger in relation to the group, therefore, permits him a view of the host that escapes that of both the carefully crafted representation of the front stage and the staged authenticity of the back stage. Thus, within the host gaze, the stranger appears as a problematic figure whose gaze cannot be managed.

More disturbingly, perhaps, the objectivity of the stranger has the potential to disrupt the group's notion of self. His freedom and bird's eye view permit the perception of a more genuine image of the host group than that accessible to full members. The disturbance resulting from this objective gaze of the stranger is not only that he may be in a position to dispute the veracity of particular cultural representations or conceptions of host identity. Rather, the gaze of the stranger has the capacity to produce feelings of uneasiness, self-consciousness and even shame. Like all gazes, the gaze of the stranger is an objectifying gaze. As Sartre (1943) describes in his famous phenomenological account of the gaze, the realization of being an object within the gaze of the Other amounts to a loss of freedom. The awareness of the gaze of the Other produces not only a feeling of being judged, but also an understanding that one's identity is something that is largely imposed from the outside. While all tourist gazes, and particularly those of extended-stay visitors, involve objectification of the host, it is possible for the host to spatially escape these gazes and to mediate their effects through the use of various masks and screens. The structural position from which the stranger gazes, however, renders such evasions ineffective. In the presence of the stranger, therefore, the host is perpetually in the unsettling position of a fully exposed object within the tourist gaze.

The social position of the stranger also appears threatening within the host gaze as a potential contaminant. In others, what is disturbing is the potential for the presence of the stranger to alter the nature and image of the host. As Simmel ([1908] 1950, p. 402)

asserts, the stranger's position in relation to the group is 'determined, essentially, by the fact that he has not belonged to it from the beginning'. As such, he is an external element whose incorporation into the group threatens to alter its pre-existing characteristics. Through 'importing qualities into [the group], which do not and cannot stem from the group itself' (Simmel, [1908] 1950, p. 402), the stranger threatens to contaminate the host with foreign elements. Within the host gaze, therefore, the stranger appears both as a figure whose presence must be carefully managed in order to maintain the consistency and purity of carefully established cultural representations, and to limit the disturbing effects of his objective and objectifying gaze.

The above-mentioned features of the stranger render this figure particularly disturbing within the host gaze. The recent interventions of the Thai state into tourism policy should be seen as responses to the perceived risks posed by strangers and potential strangers. Through exploring the host's perceptions and subjective experiences, it was possible within this chapter to demonstrate the manner in which the Thai–tourist encounter in general, and the recent direction of Thai tourism policy in particular, are the product of particular relations of alterity. The efforts of the Thai state to govern visitors and the image of Thailand are the manifestation of particular discourses of otherness and governance, within which desirable and undesirable figures of the visitor emerge. The host's perception of the tourist is, like the tourist's perception of the host, the product of particular discourses of travel and otherness. Within the host gaze, different figures of the visitor are discerned as belonging to various categories of desirability, each marked by particular costs, benefits and risks. It is on the basis of this categorization of visitors within the host's gaze, and the attempt to optimize the impact of tourism, through maximizing the benefits of the desirable and minimizing the risks of the undesirable, that the recent interventions of the Thai state in tourism policy were formulated.

References

Adler, J. (1989) Origins of sightseeing. *Annals of Tourism Research* 16, 7–29.

Boorstin, D. (1964) *The Image: a Guide to Pseudo-Events in America*. Harper, New York.

Bruner, E. (2005) *Culture on Tour: Ethnographies of Travel*. University of Chicago Press, Chicago, IL.

Cohen, E. (1979) A phenomenology of tourist types. *Sociology* 13, 179–201.

Cohen, E. (1988) Authenticity and commoditization in tourism. *Annals of Tourism Research*, 15, 371–386.

Cohen, E. (1996) *Thai Tourism: Hill Tribes, Islands and Open-Ended Prostitution*. White Lotus, Bangkok.

Crawshaw, C. (1994) *Altered Images: Tourism and Photography in the Lake District*. Lancaster University, Lancaster.

Crawshaw, C. and Urry, J. (1997) Tourism and the photographic eye. In: Rojek, C. and Urry, J. (eds) *Touring Cultures: Transformations in Travel and Theory*. Routledge, London and New York, pp. 176–195.

Czajka, A. and Gardner, A.R. (2011) *The Age of Security: Frontex and the Governance of European Migration*. Paper presented at the International Studies Association Conference, Montréal, 17 March.

Duke, P. (2007) *The Tourists Gaze, the Cretans Glance: Archaelogy and Tourism on a Greek Island*. Left Coast Press, Walnut Creek, CA.

Foucault, M. ([1963] 1976) *The Birth of the Clinic: An Archaeology of Medical Perception*. Tavistock, London.

Foucault, M. ([1966] 2002) *The Order of Things*. Routledge, London.

Foucault, M. (2009) *Security, Territory, Population: Lectures at the Collège de France, 1977–1978*. Picador, New York.

Hall, C.M. (2002) Gender and economic interests in tourism prostitution: the nature, development and implications of sex tourism in South-East Asia. In: Apostolopoulos, Y., Leivadi, S. and Yiannakis, A. (eds) *The Sociology of Tourism: Theoretical and Empirical Investigations*. Routledge, London and New York, pp. 265–280.

Huysmans, J. (2006) *The Politics of Insecurity: Fear, Migration and Asylum in the EU*. Routledge, New York.

Isin, E.F. (2002) *Being Political: Genealogies of Citizenship*. University of Minnesota Press, Minneapolis, MN.

Leksakundilok, A. (2004) *Ecotourism Development in Thailand*. University of Sydney, Sydney.

MacCannell, D. (1973) Staged authenticity: on arrangements of social space in tourist settings. *American Journal of Sociology* 79, 589–603.

MacCannell, D. (1976) *The Tourist. A New Theory of the Leisure Class*. Macmillan, New York.

Nuttavuthisit, K. (2007) Branding Thailand: correcting the negative image of sex tourism. *Place Branding and Public Diplomacy* 3, 21–30.

Saispradist, A. (2005) *A Critical Analysis of Heritage Interpretation and the Development of a Guidebook for Non-Thai Cultural Tourists at Ayutthaya World Heritage Site*. Silpakorn University, Bangkok.

Sartre, J.-P. (1943) The Look (Barnes, H.E. trans.) *Being and Nothingness*. Washington Square Press, New York, pp. 340–400.

Simmel, G. ([1908] 1950) The Stranger. In: Wolff, K. (eds) *The Sociology of Georg Simmel*. Free Press, New York.

Urry, J. (1990) *The Tourist Gaze*. Sage, London.

Urry, J. (2002) *The Tourist Gaze* (2nd ed.). Sage, London.

4 Turkish Host Gaze at Russian Tourists: a Cultural Perspective

Yvette Reisinger, Metin Kozak and Esmé Visser

A country's culture is made-up not simply of works of art or literary discourses, but of unwritten codes, signs and symbols, rituals and gestures, and common attitudes that fix the public meanings of those works and organize the inner life of a society (Figes, 2002)

Introduction

In this chapter, the host gaze refers to perceptions and experiences as well as cultural observations and comments made by Turkish hosts regarding Russian tourists and the cultural stereotypes and assumptions often embedded in these observations and comments. The foundation for understanding the host gaze is found in the work of Urry (1990) who states that tourists 'gaze' at locations and hosts, and their gaze is constructed in relationships of social experience and consciousness, and depends on what it is contrasted with. Following Urry's (1990) notion, hosts also 'gaze' at tourists. The host gaze is inseparably bound up with socio-cultural relations, depends on the external environment and is interpreted into internal socio-cultural experiences (Brunt and Courtney, 1999; Larsen and Urry, 2011).

The host gaze is limited to a specific context and environment in which it develops.

Observations of tourists by hosts can be carried out in socio-cultural, economic, historical and political contexts (Chan, 2006; Moufakkir, 2011), different sectors of the tourism and hospitality industry (Kozak and Tasci, 2005; Larsen and Urry, 2011), types of tourism (Butler, 1980; Maoz, 2006), on different types of tourists, their numbers, types of touristic enclave (Moufakkir, 2011), and by different types of hosts (e.g. working/non-working in tourism) (Maoz, 2006). In all instances, the host gaze reflects the place and the environment in which it occurs and the people who gaze and who are gazed upon. This chapter examines the host gaze in the cultural context. It argues that cultural influences enhance the potential for misperceptions and misunderstanding between hosts and tourists.

Tourism is a primary ground for the creation of cultural misperceptions and misunderstanding, especially in an increasingly globalized and interconnected world (Reisinger and Turner, 2003; Hottola, 2004). The potential for tensions and conflicts between culturally different people is considerable in such a world. There is high risk of conflict breaking out in many of the meeting areas (e.g. restaurants, hotels, shops), which could lay the ground for a development of considerable strife and hostility between tourists and hosts. Hospitality providers, such as hoteliers, restaurateurs or retailers have more direct and close contacts with foreign tourists than local residents and therefore their experiences with tourists should be examined (Reisinger and Turner, 2003; Kim and McKercher, 2011).

Social interaction and communication between hospitality providers and international tourists is susceptible to misperceptions, misevaluation, misinterpretation and miscommunication, especially in a culturally distinct environment (Jafari and Way, 1994; Armstrong *et al.*, 1997; Mattila, 1999a, b; Woods and King, 2002; Tsaur *et al.*, 2005; Manzur and Jogaratnam, 2006; Zhu *et al.*, 2007). As such, there is a need to analyse the interaction between hospitality providers and international tourists (Larsen and Urry, 2011) to understand the reasons for their cultural misperceptions and identify the ways to avoid these misperceptions (Reisinger, 2009). However, much of the research has been carried out on how tourists view local residents (MacCannell, 1976; Bruner, 1989; Urry, 1990; Dann, 1996; Keung, 2000; Tsang and Ap, 2007). There has been insufficient attention paid to how hosts view foreign tourists, especially in the cross-cultural context. Only a few studies have focused on the images the locals have of the tourists (Evans-Pritchard, 1989; Sweet, 1989; Kim, 1999).

Examining hospitality providers' comments and evaluations of international tourists in the cross-cultural context is important. Service providers have more direct and close contact with tourists and thus develop more opinions about tourists than local residents. Hosts' comments and evaluations of tourists allow for identification of the cultural gaps and potential for conflict with tourists. In the unique context of international tourism hospitality providers may assess tourist behaviour to be strange, deviant or even unacceptable. This may be a reflection of the cultural differences in values learnt in the country of the one who gazes upon and the one who is gazed upon.

This chapter discusses Turkish hosts' gaze upon Russian guests in the accommodation sector of the tourism and hospitality industry. It seeks to determine the most important factors that influence this gaze and explain the reasons behind it. It shows that Turkish hoteliers misperceive their Russian guests' behaviour. The cultural errors in the host gaze interpretations of tourist behaviour create misperceptions and dissatisfaction with tourists. The chapter implies that in order for hosts to assess tourists and understand how tourists perform in an alien society hosts should understand tourists' society and not apply one's own society's rules. Only an adequate knowledge of cultural background of tourists can facilitate hosts' understanding of tourists across cultural boundaries and develop positive host gaze. However, a question arises as to whether hosts should accept the cultural norms of tourists and tolerate the tourist behaviour they believe is inappropriate and unacceptable? The cultural relativism theory serves as an important theoretical framework that is used to find the answer to this question.

Cultural Influences on the Host Gaze

The host gaze is a socio-cultural phenomenon and reflects, to a different extent, the influence of (i) the national culture of the hosts; (ii) the national culture of the tourists; (iii) degree of cultural distance between tourists and hosts; (iv) 'touristic culture'; (v) cultural stereotyping and assumptions; and (vi) cultural borrowing. Understanding the cultural influences on the host gaze can be very helpful in reducing potential for cultural misperceptions and misevaluations, and enhancing hosts' and tourists' experiential values.

The Influence of National Culture of Hosts

The host gaze and its meaning is very subjective; it depends on the host's view of the world and reflects the environment in which the host lives. The national culture of hosts determines how their experiences are interpreted and evaluated. Since hosts bring their unique gazes on the world to their social interactions and communication with tourists, national culture of hosts teaches them to gaze upon tourists from their own unique cultural perspectives, which are determined by values they have adopted as they grew up. In the case of limited experience with tourists and the lack of knowledge of tourists, hosts judge tourists based on their subjective and culturally determined criteria for evaluation. The more favourable the host evaluation of tourists, the more positive the host gaze and the greater the probability that hosts are satisfied with tourists' presence. On the other hand, the less favourable the host evaluation of tourists, the more negative the host gaze and the less likely it is that hosts are happy about tourists.

The Influence of National Culture of Tourists

Scholars argue that when hosts analyse behaviour of tourists of different nationality they should take into account the national (home) culture of tourists (Pizam, 1999; Reisinger, 2009). Past studies have identified the influence of the national culture of tourists on their behaviour (Pizam and Sussmann, 1995; Pizam and Jeong, 1996; Pizam and Reichel, 1996). Significant cultural differences were identified among different nationalities of tourists in their values, rules of behaviour, beliefs, norms and communication patterns (Reisinger and Turner, 2003). The literature review indicates that many hosts' communities perceive tourists of different nationalities to be different and behave in different ways. Especially, in the destinations where the majority of the tourists are of different nationality, hosts view tourists to be different according to a variety of characteristics, such as behaviour, attitudes, morality (Pizam and Telisman-Kosuta, 1989; Kozak and Tasci, 2005). The previous studies also showed that hospitality workers evaluate services differently from international tourists (Baker and Fesenmaier, 1997) because

their perceptions of service quality differ from tourists' perceptions (Reisinger and Turner, 2003; Reisinger, 2009).

The Influence of Cultural Distance

The development of favourable and unfavourable host gaze on culturally different tourists depends upon the degree of the cultural dissimilarity between tourists and hosts and the knowledge of tourist national culture (Reisinger and Turner, 2003; Reisinger, 2009). Although it has been argued otherwise (Warden *et al.*, 2003; Moufakkir, 2011), perceived cultural similarity enhances mutual understanding, tolerance and the development of the positive gaze. On the other hand, perceived cultural dissimilarity generates misperceptions and errors in gaze interpretations and cultural misunderstanding, friction and even conflict. It is the gap between what is culturally familiar and unfamiliar that makes the development of the host gaze different. The cultural gap in the host gaze develops because of the hosts' limited experience with tourists and/or the lack of knowledge of tourists. This gap creates problems in cross-cultural tourist–host relations and determines the quality of the host gaze.

The Influence of 'Touristic' Culture

The host gaze upon tourists reflects the influence of 'touristic' culture, or how tourists behave or act during travel (Picard, 1995; Kim and Prideaux, 2003). When on holiday, tourists behave more freely and differently than at home (Kozak and Tasci, 2005). 'When tourists are away from home they are in a different state of mind and ... are in the play mode' (Reisinger and Turner, 2003, p. 10). 'They temporarily step out of social reality and retreat from the daily social obligations. Instead of duty and structure, they want to enjoy freedom and carefree fun' (Crick, 1989, p. 327). Similarly, Picard (1995) noted that when tourists are on holiday they live a different life, they are out of their normal socio-cultural context, which is distinct from the normal working day. When hosts evaluate tourist behaviour they should take into account tourist touristic culture (Pizam, 1999). Thus, the touristic culture shaped by tourists on holiday cannot be divorced from tourism itself (Picard, 1995).

The Influence of Cultural Stereotyping and Assumptions

The host gaze involves categorization or grouping tourists according to their common cultural characteristics, called stereotyping. Categorization of tourists allows distinctions to be drawn among them. Cultural categorization contains some 'kernel of truth' and often reflects objective assessment of tourists (e.g. 'Japanese tourists always travel in groups', 'Korean tourists always take pictures', 'German tourists are heavy beer drinkers'), According to Joseph and Kavoori (2001), most local gazes are based on stereotyped notions of the tourists and are often culturally biased. Hosts have the tendency to exaggerate the tourists' cultural characteristics when surrounded by culturally different tourists who speak a different language. In expectation of familiarity with like-minded people, hosts often feel uncomfortable when experiencing tourists of a different culture and are inclined to criticize tourists. Hosts' criticisms are generated by ethnocentrism, prejudice and/or even racial attitudes, which are the primary sources of cultural bias. Further, since hosts categorize or group tourists based on tourists' similar characteristics hosts cannot easily recognize any differences among individual tourists within the grouping. Hosts narrow the perception of the entire population of tourists to the individual tourists' traits, which represents another source of potential bias in the host gaze.

The Influence of Cultural Borrowing

An individual's cultural values can change after experiencing foreign cultures.

According to Mitchell (2006, p. 5), 'when sojourners leave home, they often carry with them a ... mental and emotional snapshot of home; on some level ... they can be unprepared ... for the changes that have occurred ... during their absence – changes that no longer match their image of home.' Following this, when hosts experience tourists from foreign cultures they undergo a cultural change while interacting with tourists; they learn about tourists' different worldviews and beliefs and modify their values, which contrast with the original values of the cultures they grew up in. The social contact with foreign tourists encourages hosts to borrow cultural elements from tourists' societies. Hosts may learn a new language or incorporate customs of tourist culture into their daily routine, and even adapt their behavioural patterns. Hosts can significantly change their attitudes and evaluation criteria by borrowing cultural elements from the foreign cultures of tourists. It is possible that the impact of tourist foreign culture on culture borrowing by the host society can be so pervasive that many of the elements of the host culture can originate from tourist cultures. This does not happen immediately; it depends upon the length and intensity of experiencing a new culture, hosts' cultural competence and intelligence. In the Western world, the rate of change of cultures, either through culture borrowings or dispersion, has become very significant in recent years.

Cultural Relativism Theory

It seems that cultural relativism theory can be used to explain the host gaze upon tourists, especially when tourists and hosts are of different cultural backgrounds. Cultural relativism theory belongs to the theory of relativism, which is important in understanding human experience and a major principle of human interaction in a global, multicultural world society (Rosado, 1994). Cultural relativism theory argues that an individual human's beliefs and activities should be understood by others in terms of that individual's own culture. This principle was established by an anthropologist Franz Boas in the 20th century. Boas (1911) wrote that civilization is not something absolute, but is relative, and 'our ideas and conceptions are true only so far as our civilization goes'. Different societies have different behavioural codes. All beliefs, customs and ethics are relative and need to be evaluated on the basis of the values and norms of these societies in their own socio-cultural contexts and not on the basis of other cultures; what are considered to be 'right' or 'wrong' behaviours are culture-specific. What is considered acceptable in one society may be considered unacceptable in another. There is no absolute cultural truth (Gellner, 1985). There are no universal standards of behaviour. Therefore, there is no meaningful way to judge different cultures (Gellner, 1985). No one has the right to judge another culture's standards of behaviour. No culture is superior to any other culture. It is arrogant to judge the conduct of other people. All judgements are ethnocentric (Gellner, 1985). As Rachels (1999) suggests, people should adopt an attitude of tolerance towards the behavioural practices of other cultures. Understanding of humanity must be based on appreciating individual cultures that are different from our own. All you have to do is know the context to understand what people are doing and why they're doing it (Benedict, 1934).

The theory of relativism also includes moral relativism (ethics depend on a social construct), value relativism (values have different importance), situational relativism (right or wrong is based on the particular situation), cognitive relativism (truth itself has no absolute, it is relative) as well as value, perceptual and conduct relativism.

Russian Tourists

This chapter focuses on the Turkish hosts' gaze upon Russian tourists. Currently, the Russian tourist market is one of the fastest growing international travel markets. The number of Russian tourists travelling around the world has been dramatically increased. In 2010, outbound tourism in Russia grew by 20% compared with 2009 (ATOR, 2010). In the first half of 2010, more than 5 million Russian citizens spent their holidays abroad.

Turkey is the most popular holiday destination for Russian tourists who constitute the largest percentage of guests in the country. The number of Russian tourist arrivals to Turkey increased from 676,183 in 1998 to 3.1 million in 2010 (Ministry of Culture and Tourism, 2011a). The number of Russian tourists to Turkey's Mediterranean coast has also significantly increased in the last years, overtaking the traditional German market. The most popular Mediterranean resorts in the southern province of Antalya have recently experienced a 10% increase in Russian arrivals, reaching 2.5 million tourists in 2010 (Ministry of Culture and Tourism, 2011b).

As a result of the changing economic and political situation throughout Europe (the traditional German travel market has experienced a decline in the number of its nationals visiting the Mediterranean due to the deteriorating economic situation in Germany and bankruptcies in the Eurozone), Turkey redirected its attention to attracting Russian tourists. Russians are attracted to Turkey by the country's hospitality, warm climate and unique tourist attractions. However, the Russian market has radically changed the face of the Turkish tourism industry. The behaviour of Russian tourists has caused a culture shock among the local providers and changed the way the Turkish hosts gaze upon these tourists.

Methods

Research context

The discussion of how Turkish hosts gaze upon Russian tourists is based on the findings of a study conducted in all-inclusive five-star resorts and hotels located in the holiday districts of Antalya. The study was conducted from November 2007 to January

2008. The purpose of the study was to understand how Turkish hoteliers (owners, managers and employees) viewed and felt about Russian tourists. The sample consisted of 20 hoteliers aged between 18 and 57 years.

Data collection and analysis

Participant observation, interviews and focus groups were used to investigate the host gaze. The hotel staff was randomly interviewed in different sections of the hotel industry operations (e.g. front office, restaurants and retail outlets). The focus groups and in-depth interviews started with the open question: 'How do you feel about Russian tourists staying at your hotel?', which was followed by other questions, such as 'Which are the most important factors that influence your feelings about Russian tourists?', 'How do your feelings about Russian tourists impact your desire to interact, communicate and serve them?', and 'Do you agree with general stereotypes held of Russian people?'. One hour focus groups and 30-minute interviews were conducted in English and recorded. The interview transcripts were examined using thematic analysis. Distinct concepts and ideas identified in the focus groups and interviews were categorized into specific themes. The most common themes emerged from the interviews were communication, rules of social behaviour and stereotyping.

Results

Communication

Quite often in the conversations the hotel employees noted that 'Suddenly the Russian language became the most important language spoken on the streets, in hotels, restaurants and bars'. Many expressed dissatisfaction with Russian tourists speaking only Russian. 'Russian tourists do not speak English and we cannot communicate with them'. One employee stated 'Dutch tourists speak German and English and German tourists speak English. Russians do not speak a second language. Other tourists also cannot communicate with them.' The Turkish hosts gazed at Russian tourists with disbelief and described the tourists as rude and arrogant because they didn't speak English.

The above example points to the expectations the Turkish hosts have of Russian guests: Russian tourists are expected to speak English or any other foreign language. Since most Russian guests speak only Russian, the communication between them and Turkish hoteliers presented a problem. Turkish hoteliers perceived Russian tourists as either incapable of speaking other languages, or unwilling to speak English, or not interested in speaking with others. This was viewed not only as annoying but also a sign of a lack of respect towards Turkish hosts and other international guests. Interestingly, in Russia English is taught as a second language in most schools. Many Russians speak English quite well. However, it appears that Russian tourists avoided speaking English. English-speaking Russians are often perceived as abrupt and rude; Russian discussions are fast and loud, full of emotions, affections and spontaneity; to the foreigner, Russian conversations sound like a quarrel. Because in the Russian language the intonation drops at the end of a sentence, Russians also sound assertive, if not aggressive. Thus, what may appear rude to the Turkish host is purely the result of stringing English words together using the Russian language structure and intention (King, 2007).

Since English is the universal language, the lack of communication between Russian tourists and Turkish hosts was not accepted and tolerated by the Turkish host. In fact, it was translated into a lack of skills and willingness to communicate and as a sign of total disrespect. What's worst, the hoteliers noted: 'It is not just that Russians do not speak other languages; they do not even start conversation with other Russians.' This can be explained by the fact that when surrounded by foreigners Russians feel intimidated and do not want to communicate with them. In the past, Russians of the

Union of Soviet Socialist Republics (USSR) had always been suspicious of others, especially strangers (Sevice, 2009). It is also possible that Russians do not want to be bothered about other guests when on holiday. According to one of the hotel representatives, Russian guests explained that 'kogda oddichajem, to oddichajem' (when we rest, we rest). When a Russian guest was asked why, he answered 'I am on holiday to enjoy myself, not to talk to other people whom I do not know'. Turkish hosts noted that while Dutch and German tourists try to make contact with other foreign tourists, even if they speak different languages, Russian tourists seem to totally avoid interactions with other guests. They are either suspicious of other guests, or regard interactions with others to be a hassle.

Rules of social behaviour

The inability of Turkish hoteliers to communicate with Russian tourists due to the language barrier was strengthened by different rules of behaviour that further developed hosts' negative views of tourists. All social relationships develop according to rules that play an important role in maintaining social harmony (Reisinger and Turner, 2003). Some rules, such as being friendly, open and honest are universal, while others apply to specific situations or cultures. Social interaction between tourists and service providers is particularly sensitive to social etiquette. Since rules of greeting, apologizing, asking questions, addressing people, complimenting, complaining, joking or showing emotions are all culturally bound, tourists and hosts who are unaware of the differences or are ignorant of the rules may offend each other and view others negatively despite the fact that some of these rules slowly become similar and become globally accepted (e.g. handshaking).

Hotel employees noted that Russian guests are ill-mannered because they do not know how to speak and greet politely (Aslan and Kozak, forthcoming). Some employees made comments that 'Russian tourists only rarely say "thank you" and use the word

"please", and they do not greet you.' This is quite unintentional. While the Dutch and British say 'thank you' after almost every possible favour, Russians consider saying 'thank you' to be insincere and fake. They prefer to say it only when they really mean it. When asking a question, Russians prefer to use short statements. Instead of asking 'Would you please be so kind as to open this window?' they would rather say 'Open this window' (Zhelvis, 2001, p. 23). The Russian direct manner of speech makes their requests sound like orders. Thus, they sound very curt and insensitive and are perceived as rude.

Russians question the need to greet someone they do not know. They only greet each other once a day because they see no point in repeating the greeting every time they see others (Kostromina-Wayne and Wayne, 2002). They also do not smile when greeting someone. For Russians, Westerners smile and apologize too much. This of course is another example of the expectations that Turkish hosts have of the Russian tourists. The above examples, however, do not show that Russian guests mean to be rude and their behaviour should be labelled as arrogant. Russians 'apologize immediately if they have interrupted you, they kiss your hand if you are a woman and help you when you are lost by taking you to your destination, even if it is not in the direction they are going' (Roberts, 1995, p. 19).

Furthermore, hotel employees noted that Russian guests are cranky and bold because they do not know how to eat and drink politely and, most importantly, how to be respectful of others and their rules (Aslan and Kozak, forthcoming). In many Turkish resorts, German rules of behaviour were adopted. Leaving towels on chairs by the pool indicated they were 'reserved'. People were nice to each other, greeted and respected others. However, since Russians 'invaded' the German holiday spots, the rules have changed. Russians were accused of being ill-mannered, acting like the nouveau riche, speaking loudly in non-comprehensible language, pulling chairs away from other tourists, not greeting anyone, consuming too much alcohol, and filling their plates with too much food.

Excessive drinking

A high consumption of alcohol was identified in all interviews as typically Russian behaviour (see, Nemtsov, 2003). Ali Akgun, the manager of the Kemer Holiday Club, noted 'Nobody believes me when I say this, Germans and Dutch drink beer and other alcohol from the early morning hours until late at night, as long as it is free. It is just that the Russians drink a little faster.' Many nations think Russians cannot live without a drink and are always drunk. There is almost a universal stereotype describing Russians as alcohol-loving. 'Russian society sees drinking as an integral part not only of celebration and relaxation, but also of everyday life' (King, 2007, p. 90).

The habit of drinking vodka in Russia was developed in the mid-15th century when both the state and the church took an interest in drink because of the revenue derived from the sales of alcohol. By the 18th century the number of taverns selling alcoholic drinks had increased significantly and liquor sales constituted half of the treasury's indirect tax revenues. The problem of public drunkenness also arose from the custom of east Slovaks to drink heavily at festival times. The drinking of alcohol helped the east Slovaks to escape from a monotonous existence, harsh cold climate and helped to bond them together. It was an integral part of Russian peasant life (Hosking, 2001). Today, Russian society sees drinking as a part of everyday life; no celebration or relaxation can be without alcohol drinking.

Excessive food consumption

The hotel staff found the Russian eating habits too excessive. According to some hotel staff, 'The way Russian tourists behave in the restaurants seems to indicate that they are sending food parcels back to their Mother Land.' 'They are peasants who not only steal the carpet from beneath their hotel beds and start camp fires beside hotel pools, but – worst of all – encourage their children to steal boiled eggs from the breakfast buffet.'

'Buffets are being plundered and people stopped greeting each other.' The hotel employees gazed at Russian tourists in amusement and sometimes disbelief. Although one might find the Russian eating habits excessive, food consumption is an important part of the Russian culture, which represents an emotional display of bonding and socializing, and of friendships forged for life. In Russia, during parties and celebration the tables are covered with more food than guests can eat. Feeding and even 'overfeeding the family and guests is a national tradition, exacerbated by the fact that refusing food is considered to be rude' (King, 2007, p. 97).

Noisy partying

Hotel employees expressed the view that 'Russians drink, eat and party all nights. They are noisy and do not care about others.' Employees reported that Russians were careless towards other tourists and insensitive to their needs. Russian parties are often unexpected and spontaneous. Russians regard receptions and buffet parties purely as diplomatic events. Small talk and social mingling is only a recent addition to the social repertoire of Russians who still require a lot of practice. For Russians, to eat standing, juggling plate and glass and holding a conversation, is not much of a celebration. They are used to a sit-down dinner, and celebration or a banquet, which can be literally translated as 'at the table' (King, 2007). Russians have a tradition of holding many celebrations and parties throughout the night; they party with enthusiasm. Historically, the celebrations were imposed by the Tsar's will. Massive parties and celebrations were decreed and those who weren't partying were severely punished (Hosking, 2001).

Queue jumping

Another example of the unfavorable host gaze upon Russian tourists was found in the case depicting Russians as having no concept of what a queue is. According to Leyla, a guest relations representative at Venezia Palace:

> When a buffet runs out of certain fruits, they come and complain about it immediately. If they waited five minutes they would have the problem solved. They are annoyed when they have to wait for a table in a busy restaurant. While German and Dutch tourists wait patiently and respectfully for their table, Russian tourists cut in line. How can anybody be so rude? If all guests are waiting in line, what gives Russian tourists the right to push others aside? Do they think they are better than the others?

This example shows that Russian behaviour was perceived very negatively by the Turkish hosts (see also Aslan and Kozak, forthcoming). Russians seemed not to be concerned about others' feelings and were not willing to follow what they saw other tourists did. Although in their country, Russians are used to waiting in line, while on holiday they do not want to wait either at the buffet or at a bar (Roberts, 1995). They felt they paid for services and they should not wait.

The habit of queue jumping stems from the Soviet era, when people had to 'storm' a bus or a train to get to work or push ahead in the line to buy scarce necessities in order to survive. In the Communistic regime Russians needed to be energetic, versatile and self-sustaining to survive. They have extraordinary capacity to overcome hardship by any means and despite everything, which has been proved by history. However, gone are the days of inefficient transportation and empty food stores with only canned food on displays. The historically and economically ingrained habit of queue jumping is slowly disappearing (King, 2007).

Treatment of others

Some hosts were astonished observing how Russian tourists treated other guests:

One evening before the restaurant was opened many guests decided to wait outside. The majority of guests who turned up were Russians. As soon as the doors opened there was a stampede and Russians were actually running to get a good table. Some guests stood in horror as they were getting elbowed out of the way by a little Russian lady.

'I always thought the Germans were the rudest people on this planet – not so, the Russian are.' In this case, the Turkish hosts were shocked by Russian behaviour. 'Russians do not seem to care much about other guests.' When a Russian guest was asked why, he answered 'We are on holiday to enjoy ourselves and do not want to care about others.' Turkish hosts viewed Russians tourists as 'wild' and prepared to do anything to get what they want.

Disrespecting rules and procedures

Interestingly, one of the Turkish hoteliers in Kundu (Antalya) noted that Russians think that 'jesli nelzja, no ty chotjes, to ty mozjes' (if something is not allowed, but you really want it, then you may do it). This attitude derives from a very specific attitude to authority. The Russian autocratic traditions (e.g. during the regime of Ivan the Terrible, Peter the Great or Joseph Stalin) were based on the necessity to obey orders and the rule of fear. On one hand, Russians had respect for and support of the top 'father figure' (a powerful leader, be it a tsar or a president), who provided material benefits and disciplined or punished corrupt civil servants and thieving oligarchs and, on the other, they had total disrespect for law, rules and authority. A famous Russian saying is 'A peasant will listen to what the master has to say, but will do it his own way' (King, 2007, p. 48).

Disrespecting providers

Hosts made comments about the way Russian tourists treated the waiting staff.

'Some learned to speak politely, but overall they yell at staff saying things like: "Hey you! Clean this table!" And they do not understand why the hotel prefers to cater to German tourists.'

> The way they bark at the Turks is unbeliev-able. The Dutch and British may have a bad reputation abroad, but what Russians think they can get away with is much worse! They should be ashamed of themselves. Such arrogance! We always used to pity Russians because of Chernobyl, commu-nism and the Second World War. Now, we see that Russians are not sympathetic. They are enormously arrogant and coarse people.

'They think they are the kings and queens of Turkish hotels.' In this case, Turkish hote-liers were appalled by the arrogant tourist behaviour towards the waiting staff; Rus-sian tourists did not feel they needed to ask or thank the staff 'because they have already paid them for service'. The habit of disre-specting staff stems from the Soviet era and the distinction Russians made between those in power who needed to be served and those with no power who needed to serve.

Wanting to act freely

The hotel employees also observed that when on holiday Russians do not care about the time; rather they care about being able to act freely. 'They avoid time schedules and do not like constraints.' From the his-toric perspective, Russian peasants always aimed at escaping the demanding schedules and norms of community life, beginning a new life, establishing a new household and fleeing the borders. They searched for the right to gallop off into the open steppe, the 'wild field' (*dikoje polie*), and making a liv-ing by hunting or fishing. For Russians, being able to act freely refers to both *civic* freedom, as is understood in modern demo-cratic societies, for which another word exists (*svoboda*) and also to *nomadic* free-dom (Hosking, 2001).

Russians want to act freely because for many centuries they accepted authoritarian government and experienced severe restric-tions on human rights and freedom. Indi-vidual initiatives, creativity and freedom of expression were severely suppressed under Communism. The Russian were taught communal ways of living, sacrificing indi-vidual aspirations for the sake of a common cause, such as building Communism, or winning the war. The worth of an individu-al's life and needs was significantly dimin-ished (Lenches, 1993; King, 2007). Thus, it should not be a surprise that today Russian tourists want to feel and act freely without any constraints.

Other Turkish hosts commented on the way Russian spend their free time. 'Most of them are bores. They just lie at the pool all day, and only get up to fetch something to eat or drink. When someone disturbs them, they get annoyed.' Many historians have noted the unenterprising nature of the Rus-sians; their ability to work in short bursts of intense activity with a long period of doing nothing in between (King, 2007, p. 143), a behaviour that has readily transferred to international travel. In the past, most holi-daying Russians spent their free time at dachas, translated as a 'country home', a place for weekend relaxation. Dachas were the only symbols of the right to private ownerships the Soviet system allowed. While holidaying at dachas Russians engaged in passive activities, such as hunt-ing in the woods, fishing, mushroom- and berry picking, playing cards, or visiting the bath house and going to the beach (King, 2007). These are 'very Russian sports', which have always been expressions of ones' Russianness (Figes, 2002). The Western sports games, such as tennis or baseball playing have never been popular among Russians. Russians prefer watching and talking about sports to participating in them (King, 2007).

Invading personal space

Turkish hoteliers noted that 'Russians invade others' privacy and personal space thinking this is OK to do.'

While Dutch tourists do not interfere with other tourists' activities and keep physical distance Russians try to get closer to others very quickly. When comfortable, Russians do not hesitate to sit down close to their neighbours. They like to stand or sit very close to others and pat them on their shoulders and even lean over to whisper something in their ears.

In Russia, years of communal living have accustomed people to having little personal space, be it on public transportation, standing in line or in daily conversations. People get closer very quickly (King, 2007). Many Westerners may find that Russians stand uncomfortably close to them. Russians also do a lot of shoulder patting and hugging. One can often see Russian women holding hands and Russian men hugging. During conversation Russians often touch the other person to make them feel at ease (Pavlovskaya, 2007). Interestingly, in the Russian vocabulary there is no direct equivalent of the word 'privacy'.

Us and them

Turkish hosts observed that 'Russians always distinguish between "us" and "them".' For Russian tourists the distinction between them and other tourists is of paramount importance because they feel the need to define their identity. Historically, Russians have always been conscious of the distinction between 'insiders' and 'outsiders' because the USSR's government created a sense of belonging to a supranational Soviet people. This attitude was transferred to international travel. Russians contrast between *my* (we) and *oni* (they) and judge everyone on the basis of group membership; the judgement *on-nie nash* (he is not one of us) is very noticeable. The phrase *u nas* (in our village, at our workplace, in our group or in our country) is very frequently used. Russians are always surprised that English has no precise equivalent (Hosking, 2001).

Stereotypes

It seems that many of the Turkish hosts' perceptions of Russian tourists were caused by stereotypes that Russian tourists brought along with them to their holiday destinations. In general, stereotypes enable hosts to categorize others and create borders between their own and others' social groups. Particularly when stereotypes refer to negative traits of others, they imply certain superiority of the social groups that create them (Eriksen, 2002). People use stereotypes when they face a new situation and lack deep knowledge of each other (Reisinger and Turner, 2003).

Unlike Russians, who have always been extremely curious about the lives of Western people, Westerners were less curious about Russians and their country and knew very little about them. For decades, Russia was hidden behind the Iron Curtain of the Soviet Union. The Western guidebooks were full of generalizations about the Russian national character. The country was surrounded by an atmosphere of vagueness and mystery. Mass media tended to describe Russia as a backward and corrupted country where one's safety could not be guaranteed. Russia was portrayed as a country of burglars, mafia, prostitutes, and extreme wealth and poverty. For many years, 'movie such as James Bond were showing a dark side of Russia: its evil professor, KGB agents, and seductresses of Russian life' (Pavlovskaya, 2007, p. 5). Russians were stereotyped as being harsh, miserable, drunken, gloomy, lazy, lacking pragmatism, cynical, bitter, sceptical, melancholic, furwearing, and known for beautiful women and corrupt politicians.

However, "despite all of the hardships, hunger, darkness and harshness of life, Russians are very warm-hearted people. Russians talk philosophy, read intellectual books and recite poetry. They are surprisingly generous, and are ready to share everything with you even if they have nothing' (Pavlovskaya, 2007, pp. 97–98). The true Russian is strong-spirited, compassionate, warm and open-hearted, self-sacrificing, courageous, proud, compassionate, forgiving, spiritual, romantic, passionate and child-loving (King, 2007). Although Turkish hosts viewed Russians as ignorant, drunken, irresponsible and passive they also perceived them as emotional, spontaneous, and freedom and food loving.

Since Russians are people of many contradictions, Europeans, who like to categorize people, have never been able to fit Russians into the so-called 'boxes'. According to a Dutch journalist, Peter d'Hamecourt, who has lived in Russia for the past 20 years, he still does not understand Russians even after all this time. 'I've kept my eyes and ears open the whole time, but unfortunately in Russia nothing is ever as it seems. Russians are just near to impossible to understand.' Thus, it is time to understand their strange habits and quirks and adjust the existing images. Because 'bears do not roam the streets, KGB agents are not following your every footstep, and temperatures of 20 degrees below zero do not occur year around' (Pavlovskaya, 2007, p. 8). 'Even now at the time of mass media, many foreigners are surprised to realize that Russians have the same joys and sorrows as the rest of the world' (Pavlovskaya, 2007, p. 4). Russians also have manners but they do have a different kind of manners (Roberts, 1995).

Why they behave the way they do?

There have been many attempts to explain the behaviour of the Russian people. Culturologists and social scientists have pointed to the 'binary nature'of Russian culture, to its tendency to extreme social behaviour, to seek extreme solutions to problems, and to shift from one cultural pattern to the diametrical opposite (Hosking, 2001). Historically, Russia transformed itself from autocratic monarchy through communism to an elected president and parliament. Russia has undergone revolutions, civil wars and mass terror (Sevice, 2009). 'The minds of the Russians have been set and broken so many times during all the reforms, wares,

and social experiments in Russian history, that old value, without had enough time to become fully established, were overtaken by new value systems, only for these to be destroyed in turn' (King, 2007, p.456). Russia is too complex, too socially divided, too politically diverse, too ill-defined geographically and perhaps too big for a single culture to be passed off as the national heritage (Figes, 2002). The result has been a chronic chaos, unresolved conflict between elites and masses, between the state and local communities. Change was characterized by violence and the closing of minds (Hosking, 2001). Arbitrary state power was a dominant feature in public life, where there was no place for legality, tolerance or ethnic cooperation; social relationships were extremely harsh and often violent.

The above images played a crucial role in shaping Russian identity, Russian politics, developing the notion of the self, from the personal and national identity to matters of dress or food, or the type of language used. In the Western countries, these cultural forms developed the image of Russia and the myth of its uniqueness exoticness and complexity. One should not be therefore surprised that Turkish hosts had difficulties with gazing at Russian tourists. Russians have long complained that Western hosts do not understand their culture, that they see Russia and its tourists from afar and do not want to know that they have inner subtleties, as they do with the cultures of their own domain. That complaint is not unjustified. King (2007) noted that discovering the Russian cultural character is like opening a *matryoshka*, revealing the layers, working hard to get to the gem inside.

Inexperienced travellers

The sudden massive arrival of Russian tourists left many complaining Turkish hosts confused and in culture shock, and also gave a reason for other foreign tourists to complain. For many years Western European travellers (British, German and Dutch) have set the tone for the Turkish tourism industry. The Turkish hosts gazed upon them as experienced travellers who followed the silent rules of social behaviour, such as mutual respect and appreciation (Aslan and Kozak, forthcoming). In particular, German travellers were perceived as strongly abiding by these rules. Russian tourists, on the other hand, were not gazed upon in the same way. As they have not been able to travel abroad for very long, Russian tourists were seen as lacking the experience of other tourists. They were perceived by Turkish hosts as not being aware of the rules that guests must follow in hotels, restaurants or shops. In the conversations, the hotel employees viewed Russian tourists as exhibiting unconventional and even irrational behaviour. Turkish hosts looked at Russian tourists in amusement and disbelief and could not understand why Russians behaved the way they did. The Turkish hoteliers gaze pointed to the expectations and stereotypes hoteliers had of Russia and the Russian people. In many cases the host gaze was based on a single or two encounters. Hosts narrowed down the entire Russian population to the individual tourist's excessive eating or drinking habits, noisy partying or disrespecting others. The host gaze was generalized to the entire Russian culture.

Since the Turkish hosts saw Russian tourists as 'the uncivilized people from the former Soviet Union' many were not happy about serving them. They noted that other foreign tourists sought holidays without Russians. Some Russians felt hurt by what was said and written about them and warned others not to judge too fast because not every Russian behaves badly. Although with time Russians can become more experienced travellers the Turkish hotel industry is currently facing the challenge of keeping their guests satisfied. Differences imbedded in national culture, although easy to notice, are not easy to overcome.

Discussion

The findings presented in this chapter indicate that the Turkish host gaze on Russian tourists was influenced by the Russian cultural identity and cultural underpinning of their behaviour, hosts' cultural expectations, differences between hosts and tourists in understanding what is appropriate behaviour, tourist holidaying culture, and cultural stereotyping and borrowing, as indicated in the literature review. This chapter identified a number of issues about Russian tourists, such as what is important to them, how they communicate and interact with others, how they rest and relax, and who they think holds the power in the host–guest relationship. These issues are more than just a reference; they draw attention to the importance of cultural and historical influences on the Russian tourist market. They have important implications for marketing to the Russian market.

Second, the cultural observations and comments made by Turkish hosts about Russian tourists revealed Turkish hosts' expectations of tourists and perceptions of the unique Russian behaviour and their self-centred exploitation of hosts, their culture and country. These caused daily miscommunication or lack of communication and hosts' dissatisfaction with tourists, and even anger. Turkish hosts viewed Russian tourists as perceiving the world as theirs to use based on the way they expected the hosts to accommodate to their needs.

Third, the Turkish hosts' comments and the subsequent analysis of tourist behaviour showed that the hosts' observations were culturally misperceived mostly due to the differences in understanding appropriate behaviour. Russian beliefs and activities were not viewed by Turkish hosts in terms of the tourists' national culture; they were viewed in terms of the hosts' cultural beliefs. The hosts' comments provided an incorrect frame of reference for Russian tourists and caused mutual misunderstanding. It is possible that the misperceptions of tourists occurred because of the hosts' lack of cultural understanding of the tourist world, empathy and tolerance of tourists. The issues identified in conversations have important implications for cultural interpretation, evaluation and definition of the Russian tourist market.

Next, Turkish hosts viewed Russian tourists according to their expectations of other international and culturally standardized tourists rather than gaining an authentic and cultural-oriented understanding of the Russian tourists' background. Turkish hosts did not account for the holiday context of tourists' behaviour either. Their entire view of Russian tourists and their culture was narrowed down to individual cases and based on single encounters. Turkish hosts' observations and images seem to reflect the cultural stereotypes of Russian tourists who were seen as unrefined guests lacking the experience of other tourists. The fact that the gaze is attributed to stereotypes and the host gazes negatively upon tourists was evident in other studies (Chan, 2006; Maoz, 2006; Moufakkir, 2011). Finally, the host evaluation of Russian tourists was affected by cultural standards borrowed from German and Dutch tourists; these could modify the hosts' opinions about the appropriateness of the Russian touristic behaviour.

It appears that understanding the cultural influences on the host gaze can be very helpful in reducing potential for cultural misperceptions and misevaluations of tourists. One of the major challenges the Turkish hoteliers will face in the future is to understand the cultural nature of their gaze. It seems that since they must cater to the growing Russian market in order to succeed they would do well to learn and understand the cultural discrepancies between them and their international guests. The Turkish hosts could learn the basic Russian language, familiarize themselves with Russian worldviews, emphasize Russian cultural identity and incorporate Russian customs into daily routine.

Cultural relativism

Within this context, the theory of cultural relativism was applied. The chapter shows that the hosts' cultural observations and comments were inappropriate. It seems that hosts should not apply their own society's rules or expectations to assess foreign tourists' behaviour. There are no absolute universally accepted standards for culturally appropriate behaviour by which hosts can judge tourists as 'good' or 'bad' or 'better' or 'worse' than other tourists. The attitudes and criteria hosts use to define appropriate and inappropriate behaviour of tourists and hosts' expectations of this behaviour are culturally relative. The hosts' views of standards for appropriate behaviour develop as a result of customs and traditions in a host society and can change over time to adapt to the changing circumstances of the host culture. Since different ways of behaviour evolve differently in different communities, the host and tourist society may have different views of the concepts of appropriateness. Thus, what may be viewed as correct in a tourist culture could be viewed as incorrect in a host culture. Culture must be seen as 'webs of meanings' within which humans must live (Geertz, 1973). 'Humans are shaped exclusively by their culture and therefore there exist no unifying cross-cultural human behavioural characteristics' (Jarvie, 1983; Spiro, 1984, 1986 cited in Zechenter, 1997, p. 323) that can be used to judge others.

The above suggests that any assessment by hosts of what is right or wrong tourist behaviour must be carried out by trying to understand the meaning of that behaviour in the tourist culture. Hosts should never fall into the belief that their culture has all the answers and they know best. No culture has a complete monopoly on the truth. Values differ and change because life circumstances differ and change. To objectively analyse tourists from different cultures, judge the worth of tourists and fully understand how tourists perform in an alien society, hosts must assess the actions of tourists in terms of the tourists' culture. Hosts must apply tourists' behavioural standards and interpret tourists' behaviour in the light of tourists' motives, values and habits. The function and meaning of every behaviour is relative to its cultural setting. As Rosado (1994) noted, a trait is good or bad only with reference to the culture in which it is to function.

However, a question arises as to whether hosts should accept and tolerate the tourist behaviour they believe is inappropriate and even rude? Cultural relativism theory teaches that since everything is relative and there are no universal right and wrong behaviours, hosts must accept all types of behaviour. Many tourists around the world have different behavioural standards and it is important for hosts to accept these differences. Because there is no international agreement as to the universally correct and objective behavioural standards and there is very little reason to believe that objective standards exist, the cultural standards of others should not be rejected.

The cultural relativism perspective is appropriate in many respects, for example eating, drinking, communication, and many other rules are different within cultures, and it is important to accept these differences when one travels to other cultures although these rules are not universally 'right' and 'wrong'. No one has the right to judge these rules because all behavioural rules are relative. However, it can be argued that if all behavioural rules are relative, then there are no rules at all. If almost any rule can be justified to be relative and all cultures are accepted to be relative then chaos and instability can develop. As a result, no culture could be subjected to any values, because there could be no transcultural values to judge any particular culture (Rosaldo, 2002).

Cultural relativism approves many cultural practices, regardless of how barbaric or inhumane they are (e.g. suicide bombing of civilians). It is a philosophy of 'anything goes' (Ruggiero, 1973). However, accepting and respecting all others' practices is a mistake because many cultural practices are arbitrary, harmful or confusing. For example, some cultures (e.g. Islam) can regard Western cultural relativism as insulting because it devalues their faith by reducing it to one of many equally valid cultural systems (Rosaldo, 2002). Since some cultural practices may be harmful or even immoral, being able to judge a culture is a major advantage. That means that not all practices are relative and there are certain practices people should accept and respect.

Furthermore, according to cultural relativism hosts should be tolerant of their guests. However, tolerance implies unconditional support and agreement with all tourist behaviours, and this contradicts the idea of relativism. Those who believe all behaviours are relative cannot say that behaviours are wrong. Although cultural relativism perspective teaches tolerance of cultural standards, the theory also supports intolerant standards and asks for tolerance of non-moral standards. Following the cultural relativism theory hosts should be tolerant of the intolerable tourist behaviour and tolerate arrogant, exploitative and even offensive behaviours. Although cultural perspective can help hosts understand why some tourists' behaviour is inappropriate it does not allow them to judge that behaviour. Thus, it is impossible to argue that tourist behaviour is right or wrong when one embraces the notion that there is no 'right' or 'wrong'. A society that embraces the notion that there is no 'right' or 'wrong' loses the ability to make judgements at all.

Cultural relativism theory also places too much focus on cultural differences. Many cultural groups have similar values but apply them differently under different circumstances. Tourists and hosts may have similar values but follow them in their own unique way. By following the principles of cultural relativism judging foreign tourists by the values of hosts' culture can be very destructive. Who are the hosts to say that their way is better?

In a rapidly changing multicultural world, hosts and tourists experience many cultural standards. Cultural standards help to understand why hosts' and tourists' behaviours are considered right, to determine their responsibility to behave in a certain way and their expectations about the behaviour of others. Ignoring cultural standards of tourists is risky, however blaming others for wrong behaviour is improper. Thus, criticizing hosts for misperceiving tourists' behaviour, lacking cultural understanding, empathy and tolerance of tourists is wrong. There is no ultimate standard of good or bad, every evaluation or comment made is subject to the cultural perspective of those who make a judgement. Ultimately, no tourist behaviour can be 'right' or 'wrong'. This notion questions the hosts' criticism of tourists' cultural behaviour.

Cultural relativism teaches that it is dangerous to assume that all behavioural standards are absolute. They are not. Although every society has its absolute standards (Bagish, 1990) they differ from culture to culture (Herskovits, 1973). Also, not all absolute standards are universal (Bagish 1990, p. 34). Universal standards transcend cultures, which all cultures manifest (Herskovits, 1973, p. 32). Not all absolute standards transcend all cultures. Many standards are specific to a society; they are not the results of the absolute truth but cultural conditioning.

Although cultural relativism is an attractive theory that encourages human beings to open their minds and stops them from being arrogant, cultural relativism perspective is unable to offer real guidance as to what and whose behavioural standards to follow. Should hosts follow the tourists' standards, or vice versa? The theory claims that all standards are proper and should be followed, even when they conflict. The theory mistakenly argues that every behaviour and rule varies from culture to culture and overestimates the degree of differences between cultures. There are rules that all societies have in common (e.g. rules against lying, stealing or murder), because those rules are necessary for society to exist. The theory also mistakenly claims that there is no 'right' and 'wrong' other than the standards of one's society, implying that people cannot criticize the cultural codes of other societies. By suggesting that every society has its own standard of conduct that is important to those who live in that society (Herskovits, 1973, p. 31) the theory can lead to moral and ethical anarchy (Herskovits, 1973, p. 64).

In summary, the cultural perspective provides no solution for evaluation of other cultures and their behavioural practices and it is questionable as to whether it can be used to evaluate the host gaze in the tourism context. This clearly challenges the way hosts evaluate tourists and calls for a new

theory that could help to explain the host gaze. In the meantime, hosts should use their logic and reasoning skills to make judgements as well as instinctively knowing that some behaviour is wrong, implying that certain standards are used to make judgements.

Conclusion

While it is not possible to generalize, the case study provided in this chapter adds to the body of knowledge of the host gaze in tourism studies. The results show that the host gaze was highly influenced by cultural factors. The lack of cultural understanding of tourists on behalf of the host can result in cultural misperceptions and negative host gaze. Thus, culture influences cannot be discounted when exploring the host gaze. However, the cultural perspective on the host gaze cannot fully explain whose and what behavioural standards should be followed. A great deal of research needs to be done to understand the influences on the host gaze and its outcomes.

Implications for tourism

As the world becomes globalized and interconnected, people from different cultural backgrounds will be increasingly exposed to each other. The realistic outcome of international tourism is the development of cultural conflict rather than peace and understanding (Havel cited in Reisinger, 2009). Although the development of communication technologies can create common meanings and facilitate communication by standardizing and strengthening cultural notions, the increasing opportunities for direct face-to-face contact among culturally different tourists and hosts will present a real danger of exposing people to culturally different standards and values and creating potential for cultural friction (Reisinger, 2009).

Since there are no absolute standards of behaviour that exist transculturally or externally to the group, a question arises as to how hosts from different cultures are to get along when their behavioural standards collide with the behavioural standards of tourists? How should hosts handle these conflicts? Can hosts challenge the cultural norms of tourists and fight against them? Should hosts accept the cultural norms of tourists and tolerate the tourist behaviour they believe is inappropriate and unacceptable? These warrant future research studies.

Cultural observations of Russian tourists by Turkish hoteliers reflect the critical cultural issues and problems facing global tourism. Many hosts in different countries perceive their international guests behaving the way Russian tourists behave. For example, Moufakkir (2011) compared Dutch hosts' gaze upon German and East Asian tourists and identified negative hosts' gaze upon German tourists. Characteristics such as arrogance, a high consumption of alcohol, being loud, disrespectful of hosts and other tourists, and unwilling or refusing to speak any other language but German were identified in all interviews as typically German. There were no clear positive characteristics, such as 'friendly' or 'well-behaved' mentioned by Dutch hosts. Germans in Moufakkir's study (2011), the same as the Russians in this study were rated as the least sympathetic and were subject to the highest number of negative stereotypes compared with other nationalities. Germans were not popular in the Netherlands, as Russians were not popular in Turkey.

Similarly, Chan (2006) found that the Vietnamese gaze upon Chinese tourists was negative. Chinese tourists were viewed as 'making a lot more requests, complaints and troubles than other tourists', littering the rooms and smoking on beds (p. 195). Reference was made to antisocial Chinese behaviour. Laxon (1991) found that the Indian gaze upon Israeli tourists saw the most negative characteristics of Western culture. Israeli tourists were seen by locals as aggressive, militant, impolite, noisy, messy, exploitative, superficial, uneducated, shallow, foolish and overtly sexual. The hosts' encounter with tourists reinforced their stereotypical views of tourists and created a distance and a mistrust. Shani and Uriely (2012) revealed many negative impacts on the local residents' quality of life in the context of hosts' friends and relatives (HFR). The local hosts experienced several sorts of difficulties, including loss of privacy, extra expenditure, hard physical work and mental stress deriving from continuous worries and obligations of hosting or even the feeling of being exploited by their guests.

This raises a question about the benefits of international tourism, such as the development of intercultural communication and understanding, reduction of stereotypes and prejudice, or broadening of cultural horizons. The hosts' comments imply that the above perceived benefits of international travel may be hard to obtain. Consequently, how should international tourism be developed to benefit from it? Should international tourism development be encouraged in a globalized world? Can international tourism facilitate intercultural understanding or cultural conflict?

Future studies

Due to time and resource constraints, the study was limited by the number and locations of accommodation providers. The findings of the study cannot be extrapolated to the entire population of Turkish hosts and Russian tourists. The study should be replicated in other geographical and cultural regions, and comparative analysis conducted. Qualitative studies should identify the most critical cultural issues associated with hosts' gazes (e.g. communication patterns, host–guest relations) in order to address them correctly and avoid future conflicts. Interestingly, the most common themes that emerged in the current study were similar to those identified in Moufakkir's (2011) study: stereotypes and communication. These issues should be used as an important reference for marketing strategies. Also, the level of cultural proximity should be measured. According to Moufakkir (2011), the host is more likely to develop a positive gaze with those from a different background because of lower expectations and higher tolerance for misbehaviour.

Further, quantitative studies should measure the degree to which the hosts who gaze at tourists and tourists who are gazed upon have an accurate knowledge of each other and the degree to which their gazes differ from each other. It would be interesting to contrast the host gaze with other hosts' gazes, the host interpretation of the gaze with other hosts' interpretations, and compare all interpretations to see if the host gaze is accurate. It would also be interesting to compare the host gaze with tourists' gazes, the host interpretation of the gaze with tourists' interpretations, and compare tourists' and hosts' interpretations to see if the host gaze is accurate. In addition, since the host gaze can be distorted by culturally biased media, stereotypes and assumptions and not reflect reality, future studies should contrast the host gaze with the gazes developed by culturally correct and unbiased media. Finally, a new cultural theory should be developed to explain the host gaze.

References

Armstrong, R., Mok, C., Go, F. and Chan, A. (1997) The importance of cross-cultural expectations in the measurement of service quality perceptions in the hotel industry. *International Journal of Hospitality Management* 16(2), 181–190.

Aslan, A. and Kozak, M. (forthcoming) customer deviance in resort hotels: the case of Turkey. *Journal of Hospitality Marketing and Management.*

ATOR (2010) Analytical Service of the Association of Travel Agencies of Russia. ATOR, Moscow.

Bagish, H. (1990) Confessions of a former cultural relativist. *Annual Editions Anthropology* 90/91, 30–37.

Baker, D.A. and Fesenmaier, D.R. (1997) Effect of service climate on managers' and employees' rating of visitors' service quality expectations. *Journal of Travel Research* 36(19), 15–22.

Benedict, R. (1934) *Patterns of Culture.* Houghton Mifflin, New York.

Boas, F. (1911) *The Mind of Primitive Man.* Macmillan, New York.

Bruner, E. (1989) On cannibals, tourists, and ethnographers. *Annals of Tourism Research* 16, 438–445.

Brunt, P. and Courtney, P. (1999) Host perceptions of socio-cultural impacts. *Annals of Tourism Research* 26(3), 493–515.

Butler, R. (1980) The concept of tourist area cycle of evolution: implications for management and resources. *Canadian Geographer* 24, 5–12.

Chan, Y. (2006) Coming of age of the Chinese tourists. *Tourist Studies* 6(3), 187–213.

Crick, M. (1989) Representations of international tourism in the social sciences: sun, sex, sights, savings, and servility. *Annual Review of Anthropology* 18, 307–344.

Dann, C. (1996) *The Language of Tourism.* CABI, Wallingford.

Eriksen, H. (2002) *Ethnicity and Nationalism. Anthropological perspectives.* Pluto Press, London.

Evans-Pritchard, D. (1989) How they see us: Native American images of tourists. *Annals of Tourism Research* 16, 89–105.

Figes, O. (2002) *Natasha's Dance: a Cultural History of Russia.* Picador, A. Metropolitan Book, Henry Hall and Company, New York.

Geertz, C. (1973) *The Interpretation of Cultures.* Basic Books. New York.

Gellner, E. (1985) *Relativism and Social Sciences.* Cambridge University Press, New York.

Herskovits, M. (1973) *Cultural Relativism: Perspectives in Cultural Pluralism.* Vintage Books, New York.

Hosking, G. (2001) *Russia and the Russians: a History.* The Belknop Press of Harvard University Press, Cambridge, MA.

Hottola, P. (2004) Culture confusion: intercultural adaptation in tourism. *Annals of Tourism Research* 31(2), 447–466.

Jafari, J. and Way, W. (1994) Multicultural strategies in tourism. *Cornell Hotel and Restaurant Administration Quarterly* 35, 72–79.

Jarvie, I. (1983) Rationality and relativism. *British Journal of Sociology* 34(1), 44–60.

Joseph, C. and Kavoori, A. (2001) Mediated resistance: tourism and the host community. *Annals of Tourism Research* 28, 998–1009.

Kim, S. (1999) Impact of Korean tourists on Korean residents in Hawaii and Queensland, Australia. In: Pearce, D. and Butler, R. (eds) *Contemporary Issues in Tourism Development*. Routledge, London, pp. 257–272.

Kim, S. and Prideaux, B. (2003) A cross-cultural study of airline passengers. *Annals of Tourism Research* 30(2), 489–492.

Kim, S. and McKercher, B. (2011) The collective effect of national culture and tourist culture on tourist behaviour. *Journal of Travel and Tourism Marketing* 28(2), 145–164.

Keung, S. (2000) Tourists' perceptions of hotel frontline employees' questionable job-related behaviour. *Tourism Management* 21(2), 121–134.

King, A. (2007) *Culture Smart: Russia*. Kuperard, London.

Kostromina-Wayne, M. and Wayne, P. (2002) *Living and Working in Moscow, Culture Shock*. Kuperard, London.

Kozak, M., Bigne, E. and Andreu, L. (2003) limitations of cross-cultural satisfaction research and recommending alternative methods. *Journal of Quality Assurance in Hospitality and Tourism* 4(3–4), 37–59.

Kozak, M. and Tasci, A. (2005) Locals' perceptions of foreign tourists: a case study in Turkey. *International Journal of Tourism Research*, 7(4–5), 261–277.

Larsen, J. and Urry, J. (2011) Gazing and performing. Environment and Planning D: Society and Space 29(6), 1110–1125.

Laxon, J. (1991) How "we" see "them": tourism and Native Americans. *Annals of Tourism Research* 18, 365–391.

Lenches, E. (1993) The legacy of Communism – poisoned minds and souls. *International Journal of Social Economics* 20(5–7), 14–34.

MacCannell, D. (1976) *The Tourist: a New Theory of the Leisure Class*. Schocken, New York.

Manzur, L. and Jogaratnam, G. (2006) impression management and the hospitality service encounter: cross-cultural differences. *Journal of Travel & Tourism Marketing* 20(3–4), 21–32.

Maoz, D. (2006) The mutual gaze. *Annals of Tourism Research* 33(1), 221–239.

Mattila, A. (1999a) The role of culture in the service evaluation process. *Journal of Service Research* 1(3), 250–261.

Mattila, A. (1999b) The role of culture and purchaser motivation in service encounter evaluations. *Journal of Service Management* 13(4–5), 376–389.

Ministry of Culture and Tourism (2011a) How to capture mobile knowledge in tourism section? Co-(r)evolution of Russian tourists and high individual places (HIP) in Antalya. http://www.kultur.gov.tr/TR/belge/1-90750/turizm-istatistikleri.html (accessed 6 December 2011).

Ministry of Culture and Tourism (2011b) General Directorate of Investment and the Ministry of Culture and Tourism. http://www.ktbyatirimisletmeler.gov.tr/belge/1-77513/giris-cikis-yapan-yabanci-ve-vatandaslara-iliskin-diger-.html (accessed 6 December 2011).

Mitchell, P. (2006) *Revisiting Effective Re-Entry Programs for Returnees From US Academic Programs*. AED Center for International Training, USA.

Moufakkir, O. (2011) The role of cultural distance in mediating the host gaze. *Tourist Studies* 11(1), 73–89.

Nemtsov, A. (2003) Suicides and alcohol consumption in Russia, 1965–1999. *Drug and Alcohol Dependence* 71, 161–168.

Pavlovskaya, A. (2007) *Culture Shock! Russia: a Survival Guide to Customs and Etiquette*. Marshall Cavendish Editions.

Picard, M. (1995) Cultural heritage and tourist capital: cultural tourism in Bali. In: Lanfant M.-F., Allcock, J. and Bruner, E. (eds) *International Tourism: Identity and Change*. Sage, London, pp. 44–66.

Pizam, A. (1999) Cross-cultural tourist behaviour: In: Pizam, A. and Mansfeld, Y. (eds) *Consumer Behavior in Travel and Tourism*. Haworth, Binghamton, pp. 393–411.

Pizam, A. and Jeong, G. (1996) Cross-Cultural Tourist Behaviour: perceptions of Korean tour guides. *International Journal of Tourism Management* 17(4), 277–286.

Pizam, A. and Reichel, A. (1996) The Effect of Nationality on Tourist behavior: Israeli tour guides' perceptions. *Journal of Hospitality and Leisure Marketing* 4(1), 23–49.

Pizam, A. and Sussmann, S. (1995) Does nationality affect tourist behavior? *Annals of Tourism Research* 22(4), 901–917.

Pizam, A. and Telisman-Kosuta, N. (1989) Tourism as a factor of change: results and analysis. In: Bystrzanowski, J. (eds) *Tourism as a Factor of Change: a Socio-Cultural Study*. European Coordination Centre for Documentation in Social Sciences, Vienna, pp. 149–156.

Rachels, J. (1999) *The Elements of Moral Philosophy*. McGraw-Hill, Boston. MA.

Reisinger, Y. (2009) *International Tourism: Cultures and Behavior*. Butterworth Heinemann/Elsevier, Oxford.

Reisinger, Y. and Turner, L. (2003) *Cross-Cultural Behaviour in Tourism: Concepts and Analysis*. Butterworth-Heinemann, Oxford.

Roberts, B. (1995) *Order and Disorder after the Cold War*. MIT Press, Boston, MA.

Rosado, C. (1994) Understanding cultural relativism in a multicultural world. In: Rachels, J. (1999) *The Elements of Moral Philosophy*. McGraw-Hill, Boston, MA, pp. 15–29.

Rosaldo, R. (2002) Of headhunters and soldiers: separating cultural and ethical relativism. Adapted from: *The Cultural War on Western Civilization*. Windschuttle, K. (ed). Foundation for Cultural Review, 2005. Digital.

Ruggiero, V. (1973) *The Moral Imperative: Ethical Issues for Discussion and Writing*. Alfred, New York.

Sevice, R. (2009) *A History of Modern Russia: from Tsarism to the Twenty-First Century*. Harvard University Press, Cambridge, MA.

Shani, A. and Uriely, N. (2012) VFR tourism: the host experience. *Annals of Tourism Research* 39(1), 421–440.

Spiro, M. (1984) Some reflections on cultural determinism and relativism with special reference to emotion and reason. In: Shweder, R. and LeVine, R. (eds) *Culture Theory: Essays on Mind, Self and Emotion*. Cambridge University Press, New York, pp. 323–346.

Spiro, M. (1986). Cultural relativism and the future of anthropology. *Cultural Anthropology* 1, 259–286.

Sweet, J. (1989). Burlesquing "the other" in Pueblo performance. *Annals of Tourism Research* 16, 62–75.

Tsang, N.K. and Ap, J. (2007) Tourists' perceptions of relational quality service attributes: a cross cultural study. *Journal of Travel Research* 45(3), 355–363.

Tsaur, S., Lin, C. and Wu, C. (2005) Cultural differences in service quality and behavioral intention in tourist hotels. *Journal of Hospitality and Leisure Marketing* 13(1), 41–63.

Urry, J. (1990) *The Tourist Gaze: Leisure and Travel in Contemporary Societies*. Sage, London.

Warden, C.A., Liu, T.-C., Huang, C.-T. and Lee, C.-H. (2003) Service failures away from home: benefits in intercultural service encounters. *International Journal of Service Industry Management* 14, 436–457.

Woods, R. and King, J. (2002) *Leadership and Management in the Hospitality Industry*. American Hotel & Lodging Association. Educational Institute, Lansing, MI.

Zechenter, E. (1997) In the name of culture: cultural relativism and the abuse of the individual. *Journal of Anthropological Research* 53, 319–348.

Zhelvis, V. (2001) *The Xenophobe's Guide to the Russians*. Oval Books. London.

Zhu, T., Cole, S.T. and Card, J.A. (2007) The association of tourist' cultural tendencies and their perceived service quality of a Chinese travel agency. *Journal of Travel and Tourism Marketing* 22(2), 1–13.

5 A Host Gaze Composed of Mediated Resistance in Panamá: Power Inversion in Kuna Yala

Amy Savener

Introduction

Power is a constituent element in tourist–host interactions, yet it is usually embodied in the tourist. After all, power is usually a referential phenomenon; one group exerts it over another. The disempowered are subordinated or marginalized, coerced and threatened. These descriptors are often used in reference to indigenous people in a variety of circumstances – political, economic and educational – and in tourism destinations.

But what happens when the indigene is proud, indifferent and preoccupied with the activities of their daily life? When they outnumber the tourist and the boundaried turf they inhabit is not the tourists' playground, but the indigene's 'living room'. What happens when the indigene reacts to uninvited guests with outright indifference or subtle derision? This chapter will outline an interesting interplay between tourists and indigenes, one in which the indigene indulges the tourist's craving for authentic experience with some sleight of theatre.

For this chapter, the moniker 'host' is misleading. 'indigene' connotes more appropriately the sense of people who inhabit an area yet also those who do not necessarily welcome, invite or rearrange their lives toward being hospitable to tourists.

Kuna Yala, Panamá – known to most tourists as 'San Blas' – constitutes a parallel universe for Dean MacCannell (1999) and John Urry's (1990) mass tourist, or today's generation of tourist, who quickly realize their expectations of hospitable service are incorrect when the Kuna Indigenous people are nonchalant, preoccupied with their own affairs and ignorant or indifferent to tourists' presumptions of service or hospitality.

This chapter analyses tourist–indigene interactions in Kuna Yala from a human and cultural geography perspective and the analysis is within the traditions of those disciplines, contributing to nascent scholarship in tourism theory and tourism studies. Indeed, tourism theory is in its nascency (Aramberri, 2001; Franklin and Crang, 2001; Knudsen *et al.*, 2007). An understanding of the interplay of indigenes who assume a sense of agency countermands the status quo of tourist hegemony and privilege. This unusual dynamic contributes a new perspective on socio-cultural interaction on the stage upon which tourism is enacted.

This chapter will review host gaze scholarship as it relates to the phenomena described in this chapter and then the historic events that have contributed to a sense of communal Kuna dignity and autonomous independence. The section that follows explores tourism in the region today. These elements lead to a series of observations and conclusions about the ways that Kuna cultural identity and resistance are reflected in tourism practices and actions. Kuna and tourist behaviour is described based on participant observation, textual analysis and informal interviews with Kuna scholars, guides and fishermen conducted in Spanish and the Kuna language.

Literature Review

Theoretical and ethnographic scholarship on tourism has covered complex host–guest interactions worldwide in the last three decades, most often concluding that power lies in the hands of the paying visitor (Smith, 1989; Munt, 1994). Literature on host–guest interaction in the developing world and especially in the Caribbean nearly always conveys the trope of a supercilious, perverse self-concerned tourist that subjugates servile hosts (Smith, 1989). Whereas indigenous groups worldwide have benefited from presenting an exotic spectacle, many of these cultures have suffered in the process (Bruner and Kirshenblatt-Gimblett, 1994; Dyer *et al.*, 2003; Kirtsoglou and Theodossopoulos, 2004).

Furnham (1984) acknowledged that the amount of cultural shock experienced by host communities depends greatly on the proportion of tourists to hosts, the duration of the tourists' visit and the amount of conflict between the worldviews and cultural personalities of the two groups in contrast to each other. Racial and ethnic prejudices as well as relative wealth can also play a role in interactions.

Extensive ethnographies of indigene–tourist interactions in remote regions of Nepal, Tibet and Thailand form the backbone of host gaze scholarship. Hill tribes in Thailand were complicit in staging a tribal experience that overemphasized remoteness and feigned the preparation of traditional meals to satisfy tourists seeking contact with them (Cohen, 1989). When the Hill tribe trekkers sought to procure intimate encounters with the Karen people (Conran, 2006), the indigenes were perplexed, finding their lives unexceptional and completely normal

and so could not understand the tourist's intruding insistence. One Karen woman expressed confusion that tourists wanted to photograph them in dirty, old clothes instead of waiting for them to dress up (Hepburn, 2002). In the Langtang area of Nepal, residents were perplexed by tourists who preferred to take photographs of buildings that are particularly disheveled and did not want any signs of modernity in the photo (Lim, 2008).

Because most Nepalese only travel for trade and work and not for recreation, they saw tourism as an activity performed only by outsiders (Lim, 2008). Most interesting, though, is that tourists were not differentiated from the constellation of outsiders, 'cognitively abstracted from tourism as an industry'. They categorized tourists into a general group of outsiders, explained by sociological theory that indicates that misunderstood concepts are categorically generalized. Therefore, the Langtangpa grouped 'tourists' into the same category as other outsiders – along with the soldiers manning a checkpost entrance to a national park and those building an army camp near the village, as well as construction workers who came from far away to work on hotel construction. The soldiers were disliked for hunting for meat, since the Lantangpa consider killing animals as a sin – and those negative impressions also extended to tourists.

Miao hosts in southwestern China also categorized tourists as a group and were not cajoled into friendliness and sharing culture, as the tourists desired (Oakes, 2006). The significance of seeds offered by American tourists in hopes of helping the Miao was lost on these indigenes; they just wanted to sell their handicrafts. To the Miao, it was just another group of tourists, not much differentiated from a Japanese group earlier in the day.

Adams (1996) argued that the intimate dependency of Western climbers upon Sherpa guides in Tibet has resulted in mimesis. This refers to the interactive process of identity reproduction in which the Sherpas see themselves through the eyes of Westerners.

Remote destinations satisfy a tourist desire for experiencing authenticity – the 'back stage' that tourists covet (MacCannell,

1999), but jaded tourists have been duped too often by false fronts designed to look like back stages (MacCannell, 1973) and therefore pursue the back stage of the back stage. Sophisticated tourists seek reality, beyond orchestrated and formulated 'back stages' (Munt, 1994). Travel guides such as Lonely Planet subtly communicate an implicit anti-tourist, pro-traveller ethos (Bhattacharyya, 1997). Familiarity with the complex phenomena of being duped by tourist performances, the experiential or cultural tourist has become ever more skilled and sceptical in their pursuit of 'authenticity' (Pearce and Moscardo, 1986) – and seek remote, 'untouched' destinations. As part of this quest, they seek 'culture' in the form of indigenous people who they see, and pose for photographs with – much like wildlife (Munt, 1994). This tourist collects evidential proof of a visit to a back region in the same way that another tourist buys souvenirs.

Host gaze scholarship has rarely documented empowered indigenes who willfully utilize tourism as a means to their own ends, although this is increasingly becoming a strategy in various communities. Some Native Americans in the USA enact the stereotype of the silent Indian, invoking a mystique that is also an effective distancing manoeuvre (Evans-Pritchard, 1989). Due to the paucity of host gaze scholarship, the indigene view is sometimes best portrayed through the keyhole view of the tourist (Maoz, 2006), since the recursive view of the host is understood as an engagement or performance experienced by tourists.

Extreme staging comes in the form of the 'performative primitive' in which customs and 'traditional dress' become costumes (Desmond, 1999). Even more extreme are the cases in which locals exploit the tourist's pursuit of authenticity with an authenticified charade or facsimile of exactly that which they seek (Cohen, 1989; Maoz, 2006). Maoz analysed the interactions of Israeli backpackers with Indian locals, wherein the Indian merchants responded to an imbalance of power by manipulating the Israeli tourists and creating an exotic mystique to encourage sales.

Indigenes, who are at home and work in a touristed destination, see tourists at leisure. When these indigenes see tourists spending disposable income in a leisurely manner, it's not surprising that the indigenes rebel with mediated resistance (Joseph and Kavoori, 2001). Embodying agency and empowerment, the indigenes do not act hospitably.

Methodology

Case study research provides insights into contemporary phenomena in a real-life context, when information from multiple sources converges and boundaries between context and phenomenon are unclear (Yin, 1984). This research was conducted from the perspective of a US citizen, grounded in scholarly geographical research in tourism studies as well as Kuna research and contextualized with participant observation and interviews during four visits to Kuna Yala between 2006 and 2011. The shortest of the visits was 10 days and the longest spanned the month of May, 2011. Multiple visits and a variety of methods (textual analysis, semi-structured interviews, participant observation and conversation) allowed for a wealth of information.

Participant observation and interviews were conducted on 21 islands and 14 of the uninhabited ones (where small-scale lodging or camping accommodations are available to tourists). The majority of research was concentrated in the western-most region of Kuna Yala, the most visited by tourists. Most Kuna informants live in Nalunega and El Porvenir. A set of up to 20 open-ended questions was asked of each interviewee with enough flexibility to allow discussion. 'Where are tourists from? Why do they come here? What is interesting about them? What is confusing about them?' Other questions probed the Kuna to share experiences or interactions with tourists and opinions on the impact of tourism on the Kuna people. The results of these conversations were interpreted via theoretical understanding of power, the contributions of numerous scholars who have studied the Kuna (Sherzer, 1983, 2003; Smith, 1984; Swain, 1989; Howe, 1998, 2002a, b, 2009; Chapin, 1990; Bennett, 1999; Apgar, 2010) and tourism studies (Urry, 1990; MacCannell, 1999; Edensor, 2000; Knudsen *et al.*, 2007).

Key-informant and community member interviews were conducted with 63 Kuna identified via the snowball approach and participant observation. The research was also informed by interviews with Kuna officials and leaders, Panamanian anthropologists, observations of people living in Kuna Yala and interviews with Kuna and tourists. Interviews were limited to Kuna who speak Spanish, although three interviews with elders who only speak Dulegaya, the Kuna language, were included with the use of an interpreter.

Kuna and Their History

An insight into some deep history is necessary in order to understand how the Kuna of Panama embody such force of agency in their interactions with tourists. The Kuna have manifested stalwart resistance to outsiders for more than five centuries, waging sometimes violent and bloody battles to preserve their independence and maintain cultural unity and identity (Gallup-Diaz, 1999; Historia, 2011). Their foes were Spaniards who wanted to enslave them, missionaries who wanted to convert them and English, French and Dutch smugglers and pirates who wanted their gold reserves. They migrated to the archipelago in the mid-1800s and exacted independence from Panama in a bloody revolution in 1938. A bounded autonomous indigenous territory, Kuna Yala operates as a sovereign nation-state; the 36,000 Kuna identify more as Kuna than Panamanian.

Kuna power is demonstrated best in how they manage their greatest commodity – their land and waters. The Kuna inhabit and govern the autonomous territory of Kuna Yala, which extends along a 225-km swath of coastal mainland that extends 10–20 km south of the coast. It also includes territorial waters and an archipelago of almost 400 nearly pristine, undeveloped islands in the Caribbean Sea, including 38 island villages and 11 coastal communities. The small coral islands are south of the hurricane belt; the Kuna enjoy temperate, breezy conditions throughout the year, punctuated by a rainy season. The islands lack mosquitos, snakes or other predators.

Some scholars assert that the Kuna are one of the best-organized and wealthiest indigenous groups in the Americas (Howe, 2002a, b; Helms, 1988; Langebaek, 1991). They are highly political (Howe, 2002) and preservation of their cultural and national identity is a top priority of the Kuna government. The following affirmation, stencilled on a wall in the central part of Mamitupo Sasardi in Kuna Yala, characterizes Kuna nationalism and cultural ideology:

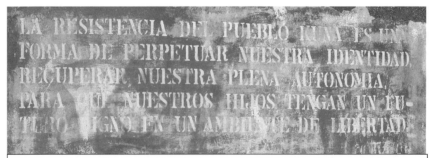

La resistencia del pueblo Kuna es una forma de perpetuar nuestra identidad, recuperar nuestra plena autonomia, para que nuestros hijos tengan un futuro signo en un ambiente de libertad.
  Translation: Kuna resistance is a form of perpetuating our identity, recuperating our autonomy, so that our children have a future constructed in an environment of liberty.

Fig. 5.1. La Resistancia Del Pueblo Kuna.

The Kuna have no colonial past and therefore should be considered non-Western. They are culturally free of colonial influences and their identity is defined by conflict and resistance. Christian proselytization has permeated somewhat; missionaries have been infiltrating the Kuna community for more than a century (Coope, 1917).

Tourism in Kuna Yala, also known as 'San Blas'

The Kuna call their home 'Kuna Yala' (which means 'Kuna land') but tourists mainly visit the islands, known to the rest of the world as 'San Blas'. A preferable reference for the purposes of this chapter–is 'the San Blas *region* of Kuna Yala', because tourists mainly visit uninhabited islands in the western part of Kuna Yala that include some tourist lodging accommodations or allow camping and the sailing waters that surround them. San Blas is a vernacular region with imprecise, subjective and nebulous boundaries. The San Blas islands represent an idyllic symbol of tranquil Caribbean life, sometimes only including a few palm trees and grass.

Tourism to the San Blas islands grew steadily, but slightly over the last 70 years – and then increased greatly in the past five years, ostensibly due to reports on the internet and even more recently, an improved road that allows a $25 2.5-h ride from Panama City. Airplanes from Panama City arrive once a day and besides the occasional helicopter arrival, all transport within the region is by sea. There are no cars or other motorized vehicles on the islands.

Kuna women dress in colourful traditional clothing, wearing handstitched molas they are known for throughout the world (Tice, 1995). Kuna women also wear uinis, which are beaded armbands and leggings, red and yellow printed headscarves and brightly patterned wrap skirts. They also wear a patterned red and yellow headscarf, a nose ring and black jagua fruit temporary tattoos on the bridge of their noses. Girls

and younger women tend to dress in Western clothing, although most young women begin to wear molas and uinis after a haircutting ceremony in their early 20s. Men go barefoot and otherwise wear Western clothing. They put on brightly coloured shirts of yellow, pink and bright blue for special occasions. Kuna men and women throughout the territory agree that the way they dress is an integral facet of femininity and Kuna cultural identity, not a costume worn for outsiders.

Most Kuna live without motors or electronics, electricity or plumbing. The majority of Kuna men still paddle daily to farm plots on the mainland to harvest fruit and vegetables, catch fish and hunt. On the islands, mothers and grandmothers spend their days sewing molas, tending houses and children and cooking. When the men return home in the afternoon, they do chores – maintaining cane buildings, carving boats from palm trunks and gathering at nightly community meetings.

Most of the islands are undeveloped; some only have a few families, although most tend to congregate in villages. There are 51 lodging facilities in Kuna Yala with a combined capacity for 854 tourists per night. Accommodations range from a $10 hut to upscale resort-style lodges that cost $240 per night. The most expensive accommodations are on uninhabited islands, with tours offered to the island villages.

The Kuna Gaze

Kuna leadership negotiates its peoples' autonomy in a myriad of ways. Their proud independence is reflected in laws governing tourist activity, public dissemination of communal strategies to benefit from tourism and even personal interactions with tourists. Governmental leadership is split into two functions – one part handles administrative politics and the other oversees, serves and protects Kuna culture and its spiritual foundation. Within the islands, caciques (chiefs) guide community politics and policy.

The Kuna government – called the Congreso General Kuna (CGK) – does not support tourism with much financial investment in the form of labour or infrastructure. The CGK resists massive tourism and makes efforts to counteract loss of traditional ways. For example, the CGK recently denied a request from regional airlines to expand runways to allow 40-seat planes to land on the islands (G. Hernandez, El Porvenir, 2011, personal communication). The largest airplanes only carry 20 passengers and arrive only once a day. The government recently initiated a programme in Kuna schools to have schoolgirls dress in traditional molas, skirts and headscarves one day a week. Just four decades ago, children dressed in traditional clothing regularly (S. Smith, California, 2011, personal communication); now they all wear Western clothes.

Kuna tourism policy is written in explicit legal language, reflecting forethought and alliances within the legal community. Kuna cultural identity is evident in their self-governance, collectively expressed autonomy and negotiation with outsiders. The Kuna government presents the front line of resistance to mass tourism and also promotes cultural unity internally, partly as an antidote to tourism. Enactment and orchestration of Kuna political standards are less certain at the local level, where the dollar sometimes holds more sway than cultural unity. The Kuna government forbids foreign investment or management of tourism projects and continually resists development proposals that would infiltrate their community. Only Kuna can own property in Kuna Yala. Several instances of conflict over these measures have occurred in the last few decades, including:

- Ongoing conflict between 1994 and 1997 over a Panamanian-financed ecoresort called Iskardup near Playón Chico; the battles quieted when Kuna took over the management (Bennett, 1999).
- The 1983 creation of a national park with funds from the United States Agency for International Development (USAID) and $150,000 of Kuna funds that protects their land from future encroachment and conserves biodiversity (Chapin, 1990).
- The 1981 night-time ambush of an American who operated a small resort wherein he was shot in the leg and chased off (Howe, 1982).
- Prevention of a 1975 Panamanian Institute of Tourism plan to build a $38 million hotel and international airport (Howe, 2009).
- The burning of a luxury lodge in the 1960s – built twice by an American entrepreneur who did not seek Kuna approval.

The Kuna accept educational resources – buildings and teachers – and some public works and health assistance from the Panamanian government, but otherwise resist tourism infrastructure. The only exception is improvements to the Llano-Cartì Highway from the Panamanian–Kuna Yala border, which was completed after three decades in November, 2010. A new bridge inaugurated the highway completion and has opened the territory to more tourists.

The Kuna government imposes entry fees and taxes on lodging establishments, but by no means has a standardized administrative system. Individual caciques (chiefs) have jurisdiction over what happens in their villages; a few require tourists to check in with them upon arrival or charge a fee of $1 to $2.

Neither the Kuna nor Panama's tourism authority promote the region with advertising, so San Blas has only appeared on international tourist consciousness in the last decade. In response, the Kuna government commissioned a three-year study on tourism in 2006, resulting in a 450-page report; a conference in August, 2010 and a new section on the Kuna governmental web site on tourism (Pereiro and de León, 2010). Travel reports from individual tourists on blogs, bulletin boards and photo-sharing sites have resulted in even greater coverage in Lonely Planet in the last five years. Most of the tourists to the region come from the USA and Europe (Pereiro and de León, 2010).

Only Kuna can benefit financially from tourism projects except in those cases where the government grants explicit permission – such as to cruises that enter Kuna waters. Regulations require Kuna entrepreneurs to present affidavits ensuring that they are the sole operators and investors and that the island is generally in support of the project. They must prove financing for the project and provide copies of loan agreements. Further laws prevent the sale of such projects or offering them as collateral for financing other projects. The penalty for breaking these laws is confiscation of the property involved.

Since the Kuna government's approach to tourism is either negligent or ambivalent, there is no plan for accommodating or hosting tourists. The Kuna lack an integrated or proactive comprehensive plan to help tourists negotiate their stay. There is no visitor information centre, no trained hospitality ambassadors, no concierge or hostess. There is no coordinated signage identifying attractions or roads or even hotels. The tourist is lucky to find an island with signs indicating where they can purchase beer or soda.

The distinction between inhabited and uninhabited islands is an important one in San Blas. While Kuna life is by no means defined by tourism, some islands are so small that many Kuna spatially elect to avoid the 'fishbowl' of encounters with tourists by living live on islands without tourist accommodations – or those islands that are geographically inconvenient to reach.

As for Kuna individuals, most do not initiate communication with tourists, treating them mostly with ambivalent indifference or mild disinterest. Tourists to the San Blas region of Kuna Yala fall into three general categories distinguished by the types of interaction they have with the Kuna: yachtees, Panamanians/backpackers and the most invasive group, ethnic tourists. These tourists come to the region hoping to learn about Kuna culture and their interests range from benign to intrusive, although most are satisfied with cursory visuals. Panamanians and backpackers, although very different in composition as far as cultural identity, have little interaction with the Kuna. The Kuna can easily manage the first two groups because their interest in Kuna culture is relatively minimal.

The yachtees group is the least complicated, as they travel within the boating community and share a network of information and resources. Their impact on the Kuna is therefore benign and mainly consumptive; they mainly stay near uninhabited islands and visit villages only to make purchases. Two Panamanian yacht cruising books feature the Kuna (Zydler and Zydler, 2001; Bauhaus, 2010). Both have rampant and often-repeated misinformation, such as that the Kuna are a matriarchal society and that the Kuna are the second-smallest group in the world after 'the pygmies'.

The local response to yachtees can be varied when a few seditious entrepreneurs step to the fore to cajole tourists with friendly smiles and service. This contingent of entrepreneurial Kuna paddle out regularly to yachts to sell vegetables, fruit, fish, crab and lobster and hot homemade bread. Kuna entrepreneurs also sell shellfish, large tarpon and turtle, threatening native populations that would otherwise feed their people. These entrepreneurs are straying from the CGK's political ideology, which advocates distance and resistance; this is, again, mediated resistance (Joseph and Kavoori, 2001).

The second group – Panamanian tourists and backpackers – also mainly visit Kuna Yala for sun, sea and sand. Some also attest to casual interest in Kuna culture. These visitors are interested mostly in the pristine, undeveloped islands and can spend happy days cavorting in azure waters with little more than quiet assistance from the Kuna. A high percentage of these backpackers are from Israel, Western Europe and the US. Since the opening of the Llano-Cartí bridge, Panamanian tourists have begun flocking to the San Blas region on weekends.

The Kuna react to tourist arrivals rather than proactively seeking to accommodate tourists, so travel to the islands is a confusing experience for backpackers and ethnic tourists. There is no travel ambassador at the borders or airports; intrepid backpackers or other travellers who arrive without planning accommodations ahead of time are often perplexed at the lack of signage, advertising and clear direction as to where they should go – and how to get there. El Porvenir has the most organized immigration office, where tourists show passports and pay a $2 usage fee. That office has a list of the 51 cabanas, hotels and lodges with phone numbers.

But these backpackers and ethnic tourists might not notice the handwritten list posted on the wall unless they ask about lodging. The options are plentiful, but the only information listed on the menu is a name and telephone number. It is incumbent on this tourist to ask questions. The lodging options are stratified by distance from the airfields or ports or roads (and the cost they must negotiate with a Kuna boatman to get there), the level of accommodation they desire (Hut or hotel? Bed or hammock? Sandy beach floor or concrete? Are running water and electricity necessary? How many meals do they require? How much do they want to pay per night? How much will they spend to get there? Do they want to visit a village or uninhabited island? If inhabited, does the tourist want a quaint island with a few families or a village of 300 with some activity, but no concrete block structures? Or do they want to go to the Kuna city of Ustupu, with 8,000 people?) Most of these conversations devolve into aporia, so the tourism inspector or boatmen make the decision for the tourist. Tourists who find their accommodations unsatisfactory usually negotiate a move elsewhere.

The Kuna are stymied by tourists who ask clarifying questions about lodging. 'They have so many questions. It is just a bed for the night, but they want to know what the island is like, what the bed is like, where the bathroom is, whether they will have privacy, whether the doors lock…" a Kuna guide named Eric Diaz Burgos explained. Burgos is the grandson of Luis Burgos, who built the cinderblock, 32-bed San Blas Hotel on Nalunega in 1966. Oftentimes, he delivers tourists to an island, yet they are dissatisfied and demand other accommodations.

Geographic and linguistic barriers support those Kuna who do not want to be bothered with tourists; they seek solace in distant villages that lack tourist lodging. Spanish-speaking Kuna men manage border crossings, manage hotels, serve as guides and interact with the outside world; more and more are learning English. Although some Kuna women work in hotels and lodges, the most contact women have with tourists comes in the form of selling molas. When tourists arrive, word spreads quickly. While some Kuna women hurry to hang molas; others go inside their houses. Kuna mothers often pull toddlers inside, closing windows and doors to prevent the peering, curious faces of tourists.

The entrepreneurial Kuna in western San Blas are self-elected representatives of the Kuna and therefore appear regularly in tourist photos shared on Flickr, Travelpod and other travelogue photo sites. Kuna transport boats also direct traffic towards villages that welcome tourists and do not tell tourists about the others. Those Kuna who interact with tourists have discovered that tourists' needs and interests are complicated, varied and sometimes contradictory.

Both groups of tourists – the yachtees and the backpackers – appeal to the Kuna because they prefer uninhabited islands and therefore intrude very little on Kuna life. The tradeoff is that they prefer cheap accommodations, buy fewer and less expensive handicrafts and tend to be less concerned about their environmental impact, leaving garbage behind. There are other negative impacts, such as social intrusions. For the most part, tourists tend to be respectful – but there are occasional transgressions. In 2011, some Americans put up a US flag on Nalunega; the village chief ('saila') told them to remove it. The saila has ultimate authority over tourist infractions on village life, although the response of such sailas varies with personality and whim.

Ethnic tourists who visit inhabited islands are the most invasive group. They want more contact with the Kuna – and the contact is more casual and less ritualized than the Kuna who sell to yachts and manage backpacker havens.

Several western islands are amenable to tourist visits –Wichub-Huala, Corbiski, Mamitupu, Carti Yandup, Carti Sugdup, Soledad Mandingo, Vanuatu, Isla Yierba, Kuanidup, Isla Pelicano, Isla Perro and Nalunega. The island village of Nalunega is a six-minute motorized boat ride from the airfield at El Porvenir, the western-most landing strip.

Apart from the minority of ambassadors and ambassadresses, interactions are generally quiet standoffs, with Kuna women holding up handstitched reverse appliqué molas or bamboo stims wrapped with material and uinis. They might also blithely pose with a parrot for a photograph, for which they demand $1 with an index finger. Actual contact consists of a few uncomfortable minutes, extended perhaps by purchases. Tourists stand several feet away, admiring and smiling, but can only communicate in Spanish occasionally with the few Kuna women who speak Spanish (as most do not).

The Kuna maintain solidarity through their unique language, which related to other nearby languages. Kuna men and children speak Spanish and Dule; most Kuna women only speak Dule. Until recent decades, Dulegaiya was rarely written. The Kuna government has published several books in the last five years about Kuna culture, including a Spanish–Dule dictionary. This is part of the governmental effort to preserve, protect and promote Kuna culture. The emergence of documenting language in print can contribute to a sense of nationalism (Anderson, 1983).

Kuna 'hospitality' provides a bed or hammock and meals and maybe a ride to a neighbouring island to swim and sunbathe for the day – and little more. They barely communicate with guests. Many tourists from the industrialized occident are confused when their modern expectations of hospitality are misguided or irrelevant. As a recent visitor noted on a blog, after arriving with rental reservations to find a busily indifferent indigene family:

> When we arrived at 'Diablo Island' we were greeted by, well, no one. Metres away, the abuela (grandmother) of the family dressed in her traditional attire of a colourful [sic.]

and arms and legs strangled from joint to joint in beaded bangles, watched us curiously from inside her cabana. We were escorted to our cabana, complete with inflatable mattresses and left to our own devices, though a family of nine lived not 10 metres away. You actually feel a bit intrusive – it's like wandering around in someone's home and they keep very much to themselves which makes it all the more awkward. Especially when they call you for the breakfast, lunch or dinner that they have prepared for you and you come to the table to find your food just sitting there with no one to thank for it. (http://beccurrey.blogspot.com/2010/06/sunning-it-up-in-san-blas.html, 2010)

Although it appears that there are very few cases of a constructed tourist gaze in Kuna Yala; a few groups dance for tourists and play panpipes, a traditional instrument (Smith, 1984). Some children in the western islands demand $1 per photo.

The Kuna will often feign ignorance if questioned about kinship, folkloric wisdom and communal values. A tourist who had researched the Kuna online before her arrival asked a guide to translate her questions to the Kuna skipper from from Isla Carti who works on the sailboat. She wanted to ask if Ibeorgun, a prophet that plays a significant role in Kuna folklore, is considered their god.

The guide hesitated – Kuna folk tales are intricate, interwoven and a complex foundation of their worldview. At nightly community meetings, they repeat stories about heroes and mythological figures such as Bab Dummad, Ibeorgun and Bab Igar. Kuna mythology involves complex perceptions of geographic spirit regions, Kuna attachment to the sea and land, their reliance on the earth and sea to feed and sustain them. These stories are a favourite topic of the Kuna and are integral to nightly community meetings in a central meeting house.

There was no simple answer to the tourist's question. To answer thoroughly would require a historic review of Kuna mythology, symbolism and a nuanced history of that particular prophet. The Kuna man smiled and answered, 'We didn't learn that in school.'

Although many of these tourists come to learn about the Kuna (Pereiro, 2010), what they learn is limited to myopic observations of traditional dress, the landscape of clustered palm-thatched cane houses and a few personally constructed museums on various islands.

Several Kuna men explained that Kuna families have historically been very protective of Kuna women, discouraging them from interacting with foreigners. A Kuna woman explained via an interpreter that the lack of common language keeps bargaining sessions to a minimum. She insists on a price by holding up fingers or writing hash marks on paper. The Kuna's quiet countenance deters haggling.

The Kuna do not allow tourists to participate in community rituals or celebrations, although some occasionally are permitted to watch. They clearly forbid tourist cameras at communal chicha preparations – an elaborate and athletic process involving jumping on logs to press sugar cane juices and boiling the frothy juice over an active fire – a process overseen by dozens of Kuna men and women.

Many visitors to Kuna Yala will disagree with the above paragraph – and this is a phenomenon unto itself. Tourists want to like the Kuna and generally find the Kuna friendly because of a minority of entrepreneurial Kuna who are increasingly finding that being friendly to tourists is highly profitable. These tourists tend to idealize this contact and conflate it to tell the world of their marvelously intimate interactions with 'the natives'.

Enchanted by the spectacle of this pure, indigenous group, many yachtees and ethnic tourists write fanciful reports of the spectacle they observe. A textual analysis of 346 such reports revealed that the word 'paradise' appeared in 282 of them and 'primitive' appeared in 201. So 'learning about the Kuna' consists of seeing them in their traditional clothing, maybe offering a gift, buying some handicrafts, taking a photo. This is hardly the basis for insightful knowledge about a culture – and yet blog reports appear weekly about how wonderfully 'primitive' life is 'in paradise'. After

all, the destination is notorious for prompting visions of exoticism and visions of paradise in tourists (Pereiro and de León, 2007). (For more information on the tourist experience in Kuna Yala, see Savener, 2012.)

The Kuna have little patience for irritation, demands or orders; the independent traveller who delights in the freedom of unplanned travel may encounter some turbulence in Kuna Yala. Those tourists who expect a level of hospitality experienced in other destinations sometimes take offence – and take this up with their Kuna hosts. When their dissatisfaction escalates to complaints and raised voices, the resulting interaction can be comical. A Kuna man does not take offence or take umbrage; they just go away. They might even laugh. They will definitely joke about the tourist later. The Kuna have a great sense of humor (Sherzer, 1983). Burgos, who works as a guide, said many tourists come to Kuna Yala seeking exotic culture – 'Caníbales! Sacrificios!' with a wink. Later, he pointed out a destroyed building emerging from the water, no island around it, calling it 'las ruinas de San Blas', mocking the staged performance of tour guides (Edensor, 2000).

Entrepreneurial Kuna

Without much firsthand knowledge of the hospitality industry or norms of tourism management or guest services norms, entrepreneurial Kuna learn how to interact with tourists via trial and error. One family on Nalunega – the Iglesias family – runs a cultural museum and keeps their gate wide open in the daytime when tourists may arrive. When tourists are spotted, news travels quickly and women rush to hang dozens of molas outside their family compound of huts, strung along bamboo gates. The patriarch of the family instructs his adult children not to approach tourists initially to sell. He explains that he must beckon to tourists in an open, friendly manner without indicating that he has anything to sell.

'No ... they don't like that. They feel pressured. We just say "Hello!" and invite them in, ask them where they are from," said

Arkimedes Iglesias, a 74-year-old grand-father. He often invites tourists to stay with his family, sleeping in the same hut with his family of 10. When tourists stay with his family, he makes sure to acquire fish or lobster to serve them, a lesson he learned through trial and error. 'They only like seafood. Tourists don't want canned food,' he said in Spanish. Iglesias learned a few words of English working as a cook serving American workers at the Panama Canal in the 1960s.

Iglesias has and the younger Burgos have learned, in the last five years, that 'travellers' to Nalunega share idiosyncrasies and particularities that they, as Kuna, cannot quite interpret. The motives are unclear, but they know that (i) they dislike being called tourists – or seen as tourists.

"They want to be called 'travellers' ('viajeros'), Burgos laughed. 'I call them "clients",' he said, winking mischievously. These Kuna recognize these tourists' quest for authentic experience – and indulge it, finding evasive and illusory ways to comply with the tourist's preference to believe his experience is authentic.

Study Contributions

Although this is not the first instance of a host community displaying agency and will, the Kuna are certainly admirable in the manner that they stand apart from other indigenous groups in asserting will and not yielding to marginalization and outside control. The unusual circumstances of tourist–Kuna interactions allow reconsideration of long-held assumptions about the nature of those who are visited by tourists and their role in what should be a negotiated compromise. The tourist does not necessarily hold power because they hold funds, and the Kuna make that clear.

Study limitations

This phenomenographic analysis can only be considered a snapshot in time, since tourism and other aspects of globalization are transforming life in Kuna Yala rapidly. This research was conducted with careful and wary acknowledgement of the dangers of etic presumption. An outsider sees with unintentional myopia and can therefore be so distracted or fascinated as to be oblivious to important cues, happenstance or underlying meaning, deaf to the symphonic chords that are integral to the fundamental structure of the symphony. I am wary, as an outsider, of the danger of conflating, misinterpreting or distilling the rationale and intentions of a cultural group to which I do not belong. Efforts were made to ameliorate these risks with methodical awareness to instances where data might be misinterpreted due to etic presumption or transference of cultural expectations, particularly where lack of common language hindered understanding. A more accurate Kuna gaze perspective will hopefully be written by a Kuna ethnographer, sometime in the future.

Future study

Further research on tourism in Kuna Yala will certainly follow; an in-depth analysis of Kuna cultural identity as expressed through governance is warranted. An analysis of the Kuna via Hofstede's National Culture Index (Reisinger, 2010) would be a fruitful pursuit for further research. And, as this study is limited in scope, a further researcher could easily expand on the findings in this short chapter.

The implications of this study for the tourism and hospitality industry would be improved respect for preserving authentic representations of host communities and recognition of their agency. Another future study could focus on Kuna culture brokers and the way that they negotiate the desire to profit financially from tourists and also respect their brethren's privacy.

Conclusion

Centuries of resistance and distrust of outsiders have coalesced into communal introversion in Kuna Yala; this has been reinforced by geographic isolation. Today's tourist is only the most recent incarnation of threatening invaders to invade Kuna territory. The problem is – these harbingers wear smiles and offer money instead of pirating gold or ripping them from Kuna women's necks or slaughtering the Kuna who show them to mineral deposits.

The Kuna see themselves reflected in tourist's eyes and consequently, the elements that interest tourists are dramatized and brought to the forefront of tourist consciousness. The Kuna national museum guides and those who work in lodging have found that tourists are immensely satisfied with stories about community chicha celebrations to celebrate a girl's first menstruation, the haircutting ceremony, weddings and divorces. The ritual for celebrating the first menstruation is a tourist favorite, often told and often repeated in blogs, with varying accuracy and detail. The shortest versions tell of a village party that lasts all day and night with everyone drinking to extreme inebriation. The actual ceremony is a four-day sequence of rituals begins by isolating the girl, blowing smoke over her, dancing, purity rituals and sometimes her first haircut.

In the case of the Kuna, silence is sufficient. The tourists are appeased with a glimpse at them before getting back on the boat or airplane to return to electricity and plumbing. For the most part, the Kuna lack the interest or financial need to serve tourists.

Georg Simmel's (1971) sociological theory about the tendency to generalize about groups of individuals so different from one's experience applies to the Kuna. Most Kuna do not attempt to speak with tourists.

Every day brings a new parade of tourists through Nalunega. Since 2006, when the Kuna appeared curious when a tourist arrived, the people who live on Nalunega have seen enough tourists that they have progressed to benign disinterest. Urry (1990) wrote that the tourist gaze was constructed of difference, but the Kuna gaze alights on a generalized, dehumanized group of tourists who basically appear the same to them as other tourists. And tomorrow, a new group of faces will come and go.

Kuna Yala is a vector of power inversion for the tourist experience. The Kuna remind tourists that they are only not at home; they are not necessarily welcome. Kuna Yala is not a home away from home. The tourist is a visitor and the power balance created by mass tourism is inverted. The Kuna challenge normative expectations of tourists benignly and nonchalantly. Kuna autonomy has historic roots and is also based in their subsistence and barter economy. Kuna success at resisting cultural diffusion is due partly to their voluntary spatial isolation, but also depends on their exemplary manner of communicating only *in ways that serve them*.

References

Adams, V. (1996) *Tigers of the Snow and Other Virtual Sherpas: an Ethnography of Himalayan Encounters*. Princeton University Press, Princeton, NJ.

Apgar, J.M. (2010) Adaptive capacity for endogenous development of kuna yala, an indigenous biocultural system. Unpublished PhD thesis, Lincoln University, Lincoln.

Anderson, B. (1983) *Imagined Communities: Reflection on the Origin and Spread of Nationalism*. Verso, London.

Aramberri, J. (2001) The host should get lost: paradigms in the tourism theory. *Annals of Tourism Research* 28(3), 738–761.

Bhattacharyya, D.P. (1997) Mediating India: an analysis of a guidebook. *Annals of Tourism Research* 24 (2), 371–389.

Bauhaus, E. (2010) *The Panama Cruising Guide: a Complete Sailors Guide to the Isthmus of Panama*. Self published.

Bennett, J. (1999) The dream and the reality. Cultural Survival Inc, http://www.culturalsurvival.org/ourpublications/csq/article/the-dream-and-reality-tourism-kuna-yala (accessed 22 March 2010).

Bruner, E.M. (1991) Transformation of self in tourism. *Annals of Tourism Research* 18, 238–250.

Bruner, E. and Kirshenblatt-Gimblett, B. (1994) Maasai on the lawn: tourist realism in East Africa. *Cultural Anthropology* 9(4), 435–470.

Desmond, J.C. (1999) Staging Tourism. Bodies on Display from Waikiki to Sea World. The University of Chicago Press, Chicago, IL

Dyer, P., Aberdeen, L. and Schuler, S. (2003) Tourism Impacts on an Australian Indigenous community: a Djabugay case study. *Tourism Management* 24(1), 83–95.

Chapin, M. (1990) *The Silent Jungle: Ecotourism Among Kuna Indians of Panama. Cultural Survival Quarterly* 14(1), 42–45.

Chapin, M. and Threlkeld, B. (2001) *Indigenous Landscapes: a Study in Ethnocartography.* Center for the Support of Native Lands, Arlington, VA.

MacCannell, D. (1973) Staged authenticity: arrangements of social space in tourist settings. *American Journal of Sociology* 79(3), 589–603.

Cohen, E. (1989) Primitive and remote hill tribe trekking in Thailand. *Annals of Tourism* 16, 30–61.

Coope, A. (1917) *Anna Coope: Sky Pilot of the San Blas Indians.* American Tract Society, New York.

Conran, M. (2006) Commentary: beyond authenticity: exploring intimacy in the touristic encounter in Thailand. *Tourism Geographies* 8(3), 244–285.

Edensor, T. (2000) Staging tourism: tourists as performers. *Annals of Tourism Research* 27(2), 322–344.

Evans-Pritchard, D. (1989) How 'they' see 'us': Native American images of tourists. *Annals of Tourism Research* 16, 89–105.

Franklin, A. and Crang, M. (2001) The trouble with tourism and travel theory. *Tourist Studies* 1(1), 5–22.

Furnham, A. (1984) Tourism and culture shock. *Annals of Tourism Research* 11, 41–57.

Gallup-Diaz, I. (1999) the door of the seas and key to the universe: Indian politics and Imperial rivalry in the Darién, 1640–1750. Unpublished PhD thesis, Princeton University, http://www.gutenberg-e.org/gdi01/ (accessed 13 November 2009).

Hepburn, S.J. (2002) Touristic forms of life in Nepal. *Annals of Tourism Research* 29(3), 611–630.

Helms, M.W. (1988) *Ulysses' Sail: an Ethnographic Odyssey of Power, Knowledge, and Geographical Distance.* Princeton University Press, Princeton, NJ.

Historia (2011) Origen del Pueblo Kuna (History: Origin of the Kuna) on web site of Congreso Kuna General, http://www.congresogeneralkuna.com/historia_kuna.htm (accessed 16 April 2011).

Hobsbawm, E.J.E. (1992) *Nations and Nationalism Since 1780.* Cambridge University Press, Cambridge.

Howe, J. (1982) Kindling self-determination among the Kuna. *Cultural Survival Quarterly* 3(6), 15.

Howe, J. (1998) *A People Who Would Not Kneel.* Smithsonian Institution Press, Washington, DC.

Howe, J. (2002a) The Kuna of Panama: continuing threats to land and autonomy. In: Maybury-Lewis, D. (eds) *The Politics of Ethnicity: Indigenous Peoples in Latin American States.* Harvard University Press, Cambridge, MA

Howe, J. (2002b) *The Kuna Gathering.* Fenestra Books, Tucson, AZ.

Howe, J. (2009) *Chiefs, Scribes and Ethnographers: Kuna Culture From Inside and Out.* University of Texas Press, Austin, TX.

Joseph, C.A. and Kavoori, A.P. (2001) Mediated resistance: tourism and the host community. *Annals of Tourism Research* 28(4), 998–1009.

Kirtsoglou, E. and Theodossopoulos, D. (2004) They are taking our culture away. *Critique of Anthropology* 24(2), 135–157.

Knudsen, D., Soper, A.K. and Metro-Roland, M. (2007) Commentary: gazing, performing and reading: a land-scape approach to understanding meaning in tourism theory. *Tourism Geographies* 9(3), 227–233.

Langebaek, C.H. (1991) Cuna long distance journeys: The result of colonial interaction. *Ethnology* 30, 371–380.

Lim, F.K.G. (2008) Of reverie and emplacement: spatial imaginings and tourism encounters Nepal Himalaya. *Inter-Asia Cultural Studies* 9(3), 375–394.

MacCannell, D. (1999) *The Tourist: aNew Theory of the Leisure Class.* University of California, Berkeley, CA

Maoz, D. (2006). The mutual gaze. *Annals of Tourism Research* 33(1), 221–239.

Munt, I. (1994) Eco-tourism or ego-tourism? *Race & Class* 36(1), 49–60.

Oakes, T. (2006) Get real! On being yourself and being a tourist. In: Minca, C. and Oakes, T. (eds) *Travels in Paradox: Remapping Tourism.* Rowman and Littlefield, Lanham, MD, pp. 229–250..

Pearce, P.L. and Moscardo, G.M. (1986) The concept of authenticity. *Journal of Sociology* 22(1), 121–132.

Pereiro, X. and de León, C. (2007) La Construcción Imaginaria Del Lugar Turístico. Tareas; Revista de Ciencias Sociales de Panamá, 127, http://www.biblioteca.clacso.org.ar/ar/libros/panama/cela/tareas127.pdf (accessed 10 April 2011).

Pereiro, X. and de León, C. (2010) *Estudio Estrategico del Turismo en Kuna Yala: Primera Version del Informe de Investigacion 2008–2010.*

Reisinger, Y. (2010) Applying Hofstede's National culture measures in tourism research: illuminating issues of divergence and convergence. *Journal of Travel Research* 49(2), 153.

Savener, A.M. (2012) Discovering Kuna Yala. *Transformational Tourism* (in press).

Sherzer, J. (1983) *Kuna Ways of Speaking: An Ethnographic Perspective.* University of Texas Press, Austin, TX.

Sherzer, J. (2003) *Stories, Myths, Chants, and Songs of the Kuna Indians.* University of Texas Press, Austin, TX.

Simmel, G. (1971) *On Individuality and Social Forms.* University of Chicago Press, Chicago, IL, and London.

Smith, V.L. (1989) *Hosts and Guests, The Anthropology of Tourism.* University of Pennsylvania Press, Philadelphia, PA.

Smith, S. (1984) Panpipes for power, panpipes for play: the social management of cultural expression in Kuna society. Unpublished dissertation. University of California, Berkeley, CA.

Swain, M.B. (1989) Gender roles in indigenous tourism: Kuna Mola, Kuna Yala, and cultural survival. In: Smith, V. (eds) *Hosts and Guests: The Anthropology of Tourism.* University of Pennsylvania Press, Philadelphia, PA, pp. 83–104.

Tice, K. (1995) *Kuna Crafts, Gender and the Global Economy.* University of Texas Press, Austin, TX.

Yin, R. K. (1984) *Case Study Research: Design and Methods.* Sage, Newbury Park, CA.

Urry, J. (1990) *The Tourist Gaze.* Sage, London.

Zydler, N.S. and Zydler, T. (2001) *The Panama Guide: a Cruising Guide to the Isthmus of Panama.* Seaworthy Publications, Port Washington, WI.

6   The Host Gaze on Current Christian Pilgrims in Israel: Tour Guides Gazing

Alon Gelbman and Noga Collins-Kreiner

Introduction

The main aim of this article is to describe, examine and analyse the manner in which tour guides in Israel gaze on the Christian Pilgrims groups that they lead in light of their familiarity and cumulative experience. The Holy Land has always been the main destination for Christian pilgrims from around the world, and religious tourism remains the main market segment of tourism to Israel as 31% of all tourists to Israel in 2010 describe themselves as pilgrims (Ministry of Tourism, 2011).

Urry (2002) elaborates on the processes by which the tourist gaze is constructed and reinforced and addresses the consequences of this gaze for the place being visited. In this study, we explore the other side of the coin: a group of people who form part of the tourists' gaze – their tour guides. Little has been written on how hosts view tourists in Israel, and we have chosen to focus on a group of professional hosts – tour guides – as they usually represent the most important local figure and host for tourists, especially groups of tourists, who arrive with an intensive and fully planned schedule with little time for significant contact with other local hosts. The chapter contributes to the current literature by understanding the hosts gaze: how tour guides view

different types of Christian pilgrims, their behaviour and their worldview.

Christian Pilgrims as Tourists

Religion and tourism today are inextricably bound up together. Religion is still among the most common motivations for travel. Thus, pilgrimage, which is one of the basic and oldest population motilities in the human world, motivated by religious reasons, is becoming a large tourism phenomenon in the 21st century and religious sites are becoming main tourist attractions visited by both religious visitors and tourists (Collins-Kreiner et al., 2006; Timothy and Olsen, 2006).

The study of the relationship between religion, pilgrimage and tourism has frequently focused separately on the issues of religion or tourism, with little equal or comparative treatment of the two together. This is surprising, as the development of tourism is hard to understand without a study of religion and the practice of pilgrimage in ancient times (Vukoni'c, 2002; Timothy and Olsen, 2006). As a result, the relationship between tourism and religion has focused primarily on the question of the similarity and difference between the tourist and the pilgrim (Cohen, 1992, 1998; Smith, 1992; Collins-Kreiner and Kliot, 2000).

Smith (1992) identifies tourism and pilgrimage as opposite ends on a continuum of travel. The polarities on the pilgrimage–tourism axis are labelled sacred vs. secular; between which are an almost infinite number of possible sacred–secular combinations, with the central area now generally termed 'religious tourism'. These positions reflect the multiple and changing motivations of travellers whose interests and activities may switch from tourism to pilgrimage and vice versa, even without their being aware of the change.

Most researchers identify 'religious tourism' with the quest of individuals to visit shrines and locales where, in lieu of piety, they seek to experience a sense of identity with sites of historical and cultural significance (Nolan and Nolan, 1989). Smith (1992) understands the difference to be based on individual beliefs and views of the world.

Accordingly, Israel's main attraction relies on its identification as the land of the Bible, the place where the monotheistic religions of Western culture evolved and where impressive and easily visible remnants of the past can bring the heritage alive. According to data published by the Ministry of Tourism, the distribution of incoming tourism to Israel in 2010 indicated that the main aim of the visit was pilgrimage (31%) and most visitors (66%) belonged to one of the various sects of Christianity.

The present study explores tour guides' perceptions of Christian religious tourists, as this group currently constitutes the largest market segment of incoming tourists to Israel. Although researchers have examined tourists' traits, images and perceptions of their visits to the Holy Land (Collins-Kreiner and Kliot, 2000; Fleisher, 2000), limited work has been directed to the gaze of hosts, as individuals and as a community, on these religious tourists.

The Host Gaze on the Tourist

The gaze is the way in which people view the world and when focused, it may include both visual and non-visual elements (MacCannell, 2001). The gaze develops towards the end of an infant's first year of life, at which time he seems to understand that a gaze yields meaningful information. Gaze contact between mother and baby is of maximal importance in their interaction and for ensuring essential sociological and social development. This unified gaze is essential for developing ties with other people. It not only transmits information, it also regulates interaction, practices social control and helps to attain goals (Flom, 2007).

Urry (2002) compares the tourist gaze to a clinical observation where the individual is the object of the medical gaze (scrutiny) in order to find tiny anomalies not visible to the ordinary person (Moufakkir, 2010). He thus conveys the notion that the tourist gaze is dynamic and structured. Urry used the gaze as a way of looking at tourism that simultaneously forms what is seen and is the *way* of seeing. Urry contends that as there are different types of tourists, tourists have different ideologically negotiated ways of looking at touristic things. Many factors, including gender and socioeconomic class, interact to construct this look. There is, in fact, no single tourist gaze. The gaze varies by and is dependent on social group and historical period (Urry, 2002, p. 1).

Urry's gaze is also a way of investigating typical forms of tourism, for a departure from the obvious 'requires the use of counter-intuitive and surprising methodologies' (Urry, 2002, p. 2). Like the gaze of the medic the tourist gaze can be used to interpret a whole way of life (Moufakkir, 2010). Urry emphasizes that while the study of tourism deals with pleasure, which is less important than life-and-death medicine, it is also a serious business guided by professional experts. It is the work of the tourist professional and academic to deconstruct these gazes (Moufakkir, 2010). This notion of the tourist gaze has been adopted by tourism academics to also study the host gaze (Enevoldsen, 2003; Kingsbury, 2005; Chan, 2006; Maoz, 2006; Moufakkir, 2010). Moufakkir argues that despite a few attempts to deconstruct the host gaze, it remains within the realm of surveys of residents' attitudes. A gaze study, however, *must* go beyond the hows to uncover the whys of attitudes and perceptions.

Stylianou-Lambert (2011), in the study of museums, suggests that no dichotomy exists between daily life and behaviour at home, and touristic behaviour. According to Urry (2002), tourists allegedly adopt a gaze the moment they leave their home and familiar landscape for the unknown. Stylianou-Lambert sees things differently. He does not negate Urry's touristic gaze but contends that it is composed of more strata because in essence tourists do not abandon their conceptions or other gazes when they arrive at a new landscape. Stylianou-Lambert maintains that creating a dichotomy between daily life and tourism is an unnecessary and artificial concept. Previously, Cohen (1979) categorized tourist types according to what he conceptualized as 'a home spiritual centre'. He argued that different people bring different 'baggage' from home, but it does not matter to what extent people are freed of this home baggage. They cannot change their cultural routine and feelings of identification with it, even when their main motivation for travelling is to leave their daily life behind. Another reason that no dichotomy is needed, Stylianou-Lambert says, is the understanding and knowledge that tourists' past experiences, motivation, distinctions and behaviours are not left behind when they are on tour (Stylianou-Lambert, 2011).

Maoz (2006) studied the gaze of locals and backpackers in India and found that the locals' gaze is closer to reality than that of the tourists. As a result, tourists are nourished by media information and the locals are nourished only by the meetings. But even this gaze is not completely lacking in information because there are those who still think about the colonial period when they see Westerners. The locals' gaze, as it was found in India, is composed of images of the tourists. It differs with the type of tourist and is eye-dependent, meaning that those in the tourist industry gaze at tourists differently than do others. They are more impatient towards tourists than are locals who are not engaged in the industry.

The locals' gaze may not be perceived by tourists to the same extent as the tourists' gaze is perceived by the locals, but the tourists are indeed exposed to it and may unknowingly perpetuate and manifest the stereotypes that the locals have of them (Maoz, 2006).

The potential of tourism social interactions may lead to cross-cultural understanding and host-gaze respect. This is supported by Allport's (1954) contact theory, according to which assembling people of different races, colours, religions and nation origins might change previous opinions and stereotypes and lead to friendships. Amir (1969) found that the results of such contacts are not always positive and in some conditions might lead to increased prejudice. What effect contacts have depends in part on conditions like: the social status of the two parties, goals (cooperative or competitive), the type of contact (intimate or casual, voluntary or forced) and the existence of pre-existing attitudes towards the other side (Allport, 1954; Amir, 1969; Riordan, 1978).

Previous research on contact theory in tourism yielded ambiguous results, with some studies indicating that touristic social contacts had a positive influence (Carlson and Widaman, 1989), while others indicated no improvement in attitudes and stereotypes or even a negative influence (Ap and Var, 1990; Pizam *et al.*, 1991). Most recent studies have yielded mixed results, with positive attitudes towards some people and negative attitudes towards others (Milman *et al.*, 1990; Litvin and Kar, 2003).

Tour Guides as Hosts

The role of tour guides in conveying information, offering explanations and developing narratives has become a current research theme. A guide's role, it is generally agreed, extends well beyond welcoming and informing tourists. The guide is entrusted with the public relations mission of summarizing the essence of a place and serving as a window onto a site, region or country (Pond, 1993; Dahles, 2002).

The focus is on the guide's role as information-giver and fountain of knowledge, teacher or instructor, missionary or ambassador for the country (Holloway, 1981). But the guide is also introduced as a 'translator' of the culture, who has the crucial task of selecting, glossing and interpreting sights (Schmidt, 1979; Holloway, 1981; Cohen, 1985, 2002; Bowman, 1992; Salazar, 2005; Gelbman and Maoz, 2012). The guide directs the tourists' gaze (Urry, 2002), telling them what to observe and what to ignore, and more importantly – how to interpret what they see.

Smith (2001) used the term 'cultural broker' to identify the responsibility for ethnic imaging and cultural trait selection. At the local level, guides are cultural brokers. A cultural broker is a mediator between the demand and supply sides of tourism. Cultural brokers are primary decision makers, selectively identifying segments of the cultural content to be shared with outsiders, and many serve as guides. 'Marginal men' and women are cross-cultural mediators between Western and Indigenous societies. Usually bilingual, special circumstances (or interests) have afforded these individuals the opportunity to know, move through and live in and between two cultures. An example for this are Chinese who have become the 'marginal men or women' guides in Dyak villages of Borneo.

The aspect of tourist guides as hosts and their 'host gaze' has rarely been researched in the past. Pizam (1996) studied the attitude of tour guides in Korea, and how they perceive Japanese and American tourists who visit the place. In essence, he examined the intercultural behaviour of the tourists as reflected in the eyes of the guides hosting them. Like organizations, nations and industries, groups also have a culture. Groups of tourists have not only their own national culture but also a 'touristic culture'. National culture belongs to a nation, belief, religion and culture. Touristic culture comes from the unification of a group of people seeking a similar experience as they tour a given destination. Pizam found that national culture has more of an influence on tourists' behaviour than does touristic culture. Understanding the behaviour of tourists can improve the touristic product and its marketing. Where tourists of different nationalities share similar characteristics or qualities, it is possible to develop homogeneous groups for touring (Pizam and Jeong, 1996).

A few years later Pizam (1999) expanded his study about tour guides' perceptions of nationalities. He realized that the ethnic origin of the interviewees – their nationality, opinions about other nations and globalization in general – affected how they perceived the tourists. Many researchers have tried to examine the host gaze using methods like daily logs, and questionnaires, but it appears that in order to draw concrete conclusions it is necessary to continue to study the phenomenon.

This study is based on the manner in which local tour guides perceive Christian pilgrims. Local tour guides were selected because they are the element of the host community with the closest connection – and in some cases the *only* connection – with the tourists themselves. Thus, understanding their perceptions may help us to better understand the host gaze. We refer to the tour guides as 'professional hosts'. Their role in conveying information and developing narratives has emerged as a research theme in the literature over the past few years. Their role, it is clear, goes well beyond merely welcoming and informing tourists. This study examines the tour guides' gaze on their tourists.

Research Methodology

The study methodology is based on in-depth interviews with a sampleof 15 tour guides regarding their attitudes, perceptions and images of the Christian pilgrims groups. Its aims are help us understand their gaze: how tour guides view different types of tourists, their behaviour, and their worldview.

The specific questions we asked tour guides include: How would you describe the tourists' behaviour? Do they interact with the local population or keep to themselves and their group? Do they socialize? Are they interested in people or only in sites and artefacts? Are the religious tourists interested in non-religious sites as well? Do they display any interest in the tourism infrastructure, or are they only interested in the religious experience? By understanding the tour guides' perceptions of pilgrims to the Holy Land, we gain a better understanding of the gaze of the host community on religious tourists currently visiting Israel.

The research method used was 'grounded theory', which refers to a theory that is developed inductively from a corpus of data. This contrasts with theory derived deductively from grand theory, without the help of data, and which could therefore turn out to fit no data at all. Grounded theory takes a case rather than variable perspective, although the distinction is nearly impossible to draw. This means in part that the researcher takes different cases to be wholes, in which the variables interact as a unit to produce certain outcomes. A case-oriented perspective tends to assume that variables interact in complex ways. The basic idea of the grounded theory approach is to read (and re-read) a textual database (such as our interviews) and 'discover' or label variables (called categories, concepts and properties) and their interrelationships. Open coding is the part of the analysis concerned with identifying, naming, categorizing and describing phenomena found in the text. Essentially, each line, sentence, paragraph, and so on is read in search of the answer to the repeated question 'What is this about? What is being referenced here?' Part of the analytic process is to identify the more general categories that these things are instances of (Glaser and Strauss, 1967; Strauss and Corbin, 1990).

The profile of the tour guides who were interviewed was varied and included young and older tour guides with few and many years of experience. Most of them had more than ten years of experience and some more than 20 years. The sample included men and women (but mostly men), most of them guides for groups of 20 or more tourists, Christian pilgrims but also groups of Jews and culture and history tourists.

The average duration of each interview was   minutes. All our respondents found the topic interesting and were willing to participate. We interviewed until theoretical saturation was reached (Rubin and Rubin, 1995). The interviews were conducted between March 2011 and August 2011 and were analysed using a manual colour-coding process (Creswell, 1994). The interview transcript was read separately by the two authors. We separately marked off concepts, themes and ideas each time they occurred in the interview, and then reassembled the data into specific themes. The most common themes that emerged from the interviews and that we unanimously agreed upon centred on stereotypes and culture.

Israeli Tour Guides Gazing on Current Christian Pilgrims

Analysis of the in-depth interviews with the tour guides indicated that it is possible to relate to the findings through a number of salient elements that emerged from the descriptions of the hosts' (tour guides') gaze on the tourists. The main factors that found to affect their gazes were: previous experience, prior opinions and stereotypes, personal philosophy and cultural familiarity.

If guides use the initial gaze (external appearance) to identify and differentiate between religious and non-religious tourists or to identify religious affiliation, a deeper gaze treats tourists according to their affiliation with one sect or another, such as Catholics, Protestants, Greek Orthodox and Mormons. It should be noted that the religious factor in a visit to Israel, or what many tourists call the Holy Land, is of great significance (Collins-Kreiner et al., 2006).

Although the guides noted that gazing on external dress did not reveal a lot, unless the dress was something blatant or extreme, in fact external identification of religious signs did help the guides to learn faster about the tourists they were meeting. As one of the guides stated in the interview:

When I first see a group arriving, I look for religious indications, to see if they are wearing *yarmulkas* [skullcaps worn by some Jews]. If the tourists are Christian, I gaze at the type of dress and I adapt myself to the nature of group as I identify it. For example, in terms of dress – on the first day I will dress a little more formally, and according to what they wear during the tour I will adapt my own type of clothing. If they wear button-down shirts on the first day, and then on the second and third day too, I will also dress accordingly. But if on the second day they change into jeans and t-shirts I will also dress less formally.

External dress served as a message for the guide and his response was to adapt himself to the style adopted by the tourists in his group.

External identification, explained one of the guides, can express a measure of religiosity or affiliation to a given sect. One of the guides gave this description:

Religion has a very clear agenda and I know exactly what their expectations are and what will excite them and what will make their day. Everything is predictable and structured. On the other hand, secular tourists are much less predictable. You have to take their pulse much more often and learn what interests them. I have to be much more careful and varied, for example, giving equal time to all three religions in Jerusalem.

In other words, it is possible to distinguish a type of standardization in the gaze on religious groups, which are viewed as being uniformly interested in the same things. This is a perception that may help in coordinating expectations but some of the guides complained about it, because they felt it came at the expense of their ability to transmit information and their interpretation of the place, so that in essence part of the substance of their role as tour guides could not be fully expressed.

While tour guides have experience and great skill in guiding groups of religious tourists and especially Christians, it is interesting to see that the non-religious tourists are perceived as easier to work with than religious tourists, as one of the interviewees described: 'The non-religious tourists are

easier than the religious ones, who need prayers and passages read out in many places, such as before each meal. I understand their needs and accept them and it's totally OK with me.' It appears that this can be explained mainly by the fact that schedules when guiding religious groups must to be adapted to religious rituals and beliefs, which dominate both in terms of the route and content of the tour.

In many cases the group is accompanied by its community priest or pastor, who plays a central role in the pilgrimage tour experience. This, of course, comes at the expense of – and often instead of – a greater and multidisciplinary familiarity with the cultural space that they are visiting.

In guiding pilgrimage groups, tour guides have fewer opportunities to serve as what Smith (1992) describes as cultural brokers that are primary decision makers, selectively identifying segments of the cultural content to be shared with outsiders, in addition to being guides.

Tour guides view these tourists as individuals whose main purpose on the trip is to expose themselves to a religious experience. They are so busy with rituals and prayers that they are perhaps, to some extent, cut off from the space they are in – the modern State of Israel. Therefore, guides often prefer non-religious tourists who are open to broader and more varied cultural messages. As one of the guides said:

I prefer the non-pilgrimage tourists because the dialogue is more interesting. It is possible to discuss issues with them, not only to talk about religious places and religion, but also about contemporary Israel. I love to combine – that is part of the profession. But the pilgrims mainly want to go into the religious aspect only, the period of Jesus, what Jesus did and where. They don't have much interest in the State of Israel that they are visiting.

The literature often mentions this difference between the pilgrim and the secular tourist (Cohen, 1992, 1998; Smith, 1992; Collins-Kreiner and Kliot, 2000).

Another element that arose in this context, and also reinforces it, was mentioned by several guides. They perceive religious tourists – whether Jewish or Christian – to be more conservative and more right-wing politically. As the following guide said:

> Many of the religious ones [tourists] are more conservative. There is a link between religion and conservatism and being right-wing, not only among Christians including Mormons and other sects, but also among Jews. I do not identify with this set of values but I accept it, I truly believe there is no right side; each side pays a price.

In the guide's gaze, this is another element that limits tour dynamics and makes relations between him and these tourists more difficult. It is important to note that the guide clearly states that while he does not identify with their values, he certainly accepts them with great understanding. His extensive experience with views that differ from his own values has taught him to accept others with different views. This is similar to what Allport (1954) describes in his contact theory, about the positive effect of inter-cultural contacts, which in this case are part of the tourism experience.

The tour guides' gaze on Christian tourists clearly indicates distinctions they make as they gaze on different sects of Christianity. Some of the guides expressed amazement at the importance pilgrims attribute to differences in beliefs and customs, including the exact location of a given mythological event. This is how one guide describes it:

> It is amazing to see how in various sites there are two churches side by side for each sect, to mark the exact place in which, according to their belief, the same event occurred, for example, in Capernaum, the home of Peter's mother in law, or in Cana of the Galilee, where they believe that Jesus performed the first miracle [of turning water into wine]. It is simply astonishing to me, to see such duplication between Catholics and Greek Orthodox, where each one believes that the location of *his* church is the authentic one.

Guides gaze differently on Catholic and Protestant Christian tourists:

> Among the Catholics and Orthodox, the demand is to visit more holy places. If there are seven religious sites around the Sea of Galilee, they want to visit each and every one, without exception. It's in their itinerary. On the other hand, the Protestants are satisfied with visiting only two sites and passing by the other sites with a short explanation given on the bus; for example, the site where they believe Jesus walked with the apostles after His resurrection. Catholics and Greek Orthodox want to touch the very stones.

The guides also use everything they know to explain one sect to the other, as one of the interviewees describes:

> With the Protestants I am not allowed to talk about Mary and if I take them to a Catholic site I have to explain to them why in some cases Mary is more important for the Catholics than Jesus. There aren't any Protestant churches to Mary... With Protestants I usually dig deeper in the Bible, and they laugh more at the Catholics. On the other hand, the Catholics do not even recognize the existence of the Protestants, and they don't laugh. For example, the Catholics get upset that the Greek Orthodox or others have a section in the Church of the Holy Sepulcher.

Another interesting phenomenon is the specialization that some guides develop for members of a particular Christian sect, such as the Mormons. They have developed professional and social ties with the communities in Israel and abroad (usually the USA, in this case). Thus, their familiarity with and gaze on Mormon tourists are based on deep knowledge and close contact resulting from these ties. One of the tour guides who specializes in Mormon pilgrimages has developed friendships with Mormon communities in the USA over the years and has even visited them in their country. This is how she describes the situation:

> I prefer Mormons. I love people who are spiritual and have values. I really feel close to that, and most Mormons are like that. In their priorities, spiritual matters take precedence over concrete ones: ties between one person and another, mutual assistance and helping others.

In other words, the explanations she gives for her gaze are deep and a result of more than work relations with them as a tour guide. Here we can discern a very positive process that was described by Allport (1954) in his contact theory, in which social interactions lead to cross-cultural understanding, host gaze respect and even real friendship.

The Mormons are perceived as a unified family community and very pro-Israel. These beliefs are anchored in their religious tenets, as one of the tour guides who works with Mormon tourist groups describes:

> The Mormons are different from non-Mormons in that they are much more family oriented. I once entered a hotel with a group of American Protestants, in July – and the Americans were surprised: Why were so many children there? Couldn't their parents have found some sort of arrangement for them? Mormons would not have asked that – they go on holiday with their children. The Mormons are very pleasant, direct, easy to work with and very polite. They are very pro-Israel theologically, which makes working with them easy. Some Christian sects are more pro-Jewish or neutral, but it is hard to work with those who are anti – they're more pro-Arab. There are some groups like that among the Protestants – but not all. Among the British it's a mixed bag.

The Mormons are also very interested in Israel in part because it is a part of their religious outlook, as one of the guides related: 'The Mormons come very prepared. They receive a folder from which they learn about everything – the kibbutz, the Druze, everything – they prepare a year in advance.' In other words, this is an exceptional example of a tourism group that is perceived as having prior knowledge and a high level of interest in the tourism destination.

The Religious Factor

The study shows the great weight of religious characteristics on tour guides' gaze on religious tourists arriving in Israel. Previous studies found the effect of religious characteristics on the intensity of the touristic experience (Cohen, 1998; Fleischer, 2000; Collins-Kreiner et al., 2006) but apparently without relating to the religious dimension of the host's gaze.

The picture that emerges indicates a perception of non-religious tourists as easier to work with than religious tourists, apparently because work with religious groups must be adapted quite significantly to religious rituals and beliefs (Cohen, 1992, 1998; Smith, 1992; Collins-Kreiner and Kliot, 2000), both in terms of tour itinerary and content. In many cases religious groups are accompanied by their community pastor or priest, who plays a central role in the tour and in the pilgrimage experience. From the vantage point of the hosts, such an addition to the group comes at the expense and often in place of a broader familiarity and more multidimensional acquaintanceship with the cultural space being visited. The tour guides feels that their role in transmitting intercultural messages (Smith, 1992) is more limited than with secular tourists.

Noy (2011) writes critically about the dominance of imagined spaces made up of mindscapes, memory and fantasy in modern tourism. These imaginary spaces have taken root in the imagination of individuals and of groups. It would appear that tour guides are critical of the dominance among pilgrims arriving in Israel of the imagined space experience as opposed to the actual material space. Thus, many of these pilgrims have a better sense of the imagined space, which they call the Holy Land, than of the actual space of the State of Israel.

In the tour guide hosts' gaze, Christian tourists are clearly differentiated according to their sect affiliation. The tour guides gaze differently on Catholic tourists and Protestant tourists. It is also interesting that some tour guides specialize in groups from a specific sect within Christianity, such as the Mormons, where certain of the tour guides have developed professional and social ties with communities in their country of origin (usually the USA). Here we can discern a highly positive process that was created in the manner described in Allport's (1954) contact theory, in which social interactions lead to cross-cultural understanding and host gaze respect and even real friendship.

This chapter show that the religious factor has a great effect on much of the tour guides' impression of the tourists, and especially when the tour destination is of a pilgrimage or religious nature for most of the group. Religious affiliation and sect is also connected to many stereotypes about tourists' conservatism, political bent, the nature of the itinerary, prior knowledge and communication with the tour guides. Its findings definitely indicate the existence of clear stereotypes among professional hosts as they gaze on tourists.

Discussion: Dividing the Gaze

The basic idea of this research as a grounded theory approach was to read the textual database of our interviews and 'discover' or label the different gazes and to identify the more general categories. Accordingly, an analysis of the in-depth interviews with the tour guides indicated that it is possible to relate to the findings through a number of salient elements that emerged from the descriptions of the hosts' (tour guides') gaze on the tourists.

On the basis of these descriptions we developed four main types of host gazes on tourists. They were: (i) the 'initial gaze', which reveals the hosts' impression of the tourists' external appearance; (ii) the 'distinguishing' gaze, which identifies and distinguishes between religious and secular tourists and between religions and religious sects; (iii) the 'overall gaze', which forms an impression of the tourists' culture, education, previous knowledge and interest in the local culture of the visit destination; and (iv) the 'differentiating and analysing gaze', which identifies and analyses differences between people of different nationalities.

Thus, using grounded theory while researching the host gaze means that the researcher takes different cases to be wholes, in which the variables interact as a unit to produce certain outcomes. One of the outcomes is that personnel in the tourism industry, who serve as professional hosts, as Maoz (2006) found in her study, gaze differently on tourists than do other locals, and it is her contention that the professional hosts are usually less patient towards the

tourist. Furthermore, she maintains that exposing tourists to the gaze of locals only strengthens and perpetuates prejudices and stereotypes. Although this study did not examine the issue, its findings definitely indicate the existence of clear stereotypes among hosts as they gaze on tourists.

The findings also showed that in their gaze on tourists, tour guides tend to not filter out their own philosophical world-view on a given subject, so that their gaze may distort reality, making it more positive or more negative. The tour guide's spiritual beliefs may cause him to feel like a messenger of good will, for example, and his work as a tour guide is for him is the most suitable place for this mission, as was described by Cohen (1985), who referred to tour guides who are not only navigators who lead tourists to places and sites, but also guides who lead tourists into the inner depths of ideas and places and imbue them with a comprehension of the spiritual essence of a place. The tourists' gaze is often translated into communication strategies and behaviours that hosts adapt specifically to the tourists and their characteristics as these were identified in their gaze.

Summary: the Unique Contribution of Professional Hosts

The chapter addresses the unique contribution of the analysis of the professional hosts to the overall theory of host gaze. It proposes a four-stage gaze in order to describe the processes and elements that are reflected in the gaze of hosts on the tourists with whom they come in contact. As with Urry (2002), who noted that there is no one tourist gaze, and that in fact the gaze is a function of many factors that come into play, the findings of this study also lead to a similar conclusion. The findings also support the idea that gazes entail a chain of interrelated processes that occur over time.

While this 'divided gaze' was developed in the light of findings that emerged from interviews with Israeli tour guides about the groups they meet, it might also be applicable in other cases pertaining to other hosts, such as hoteliers or service personnel in souvenir stores, as well as to host gazes on tourist types other than those characteristic of the Israeli destination. These findings can also provide important information for communications between the two parties. Thus, we propose that future studies explore the different types of gaze that were identified in this study, among other kinds of hosts. The gaze of professional hosts on pilgrim tourists in the Holy Land also adds knowledge that can serve for comparisons with the gaze on pilgrim tourists in other places. It also adds to the understanding of the profile of religious tourists in modern times.

References

Allport, G.W. (1954) *The Nature of Prejudice*. Addison-Wesley, Cambridge, MA.

Amir, Y. (1969) Contact hypothesis in ethnic relations. *Psychological Bulletin* 71, 319–342.

Ap, J. and Var, T. (1990) Tourism and attitude change: Greek tourists visiting Turkey. *Annals of Tourism Research* 19, 629–642.

Bowman, G. (1992) The politics of tour guiding: Israeli and Palestinian guides in Israel and the occupied territories. In: Harrison, D. (eds) *Tourism and the Less Developed Countries*. Belhaven, London, pp. 121–134.

Carlson, J.S. and Widaman, K.F. (1989) The effect of study abroad during college on attitudes towards other cultures. *International Journal of Intercultural Relations* 12(1), 1–17.

Chan, Y.W. (2006) Coming of age of the Chinese tourists: the emergence of non-western tourism and host–guest interactions in Vietnam's border tourism. *Tourist Studies* 6(3), 187–213.

Cohen, E. (1979) A phenomenology of tourist experiences. *Sociology* 132, 179–201.

Cohen, E. (1985) The tourist guide: the origin, structure and dynamics of a role. *Annals of Tourism Research* 12, 5–29.

Cohen, E. (1998) Tourism and religion: a comparative perspective. *Pacific Tourism Review* 2, 1–10.

Cohen, E. (1992) Pilgrimage centres: concentric and excentric. *Annals of Tourism Research* 19(1), 33–50.

Cohen, E. (2002) A new paradigm in guiding: the Madrich as a role model. *Annals of Tourism Research* 29(2), 919–932.

Collins-Kreiner, N. and Kliot N. (2000) Pilgrimage tourism in the Holy Land: the behavioural characteristics of Christian pilgrims. *Geo Journal* 50, 55–67.

Collins-Kreiner, N., Kliot, N., Mansfeld, Y. and Sagie, K. (2006) *Christian Tourism to the Holy Land: Pilgrimage During Security Crisis*. Ashgate Publishing, Aldershot.

Creswell, J.W. (1994) *Research Design: Qualitative and Quantitative Approaches*. Sage Publications, Thousand Oaks, CA.

Dahles, H. (2002) The politics of tour guiding – image management in Indonesia. *Annals of Tourism* 22(3), 783–800.

Enevoldsen, K. (2003) See no evil, hear no evil: an 'outsider's' encounter with cultural tourism in South Africa. *Cultural Studies Critical Methodologies* 3(4), 486–502.

Fleischer, A. (2000) The tourist behind the pilgrim in the Holy Land. *Hospitality Management* 19, 311–326.

Flom, R.L. (2007) *Gaze Following Its Development and Significance*. Lawrence Erlbaum Associates Inc., Hillsdale, NJ

Gelbman, A. and Maoz, D. (2012) Island of peace or island of war: tourist guiding. *Annals of Tourism Research* 39(1), 108–133.

Glaser, B. G and Strauss, A. L. (1967). *The Discovery of Grounded Theory: Strategies for Qualitative Research*. Aldine Publishing Company, Chicago, IL.

Holloway, J. (1981) The guided tour: a sociological approach. *Annals of Tourism Research* 8, 377–402.

Kingsbury, P. (2005) Jamaican tourism and the politics of enjoyment. *Geoforum* 36, 113–132.

Litvin, S.W. and Kar, G.H. (2003) Individualism/collectivism as a moderating factor to the self-image congruity concept. *Journal of Vacation Marketing* 10(1), 23–32.

MacCannell, D. (2001) Tourist agency. *Tourist Studies* 1(1), 23–37.

Maoz, D. (2006) The mutual gaze. *Annals of Tourism Research* 33(1), 221–239.

Ministry of Tourism (2011) *Incoming Tourists – 2010, Final Report*. Jerusalem, Israel.

Milman, A., Reichel, A. and Pizam, A. (1990) The impact of tourism on ethnic attitudes: the Israeli Egyptian case. *Journal of Travel Research* 29(2), 45–49.

Moufakkir, O. (2011) The role of cultural distance in mediating the host gaze. *Tourist Studies* 11, 73–89.

Nolan, M.L. and Nolan, S. (1989). *Christian Pilgrimage in Modern Western Europe*. The University of North Carolina Press, Chapel Hill, NC.

Noy C. (2011) Imagined spaces as commodity: some critical comments on (in)visibility in tourism. In: Soffer, A., Maos, J.O. and Cohen-Seffer, R. (eds) *Cultural Landscape Patterns*. Chaikin Chair in Geostrategy, University of Haifa, pp. 221–232.

Pizam, A. (1999) The American group as viewed by British, Israeli, Korean, and Dutch tour guides. *Journal of Travel Research* 38, 119–126.

Pizam, A., Jafari, J. and Milman, A. (1991) Influence of tourism: US students visiting USSR. *Tourism Management* 12(1), 47–54.

Pizam, A. and Jeong, G. (1996) Cross-cultural tourist behavior perception of Korean tour guides. *Tourism Management* 17(4), 277–286.

Pond, K. (1993) *The Professional Guide: Dynamics of Tour Guiding*. Van Nostrand Reinhold, New York.

Riordan, C. (1978) Equal-status interracial contact: a review and revision of the concept. *International Journal of Intercultural Relations* 2(2), 161–185.

Rubin, H. and Rubin I.S. (1995) *Qualitative Interviewing: the Art of Hearing Data*. Sage Publications, Thousand Oaks, CA.

Salazar, N. (2005) Tourism and glocalization: 'local' tour guiding. *Annals of Tourism Research* 32(3), 628–646.

Schmidt, C. (1979) The guided tour: insulated adventure. *Urban Life: a Journal of Ethnographic Research* 8, 441–468.

Smith, V. L. (1992) Introduction: the quest in guest. *Annals of Tourism Research* 19, 1–17.

Strauss, A. and Corbin, J. (1990) *Basics of Qualitative Research Grounded Theory: Procedures and Technique*. Sage, Newbury Park, CA.

Stylianou-Lambert, T. (2011) Gazing from home: cultural tourism and art museums. *Annals of Tourism Research* 38(2), 403–421.

Smith, V.L. (2001) The culture brokers. In: Smith, V.L. and Brent, M. (eds) *Hosts and Guests Revisited: Tourism Issues of the 21st Century*. Cognizant Communication Corporation, New York, pp. 275–278.

Smith, V.L. (1992) Introduction: the quest in guest. *Annals of Tourism Research* 19, 1–17.

Timothy, D.J. and Olsen, D.H. (2006) *Tourism, Religion and Spiritual Journeys*. Routledge, London and New York.

Vukoni'c, B. (2002) Religion, tourism and economics: a convenient symbiosis. *Tourism Recreation Research* 27(2), 59–64.

Urry, J. (2002) *The Tourist Gaze*. Sage Publications, London.

7 Picturing Tourism: Conceptualizing the Gambian Host Gaze through Photographs

Helen Pattison

Introduction

In general, the current approaches to tourism research do not adequately explore, theorize or conceptualize the complexity inherent to local tourism spaces in the non-West as tourism studies have (largely) failed to engage meaningfully with the agency of the non-Western 'host' (Franklin and Crang, 2001; Tribe, 2006; Pritchard and Morgan, 2007). Indeed with the absence of a sophisticated engagement with ontology, epistemology and methodology, tourist studies can often be accused of, 'fixing the "ethnic" identities of peoples in tourism destinations into perpetual "otherness"' (Tucker and Akama, 2009, p. 513). The host–guest paradigm is framed by Western discourse that influences the way the researcher understands and conceptualizes the relationship between the host and guest, the definition of a host and the experience of the host in tourism space and place (McNaughton, 2006). The host–guest paradigm is no longer sufficient to conceptualize the complexity of the postcolonial tourism experience. The aim of this chapter is to deepen the understanding of the host gaze by bringing together several discussions from different fields that will open and deliver new lines of enquiry from which to analyse host processes. The chapter commences by briefly suggesting that

contemporary research on alternative tourism does not go far enough in engaging with the gaze of the host, particularly from the perspective of the host. The chapter then goes on to propose that the camera can be used by hosts as a tool of recording and reflecting upon the host gaze, by approaching the research through postcolonialism and a Foucauldian notion of relational power. This approach allows the researcher to conceptualize alternative discourses (to hegemonic Western discourse), which facilitates the understanding of tourism and the host gaze in non-Western communities. Empirical research is carried out at Tumani Tenda, a community-owned tourism camp in rural Gambia. Cameras were given to several of the Gambian hosts and subsequent photo-elicitation interviews conducted so that the hosts could capture and make visible their own feelings, experiences and understandings of tourists and tourism. Through engaging with the hosts' photographs and their explanations of them it can be suggested that the villagers perceive and experience community and tourism as a process that is framed by communal values and a philosophy of communalism. These concepts are inherent to the sub-Saharan and Southern African philosophy of *ubuntu*; a philosophy, culture and way of life that characterizes the communal nature of

African communities (Tambulasi and Kayuni, 2005; Eze, 2008; LenkaBula, 2008).

The chapter illustrates that by understanding 'community' and tourism from the perspective of the hosts (by engaging with local voices, locally produced images and discourses) a more complex and nuanced conceptualization of the host gaze within a community will be possible.

Approaching the Host Gaze

Eadington and Smith (1992, p. 3) define alternative tourism as, 'forms of tourism that are consistent with natural, social, and community values, and which allow both hosts and guests to enjoy positive and worthwhile interaction and shared experiences'. Alternative tourism involves the development of locally owned, small-scale enterprises that make use of local inputs to reduce the leakages associated with foreign-owned developments, foreign inputs and expatriate labour (Koch *et al.*, 1998). It emphasizes participation, equity, self-sufficiency, autonomy, local control of resources, and appreciates social complexity (Jackiewicz, 2006). However, the notion of 'community' and alternative tourism has been largely defined by the West. There are academics who question the appropriateness of transplanting Western concepts and alternative (albeit still Western) models of development into non-Western contexts; this is just another form of top-down, Western proscribed tourism development. In addition, 'community' and 'community participation' represent a romanticized view of communal cohesion and responsiveness (Bianchi, 2003). Bianchi (2003, p. 15) acknowledges that:

> Most, if not all, studies concerned with community involvement in tourism, recognise the complex and stratified nature of communities, however, they still do not go far enough in terms of theorizing the nature of power, conflict, development and political agency in the context of tourism.

The researcher of this study argues that understanding 'community' from the perspective of a (Gambian) host will facilitate a more complex and nuanced conceptualization of the development and role of community-based tourism and the host gaze. Such an understanding may be framed by Foucault's notion of relational power and postcolonialism.

Foucault (1982a, b) presents a complex, dynamic and localized form of agency and resistance of the subject through his description of power as a relation; every subject is an object of power but also has the capacity to exercise power through acting upon another; acting upon the actions or conduct of a subject. Furthermore, the subject is constituted through this possibility of resistance within power relations. Butin (2001, p. 169) explains, 'The individual is not passively made by power, but makes herself by being able to resist within power relations.' Using a Foucauldian notion of relational power enables the power and agency of the hosts to be explored – so breaking free from the tendency of tourism research to focus on the tourist (a form of power in itself) – and also to contextualize these experiences within micro- and macro-power dynamics that influence 'community'. As power is relational, diffuse and multi-directional the non-Western host is not passive within the tourism industry, tourism research or the tourist gaze (all largely Western-based and critiqued for 'othering' the non-West) but is able to act, resist and negotiate the many influences inherent to tourism spaces; the host becomes both the object and agent of power and Western colonial binaries of 'subject' and 'object', 'active' and 'passive' are deconstructed.

Postcolonialism also enables attention to be focused on the experience of the non-Western host within the tourism industry and host–tourist encounters. Treacher (2005, pp. 44–45) defines postcolonial theory as:

> a body of work that attempts to explore the inextricably linked relations between the western people and those from the non-West. It is a way of conceptualising, understanding and speaking about the complex relations between the colonised and the coloniser... Critically, it is committed to opening up a space in which

those without a voice can speak and be heard, to extending theoretical viewpoints and analysis, to encompass knowledges and understandings developed outside of the West. (Treacher, 2005, pp. 44–45)

Listening to non-Western peoples leads to the possibilities of alternative discourses to that of Western/colonial discourse (Dirlik, 1994) and again leads away from a focus on the Western tourist and the all-pervasive tourist gaze. As Foucault (1980, p. 131) declares, 'each society has its regimes of truth, its "general politics" of truth: that is the type of discourse which it accepts and makes function as true'. For the tourist researcher to understand the host gaze it must be recognized that there is more than one way of knowing and experiencing the world. Engaging with the values inherent to an *ubuntu* philosophy may be one way to apprehend the experiences of many hosts in southern and sub-Saharan African communities.

Ubuntu Philosophy

As Ramose (1999) believes, different ethnic groups in sub-Saharan Africa share similar ideals that are embodied in *ubuntu*; *ubuntu* is the underlying foundation of African communal cultural life (Tambulasi and Kayuni, 2005). It is a philosophy, culture and way of life that characterizes the communal nature of African communities (Tambulasi and Kayuni, 2005; Eze, 2008; LenkaBula, 2008).[1] Of importance is how a person conducts relationships with others, it is the 'capacity in African culture to express companion, reciprocity, dignity, harmony and humanity in the interest of building and maintaining community with justice and mutual caring' (Nussbaum, 2003, p. 2). *Ubuntu* expresses, 'our interconnectedness, our common humanity and the responsibility to each other that deeply flows from our felt connection' (Nussbaum, 2003, p. 2). An *ubuntu* philosophy positions 'self' within a network of social relationships (particularly kinship) that influences actions; 'The concrete person is a

web of interactions, a network of operative relationships... The dignity of human beings emanates from the network of relationships, from being in community' (Louw, 2004, p. 2). 'Beings' are inextricably linked to each other and to community as each constitute the other, as Archbishop Desmond Tutu declared; 'Africans have this thing called ubuntu... We believe a person is a person through another person, that my humanity is caught up, bound up and inextricable in yours' (Tutu Foundation UK, 2007). Thus each person works toward the common good, a collective pursuit of ends shared by members of a community, as what is good for the community is good for the individual and vice versa. *Ubuntu* can be understood as individuals coming together to form a whole (a community). Wholeness 'is a process of becoming in which everybody and everything is moving towards its fullest self, its best personhood, but which can only be reached through and with others' (Krog, 2008, p. 208). Eze (2008) feels the need to stress that individual subjectivity is not determined or created by community (and neither is the good of the individual subordinate to the community) but each are mutually constitutive; 'the place of the community and individual is defined through an inter-subjective formation between them' (Eze, 2008, p. 389). Examining these connections and inter-subjective formations enables us to understand configurations of community and identity, as 'At the heart of *ubuntu* lies an understanding of identity as it emerges through relationship; that is, the principle of interconnectedness' (Lewis, 2010, p. 69). As relationships are continuously forged and re-forged, identity is also constructed, deconstructed and reconstructed; 'Identity, according to this view, is not just moulded and fixed by the forces of history, but is an ongoing process that can take place in the present and is an expression of the existential, given moment. This concept of the constant forging of identity through relationship is what defines *ubuntu*' (Lewis, 2010, p. 79).

The empirical research revealed that many elements of the philosophy of *ubuntu* were practised at Tumani Tenda, and grasping this has enabled me to understand 'community' and tourism as a process. By linking a postcolonial Foucauldian framework of relational power with *ubuntu*[2] the researcher was able to focus on the hosts as agents acting within a web of (power) relationships to create and recreate community and (re)configure contemporary power relations (i.e. the perceived asymmetrical host–guest relationship). This chapter suggests that researching tourism in Tumani Tenda provides a lens through which such complexity of (this specific) 'community' can be conceptualized, whilst at the same time an understanding of 'community' (incorporating *ubuntu*) facilitates an understanding of the development, perception and experience of tourism from the point of view of the hosts. It is also possible to grasp what it means to be a host from the perspective of the local person.

The Role of the Camera in the Host Gaze

A useful but under-utilized method of perceiving tourism through the eyes of the hosts is to provide the hosts with cameras. The camera, as a scientific instrument and technology of research, was perceived as an appropriate method for conducting the objective, scientific research characteristic of the colonial moment. The camera played a central role in objectifying and 'othering', constructing and reinforcing binaries of primitive/modern, civilized/uncivilized, inferior/superior, and disseminating these to the Western public. The early tourist practice of taking photographs and consuming postcards reinforced racial stereotypes, reflecting the legacies of imperial representation (Ryan, 1997; Whittaker, 2009). These representations may also be traced in contemporary tourism images. Enwezor (2006) also writes about how touristic images have played their part in a 'vampiric machine'. Such images suffocate Africa; they stand in for a larger collective scene that generalizes the experiences of Africa and places Africa in a different time frame to the West. They provide signs for how the rest of the world

comes to know Africa thus, 'turning the practice of photography into a mythology factory' (Enwezor, 2006, p. 15).

The researcher of this study argues that the camera may be appropriated by different agents and embody alternative discourses and subjectivities so that multiple ways of knowing become available. The camera becomes a site, or tool, of resistance (to the hegemonic Western worldview). Postcolonial theory enables us to 'open up the notion of agency' and 'deepen our understanding of subjectivity by looking at its multiple forms, influences and meanings and opening up spaces where ... subjects are constructed' (Power, 2003, p. 126). Pinney and Peterson (2003) believe that analysing the uses of the camera provides a path for understanding subjectivity and recognizing agency. Postcolonial theory provides a framework for the decolonizing of the camera and also recognizes the camera's 'other' histories (Pinney and Peterson, 2003). Photography can be used to conceptualize alternative discourses to hegemonic Western discourses that involves 'exploring subaltern readings and re-uses of photography. It also requires exploring local modifications of a globalized technology and the ways in which photography can be transformed so it becomes a tool of local empowerment' (McEwan, 2009, p. 158).

Enwezor organized an exhibition of African photographers who engage with 'the continent's vast and complex visual world' (Enwezor, 2006, p. 18). Enwezor (2006, p. 18) describes the aim of the exhibition:

> I want us to direct attention to the multiple ways of representing African life and space, to enunciate forms of visual practice that open up to the facts that we not only share the same space but also the same time. In other words, I am speaking about visual practices that recognise coevalness, that reach beyond the stock images that have endured until now as the iconography of the 'abandoned' continent. (Enwezor, 2006, p. 18)

The photographs in the exhibition show us the diverse ways we can look at contemporary Africa, taken from an African perspective; a self-representation that presents

Africa in all its heterogeneity and multi-plicity. The exhibition arose through a desire to create a postcolonial culture and identity (Enwezor, 2006).

While visual methods have been used as a research technique within the social sciences, in tourism research they are 'simply not on the agenda' (Feighey, 2003, p. 78). The visual as a method in tourism is largely confined to content analysis and semiotic analysis of tourist media (Scarles, 2010). Photo-elicitation interviews (using researcher and tourist photographs and tourist media), have also been employed to gauge tourists' perceptions of landscape aesthetics in tourist destinations (MacKay and Couldwell, 2004; Jacobsen, 2007), the meanings that are attached to place (Stedman *et al.*, 2004), and the tourist's holiday experiences (Cederholm, 2004). The camera is an important part of the everyday tourist experience and can serve to reinforce colonial representations as tourists seek to capture the 'authentic' and exotic. However, the camera can be used by hosts to challenge the hegemonic Western representations of 'other' people and places. There have been few examples of this practice in tourism research and 'as a consequence [of the lack of visual methods in tourism research in general], a potentially rich seam of evidence that can inform our understanding of tourism as a social construct and set of phenomena has been under-utilized, not to say undermined' (Burns and Lester, 2005, p. 50).

Methodology

The field research was conducted at Tumani Tenda village and tourism camp, located in Kombo East, the western division of The Gambia. The village is approximately 45 years old, founded by the Sanyang and Sonko families who migrated from the Casmance region of southern Senegal. The village is currently inhabited by 300 people from seven families; all belong to the cultural group of the Jolas.[3]

Since official independence in 1965 the Gambian government has largely neglected the socio-economic development of rural Gambia, prioritizing investment in the development of the Tourism Development Area (TDA) to attract foreign transnational tourism corporations. In the TDA the government has invested in infrastructural development such as roads, communications systems, electricity supply and the expansion of an international airport. Up-country there is a visible lack of infrastructure, including poor roads and an inefficient public transport system. Tumani Tenda is a relatively isolated community with no running water or electricity supply. Rural areas, including Tumani Tenda, are dependent on agriculture for subsistence and their livelihood. However, there is a dependency on a single cash crop (ground nuts) and this is experiencing continuing losses. Rural areas appear to have been neglected by the government and the rural population marginalized. In addition, the Western tour operators do not encourage tourists to travel up-country by themselves; people and place are imaged as dangerous, unknown and 'other'.

Tumani Tenda tourism camp was established in 1999 to provide an alternative source of income for the village; it is the only example of tourism in The Gambia that is owned, developed and managed by the community. The camp is half a mile from the village situated next to a tributary of the River Gambia. It consists of seven huts made from walls of dried mud and thatched roofs and there is a central restaurant/bar that serves cold drinks and traditional Gambian food. Each family has one or more members that are involved in tourism and/or volunteer at the tourism camp. The core camp workers consist of a camp manager, four guides (one of whom is also the camp accountant), two cooks, a bartender/maintenance man and two cleaners. However, many of the villagers help out directly at the camp and also indirectly through growing and providing food for the camp and tourists and greeting tourists when they walk through the village. The majority of the villagers described themselves as 'hosts' regardless of the amount of contact they have with tourists; the villagers become hosts when tourists visit their community.

The research was conducted in 2008 over a two-month period within the peak tourism season in The Gambia (mid-January to mid-March). Disposable cameras were given to 16 Gambian hosts. Each camera had 27 exposures that were taken over 10 days. The camp manager and Pap, a local person who volunteers as a guide at the camp, decided who I should give the cameras to. These were all either camp workers or villagers who were under the age of 40.[4] The participants who are specifically referenced in this chapter include Pap and Sidou, two camp guides in their mid-20s who have extensive contact with the tourists. They take tourists on village tours, fishing and boat trips, nature walks and tours around the community garden, forest and farm. Pap and Sidou also take all their meals with the tourists at the camp and are on hand at the camp throughout the day. Another participant, Yassim (in her late 30s), is the camp cook and sister to the camp manager although she cannot easily communicate with the tourists as she does not speak English. Ente (a female in her early 30s) Mai (17) and Alieu (14) and Modou (nicknamed 'Teacher' by the villagers), are villagers who will greet tourists, talk to them and often help out indirectly at the camp (see the following sections for their role within the community and tourism).

For each participant the researcher demonstrated the technicalities of using the camera and gave them the same brief; to take photographs that encapsulated their perception of, feelings towards, and experience with tourists, their role in the tourism industry and the importance of tourism to their everyday lives. Once the films were developed, photo-elicitation interviews (PEIs) were held with each participant, varying in duration from 30 to 90 minutes. All of the interviews were recorded and the researcher's guide (Pap) acted as translator for one of the interviews (with Yassim). The most interesting discovery was the obvious absence of tourists in the hosts' photographs. However by asking 'Why the absence of tourists? What is being captured in their place?' an understanding of the host gaze (that explores dimensions of the gaze other than the imaging of tourists) can be gleaned.

Tape-recorders were also given to eight of the hosts asking them to record a 2-week diary of their daily involvement in tourism. However, as the researcher listened to each tape it became apparent that the audio-diaries were taking on a life of their own, becoming part diary, part autobiographical. The participants took it upon themselves to tell their own stories and reflect upon their perceptions of tourists and their role in the tourist industry; this resulted in many valuable and thick descriptions.

The following exploration of the host gaze is based upon reflection and analysis of the hosts' photographs (by both the researcher and the host participants through PEIs), audio-diaries, interviews and the researcher's observations, framed within critical postcolonialism and a Foucauldian notion of relational power.

The Host Gaze at Tumani Tenda: the Influence of an (Invisible) External Gaze

At Tumani Tenda there is an apparent absence of external influences directing the development of tourism and the construction of the host gaze. The community initiated the tourism camp in 1999 and own and manage it themselves. However, although the government and foreign tour operators do not have direct, visible power over Tumani Tenda with regards to tourism, there is evidence of an invisible presence of power, or an invisible gaze. This has influenced the actions and gaze of the local people as they utilize their productive relational power in a form of resistance; entering into national and global systems through community-based tourism.

Sidou tells of how the actions of the tour operators based at the coast influence the movement of tourists up-country:

> Tour operators they normally tell them moving from the beach to the local people is not safe... It's not safe to travel up-country because they don't want them to move from the beach to up-country. These are the

things they normally encourage them also not to move from the beach to the local people, to meet with the local people.

Sidou goes on to say of the tour operators:

> They want to keep the money for themselves, they don't want the money to come back to the local people, yeah. Because the money they are getting there it's not benefitting the Gambian people, money normally go back to ... the UK or outside the country to other countries.

Sidou believes that, 'nobody will be coming out to develop your community, your project; you have to do it for yourself'. This is an attitude of self-reliance that seems to be consistent with the practice of *ubuntu* by the community. Resistance to the marginalized and isolated position of Tumani Tenda at a national and international level has taken a form of productive action. Community members have taken the development of the community into their own hands effecting change in order to reach their full potential and open up new opportunities.

Picturing Tumani Tenda: a Sense of Community

When viewing discussing the hosts' photographs it came apparent that in order to understand the host gaze at Tumani Tenda

notions of 'self' and 'community' must also be understood from the perspective of the hosts. As this chapter goes on to illustrate, the hosts understanding and experience of tourism is inextricably linked to their conceptions of power, community, self and other as evidenced by the following photographs taken by the participants.

The hosts' photographs reflect the philosophy of *ubuntu*; the interconnectedness between individuals, the strong social bonds, kinship and a 'family atmosphere'. At Tumani Tenda *ubuntu* has become a way of life; a philosophy and a culture that defines the community and influences the values and actions of each community member. In the photographs each person has their own role and responsibility within the community. Alieu (Fig. 7.2) is responsible for tending to the cattle and he also has a role to play in the community garden.

Fig. 7.2. Self-portrait of Alieu tending to cattle.

Fig. 7.1. Mai's brothers and their friends play in the village. Photograph taken by Mai outside her family compound.

Ente works in the community garden and is also responsible for pounding couscous at the farm (Fig. 7.3). Mai cooks for her whole family daily. 'Teacher' teaches at the local primary school and is also responsible for distributing medicine to the community when it is needed. Each person is a valuable member of the community participating in community life and contributing to the well-being of the community as a whole; everyone has a part to play to enable the community to function effectively. Mai, Ente, Alieu and Yassim all took photographs of the community garden. The garden is the heart of the community; it is communally owned and each family has its own plot on which to grow vegetables. Despite the division of land into family plots the community works together as a whole, to enable its members to be self-sustaining.

The villagers participate in shared labour that spans across different generations.

Ente pounds the couscous with her family, ranging from young children to her grandmother. Mai's grandmother works with Mai in the community garden and her grandfather works at the farm. Children are instilled with communal values at a young age; to work together as a community for the benefit and development of the whole community. 'Teacher' takes photographs of community projects, including a fence. He explains:

Fig. 7.3. Photograph taken by Ente: pounding couscous.

I take this picture because it is work by the students. It is a fence ... it is made by the students in the school helping the teachers have a comfortable bathroom... That is also a big operation between the students and the teachers because they are always helping each other. When the teachers have work like this they organise the children to do it with them.

By participating in such projects the school children are gaining practical knowledge and skills and learning that the development of the community is in their own hands. This is a knowledge and attitude that is intrinsic to the community and as I will go on to describe, is an inherent part of the host gaze in tourism.

At Tumani Tenda there is a complex web of power between 'self', 'other' and 'community', which is framed by a philosophy of *ubuntu*. Foucault states that power is relational, that it can be analysed through people engaging and interacting with each other. Through this relational power each person can influence the other through their actions, and their ability to act (and react) constitutes the self. Perceived 'truths' can constrain or define possibilities for action; they can, 'govern the ways in which we can reflect on others and ourselves and, thereby, define a field of possible ways of acting on others and ourselves' (Owen, 1994, p. 156). Tumani Tenda's interpretation of *ubuntu* is internalized by the villagers; it becomes the norm, a perceived 'truth'. This communal philosophy guides the action of self and self's interaction with others. Self and other become inextricably linked to each other and to the community as each is interdependent on the other for their welfare and development. At Tumani Tenda interaction between individuals creates a collective action that is utilized to develop the community as a whole and also to ensure the welfare of 'self'. Power (networks) between selves (relational power) is productive; there is power *to*.

Understanding the Host Gaze: Community, Tourism and *Ubuntu*

This understanding of power and the relationships between self, other and community described in the previous section is intrinsic to explaining the host gaze and the development and role of tourism within Tumani Tenda. Few of the photographs taken by the villagers captured tourists. This is not because tourism is unimportant to these community members but rather that they have a certain way of understanding tourism based on the philosophy of *ubuntu*. As the photographs, diaries and interviews conducted at Tumani Tenda were analysed, and as the importance of the villager's definition of 'community' to all aspects of life became increasingly apparent, the researcher began to question her own (Western) assumptions of the host gaze and how the research methods were used. To ask participants to take photographs of tourists (even if it was to try and elicit local voices, experiences and perceptions) was to subconsciously assume that there was only one (Western) way to perceive of and understand tourism and the host gaze. This was perpetuating the Western notion of there being one 'truth' and by focusing on tourists as the subject of the photographs (and indeed the host haze), reinforcing the centrality of the tourist inherent to most tourism research. This reinforced the importance of enabling the participants to take the research in the direction they wanted it to go; enabling them to speak, and for the researcher to listen to the participants explain tourism through their own worldview, or particular 'truth(s)'.

In the participants' photographs the intangibles of tourism are often captured rather than the tourists. The intangibles – such as cooperation, social relationships, community cohesiveness and a work ethic – are the characteristics of the community that make tourism possible. Importance is placed on tour*ism* rather than tour*ists*; tourism is approached and understood holistically. It is part of a process that is integrated into the daily functioning of the community to achieve the common goals of self-sufficiency and community development. The series of photographs taken by Yassim (Figs 7.4–7.6) illustrate how tourism and community are entangled together into a holistic process, as she captures the various community inputs that go into producing a meal for the tourist's consumption.

Fig. 7.4. Vegetables for the tourists' meal are grown in the community garden. Photograph taken by Yassim.

Fig. 7.5 Fishermen (including Mola – see below) repair the nets that are used to catch fish to sell at the market and to feed the community and tourists. Photograph taken by Yassim.

Fig. 7.6. The grain store is representative of the farm labour that goes into producing porridge and bread for the community and the tourists. Photograph taken by Yassim.

In addition, the community processes shown in the photographs *are* tourism; they provide activities and attractions for the tourists. For example Mola, a village fisherman, combines fishing (for the consumption of the villagers) with taking tourists out in the fishing boat and teaching them how to fish with the nets and also how to make and repair the nets.

Encounters with Tourists and Tourism: an Opportunity for 'Creative Subjectivity'[5]

How the hosts perceive tour*ists* is entangled with the values inherent to *ubuntu*. A person with *ubuntu* is open to others; open to discovering and understanding alternative viewpoints through creative dialogue while maintaining their own culture/way of life (Eze, 2008; Lewis, 2010). Eze (2008, p. 395) calls this 'creative subjectivity'. At Tumani Tenda tourism has contributed to generating possibilities for 'creative subjectivity' of which many of the villagers have taken advantage. The desire for alternative (Western) knowledges and understanding though cross-cultural collaboration is reflected in the photographs and interviews.

Pap sees the value in exchanging ideas with the tourists; 'late in the evening then we all sit together and just a matter of discussing, exchange ideas what we see and how we see all our activities we have been to … if they have a good idea they can impose it to us'. 'Teacher' took a photograph of a half-built community computer laboratory that is being constructed near the school in Tumani Tenda. 'Teacher' believes that the computers will benefit the community, enabling them to access the internet and (inter-)connect and communicate with a global community. The computer laboratory is perceived as 'modern' and the computers are to be donated by a Dutch tourist, however its construction and use embodies the communal philosophy integral to Tumani Tenda. Thus the laboratory is a cooperative project between the community and the West that interrelate

'modernity' with communal values and a communal work ethic. In a similar vein Ente, Yassim and Alieu take photographs of the mechanical pumping system in the community garden. The pump was donated by a tourist and creates a more efficient communal watering system; the pump enables communal work but it also would not function without communal input. With these community projects technology is adopted and adapted to work within the value system of Tumani Tenda so that development (and productive power) is harmonious with community (and the *ubuntu* philosophy).

It is emphasized that Tumani Tenda does not want its culture to evolve into a Western culture:

> We have to maintain our culture; we teach them our culture and also they teach us their culture just to change our ideas on how we do our culture, but we cannot change our culture because our culture has started since our grandfather's grandfather's grandfather (interview with Abiyatou).

Fatou says she wants 'to know about Europe and what is going on in Europe', but she never wants to go and live there.

At Tumani Tenda the emphasis is on gaining new ideas and knowledge (about the West) that will have a practical use in the community. Knowledge of 'modern' technologies and culture that the Western tourists bring (to conversations and exchanges) are perceived of as different but not necessarily superior to, or incompatible with, the villagers' own way of life. There is no strict demarcation between host and guest, tradition and modernity, but an intertwining and blurring. There is a perceived equality of 'difference' that enables a reciprocal relationship as each benefits from the other. For example, for the tourist a tour around the community garden is an opportunity for an embodied experience of local daily life. Yassim explains that she is, 'very happy to show them and teach them'. For the local person the interaction with tourists is an opportunity to demonstrate the physical demands of such work through first-hand experience and point out the improvements that could be made to make life easier. In her audio-diary Amie talks about the benefits that tourism brings to the community: 'They [the tourists] come and ask what were the problems and we said water. They sponsor us with a generator which will pump water to the camp and also supply for garden. Now we can grow more vegetables and we have a good harvest.'

A part of the community's identity is its productive relational power and forward thinking. The host gaze becomes a gaze into the future, or a gaze that paves the way forward; a process rather than a static image of tourists or tourism. As Awa explains; 'We are now growing up further, not backward but we are going further because of the eco-tourism camp.' Amie (in her audio-diary) believes that, 'If we continue Tumani Tenda will become the best village in the whole country.' The Alcalo, Amie, Awa, Abiyatou and Yassim all agree that the productive power of Tumani Tenda should be emulated by others and they believe that it is their responsibility to impart their knowledge and experience of tourism for the good of the wider community. Again, the host gaze should not be thought only as a gaze upon tourists but (to the Tumani Tenda villagers at least) the host gaze involves sharing a gaze of responsibility and pride in community and nation. In her audio diary Amie reveals; 'This [tourism] is a great idea. This is the only example I've seen in The Gambia; we are trying to call people to come and learn what we are doing ... all the lodges that are here and the camps are owned by individual people, only TT is owned by the community so let them come and learn from us.' Amie goes on to say:

> Other villages come to learn from us, for example Kartong, they want to do the same thing. Limbangbolu[?] came to learn from us, from up-country. We tell them how we work, how we started the project ... even Guinea Bissau heard about Tumani Tenda and they say we will have to visit Tumani Tenda to learn and get experience from what they are doing... Today here in The Gambia, anywhere they are talking about TT now we are getting benefit from tourism.

The Mediation of the Host Gaze by the Local Guides

At Tumani Tenda three tour guides (Pap, Sidou and Sanna) all from the local community, mediate between the tourists and the local people. It is their role and responsibility to facilitate the cross-cultural exchange, interaction and communication between the local people and the tourists. This they do by guiding the tourists around the village and surrounding land, and accompanying them on various activities (such as cooking lessons, fishing trips). It is the guides who have the most contact with tourists and thus also facilitate the tourists' experience, interpretation and understanding of the people and place. The local guide has a dominant role in representing and communicating the host gaze, and their actions add another dimension to the social processes, interactions and productive relational power of 'community'.

The guides encourage the tourists to engage with their surrounding environment, to develop an embodied encounter with nature, one that surpasses the visual and the metaphorical, to engage the senses and make the tourist feel they are really 'doing' tourism. Tourists participate in activities that are represented by the guides to be the everyday for the local people of Tumani Tenda but are in a different time and place for the tourists. 'Back'-to-nature implies travelling back to a different time, escaping their modern (Western) lives to take up 'primitive' tools to work and sweat with the earth.

Pap and Sidou subtly advertise Tumani Tenda as a 'little piece of paradise' (comment in visitor book). Places outside of Tumani Tenda are dubbed as dangerous and 'other' by Pap, the safety of the tourist is only ensured if a guide is there to shield and protect the tourist: 'some of them they will tamper you, when they are hassling you asking for something ... those guys they will just watch you and the man will do whatever he want to do to you and then take money away from you by force'.

Fig. 7.7. Tourists and villagers participate in a forest clearing day. Photograph taken by Pap, a camp guide.

Fig. 7.8. Fajara Beach. Taken by Pap, a camp guide.

There is a clear contrast between the active, participating and interacting tourists at Tumani Tenda and the prone bodies lying on the beach at the coast (see Figs 7.7–7.8). Through the visual (reinforced through the PEI), Pap constructs his own binaries: dynamic, traditional, community values and embodied experiences at Tumani Tenda with an individual hedonistic tourist on display at the coast. In general the hosts believe either that beach tourists are lazy and that they cannot be 'bothered' to experience the 'real Africa', including the culture, food and people when they have everything they need at the resorts, or that the tourists are afraid for their own safety if they move

away from the beach resorts (not helped by the tour guides. For Sidou also, the tourists that lie on the beach are different from the tourists who come to Tumani Tenda: 'for them they don't want to interact with the local people because they have been fond of sitting on the beach because they don't use to these kind of things, to meet with the local people and discuss'. Both the guides encourage the tourists who visit Tunani Tenda to discuss the differences between their experiences at the coast and their experiences of Tumani Tenda.

Through the subtle construction and representation of place by the guides (by encouraging the negotiation of experiences between Tumani Tenda and the coast through discussion, and enabling an embodied encounter with nature and community) tourists are made to feel different and distanced from the coastal tourist and the negative images associated with them; the tourists that come to Tumani Tenda are special.

(Mis)representation and (Mis)use of 'Community' and *Ubuntu*: Latencies of Power Within Tumani Tenda Community

In appearance (an appearance constructed by the guides) the tourists become part of the community. However, the place and experience that the guides create for the tourists differs from that which the villagers wish to portray to the tourists. The guides (mis-)represent Tumani Tenda as a state of 'being' rather than in a process of 'becoming', reconstructing binaries and boundaries that many local people perceive of as discontinuous. For example, the guides construct a certain image of Tumani Tenda (for the tourists) by presenting carefully selected snapshots of community life. The guides accompany tourists on a tour around the village; it was observed that each group of tourists is taken to the same sights/sites (the central meeting area, the community garden and the school) every time. After participating in several of these tours the researcher came to realize that the guides were representing a different community to that which the local people had captured in their photographs. For example the oldest (so perhaps more 'primitive' or 'authentic') woman in the village (Fig. 7.9) was shown, as was the baker (who was asked by the tourist to take his top off exactly so he would look more 'primitive' and 'authentic'; Fig. 7.10).

On the village tours the guides did not point out any of the symbols of modernity that were captured in the villager's photographs; the (half-built) computer lab is bypassed, as is the new milling machine. The guides did point out the mechanical water pump in the community garden and explain the watering system however, the tourists had a superficial understanding as to the importance and meaning of this system; believing it to be 'primitive'. du Toit (2005, p. 849) writes within an *ubuntu* framework, a non-Western use of 'technology' 'is integrated with people's beliefs, customs, values and social life'. 'Modernity' embedded within an *ubuntu* philosophy; an extension of community life, may not be recognized or understood by Western tourists (in the same way as the

Fig. 7.9. Tourists photograph the oldest woman in the village. Researcher's photograph.

Fig. 7.10. Tourists photographing the 'authentic'. Researcher's photograph.

local people) and the guides did not explain to them the importance or context surrounding the water pump. An absence of (a contextual) explanation as to what the tourist gaze is being directed to may be just as much a misrepresentation of community culture (or the host) as what is left out of the tourist's gaze. To the tourists the village remains a place untouched by modernity as the guides create an alternative identity for Tumani Tenda based on Western images of the authentic 'other'; the villagers' host gaze is obscured and only partially influences the tourist's experience. Adding to this is the language barrier (the guides are proficient in English, while many of the villagers are not) and strong kinship ties. Lutz (2009, p. 324) believes that the *ubuntu* philosophy can be exclusionary as 'While traditional societies are non-individualistic, love-of-neighbour is often limited to a relatively small circle of neighbours.' At Tumani Tenda the presence of kinship and intimate friendship ties has excluded some community members from participating in tourism. Tension has arisen in particular over the lack of transparency over the decisions taken by the tourism camp manager. As one villager describes: 'We don't sit and discuss tourism and the camp, we don't discuss village development ... no one knows where the money is going to. We don't know how much the camp is earning and how much goes to the community.'

The research participants from the village made it clear that they benefit from tourism, and they emphasized the cross-cultural exchanges between themselves and tourists that contribute to productive relational power and the development of the community. However, this section has also discussed the role of the guides in constructing and mediating superficial interactions, and the inability of tourists and local people to communicate in any depth. In her audio diary Amie describes the type of tourists with whom she interacts: 'Some tourists will stay for one month researches. They learn Jola so when they go to the village they can interact. When they come to the village they will eat together and interact,

and come from the camp at night and sit with people and gather together and chat.' This is what the researcher of this study personally experienced, although most conversations were still mediated by a guide. The villagers appear to have the most interaction with and receive the most benefits from researchers and NGO workers rather than tourists who visit Tumani Tenda as part of their holiday. Most developments in the village were donated by NGOs, or sponsored by those who had stayed at the village for a few weeks at a time. These 'tourists' participate extensively in community life with the aim of understanding the community and there is a mutual desire by the 'tourists' and the local people to exchange knowledge.

Conclusion

While many authors have addressed the persistence of power in the West's construction of knowledge 'about' subaltern tourism spaces and places, there is limited in-depth understanding of the intricacy and dynamism of power, perceptions and experiences *within* these spaces and places. Particularly weak is how the hosts experience, create and negotiate power relations based on their local discourses and understandings of tourism and tourists. Franklin and Crang (2001) blame the narrow theoretical and methodological basis of tourism research for this deficiency, stating that tourism researchers lack the tools necessary 'to analyse and theorise the complex cultural and social processes that have unfolded' (Franklin and Crang, 2001, p. 5).

The research within The Gambia has illustrated the importance of moving away from the outdated host–guest paradigm to utilize a more sophisticated theoretical framework and a relatively innovative method (within tourism studies) that enables the researcher to gain a deeper insight into the complex web of power, relations and processes that occur at a local level within tourism spaces, with a particular focus on the host's experiences.

Attention should be placed on conceptualizing the host gaze as a process. At Tumani Tenda the host is not a static or passive 'being' as is portrayed by much tourism literature on subaltern hosts. Rather, the hosts continuously negotiate, work and rework influences such as various forms and relations of power (local, national and international), the discursive influences of the tourism industry, subjects (tourists and other 'hosts') and various concepts and values (such as tradition, modernity, *ubuntu*). The community has used its conceptualization of *ubuntu* as a resource to overcome the marginalizing power of the government and create a strong communal work ethic and the interconnectedness of individual roles and responsibilities (to form a functioning whole), which has contributed to the development of tourism. The villagers' understanding of tourism is inextricably linked to their notions of power, 'community', self and other (a holistic process guided by *ubuntu*) that is evidenced in the photographs that the participants took. The 'hosts', rather than 'being', are in a continuous 'process' as they consciously and unconsciously adjust their identities to adopt, adapt to and attempt to benefit from tourism within the context of such influences. Tourism researchers would benefit from using the term 'process' as a conceptual framework in order to gain deeper understandings of the multiple actions, identities and experiences of hosts within tourism encounters and tourism spaces. Utilizing this approach will give meaning to the term host, which is used loosely in much tourism literature, and also the host–tourist encounter.

In addition, the dynamic process of 'becoming a host' (and the power, practice and process involved in this) directly and indirectly influences the actions, perceptions and experiences of the tourists. Tourism space is continuously created and recreated to form various tourism places, as the 'hosts' utilize and display their various identities to the tourists, the tourism industry and each other. How tourism is approached and understood by the hosts may be different to Western conceptualizations (by the academy, the industry and tourists) of community-based tourism in a non-Western community. The Western tourism industry and tourism researchers should take note of this if successful, viable tourism projects are to be achieved in non-Western communities.

At Tumani Tenda the host gaze must be understood as a process rather than a narrowly defined gaze. The gaze is a gaze into the future, a gaze of responsibility to impart knowledge of tourism to other communities, a gaze towards Europe, a gaze upon tourists – of which there are different types: a short stay tourist, a researcher/NGO worker, a coastal tourist. There is also a simultaneous inward and outward gaze; towards self, community and towards a process of creative subjectivity. The host gaze can simultaneously be all of these gazes (along with others that may not have been uncovered through the research). The villagers' host gaze is often undermined by the host gaze of the tourist guides – their status as guide, and close contact with tourists gives them power to communicate their own version of Tumani Tenda. This version is based on the tourist gaze – the community is represented as authentic and traditional, a lost way of life for the Western tourists to experience bodily. The binaries of host–guest, tradition–modernity and self–other that the villagers deconstruct, are reconstructed by the guides.

This chapter has illustrated the importance of moving away from the outdated host–guest paradigm and the tourist gaze in order to gain a deeper insight into the host gaze. Such an aim may be realized by engaging with postcolonialism and a Foucauldian notion of relational power. The chapter has mainly concentrated on empirical research. The extent to which such an approach can lead to deep insights into the diverse and dynamic host gaze(s) needs further theoretical consideration. As does the conceptual value of broadening the understanding of tourism and community as a holistic process and of the host gaze as influenced by alternative discourses (to that of the West – e.g. *ubuntu*).

The camera was a site of experimentation during this research process, both for the research participants and myself; the process has demonstrated the potential value of utilizing cameras as a method that opens up and delivers new lines of enquiry regarding the host gaze(s). Tourism research would benefit from adopting and adapting the camera as a method, while critically relating its use to other tools of inquiry, such as conventional interviews. The research has illustrated that contextual information, in particular the explanation of photographs through interviews was crucial to understanding the meanings captured within the photographs from the 'host's' perspective. Conversely, images present a powerful means of conveying messages. Through the lens of the camera hosts can capture or create the 'realities' of tourism spaces as they 'see' and experience them; the hosts direct the research and bring attention to objects, spaces and practices that may be overlooked in the researcher-directed interview process. Thus this chapter suggests that further work should involve relating the utilization of cameras and traditional research methods and also reflecting critically on the utility of cameras and photography as contributing to the conceptualization of the 'host's' gaze(s) and alternative understandings of tourism spaces, encounters and experiences.

References

Bianchi, R.V. (2003) Place and power in tourism development: tracing the complex articulations of community and locality. *PASOS* 1, 13–32.

Burns, P. and Lester, J. (2005) Using visual evidence: the case of cannibal tours. In Ritchie, B. W., Burns, P. and Palmer, C. (eds) *Tourism Research Methods: Integrating Theory with Practice*. CABI, Wallingford, pp. 49–62.

Butin, D.W. (2001) If this is resistance I would hate to see domination: retrieving Foucault's notion of resistance within educational research. *Educational Studies* 32, 157–176.

Cederholm, E.A. (2004) The use of photo-elicitation in tourism research – framing the backpacker experience. *Scandinavian Journal of Hospitality and Tourism* 4, 225–241.

Dirlik, A. (1994) The postcolonial aura: third world criticism in the age of global capitalism. *Critical Inquiry* 20, 328–356.

du Toit, C.W. (2005) Implications of a technoscientific culture on personhood in Africa and in the west. *HTS Teologiese Studies/Theological Studies* 61, 829–860.

Eadington, W.R. and Smith, V.L. (1992) *Tourism Alternatives: Potentials and Problems in the Development of Tourism*. University of Pennsylvania Press, Philadelphia, PA.

Enwezor, O. (2006) *Snap Judgements: New Positions in Contemporary African Photography*. Steidl, New York and Gottingen.

Eze, M.O. (2008) What is African communitarianism? Against consensus as a regulative ideal. *South African Journal of Philosophy* 27, 386–399.

Faal, D. (1999) *A History of The Gambia AD 1000–1965*. Edward Francis Small, Serrekunda.

Feighey, W. (2003) Negative image? Developing the visual in tourism research. *Current Issues in Tourism* 6, 76–85.

Foucault, M. (1980) *Power/Knowledge: Selected Interviews and Other Writings, 1972–1977*. Pearson Education, Harlow.

Foucault, M. (1982a) Why study power: the question of the subject. In: Dreyfus, H. and Rabinow, P. (eds) *Michel Foucault, Beyond Structuralism and Hermeneutics*. University of Chicago Press, Chicago, IL, pp. 208–216.

Foucault, M. (1982b) How is power exercised? In: Dreyfus, H. and Rabinow, P. (eds) *Michel Foucault: Beyond Structuralism and Hermeneutics*. University of Chicago Press, Chicago, IL, pp. 216–226.

Franklin, A. and Crang, M. (2001) The trouble with tourism and travel theory? *Tourist Studies* 1, pp. 5–22.

Jackiewicz, E.L. (2006) Community-centered globalization: modernization under control in rural Costa Rica. *Latin American Perspectives* 33, 136.

Jacobsen, J.K.S. (2007) Use of landscape perception methods in tourism studies: a review of photo-based research approaches. *Tourism Geographies* 9, 234–253.

Koch, E., de Beer, G and Elliffe, S. (1998) International perspectives on tourism-led development: some lessons for the SDIs. *Development Southern Africa* 15, 907–915.

Krog, A. (2008) '... if it means he gets his humanity back...': the world-view underpinning the South African truth and reconciliation commission. *Journal of Multicultural Discourses* 3, 204–220.

LenkaBula, P. (2008) Beyond anthropocentricity – *botho/ubuntu* and the quest for economic and ecological justice in Africa. *Religion & Theology* 15, 375–394.

Lewis, B. (2010) Forging an understanding of black humanity through relationship: an *ubuntu* perspective. *Black Theology: An International Journal* 8, 69–85.

Louw, D.J. (2004) *Ubuntu*: an African assessment of the religious other. www.bu.edu/wcp/Papers/Afri/AfriLouw.htm (accessed 18 November 2010).

Lutz, D.W. (2009) African *ubuntu* philosophy and global management. *Journal of Business Ethics* 84, 313–328.

MacKay, K.J. and Couldwell, C.M. (2004) Using visitor-employed photography to investigate destination image. *Journal of Travel Research* 42, 390.

McEwan, C. (2009) *Postcolonialism and Development*. Routledge, London and New York.

McNaughton, D. (2006) The "host" as uninvited "guest"; hospitality, violence and tourism. *Annals of Tourism Research* 22, 645–665.

Nussbaum, B. (2003) African culture and ubuntu: reflections of a South African in America. *World Business Academy* 17, 1–12.

Owen, D. (1994) *Maturity and Modernity: Nietzsche, Weber, Foucault and the Ambivalence of Reason*. Routledge, London.

Pinney, C. and Peterson, N. (2003) *Photography's Other Histories*. Duke University Press, London.

Power, M. (2003) *Rethinking Development Strategies*. Routledge, London and New York.

Pritchard, A. and Morgan, N. (2007) De-centring tourism's intellectual universe, or traversing the dialogue between change and tradition. In: Ateljevic, I., Pritchard, A. and Morgan, N. (eds) *The Critical Turn in Tourism Studies: Innovative Research Methodologies*. Elsevier, Amsterdam, pp. 11–28.

Ramose, M.B. (1999) *African Philosophy Through Ubuntu*. Mond Books, Harare.

Ryan, J.R. (1997) *Picturing Empire: Photography and the Visualization of the British Empire*. Reaktion Books, London.

Scarles, C. (2010) Where words fail, visuals ignite: opportunities for visual autoethnography in tourism research. *Annals of Tourism Research* 37, 905–926.

Stedman, R., Beckley, T., Wallace, S. and Ambard, M. (2004) A Picture *and* 1000 words: using resident-employed photography to understand attachment to high amenity places. *Journal of Leisure Research* 34, 580–606.

Tambulasi, R. and Kayuni, H. (2005) Can African feet divorce western shoes? The case of 'ubuntu' and democratic good governance in Malawi. *Nordic Journal of African Studies* 14, 147–161.

Treacher, A. (2005) On postcolonial subjectivity. *Group Analysis* 38, 43–57.

Tribe J. (2006) The truth about tourism. *Annals of Tourism Research* 33, pp. 360–381.

Tucker, H. and Akama, J. (2009) Tourism as postcolonialism. In: Jamal, T. and Robinson, M. (eds) *The Sage Handbook of Tourism Studies*. Sage, London, pp. 504–520.

Tutu Foundation UK (2007) Ubuntu: putting ourselves back together. http://www.tutufoundationuk.org/ubuntu.html (accessed 18 November 2010).

Whittaker, E. (2009) photographing race: the discourse and performance of tourist stereotypes. In: Robinson, M. and Picard, D. (eds) *The Framed World: Tourism, Tourist and Photography*. Ashgate, Farnham, pp. 117–136.

Endnotes

[1]Of course as Lutz (2009, p. 315) states, 'To say that African cultures are communal is not to deny that they differ from one another. Believing that all African cultures are alike would be as mistaken as believing that all European cultures are alike.' However, 'it is true generally that Africans are less individualistic, more communal than Westerners'.

[2]The local people of Tumani Tenda did not use the term *ubuntu* themselves but they did describe a way of life that is underpinned by communal values and a philosophy of communalism (features of *ubuntu*). I do not wish to impose a label upon them or define the local people with this term. I use the word *ubuntu* with

sensitivity; it is simply a *word* or one way to describe an abstract *feeling*, a philosophy or a way of life that is hard to pin down and a concept that changes in meaning in different contexts/places (Tambulasi and Kayuni, 2005).

[3] Tumani Tenda is located on the border of the pre-colonial boundary of the Kingdom of Fogny, a settlement of the Jola group. The Jolas have their own distinct language, culture and customs, and their social organization is based on a communal system with particularly strong kinship ties (Faal, 1999).

[4] The practice of giving the hosts cameras revealed the dynamic nature of power in both the community, between the community and the guides based at the tourism camp, and in the research process (including my own positionality and the ethics of using visual methodologies). This process alone shed light on several gazes and is deserving of more attention

[5] Eze, 2008, p. 395.

8   You Never Know Who is Going to be on Tour: Reflections on the Indigenous Host Gaze from an Alaskan Case Study

Alexis Celeste Bunten

Introduction

From May through September each year, approximately 1.25 million people travel to Southeast Alaska's famed 'inside passage' via cruise ship. Market research reports that visitors to Alaska hope to experience wilderness, wildlife and scenic beauty followed by meeting Native Alaskans. Sitka, arguably the most beautiful coastal city in Alaska, is known for all of these factors in abundance. Home to the Tlingit Indians famous for their monumental northwest coast carvings and Potlatch ceremonies, it was once the capital of Russian America, and the city retains this cultural and historical past through its architecture and traditions. One Southeast Alaskan tour company, Tribal Tours, appeals to these desires by offering tours guided by local Alaska Natives, whose ancestors have called this area home for at least 10,000 years. Tribal Tours prides itself in delivering 'an opportunity to experience Alaska with real Alaskans'. 'Our Alaska Native guides have a personal connection to Sitka's history and culture, and you can feel the difference' according to its web site. Sitka Tribe of Alaska (STA) (2006) founded Tribal Tours in 1994 offering tours that focus on Sitka's history, culture, wildlife and nature from a local, Indigenous perspective. STA's general manager at the time, Ted Wright, remarked, 'tourists are looking for [the Native perspective], and too often they don't find it. We have exactly the right people in the right place to do that.'

STA must take part in Sitka's tourism industry under the constraints of existing international and national structures, which dictate the framework in which Tribal Tours may operate. At the international level, cultural tourism typically conforms to a format familiar to consumers and middlemen (such as planners, marketers and hoteliers). Typically, this takes the form of staging the world as a museum in which Indigenous cultures are experienced in a uniform, sanitized, synchronic design regardless of location, ethnicity and history. Thus, cultural tourism venues often invites visitors to imagine travelling 'back in time' before the 'contamination' of colonization through tactics such as entering a life size model of traditional housing, listening to hosts speak their ancestral language and watching them perform traditional dances in costume/regalia. Several scholars (Handler and Saxon, 1988; Kirshenblatt-Gimblett, 1998) have remarked upon this 'museumizing' of Indigenous groups through the paradigm of tourism, noting that heritage politics are, according to Appadurai (1990, p. 304), 'remarkably uniform throughout the world'.

By touring the sites of this global 'museum', tourists can ultimately affirm and reinforce what they think they already know about the world presented in a predictable format (Bruner, 2005). Perhaps more importantly, tourists are more likely to visit *the Natives* when they are presented in a familiar and comfortable mode.

Tribal Tours has worked, in part, to fit this mould by constructing the Sheet'ka Kwaan Naa Kahidi Community House, as a venue for the Sheet'ka Kwan Naa Kahidi dancers. In addition to the dance performance, Tribal Tours offers a number of tour products, mainly tours showcasing Sitka history and culture by motorcoach. These tour products capitalize upon Sitka's numerous attractions such as the Totem Heritage Center at the Sitka National Historical Park, the Sheldon Jackson Museum, the Alaska Raptor Center and others that have not been a part of conspicuous tourism development including the Tlingit "village" where Native people still live, and the Alaska Native Brotherhood Hall where local Natives still conduct meetings and events. In addition to built edifices, these tours highlight sites of historical interest as well as features of the natural environment including Mount Edgecumbe volcano, Indian River, Sitka Sound, and the flora and fauna that make up the Indigenous subsistence diet and medicine. While focused on the Native point of view, tour content includes Sitka history, the Tlingit culture, weather patterns, stories, jokes and general information selected by guides.

The tourist gaze has special implications for hosts living the aftermath of colonization and cultural genocide. Drawing from two seasons of fieldwork working for Tribal Tours, this chapter argues that hosts are not powerless in their responses to the tourist gaze. Rather, they draw upon their own conceptions of tourists through a reverse and parallel 'host gaze'. If the tourist gaze is a front stage activity, the host's gaze plays out in the back stage. Just as the tourist gaze reproduces asymmetrical power relations between visitors and members of subaltern cultures on display, the host gaze is an attempt to take back a modicum of power to define oneself and have a say in one's working conditions.

Scholars writing about Native American tourism point out that interaction between tourists and Natives may result in enhancing and upholding negative colonialist/Victorian/orientalizing stereotypes concerning Native peoples (Evans-Pritchard, 1989; Laxson, 1991; Lujan, 1993; Babcock, 1994; Nicks, 1999). John Urry (1990, 1992), discusses the power of 'the tourist gaze' whereby tourists wield power over locals through the way they look at them coupled with expectations of authentic appearance and behaviour. According to this model, tourists are understood to shape the outcome of cross-cultural encounters by giving preference to locals who look and behave in ways that are, in their minds, authentically indigenous or ethnic. Repeatedly meeting tourist expectations, in turn, attracts more tourists, but may irrevocably alter the hosts: a process Dean MacCannell (1984) refers to as 'reconstructing ethnicity'. As part of the process of succumbing to the tourist gaze, Indigenous tourism workers may unconsciously internalize the West's false images of them. In other words, in order to participate in the tourism market, Indigenous cultural tourism workers must become, to a degree, Westernized.

Nick Stanley (1998) refers to this perspective as 'the tradition of melancholia' in which ethnographic display is situated within a hegemonic global system that does not allow plural meanings to emerge for both host and guest participants in the cultural encounter. According to the tradition of melancholia, cultural demonstrations in the tourism setting are inherently exploitative, and inauthentic. The concept of a 'host gaze' that is at the same time both independent of and in response to the tourist gaze refutes this notion of passive participation in the dominant economies and systems of cultural representation. The host gaze speaks back to the tourist gaze in an attempt to reframe it. Just as tourists size up and coerce their hosts with the power of the tourist gaze, hosts interact with visitors based on a set of systematized beliefs about their guests.

Like the tourist gaze, which can change over the course of the touristic experience, the host gaze is not static. The host gaze gradually shifts from generation to generation, season to season and day to day. As the tourist gaze is informed by long-held stereotypical motifs about the culture being consumed, the host gaze is generated well before the tourist encounter. Native tourism workers' ideas about visitors are informed by cultural attitudes towards guests and how to treat them, as well as historical relations between Natives and non-Natives. These ideas are refined through customer service training designed to 'humanize' visitors, and improve communication between hosts and guests. The host gaze continues to shift through interaction with guests, and over the course of a tourism season. Ultimately, it becomes a memory of visitors long gone, and expectations for those to come. This chapter builds upon G. V. Doxey's (1976) evolutionary model of changes in locals' attitudes towards tourists (from euphoria, to apathy, annoyance and antagonism), and builds upon it arguing that the shifting nature of the host gaze can be a valuable psychological mechanism that helps hosts to better accommodate guests, protect them from the alienation resulting from self-commoditization, resist touristic stereotyping, define themselves vis-à-vis the dominant society and enjoy the positive aspects of working in tourism.

Historical Relations of the Host Gaze

Just as elements of the tourist gaze exist in their minds long before visitors ever encounter their hosts, hosts' assumptions about visitors are likewise formed over prolonged periods. Although Tribal Tours is the first company in Sitka to market tours from an Indigenous perspective, the city's Native peoples already had over a century of experience of hosting Euro-American visitors. This engagement in tourism, combined with over 200 years of relations with Russian then American colonizers, helped to shape Tribal Tours workers' suite of

understandings, expectations and imaginings of today's visitors encapsulated within the host gaze.

Formal tourism began in Sitka shortly after the USA's 1867 purchase of the territory of Alaska from Russia.[1] While the Russian colonizers profited mainly from the fur trade, the Americans were interested in exploiting all of Southeast Alaska's natural resources through permanent settlement of the territory. American settlers, backed by the US military might, quickly relegated Sitka Natives to the lowest social status, systematically disenfranchising them from equal political and economic participation in Euro-American settler society.[2] Sitka's Tlingit people began to entertain the earliest tourists against this backdrop of inequality, selling their handicrafts to visitors seeking mementos from their trip.

News of Alaska's natural wonders began to trickle down to the lower 48 states as military men, outdoorsmen, adventurers, prospectors and surveyors wrote home to tell about their experiences in America's newest territory. The first tourists arrived in the 1870s with the advent of regular steamship passage between west coast ports and Alaska. As the territorial capitol, Sitka was a major port of call on these itineraries that only the wealthiest members of American society could afford. As word of mouth spread about the monumental glaciers, soaring mountains, exotic wildlife and peoples of the Alaska's famed 'inside passage', more and more Americans came to see Southeast Alaska for themselves. By 1890, some 5,000 visitors had already come to the region (Hinckley, 1965, p. 71). By this time, Southeast Alaska Natives had experienced a great deal of change. In less than 25 years since the sale of Alaska to the USA, Southeast Alaska Natives had already lost much of their lands, subsistence economy and civil rights to become second-class citizens in their ancestral homelands while forced to assimilate to a new American society and its cash economy, beliefs and way of life.

Travel brochures capitalized upon Victorian notions of progress to help sell the steamship passage. One reprinted passage from the Juneau *Free Press* describes the

Tlingit as 'the artistic savages of the world' whose 'marvels of savage work' would serve as perfect 'romantic remembrances of a yet more romantic journey back to civilization' (1887, p. 12 in Kan, 2004). The widespread belief that tribal peoples were living examples of mankind's evolutionary path from primitive society to civilization highlights the influence of evolutionary theory on emerging social sciences that confused biology with culture and codified 'social progress' with the racial hierarchies of physical anthropology through pseudo-scientific measurements of different 'races'.

The tourist gaze of the Victorian era positioned Alaska Natives as 'savages' in the process of assimilating to the American way of life. This ideology of Native American 'progress' along a path to civilization justified US Federal policy to appropriate Indigenous peoples' resources while 'educating' them in US-run schools designed to assimilate them to the dominant society. The American public viewed Native Americans dichotomously as closer to nature and therefore doomed to extinction, and able to be acculturated into mainstream American society. Within this paradigm, Indigenous arts and handicrafts were considered both as artefacts of a dying race, and as a pathway to civilization that 'teaches' Natives how to engage in a cash economy.

Tlingits were savvy profiteers, greeting tourists as they walked off the gangplanks of their steamships and onto the docks where Native women sold a 'great many wares of their own manufacture, such as baskets, hats, and stockings, also canes and miniature totem poles, manufactured by their husbands or brothers' (Hinckley, 1996, p. 255). In addition to artefacts, tourists could pay to take a picture with a Native, or sometimes view a dance performance staged during summers when dancing was not a ceremonial feature.[3] Though their views of tourists can only be conjectured, these records indicate that Sitka Natives understood visitors' relative wealth and did not relinquish their goods without attempting to gain the best price possible. Several 19th century tourists noted the shrewdness of Sitka Tlingits selling their wares. Travel

writer, Eliza Ruhamah Scidmore, pointed out that 'there was no savage modesty or simplicity about the prices asked' (1885, p. 90). Echoing this sentiment, Septima Maria Collis observed in her 1890 memoir of her trip to Alaska that the prices Tlingit women asked for their baskets, spoons, bracelets, rings, miniature totem poles, and so forth, 'were exorbitant in the extreme, and they [the sellers] seemed to have a trades-union understanding among themselves that, having once fixed a price, they would adhere to it to the last' (Collis, 1980, pp. 97–98, in Kan, 2004). Another visitor, Kate Field, determined that Sitka Indians grew so greedy under the influence of tourists that they covered up some of their best relics, '"pay quarter you see. You no pay quarter, you no see..." was a squaw's laconic comment' (Hinckley, 1965).

Wealth and status are integral aspects of traditional northwest coast North American cultures, and the Tlingits proved to be astute traders. Before contact with Europeans, they traded extensively among themselves and other tribes for practical and prestige goods. By the time tourism arrived, Tlingit men and women had been working in the fishing, canning, mining and timber industries for a number of years. They developed ways to attribute monetary value to northwest coast handicrafts as well as how to bargain for handmade curios through prior interactions with professional museum collectors who swarmed the region throughout the final quarter of the 19th century.[4] Sitka even boasted an 'Indian Princess', Thom, a high caste woman who became wealthy by acting as an intermediary between Native artisans and prospective buyers (Hinckley, 1965, 1996; Kan, 2004). After her 'image' was codified by a portrait that was published in *The Thlinkets of Southeastern Alaska* (Knapp and Childe, 1896), Princess Tom became a tourist attraction in her own right with tourists visiting her home to purchase baskets, bracelets, earrings and carvings she purchased from Tlingit artisans in other villages along the coast (Gmelch, 2008, pp. 64, 162). The photographers who made the image of Princess Thom 'famous'

admitted that local Euro-American residents were well aware of the fact that the
noble origin and wealth of this woman was
blown out of proportion by naive visitors
(e.g. Knapp and Childe, 1896, pp. 106–107)
providing evidence that Princess Thom
consciously crafted her image to capitalize
upon the Victorian era tourist gaze. Though
what she thought of her visitors is unknowable, it is likely that Princess Tom consciously capitalized upon narratives of
social Darwinism that heralded Native art
as evidence of a dying race. She sold Tlingit objects out of her home in the Tlingit
'village' or 'ranche', marketed by the town's
white leaders as a place where 'savage'
Indians still resided.[5]

By the turn of the 20th century, Sitka's
civic leaders saw tourism as a source of
extra cash as well as an incentive to keep
Natives busy making souvenirs and enter-
taining tourists instead of engaging in 'antisocial' behaviour. Although Sitka boasted
more tangible sites of historical interest to
the traveller than most other ports of call at
the turn of the 20th century, tourism in
Sitka ground to a halt during the Second
World War. While some people continued
to visit Southeast Alaska after the Second
World War via air service and ferry, tourists
would not return to Sitka in measurable
numbers until 1970 with nearly 150,000
arrivals. With demand outpacing transport
options and infrastructure, cruise companies began to operate in Southeast Alaska,
growing throughout the 1980s and 1990s to
stable numbers around 200,000 throughout
the 2000s. However, these numbers have
been impacted by the economy. Cruise
numbers were around 135,000 in 2010,
down 30% from 220,000 the year before.
Tribal Tours mainly caters to the cruise ship
passenger.

Although the demographics are not
static, today's average cruise ship passengers to Alaska can be described as a middle
aged, white, married, ethnically Christian
from middle America. Typically affable,
they may know a little about the region's
specific ports of call through advertisements
and brochures on board the cruise ship.
They are familiar with a set of informal

norms and rules that regulate interaction
between tourists and tourism workers at
cruise ship destinations. On the surface, the
throngs of people arriving in Sitka by cruise
ship may appear similar, but upon deeper
examination, even those arriving by cruise
ship compromise a diverse crowd.

Mitigating the Host Gaze

Indigenous involvement in Sitka's early
tourism mirrored their lives in many ways
– they had scant control over both. Under
the military might of the US Army and
Navy, economic pressures brought forth by
the cash economy, religious conversion and
cultural assimilation through the boarding
school system, Tlingits were politically
weakened during the 'Americanization' of
Alaska. Alaska Natives were not allowed to
own land according to the 1884 Organic
Act, nor did they enjoy the benefits of
citizenship. White racism against Natives
was blatant, and the graduates of the Sitka
Industrial Training School often found it
difficult to attain the mainstream acceptance promised to them. While Sitka's
Tlingit population did not accept this way
of life, they resourcefully came to work
within the structures of the American political economy eventually becoming powerful lobbyists for themselves, and all Alaska
Natives in issues of civil rights, land claims
and participation in the mainstream economy. The legacy of this historical backdrop
can be detected within the dynamics of the
host gaze within this setting.

Oftentimes Indigenous tourism workers feel ambivalence towards their clients.
Sherry Ortner, writes, 'in a relationship of
power, the dominant often has something
to offer, and sometimes a great deal (though
always of course at the price of continuing
in power)' (1995, p. 175). On one hand,
Indigenous tourism workers feel a sense of
pride in sharing cultural excellence with
admiring visitors, who frequently compli-
ment their guides on their appearances,
traditions and values. Native American
tourism workers tend to embrace some of

the stereotypes that play out through the tourist gaze, that they are 'closer' to nature than non-Natives, or that they must somehow lead 'simpler' lives than members of the dominant ethnicity. On the other hand, facing the demands of interpersonal service work coupled with more negative stereotyping tears at positive feelings of self-worth and may invoke deep-seated intergenerational psychological pain associated with the after effects of colonization. For example, one Tribal Tours' guide reported a tourist who insisted on loudly repeating aspects drawn from colonial accounts of a very traumatic event when her ancestors marched across Baranoff Island in retreat after the battle of 1804 against the Russian invaders. Without allowing this guide to explain, the tourist informed the entire tour group that this group of Tlingits murdered their own children to prevent the Russians from following the sounds of their cries, slayed the elderly to keep them from slowing the group down, and then ate the remains of the dead. The guide cried as she recounted this story, and did not come back to work the next day, too emotionally drained from the previous day's events. For Indigenous tourism workers, serving visitors who belong to the dominant society runs the risk of exposure to harmful stereotypes and ideologies used to justify the horrific and inhumane acts of colonization. Although they represent a minority, visitors who maintain these racist ideas usually justify them by twisting the social outcomes of colonization (such as poverty, alcoholism, inability to contribute to the dominant economy, and so on) into 'evidence' to substantiate their racism.

Tribal Tours' management understands that some of their workers may have ambivalent and even negative feelings towards non-Native visitors to whom they are obligated to offer excellent customer service. Management understand that workers may feel sensitive about elements of the tourist gaze that relegate them to the status of the colonized 'Other', or more modern stereotypes such as the lazy 'rich' Indian. They are also aware that some of their workers

may have limited experience working in the service industry. For these reasons, and to maintain a high quality of customer service among its employees, Tribal Tours includes an 'Alaskahost' hospitality certification component during staff training. As the primary mode of intervention management can employ to shape the host gaze, AlaskaHost is arguably the most important part of the overall training process. Once new employees interact with tourists, they tend to shape their own ideas about their guests based in part on the dynamics of the workplace, but also informed by their emotional responses to the postcolonial conditions of colonization. Therefore, it is essential to set in motion ways of thinking about guests that help tourism workers to avoid equating visitors with any pre-existing ambivalent feelings about representatives of the dominant society.

The AlaskaHost programme web site describes it as customer service instruction that helps employees to understand the importance of providing quality customer service, recognize and anticipate customer needs and expectations, understand the economic value of the visitor industry to the State of Alaska and learn how to deal with dissatisfied customers in a professional, helpful manner. The programme teaches the meaning of customer service, the economic benefit of tourism to the state of Alaska, the power of first impressions, and how to recognize and assist different types of angry customers. One of the first impressions exercise handouts states:

> To your customers YOU are the business you work for, and perhaps the only contact they may have with your company or community... From the first impressions made through your personal and telephone contact, customers will come to conclusion about what kind of person is serving them, what they may expect in the way of service and whether or not you intend to pay attention to their needs.

One exercise simulates real life situations in which a tourist might become difficult. This lesson simulates irritated tourist 'types' including 'the passive complainer', 'the aggressive complainer' and 'the constructive complainer', along with advice about how to de-escalate them. One of the most effective de-escalation techniques emphasized in AlaskaHost training is to express sympathy with the tourists' point of view. The handout reads:

> Imagine you've gone through a year of scrimping and saving, three months of debating, two months of planning, one month of budgeting, three weeks of preparing, two weeks of mapping, one week of packing and days of travelling...
> A little warm hospitality could do wonders, couldn't it? After all, visitors are customers and people just like you.

Most of the strategies that Alaska Host training imparts can be understood under the general category of 'emotion work', a critical component of the service industry in which the emotional style of offering the service is part of the service itself. Arlie Hochschild describes emotional labour as requiring one 'to induce or suppress feelings in order to sustain the outward countenance that produces the proper state of mind in others – in this case, the sense of being cared for in a convivial and safe place' (1983, p. 7). Successful emotional labour, thus, invokes an artificial intimacy within a setting normally associated with polite, public distancing. When tourism workers treat visitors like old friends through the telling of personal jokes and stories, they transmute the private emotional behaviour of intimate conversation, to the public act of tour guiding. They invoke the host–guest paradigm.

To consistently summon friendly feelings towards visitors, the tour guide must summon good feelings for her customers. Emotion work requires some self-deception on the part of the worker, akin to method acting. Also referred to as 'deep' acting, Russian director, Constantin Stanislavski, developed the technique that urged actors to self-induce real feelings. Deep acting, according to Hochschild, 'has always had the edge over simple pretending in its power to convince ... in jobs that require dealing with the public, employers are wise to want workers to be sincere, to go well beyond the smile "that's just painted on".' Once the tourism worker learns, and eventually masters the techniques of emotion work, their emotional activities are, to a degree 'under the control' of the employer. By training themselves to feel positive emotions towards visitors, tourism workers insert a stop-gap into unconstructive patterned thought processes about strangers and members of the dominant society who tend to make up the majority of visitors.

Mediated by the customer service skills such as those taught in AlaskaHost training, the host gaze is under more conscious control than the tourist gaze. After all, hosts' livelihoods depend upon their success in the workplace. Before hosts and guests ever meet face to face, the tourist and host gazes are being formed. Motifs about the exotic Other feed the power of the tourist gaze through mass media, entertainment and official doctrine codified through the 'official' history taught in schools and beyond.[6] Even at this stage before the tourist encounter, the Indigenous host gaze is quite complex, 'from at least three worlds: the world of their own culture which provides a traditional sense of identity, the post-modern world of Western dominated business practice and consumerism, and a world of interaction between these two cultures' (Ryan, 1997, p. 259). Hosts share the same media as their guests, and are therefore very familiar with dominant society tropes about Native Americans and Indigenous peoples in general. These understandings are further mitigated by intergenerational, first-hand experience of these stereotypes (whereas tourists do not necessarily trace a direct line of descent to the acts of colonization, the colonized always do). Finally, the host gaze requires Indigenous tourism workers to engage in some degree of conscious rewiring of their emotional circuitry to manage their conceptions of visitors. This emotion work must override any negative associations with legacies of colonialism that Indigenous workers may feel in regard to the dominant society, and it helps them to respond to the tourist gaze via the host gaze.

Shaping the Host Gaze

The summer tourism season begins shortly after workplace training ends. Recently trained workers are eager to meet the tourist gaze, their own host gaze adjusted to include idealized notions of their customers, but they quickly come to learn that most tourists do not wish to experience Indigenous cultures on Indigenous terms. Faye Ginsburg (2002, p. 48) describes a 'the burden of representation' in which Indigenous cultural producers must create an Indigenous presence in an industry that is dominated by non-Indigenous institutions and agencies. In order to participate in the global economy of tourism, local tour vendors must package their product according to industry standards.[7] Indigenous tourism sites around the world seem to share the same techniques for staging and presenting culture to outside audiences. This 'cultural tourism formula' includes: (i) the greeting; (ii) the Native guide; (iii) demonstrated use of the heritage language; (iv) traditional architecture; (v) a performance; (vi) a gift shop or souvenirs for sale; and often (vii) demonstrations of traditional Native crafts (Bunten, 2010).

Part of Tribal Tours' sustainability can be attributed to following the cultural tourism formula. Visitors begin their experience with Tribal Tours with a Native tour guide who greets them in both Tlingit and English. The guide then drives the tour group through Sitka pointing out historical sites of interest (in the same manner as any motor coach tour anywhere in the world). The Native dance performance takes place in the *Sheet'ka Kwaan Naa Kahidi* Community House, a replica of a pre-contact Tlingit clan house. After the performance, the dancers take pictures and chat with the tourists. While the Tribal Tours experience is unique in cultural, spatial and historical content, it resembles many cultural tours throughout the world.

Dramaturgical analysis sheds light on the predictable uniformity of exchanges that take place between the host and guest. 'Front stage' and 'back stage' are defined as 'a place relative to a given performance, where the impression fostered by the performance is contradicted as a matter of course and is hence, hidden from tourists' (Goffman, 1959). Tribal Tours' workers are thus, 'on stage' from the moment they interact with visitors. For most workers, going onstage means projecting a persona, from their appearance to tour content, that satisfies aspects of the tourist gaze.[8] Likewise, tourists assume pre-determined roles and generally understand a set of informal rules of conduct within the tourism setting.[9] Because both hosts and guests typically follow unspoken conventions of the tourism format, one tour often resembles the next from the content presented, to the way it is presented. Crang (1997, p. 143) refers to this communicative structure within the tourism setting as product performances, 'pre-established, if rarely tightly fixed, social definitions of the settings being produced and consumed'.

The predictability of the tourism formula and the product performances that take place within it establishes a discursive space within the cross-cultural encounter. Visitors pay to fraternize with 'real Natives', but they are afraid of 'real' difference. Laura Peers elaborates:

> [tourists] may be further discomfited by being face to face with a Native person for the first time in their lives; by feeling uncomfortable because they are unfamiliar with Native culture; and by being afraid that they will say something to offend the Native interpreters. Suddenly, there are a lot of 'real' – but also uncertain –things going on. (Peers, 2007, p. 146).

While they are eager for an encounter with 'the Other', tourists often do not willingly shed their culturally dictated attitudes towards Indigenous peoples and modes of interaction with strangers. They want their hosts to have a voice, but still conform to stereotypes implicit in the tourist gaze.

Although Indigenous hosts employ emotional labour to buffer themselves against the forced intimacy of the tourism encounter, they run the risk of self-alienation amplified by visitors' desires for the Other. Alienation occurs when there is an increasing disparity between the worker's power over the product of their labour and the demands for it through capitalist expansion. In other words, as the tourism workers' identity becomes less something that simply exists under the workers' sovereign control and more something commanded by the dictates of the tourist gaze, it becomes commoditized. Dean MacCannell argues that emphasizing ethnic difference can cause a 'distinctive modern form of alienation, a kind of loss of soul' (1992, p. 168). In a similar reverse process, the host gaze mitigates against this alienation by dehumanizing visitors as ideal types.[10] If the tourism worker understands the touristic interaction as between ideal types projected through the tourist and the host gaze, then his or her real identity, or soul, is no longer at stake through the activities of self-commodification.[11]

Tribal Tourism workers' categorize visitors into broad types according to class, age, race and nationality. Although nearly all tourists fit into a very broad middle class bracket, they represent a wide range of incomes and lifestyles. Some cruise companies cater to the budget tourist, those who cannot regularly afford lavish vacations. These visitors tend to sign up for Tribal Tours' inexpensive, 1-h city tours. Other cruise lines cater to wealthy world travellers who take several lavish vacations a year. These more cosmopolitan tourists tend to pre-book Tribal Tours' exclusive tours, and often have a specific interested in learning about Indigenous cultures. Many of them invest in high-end Indigenous art objects, and are therefore, more likely to 'do their homework' before coming on vacation. Tribal Tours guides enjoy interacting with both high and low end visitors for different reasons. Guides spend more time with these customers due to the structure of exclusive tours, which are often longer in duration, smaller in passenger numbers and catered to the customers' wishes. This personal interaction fosters positive cultural exchanges between hosts and guests. On the other hand, tourism workers also feel some solidarity with their more frugal customers on the shorter, more crowded 1-h city tours where the dialogue sticks closer to more working class interests and patterns of speech.

Tourists travelling to Sitka are representative of larger racial patterns throughout the US. While most visitors are Euro-American, there are a few African-American, Hispanic, Asian American and Native American tourists. As such, Tribal Tours guides clamour to give tours to the occasional African-American and Hispanic tourists (there aren't enough Indigenous tourists to fight over). Encounters with these visitors provide Tribal Tours' workers an opportunity to interact with other Americans of colour with whom they feel some solidarity relative to larger patterns of American structural domination.[12] When the entire tour is made up of a minority group, Tribal Tours guides sometimes 'flip the script', inviting their guests to compare their experiences as a minorities living in America to its Alaska Native counterpart.

International tourists arrive in smaller numbers than domestic visitors. Tribal Tours guides tend to avoid them due to communications and cultural barriers. Most foreign tourists talk over their guides throughout the tour. This scenario only became a real problem when non-English speaking foreigners are on tour with English-speaking passengers who want to listen to the tour narrative. When this happens, English-speaking American tourists often scold foreign tourists who do not know the 'script' and rules of their guides' 'product performances'. As both groups interrupt each other, neither is satisfied, and guides earn fewer tips for their effort.

Tribal Tours workers further typecast foreign visitors into 'nationalities' that may or may not correspond to visitors' actual countries of origin. Although Tribal Tours workers make a living promoting cross-cultural understanding, many of them having never ventured very far from Alaska are simply not exposed to enough different kinds of people to discern the nuances between some ethnic groups. Similarly, certain nationals are viewed as 'non-tippers', middle easterners regardless of national and ethnic origins are often referred to as 'Arabs', and so forth. This aspect of the host gaze reflects stereotypes and imaginary con-structs circulated through local and national discourse and refined into ideal types through multiple interactions, revealing that these Indigenous tourism workers share as many assumptions about their visitors as guests have towards their hosts!

Categorizing visitors is not a knee-jerk response to cross-cultural interaction medi-ated within the rules of the service industry and ideological tropes of the dominant soci-ety. Tourism workers use these typologies and the behavioural expectations that accompany them to manage the commodi-fied cross-cultural interaction. It prepares them to give certain tours tailored to specific groups, and what kinds of tips to expect for their efforts. If workers are primed knowing that a particular group of visitors may not pay attention, and that this is not a reflection of their' labour, workers are less likely to feel alienated. Typecasting tourists allows hosts to exercise a certain small power over the demands of a service industry job – a power in which they can determine which visitors to serve regardless of supply and demand.

The Host Gaze as Meta-Discourse

Each year, Tribal Tours' tour guides are sur-prised by the people they meet on tour from leaders, to celebrities, wealthy industrial-ists and world-renowned scholars to every-day people. Visitors arrive in every size, colour, gender and age from around the world. They travel alone, with their fami-lies, lovers, alumni, business partners, col-leagues, clients, friends, entourages and interest groups. They belong to different social classes, represent different educa-tional levels and have very different ideas about what to expect when they meet a 'real Native'. For these reasons, despite the care-ful calculations concerning which tour groups to take and which to avoid, tour guides try to treat each group on a one-by-one basis following the oft-repeated mantra, 'you never know who is going to be on tour!'

Metacommentary refines the host gaze as workers constantly shift between public

and private displays of identity for different audiences and develop a heightened aware-ness of multiple discourses of their identi-ties. They come to the workplace with their own ideas about what it means to be Indig-enous gained through personal experience. Workplace training adds another layer of interpretive understanding. Codified in the tour script and reinforced through Alaska Host training and cultural workshops organized by management, workers absorb Tribal Tours' narrative of collective iden-tity. Throughout these processes, tourism workers converse with each other, generat-ing moments of metacommentary. 'Back stage' conversations provide tour guides the means to self-reflexively replay parts of their tour presentations to each other, load-ing the replayed spoken text with new lay-ers of meaning through discussion.[13] They talk about who does their job well and who doesn't, who makes scheduling mistakes, how to improve the timing of tours, how to glean more tips, ticket sales techniques, the funny things tourists say, where to show visitors wild animals, and so on. These con-versations help tourism workers to better perform their jobs and they serve as the main forum in which they negotiate how to present themselves as representatives of Native Alaskan cultures to tourists.

Through these discussions, tourism workers work out the protocols and ethics of cultural transmission across contexts. What material to include and how to broach sensitive subjects is a common challenge for workers at cultural tourism venues in places of colonial conquest. For example, some Tribal Tours guides stated that their tour groups might view them as 'hostile' if they express too much charged emotion against European colonizers of the past. Guides also know that if they discuss tragic events in history, they are in danger of calling forth internalized, intergenerational pain attached to these events. Once these feel-ings rise to the surface, emotional labour cannot always suffice to bring guides back to their personas for the rest of the tour. Dis-cussing Native inclusion at historical re-enactment sites in the Great Lakes region, Laura Peers writes:

Equally challenging has been the question of to what extent sites should communicate the damage caused to Native peoples by the historical eras and processes they represent: showing agency, adaptation, and resilience is a good balance to older messages that Native peoples became either extinct or assimilated as the result of European contact, but such positive messages now tend to veer away almost entirely from the darker aspects of Native–White relations: alcohol abuse, disease, dispossession, and racism are touched on, but seldom incorporated into the central messages of public history sites (Peers, 2007, pp. 50–51).

These moments of negotiation among cultural producers over the transmission of local knowledge transforms the workplace into a 'crucial site' (Hall, 1986) where 'discursive consciousness' (Giddens, 1979) arises from cross-cultural interaction mediated by consumer demand. Crucial sites of metacommentary invoke a high level of awareness among tour guides of the activities and ideologies surrounding cultural perpetuation and representation. Indigenous people working in tourism display a sophisticated understanding of 'what it means to be Indigenous' from both a local viewpoint, as well as those of tourists. This critical reflexivity produced in response to the tourist gaze renders the tourism site as a

'new space for defining new parameters of identity, livelihood, and meaning' (Adams, 2003, p. 571).

The 'tourist gaze' is a form of power, but there is also an inherent empowerment in presenting one's own culture for outside consumption. Operating in conflict with the demands of the tourism industry to always remain friendly, approachable and polite, the host gaze is a tool that workers use in the back stage to control their emotional and physical labour in the front stage. In an industry whose profit is driven by both customer volume and satisfaction, the host gaze serves as a way to keep the product of workers' labour within boundaries erected to prevent alienation. It helps hosts release negative feelings through mental categories applied to certain groups of tourists who do not play by the generalized, unwritten social 'rules' of the tourism encounter. The host gaze is dynamic; metacommentary helps hosts to adapt their feeling about their guests over time preventing them from objectifying their clients over repeated interaction. Ultimately, Indigenous tourism workers' responses to the tourist gaze often result in positive feelings of self-worth, and as part of a larger project to promote their identities as something special, worth passing on within and across cultures.[14]

References

AlaskaHost Program (nd) AlaskaHost Program www.dced.state.ak.us/ded/dev/AlaskaHost/home.htm (Accessed 28 July 2011).

Adams, K. (2003) Cultural displays and tourism in Africa and America. *Ethnohistory* 50(3), 567–573.

Appadurai, A. (1990) Disjuncture and difference in the global economy. In: Featherstone, M. (eds) *Global Culture*. Sage Publications, London, pp. 295–310.

Babcock, B. (1994) Pueblo cultural bodies. *Journal of American Folklore* 107, 40–54.

Bailey, B. (2001) The communication of respect in interethnic service encounters. In: Duranti, A. (eds) *Linguistic Anthropology: a Reader*. Blackwell Publishers, Malden, MA, pp. 119–149.

Bruner, E. (2005) *Culture on Tour, Ethnographies of Travel*. University of Chicago Press, Chicago, IL.

Bruner, E. and Kirshenblatt-Gimblett, B. (1994) Maasai on the lawn: tourist realism in East Africa. *Cultural Anthropology* 9, 435–470.

Bunten. A. (2008) Sharing culture or selling out? Developing the commodified persona in the heritage industry, *American Ethnologist* 35(3), 380–395.

Bunten, A. (2010) More like ourselves: indigenous capitalism through tourism. *American Indian Quarterly* 34, 285–311.

Cole, D. (1995) *Captured Heritage: The Scramble for Northwest Coast Artifacts*. University of Oklahoma Press, Normal, OK.

Coser, L. A. (1977) *Masters of Sociological Thought*. Harcourt, Brace, Jovanovich, San Diego, CA.

Craik, J. (1997) The culture of tourism. In: Rojek, C. and Urry, J. (eds) *Touring Cultures: Transformations of Travel and Theory*. Routledge, London, pp. 113–136.

Crang, P. (1997) Performing the tourist product. In: Rojek, C. and Urry, J. (eds) *Touring Cultures: Transformations of Travel and Theory*. Routledge, London, pp. 137–154.

Drew, P. and Heritage, J. (1992) *Talk at Work: Interaction in Institutional Settings*. Cambridge University Press, Cambridge.

Doxey, G. V. (1976) A causation theory of visitor-resident irritants: methodology and research inferences. In: *The Impact of Tourism, Proceedings of the 6th Annual Conference of Travel Reservation Association*. San Diego, CA, pp. 195–198.

Evans-Pritchard, D. (1989) How 'they' see 'us': Native American images of tourists. *Annals of Tourism Research* 16, 89–105.

Giddens, A. (1979) *Central Problems in Social Theory*. University of California Press, Berkeley, CA.

Ginsburg, F. (2002) Screen memories: resignifying and traditional in indigenous media. In: Ginsberg, F., Abu-Lughod, L. and Larkin, B. (eds) *Media Worlds: Anthropology on New Terrain*. University of California Press, Berkeley, CA, pp. 39–54.

Gmelch, S. B. (2008) *Tlingit Encounter with Photography*. University of Pennslyvania Museum of Archeology and Anthropology, Philadelphia, PA.

Goffman, E. (1959) *The Presentation of Self in Everyday Life*. Doubleday, Garden City, NY.

Hall, S. (1986) Gramsci's relevance for the study of race and ethnicity. *Journal of Communication Inquiry* 10, 5–27.

Handler, R. and Saxon, W. (1998) Dyssimulation, reflexivity, narrative, and the quest for authenticity in living history. *Cultural Anthropology* 3(3), 242–60.

Hinckley, T. C. (1965) The inside passage: a popular gilded age tour. *Pacific Northwest Quarterly* 56, 67–74.

Hinckley T.C. (1996) *The Canoe Rocks: Alaska's Tlingit and the Euramerican Frontier 1800–1912*. University Press of America, Inc., Lanham, MD.

Hochschild, A. R. (1983) *The Managed Heart: Commericalization of Human Feeling*. University of California Press, Berkeley, CA.

Johnson, K. and Underiner, T. (1994) Command performances: staging Native America at Tillicum Village. In: Jones Meyer, C. and Royer, D. (eds) *Selling the Indian: Commercializing and Appropriating American Indian Cultures*. University of Arizona Press, Tuscon, AZ, pp. 44–61.

Kan, S. (2004) 'Its only half a mile from savagery to civilization': American tourists and the southeastern Alaska Natives in the late 19th century. In: Mauzé, M. and Kan, S. (eds) *Coming to Shore, Northwest Coast Ethnology, Traditions, and Visions*. University of Nebraska Press, Lincoln, NE, pp. 201–220.

King, J. (1997) Marketing magic: process and identity in the creation and selling of native art and material culture. In: Mauzé, M. (eds) *Present is Past; Some Uses of Tradition in Native Societies*. University Press of America, Lanham, MD, pp. 81–94.

Kirshenblatt-Gimblett, B. (1998) *Destination Culture: Tourism, Museums, and Heritage*. University of California Press, Berkeley, CA.

Knapp, F. and Childe, R. L. (1896) *The Thlinkets of Southeastern Alaska*. Stone and Kimball, Chicago, IL.

Laxson, J. D. (1991) How 'we' see 'them': tourism and Native Americans. *Annals of Tourism Research* 18, 365–391.

LeFevre, T. (2004) Seizing identity, manipulating globalization: The Wetr Dance Troupe in Lifou, New Caladonia. BA thesis, Dartmouth College Department of Anthropology, Hanover, NH.

Lujan, C. C. (1993) A sociological view of tourism in an American Indian community: maintaining cultural integrity at Taos Pueblo. *American Indian Culture and Research Journal* 17, 101–120.

MacCannell, D. (1973) Staged authenticity: on arrangements of social space in tourist settings. *American Journal of Sociology* 79, 589–603.

MacCannell, D. (1984) Reconstructed ethnicity tourism and cultural identity in third world communities. *Annals of Tourism Research* 11, 375–391.

MacCannell, D. (1992) *Empty Meeting Grounds: The Tourist Papers*. Routledge, New York, NY.

Nicks, T. (1999) Indian villages and entertainments: setting the stage for tourist souvenir sales. In: Phillips, R. B. and Steiner, C. B. (eds) *Unpacking Culture: Art and Commodity in Colonial and Postcolonial Worlds*. University of California Press, Berkeley, CA, pp. 31–15.

Nuttal, M. (1997) Packaging the wild: tourism development in Alaska. In: Abram, S., Waldren, J. and MacLeod, D. (eds) *Tourists and Tourism; Identifying With People and Places*. Berg, Oxford, pp. 223–238.

Ortner, S. B. (1995) Resistance and the problem of ethnographic refusal. *Comparative Studies in Society and History* 37, 173–193.

Peers, L. (2007) *Playing Ourselves: Interpreting Native Histories at Historic Reconstructions.* Alta Mira Press, Lanham, MD.
Rossel, P. (1988) Potlatch and the totem: the attraction of America's northwest coast. In: Rossel, P. (eds) *Tourism: Manufacturing the Exotic.* International Work Group for Indigenous Affairs, Copenhagen.
Ryan, C. (1997) Maori and tourism: a relation of history, constitution, and rights. *Journal of Sustainable Tourism* 5, 257–278.
Skidmore, E. (1885) *Alaska: Its Southern Coast and the Sitkan Archipeligo.* Lothrop, Boston, MA.
Silver, I. (1993) Marketing authenticity in third world countries. *Annual Tourism Research* 20, 302–318.
Sitka Tribe of Alaska (2006) Main. http://sitkatours.com/index.html (accessed 10 November 2008).
Spradley, J. (1975) *The Cocktail Waitress: Woman's Work in a Man's World.* John Wiley & Sons, Inc., New York.
Stanley, N. (1998) *Being Ourselves for You: the Global Display of Cultures.* Middlesex University Press, London.
Urry, J. (1990) *The Tourist Gaze.* Sage Publications, London.
Urry, J. (1992) The tourist 'gaze' revisited *American Behavioral Scientist* 36(2), 172–186.

Endnotes

[1]Tlingit Indians have inhabited the Sitka area for some 10,000–15,000 years. By the late 1700s, the Tlingit people had already experienced numerous encounters with Spanish, French, British and Russian explorers, but it was the Russians who would initially colonize Alaska. The first Russian explorers came to Sitka in 1741 drawn by the great wealth that could be generated through the sale of sea otter pelts to China. The Russian American Company (RAC) first established a settlement in 1799 whose inhabitants were massacred by the Tlingits during a sneak attack in 1802. The Russians returned in 1804 to battle once more with Sitka Natives, this time with reinforcements that included two great battleships and roughly 300 Russian and Aleut men. Although the Tlingits never acknowledged a formal defeat, 5 days after Baranov's arrival in Sitka Sound, a substantial number of Tlingits retreated to the Northern end of Shee, renamed Baranov, Island for 20 years, after which the Russians claimed deed to the Tlingit village *Sheet'ka*, renaming it *Novo-Arkhangel'sk.* Under financial pressure from increased involvement in the Crimean war and expense of maintaining a large overseas colony, Russia sold the territory of Alaska to the USA in 1867. At the time of the US purchase of Alaska, roughly three generations of Sitka's Native population had already lived alongside the Russian, Finn, Aleut and Native-Russian Creole settlers working for the RAC trading post and ship building factory, headquartered in Sitka.
[2]The territory of Alaska was maintained under martial law administered first by the US Army (1867–1877), then the US Navy (1879–1884). In a preemptive show of force, the US military attacked several Southeast Alaska Tlingit villages to prevent Alaska Natives from rebelling against the American takeover.
[3]Evenings ashore granted some sightseers a faint reminder of vanished Tlingit glories. Then it was the natives would build a large blazing fire, don their colorful wolf and bear costumes, and, while dancing to a slow, pounding beat, chant of departed splendors. Occasionally, the chief would address the white spectators, and few, if any, of his listeners were quite able to forget the poignancy and power of the Indian's unpolished rhetoric. (Wiley, Yosemite, p. 159. A. L. Lindsley *Sketches of an Excursion to Southeast Alaska c.*1881, in Hinckley, 1965, p. 72)
[4]In his 1995 publication, *Captured Heritage: the Scramble for Northwest Coast Artifacts*, Douglas Cole discusses many of the strategies used by museum collectors, and Natives in the sale of authentic artefacts. An example of such is in the passage:

> The Indians were of course, astute enough not to simply wait for collectors to come to them. Newcombe noted that the recently converted Kaigani villagers took their dance properties and sold them at high prices at Ketchikan and Wrangell. George Hunt was baffled by the high prices demanded by the friendly Cove Nootka. 'I never see any Body like these People for asking so a High Price for there things as this People, for they say that they can go to Seattle and Tacoma and get High Price for there things for What Ever they Bring there.' Despite the ability of the sellers to seek Metropolitan prices, a significant discrepancy remained. In 1886, Boas estimated that his $70 Nuwitti collection was worth $200 at Victoria Prices and Swanton in 1900 found Skidegate prices half of those in Victoria.

This back-and-forth exchange between collectors and Natives likely resulted in heightened awareness among the Natives of Western categories of value and exchange.

[5]In contrast to the 'ranche' or Indian village, Sitka's white civic leaders encouraged visitors to marvel upon the accomplishments of missionary and educational institutions. Sergei Kan writes, 'a visit to the Sitka Industrial School ... was part of every tourist's itinerary (e.g. *The Alaskan*, 1890, p. 2). Thus, a visitor to Sitka could literally make a journey from "savagery", the old Indian village, to "civilization" the Industrial School and the cottages, in less than a half-hour' (Kan, 2004).

[6]Craik makes the argument that 'cultural experiences offered by tourism are consumed in terms of prior knowledge, expectations, fantasies, and mythologies' generated in the tourist's origin culture rather than by the cultural offerings of the destination (1997, p. 119). One major source of tourist expectations is located in the marketing efforts of tour operators (Rossel, 1988; Urry, 1990; Silver, 1993; King, 1997; Nuttal, 1997). Urry (1990) writes, 'what people gaze upon are ideal representations of the view in question that they internalize from postcards and guidebooks (and increasingly from TV programmes). And even if they cannot, in fact, "see" the natural wonder in question they can still sense it, see it in their mind.'

[7]Scholars have written about some of these attractions such as the Masai attraction at Mayer's Ranch in Kenya (Bruner and Kirshenblatt-Gimblett, 1994), The Tjibao Cultural Center in Noumea, New Caledonia (LeFevre, 2004), Northwest Coast Native Tillicum Village just outside of Seattle Washington (Johnson and Underiner, 1994), the Yunaan Nationalities Village in Kunming, China (Bruner, 2005), to name a few. In order to gain a feeling for the real global presence of the formula, one need only to perform an internet search, type in a non-Western global culture and a host of web sites appear describing cultural attractions that fit the cultural tourism formula profile.

[8]Through self-commodification, people working in the tourism industry package and present their identity for outside consumption. This process entails developing a commodified persona in the tourism workplace setting in which cultural tourism workers portray themselves as representatives of an 'authentic' culture in response to tourists' desires, but they do so on their own terms. For further discussion and analysis of the commodified persona, see Bunten, 2008.

[9]For example, hosts and guests both implicitly accept that hosts explain, and guests listen, ask questions and make comments.

[10]'Ideal types' refers to a method for categorizing and analysing patterns of phenomena. Ideal types never exist in reality, but can be used as an abstract 'short hand' to describe reality. It aggregates sets of particularities within of a class of objects, people or phenomena into a unified analytical construct, allowing them to be compared with each other. Max Weber identified three kinds of ideal types along a continuum of abstraction, first those rooted in historical particularities as 'the Western city'; second, those involving abstract elements of social reality, as 'bureaucracy'; and third, behavioural predictions, as in propositions of rational actor behaviour in economic theory (Coser, 1977, pp. 223–224).

[11]I define self-commodification as 'a set of beliefs and practices in which an individual chooses to construct a marketable identity product while striving to avoid alienating oneself throughout the duration of interaction with an outside, purchasing party'. Self-commodification is a dual process; it is both an economic response to the global expansion of the service sector, and a politically motivated expression of identity. The emotional labour combined with the cross-cultural skills necessary to entertain groups of tourists contribute to the Native tour guide's construction of a 'commodified persona'. The self-commodification taking place at the tourist site is conducted within a well-ordered framework of political, economic and social structures. However, there is room at the individual level to respond to micro- and macro-structural political–economic domains, and even to confront them. Ultimately, the worker expresses free choice over the way she constructs a commodified persona, but these choices affect the market value of the self as a commodity. Finally, the commodified persona is a heuristic formed through responses to human interaction. The commodified persona is not, as so many aspects of tourism are accused of being, a simulacra. While the commodified persona meets tourist expectations to many degrees, the person behind it usually does not openly accept himself/herself as an object of commodification.

[12]African Americans make up 0.5%, Hispanics make up 4.9% and Asians make up 5.7% of Sitka's total population according to the 2010 census.

[13]Scholarly texts that examine and analyse conversation in the workplace include Spradley, 1975; Drew and Heritage, 1992; Bailey, 2001.

[14]Other scholars observing the commodification of indigenous cultures have noted that outside recognition and appreciation results in an increase in local pride among the source culture group. See LeFevre, 2004; Peers, 2006.

9 Looking Down, Looking Out and Looking Forward: Tibetan Youth View Tourism in the Future

Mao-Ying Wu and Philip Pearce

Introduction

Metaphors and similes are powerful tools to help individuals and social groups understand their worlds. Moscovici (1988) in his theory of social representations suggests that such linguistic and cognitive devices make the unfamiliar familiar. They help us convert the strange and unusual into entities we can mentally digest. Researchers as well as citizens and social groups also rely on metaphorical devices to aid their understanding of social life. Tourism researchers have been frequent users of these tools (Bowen and Clarke, 2009). In the lexicon of tourism terms there are anthropological approaches that depend on crossing thresholds and transferring between spaces (Leach, 1961; Graburn, 1977; Turner and Turner, 1978), there are psychological models employing motivational ladders (Pearce and Lee, 2005), there are theatres with front and back stages (MacCannell, 1973) and there is the concept of gaze (Urry, 1990) as an iconic statement intended to capture the process of tourist consumption.

As readers of this volume will be very aware, the concept of gaze is under its own close scrutiny in this set of chapters. To adopt a further metaphor to explain the existing one, the term gaze is being stretched, its elasticity tested and its relevance to contemporary tourism potentially at the point of over-extension. This chapter pursues three notable themes – a non-Western setting, a location with a rapid evolution of tourism and a focus on the future – to continue the exploration of the gaze concept. It explores these three themes by focusing on how young Tibetans, unused to tourism and isolated from other examples of tourism's effects, view the future of the tourism sector in their distinctive context.

The distinctive themes of the chapter can be noted in some more detail. The original formulation by Urry (1990) building on the sociological work of Foucault (1976), Walter (1982) and to a lesser but implicit extent on MacCannell (1976), was conceived within the strong traditions of Western scholarship and attendant attitudes to the environment and other people. Examining the operation of gaze within a culture considerably removed from the historical traditions of how to view other people and the world is a clear extension of the dominant research tradition. Additionally, for Urry and the authors to whom he has been linked, tourism has been a readily visible and ongoing phenomenon in their communities and their work reflects examples of tourists and communities drawn from a long history of tourism growth and expansion. In many of these communities, such as the Lake District cited in much of Urry's work, tourism has evolved slowly but inexorably over the past 100 years. In such locations the citizens as well as the tourists themselves have been subject to a long induction in how to view each other. In the research context pursued in this chapter there is a different history. Not only is the context one of Asian culture, but it is also one of massive rapid and recent evolution of the attendant tourist–local social interaction. The effects of this revolutionary and rapid learning process are likely to be more akin to an intensive short course rather than a lengthy education. Furthermore, and not unimportantly, the gaze with which the founding authors have been concerned has been retrospective. This temporal tradition of thinking about how both tourists and communities view each other has also been followed by those reworking the gaze formulation. For example concepts like the mutual gaze (Maoz, 2006), the reserve gaze (Gillespie, 2006), the local gaze (Maoz, 2006; Wu, 2012), the family gaze (Baerenholdt et al., 2004), and the host gaze (Chan, 2006; Moufakkir, 2011) are essentially backward looking, focusing on the recent past or aspects of the present interactions. The future perspectives and visions for both the tourists and the communities they visit are not well represented in the gaze-related literature.

This chapter takes a forward looking approach to viewing tourism in the community of the Old Town of Lhasa, Tibet. It focuses on the perspectives of 'post 80s' youth as the potential community and tourism leaders of the future. It provides an empirical study richly imbued with an emic perspective on the ways in which Tibetan youth, living in one of the world's highest and most austere settings, look down, look out and look forward to the future involving tourism.

Study Site: The Old Town of Lhasa

In this section, the study site is specified. The clear specification of the research context in tourism studies has been suggested

by a number of scholars (Cohen, 1979; Pearce, 2004, in press; Wall and Mathieson, 2006). The tourism context of the Old Town of Lhasa is very different from both Western countries and small island countries, and even other provinces in China. Understanding its characteristics assists in developing one of the defining themes of this chapter for contributing to the literature on gaze.

Overall View of the Old Town of Lhasa

Lhasa, or 'Lasa' in Mandarin, is the capital city of Tibet Autonomous Region, China. It covers an area of close to 30,000 km^2 with 544 km^2 of downtown region – the Chengguan district. This is also known as the city centre of Lhasa. The Old Town of Lhasa is 'the centre of the city centre', where most of the tourist attractions can be found.

Lhasa is home to the Tibetan, Han and Hui people, as well as many other ethnic groups. The Tibetan ethnic group makes up 87% of the permanent population. At the end of 2009, there were approximately 160,000 permanent residents and another 133,000 migrants living in the city area of Lhasa. In the old town of Lhasa, the population is nearly 40,000, while many people work and do business in the old town, but live in newly developed suburbs (Lhasa Municipal People's Government, 2009).

The Old Town of Lhasa has two special features. First, it is the heart, the centre core of Tibetan Buddhism. Buddhism has permeated every aspect of its life and culture for 1,300 years. Despite Lhasa's massive modernization process, to which the tourism industry is central, Buddhism is still influential and dominates many aspects of life for local Tibetans. The Old Town of Lhasa, with Potala Palace, Jokhang Temple and another dozen temples and monasteries, is the spiritual home of Tibetan Buddhists (Tiley Chodag, 1988). Second, the position of the Old Town of Lhasa is much more than the main pilgrimage site for Tibetan Buddhists. It is the pervasive centre in Tibet; the political, cultural and economic hub of the autonomous region.

Tourism in the Old Town of Lhasa

Lhasa is known for its 'mysterious, remote, Tibetan Buddhism' among tourists (Lhasa Tourism Administration and BES Consulting & Design, 2010). The main attractions in the Old Town of Lhasa are Buddhism-related architecture and Tibetan customs. The world heritage sites (Potala Palace, Jokhang Temple, Norbulinka Royal Garden), Tibetan temples and monasteries, and Tibetan traditional yards are distinctive; all have a strong Tibetan flavour.

Modern tourism in Lhasa began in 1981 when Tibet opened its door to the world. Due to large infrastructural projects in 1990s and Potala Palace's inclusion in the World Heritage list in 1994, the Old Town of Lhasa witnessed a dramatic increase in international visitors, and an even greater increase in domestic tourists. Currently tourism in Lhasa is still in a rapid development stage (from 2001 till now) (Lhasa Tourism Administration and BES Consulting & Design, 2010). With the opening of Qinghai-Tibet railway in 2006, tourism developed at an extraordinary speed (Su and Wall, 2009; Fu, 2010). It received 3.21 million tourists in 2009, which was double the tourist numbers in 2005, prior to the opening of the railway. In Lhasa, the majority of tourists are domestic, comprising 96.79% of the market in 2009. Most of the domestic tourists are the recently emerging affluent middle class in inland China (Murakami, 2008). In terms of international tourists, the leading countries generating visitors are the USA, Japan, Germany and Canada.

Due to its rapid development and economic contribution, the tourism industry has been positioned as one of Tibet's pillar industries since the late 1990s. In recent years, the tourism income accounted for more than 30% of tertiary industry, and more than 20% of local GDP (Lhasa Statistics Bureau, 2010). Local residents as well as migrants from inland China are increasingly being involved in the tourism industry.

There is a marked seasonality for tourism in the Old Town of Lhasa, as well as in other parts of Tibet. The seasonality is caused not only by the climate and altitude forces, but also by the concentration of religious and cultural celebrations in summer. As a result, taking 2009 as an example, visitation from May to October consisted 89.92% of the annual visitation, while the remaining half of the year comprised one tenth of the market.

'Post 80s' in the Old Town of Lhasa

'Post 80s' is a popular Chinese concept. It is the literal translation of '*80 hou*' in Mandarin, which represents the group of people who were born in 1980s. They were 19–29 years old in 2010 when the field trip of this study was conducted. 'Post 80s' youth are a similar cohort to 'Gen Y' (Benckendorff *et al.*, 2009) and other concepts in Western countries (Arnett, 2000).

It can be argued that age is not the most precise marker of groups (Arnett, 2000; Zhu, 2004). However, this group of young people in China are not natural extensions of former generations. They were brought up under China's dramatic social and economic changes, with roots in the government-initiated reforms in 1978 (Moore and College, 2005). They have witnessed social and economic changes perhaps unparalleled in human history (Taylor, 2008), and arguably have formed profoundly different psychological and sociological characteristics (Deng *et al.*, 2009). Most importantly, they are regarded as the potential leaders for social and economic development, including tourism, in the near future of China (Yahoo, 2010). It is argued in this research that these strong forces do effectively define a coherent cohort of young Chinese and Tibetan youth.

Migration is an important type of livelihoods diversification for youth (Wouterse and Taylor, 2008; Ellis, 2000b; Qin, 2009). It is especially true when considering the tourism industry where migrants have historically formed an important part (Williams and Hall, 2000; Janta *et al.*, 2011). Indeed, a large percentage of the 'post 80s' group in Lhasa are migrant Tibetans. In Lhasa, the Indigenous 'post 80s' group is approximately 32,400 in number. The migrant group comprise a further 13,000 people. Migrant Tibetan youth are composed of three sub-groups. The first is migrants from other parts of Tibet, attracted to Lhasa by its central position in Tibet. The second group consists of those who come from inland China, but stay and work in Lhasa after completing their higher education. The last group includes fortune-seekers from inland China, who believe that the Lhasa location is full of opportunities.

Throughout the world, youth represents a source of cultural innovation and dynamism, and are main players and 'indicators' of the future (Ono, 2003; World Bank, 2007). They are powerful agents directing the course of social change, both in cities (Tienda and Wilson, 2002) and rural areas (Jentsch and Shucksmith, 2003; Bennell, 2007a). In China, 'post 80s' youth are positioned to be leaders of a country that will have one of the largest economies in the world (Ralston *et al.*, 1999; Stanat, 2005). In Lhasa, a society at the beginning of social and economic transformation (Fu, 2010), 'post 80s' youth are believed to be in a key position and have crucial roles to play (Muilu and Rusanen, 2003; Bennell, 2007b).

Exploring the Future Gaze

As has been stated above, one of the research opportunities in gaze studies in tourism is the potential to focus on the future gaze. In terms of the future in this specific study, the 'post 80s' group in Lhasa, are the major players. Thus, an examination of their views on tourism and tourists in the future can be claimed as an initiative in developing gaze studies.

There are some persistent problems in the understanding of tourism development and its future. A long-standing concern has been how to assess and then incorporate local residents' views of the future of their setting (Pearce and Wu, 2010). In this study, social representations theory and sustainable livelihoods framework are introduced to explore the young hosts' gaze into future tourism.

Social Representations Theory

Social representations theory was developed by Moscovici (1976) from the broader sociological term of collective representations. Expressed succinctly, social representations are 'ways of world making' (Moscovici, 1988) They are shared, publicly communicated, everyday belief systems of meaning (Pearce, 2005; Quenza, 2005; Moscardo and Pearce, 2007).

At its core, social representations theory is an emic, contextual and social theory (Voelklein and Howarth, 2005). Social representations are socially produced knowledge, shared by groups within a society. It is worth mentioning however that few communities are uniformly cohesive in their views. Moscovici (1988) suggested three levels of consensus of social representation ('hegemonic', 'emancipated' and 'polemical', respectively). There are often competing and sometimes contradictory versions of reality existing side by side in the same community, culture and individual (Howarth *et al.*, 2004; Mayers, 2005; Pearce, 2009). Using the language of gaze, these varied social representations may be thought of as group gazes or perspectives on tourism and tourists.

In daily life, social representations reflect how people jointly 'see' the world. Representations help facilitate communication. The general theory of social representations can be applied to many topics, in particular to one topic which has the potential to change people's lives and social worlds – the development and growth of tourism.

The social representation theoretical perspective has been applied to tourism studies most notably by Pearce *et al.* (1996, 2005, 2007, 2009) and followed by other researchers. For Pearce *et al.*, social representations theory offers an interesting opportunity to examine how representations help structure and organize community views of tourism impacts.

In this future gaze study, social representations theory is employed to understand how many macro-organizing views the Tibetan youth hold about tourism. Questions we seek to address include: Is there a dominant view? Are there multiple and competing views? How are these views constructed? The social representation approach is particularly helpful in directing attention to the large scale perceptions and support for tourism or the lack of enthusiasm for tourism-induced change. It can be helpful in summarizing questions about the origin of the respondents' ideas and with whom they share those ideas.

Although the above academic directions highlight the suitability of social representations theory in tourism studies, the potential of the theory within tourism community future research is in need of clarification, elaboration and development. In particular social representations do not direct researchers to any specific content that constitutes people's views. A combination with other theories, frameworks or research approaches represents one possible route to help specify further ways in which this key approach to understanding social life may be enriched for tourism study. In this study, sustainable livelihoods framework was adopted as a further conceptual tool to build our approach to understand how Tibetan youth sees the future of tourism.

Sustainable Livelihoods Approach

The Sustainable livelihoods approach (hereafter referred to as the SLA or SLs) arose from the broad context of rural development, and has become central to the discourse on poverty alleviation and rural development (Scoones, 1998). Reviewing the WECD (1987) panel definition, Chambers and Conway (1991) suggested:

A livelihood comprises the capabilities, assets (including both tangible and intangible assets,), activities required for a means of living.

A livelihood is sustainable when it can cope with and recover from stresses and shocks, maintain or enhance its capabilities and assets, and provide sustainable livelihood opportunities for the next generation, and which contributes net benefits to other livelihoods at the local and global levels in short and long term. (Chambers and Conway, 1991, p.6)

The core ideas of SLF can be briefly described in a pentagram-based framework (Fig. 9.1). This *people-centred* paradigm emphasizes the inherent capacities and knowledge systems of the local community and integrates the broader environmental, social and economic context of livelihood into a holistic analysis framework. In this way, it helps to identify the 'restrictions/barriers and opportunities to SLs and reveals the multiple-sectoral character of real life, and thus offers an opportunity to promote the sort of cross-sectoral and cross-thematic approach that should be the hallmark of development work' (Helmore and Singh, 2001; cited in Tao, 2006).

For this research effort, the future of tourism in Tibet as perceived by its young generation, the livelihoods approach offers a set of well-defined areas about which questions can be asked. The kinds of resources and capital identified in the livelihood analysis have tangible and specific qualities and effectively scan a wide range of interest

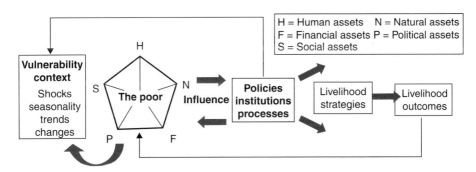

Fig. 9.1. Sustainable livelihoods framework. (Adapted from DFID, 1999 and IFAD, 2007.)

areas. The approach can help build confidence in the thoroughness of any assessment of the perception of tourism's future.

Integration of the Perspectives

The social representations theory and the sustainable livelihoods framework, complement each other when doing research in the tourism community relationships area. Social representations theory helps to understand how people 'see' and organize their view of the tourism futures. The SLF provides the content of what defines and constitutes their perceptions and preferences. It focuses more on the topics inside the social representations rather than providing a competing or parallel theory.

The two theoretical systems or conceptual schemes already considered do not directly shape the behaviour of researchers in terms of how to approach their understanding of communities. In the next section, an emic research approach is developed. This kind of research procedure facilitates the application of these theoretical systems into practice.

Research Procedure

The designing of the research procedure endeavoured to be emic; that is actually accessing the local voices. Photo-elicitation interviews, focus groups and questionnaire-based surveys were adopted in sequence. The former two qualitative methods provided a broad and critical understanding of tourism as a social phenomenon (Wearing et al., 2010). These two methods each encouraged the host to come to speak of his own life and offered an opportunity for practical engagement with the research context (Moscovici and Markov, 1998). The photo-elicitation interviews and focus groups acted as foundation studies to collect local voices concerning their gaze on tourism and tourists. Further, the approaches offered insight to help design a questionnaire that is based on local voices, rather than the researchers' judgement (Pearce et al., 1996).

Two indigenous Tibetan youth and two migrant Tibetan youth participated in the photo-elicitation interviews. During these interviews, the respondents were required to share and interpret their photos in terms of (potential) tourism attraction assets. In the interviews, photos were placed between the researcher and informants, thus reducing the asymmetry in power between the researcher and participants (Collier and Collier, 1986; Harper, 2002; Pink, 2007). Two participants in the photo-elicitation interviews worked as liaison personnel to recruit focus group members. The remaining two groups were organized through the researcher's personal network. The pre-existing friendship or sub-communities helped group members to engage freely with one another within the natural social context in which ideas were formed and discussed, and to validate information more readily (Krueger and Casey, 2000). Perceptions on tourism attraction assets, views on tourism as a livelihoods choice, preferences for tourist groups and contextual issues were widely discussed.

Content analysis was adopted to analyse the interview and focus group data. This material was then used to construct the relevant in questionnaire based survey. Questionnaires formulated in this way, incorporating local voices and interest, are more likely to be received and accepted with the support of the local community (Jennings, 2010; Mason et al., 2010; Pearce and Wu, 2010).

Pretesting the content and language of the survey was carried out with the Tibetan respondents to ensure that the emic (community) perspective was maintained in the questions (Pearce et al., 1996). Four indigenous Tibetan 'post 80s' and six migrant Tibetan youth were employed as research assistants to deliver the questionnaire to the respondents face to face. Help was also generously offered by 'post 80s' staff in some local organizations in Lhasa, such as the Lhasa Tourism Administration, the School of Tourism in Tibet University and Tibetan Academy of Social Sciences. In all, 303 copies of the questionnaires were delivered, and 258 copies of the questionnaires were returned and properly completed, by 134 indigenous Tibetan youth and 124 migrant Tibetan youth.

Compared with the photo-elicitation interviews and focus groups, which were carried out in a natural and causal environment and offered contextual detailed information, the questionnaire-based survey had the advantage of accessing a larger number of 'post 80s' Tibetan youth and providing a broader overview of that perspective.

Research Findings

In this section, Tibetan 'post 80s' youth's gaze on tourism and tourists are explored and described.

Gaze on the future and its time range

In the foundation study of photo-elicitation interviews, the definition of the future was firstly explored by asking questions such as 'How many years into the future do you think about when you hear the word "future"?' 'How far into the future do you find it difficult to clearly imagine possible futures?' All of the interviewees expressed a view that they were not accustomed to thinking about the future. Three of the participants would set personal targets for themselves and think about personal futures in 5–10 years, however, they hardly thought about the regional, national or international futures. Another respondent challenged the effectiveness of longer-term thinking, and regarded the future in shorter terms, such as 1–5 years. Considering that the Chinese government and other organizations usually adopt 5–10-year time scales when they make future plans, this study adopted 5–10 years as the future time range when exploring future gaze in the following sections.

Gaze on tourism as a livelihoods choice

In the three-fold sustainable livelihoods framework (assets, access and activity, respectively), the transformation of livelihoods assets reflects the meaning the person tries to create through their livelihoods strategies (Bebbington, 1999). It also gives people the capacity to be and to act (Sen, 1997). In this sense, the youth's gaze on tourism as a future livelihoods choice will greatly influence their gaze on tourism and tourists.

In Tibetan 'post 80s' youth's opinion, the top three income-generating opportunities in the current old town of Lhasa were wholesale and retail trading, tourism and handicrafts making. Though tourism was one of the foundation industries recognized by the government at the time of the research (2010–2011) (Lhasa Municipal People's Government, 2009), it only played a substantial, but not primary role in the respondents' livelihoods portfolio.

Questions on perceptions of tourism's role in their future livelihoods portfolio, preferred roles of tourism, willingness to work in the tourism industry and willingness to set up one's own tourism-related business in the next 5–10 years were used to explore the 'post 80s' youth's gaze on tourism as a livelihoods choice in the future. Cluster analysis was undertaken because it can isolate different groups (clusters) within a sample by examining the individuals' common features (Pérez and Nadal, 2005). Instead of examining average responses to questions, it provides a more accurate reflection by forming different units with a low degree of intra-group and high degree of inter-group variation. More importantly, it is consistent with what social representations theory suggests. Cluster analysis actually has the ability to allocate respondents to groups based on the underlying patterns to questions about their views of tourism (Fredline and Faulkner, 2003). Furthermore, it offers explicit evidence that the hosts in the community and their opinions are not homogeneous.

More specifically, a non-hierarchical clustering technique was used. Taking into account the complexity of the results and the high number of variables involved, a cluster of four groups was chosen as the clearest solution (see Table 9.1).

Table 9.1. The classification of sub-groups with differing views of tourism as a livelihoods strategy.

Sub-groups	Frequency	%
I. In-betweeners: Tourism is a livelihoods choice	81	36.7
II. Ambivalent supporters: Tourism is a livelihoods choice for others	53	24.0
III. Alternative supporters: Tourism is good but should be controlled	31	14.0
IV. Lovers: Tourism is a fantastic and important livelihoods strategy	56	25.3

Sub-group I: in-betweeners

This sub-group contained 81 respondents and formed the largest sub-group. Respondents in this sub-group realized that tourism was a potential livelihoods choice. It might be substantial, but acted as only one of the diversified livelihoods combinations. They were not enthusiastic about tourism development or working in tourism, nor were they negative towards this kind of social and economic development. If work opportunities arise, this group of respondents would consider such employment seriously and balance the benefits and costs.

Sub-group II: ambivalent supporters

The second sub-group, containing 24% of the respondents, has been labelled as *ambivalent supporters*. A sharp contrast was noticed when comparing their attitudes towards tourism development at a community level and their willingness to work in the tourism industry. In general, they thought that tourism would play a more important role in the next 5–10 years, and they welcomed further tourism development. However, they did not show any enthusiasm for working in the tourism industry, either for tourism jobs in specific areas or as tourism entrepreneurs. This group of respondents believed tourism enhanced the community and other people's well-being. However, they themselves, had more suitable livelihoods choices, and tourism was not their priority.

Sub-group III: alternative supporters

This sub-group was made up of 31 Tibetan youth. Their response patterns were quite distinctive. They were the only group who strongly advocated that the future roles of tourism in the community should be decreased or at most kept at the present level. However, they should not be considered as a group of 'haters' as has been described for some commonly identified groups in previous studies (Davis *et al.*, 1988; Fredline and Faulkner, 2003). These alternative supporters were eager to work in the tourism industry in the future, and they were also enthusiastic about tourism entrepreneurship. However, this group preferred alternative quality tourism. They advocated restricting the number of tourists and supported the adoption of low-volume tourism. For them, the current mass tourism was problematic. Hence, they preferred the kind of tourism that embraced quality interaction with tourists, more spending, minimal leakage and less negative impact.

Sub-group IV: lovers

The final cluster, sub-group IV, contained 56 respondents and could be described as *lovers* of tourism in Lhasa. They showed great support for tourism development in the next 5–10 years. They also showed their preferences for tourism as livelihoods choice. In their opinion, working in tourism offered a good career, rather than just jobs to making a living.

Using the group classification as a key dependent grouping variable, discriminant

World heritage sites

Religious sites   Tibetan traditional yards

Tibetan daily life and customs   Tibetan medicine

Fig. 9.2. Examples of tourism attraction assets. (Provided by the photo-elicitation interviewees, used with permission.)

analysis was adopted to explore which factor better predicted the group classification. The discriminant function 1 performed well, accounting for 82.6% of the explained variance ($\lambda = 5.27$, $\chi^2 = 573.01$, $P < 0.01$). In determining which predictor variable contributes the most to function 1, discriminant function coefficients and loadings were examined. It suggested that 'preferred roles of tourism in the future (Beta = 1.00)' was the most important predictor in discriminating among the sub-groups, followed by perceptions of 'tourism's role in the future livelihoods portfolio (Beta = 0.24)', 'tourism entrepreneurship (Beta = 0.16)' and 'tourism jobs (Beta = 0.12)'.

Gaze on tourism attraction assets

During the photo-elicitation interviews, the four participants provided 49 photos. Most of the photos were about (potential) tourism attraction assets. Through initial analysis and further information from the focus groups, these (potential) tourism attraction assets were identified as the world heritage sites, religious sites, traditional Tibetan yards, Tibetan daily life and customs, and Tibetan medicine (see Fig. 9.2). For these tourism attraction assets, world heritage sites were the only category that had been developed as tourism attractions at the time of research (2010–2011), while the other four attraction assets were, arguably, underdeveloped.

The values of these (potential) tourism attractions, the difficulty in developing them and the desirability of development were explored. Repeated measures one-way ANOVA was employed to detect differences between five sets of multiple correlated group means. The results show:

The world heritage sites, which have been used as tourism attractions since the beginning of the 1980s, were regarded as the most valuable, and the most desirable but the most difficult to manage for tourism's future. The value of these world heritage sites is recognized worldwide. These world heritage sites assets are the landmarks of Lhasa, and indeed of Tibet. Local youth showed great interest in using them to attract more tourists, which resulted in the highest level of desirability. Nevertheless, they thought these assets were the most difficult to develop.

The religious site assets are scattered in every corner of the old town, Lhasa. In the minds of the Tibetan 'post 80s' youth, they were the least valuable as tourism attraction assets, and perceived as very difficult to develop (at the same level with that of world heritage sites). Hence, their overall desirability in development was at a medium level. The reason it would be very difficult to develop these sites is linked to the sensitive religious and political issues and concerns of Lhasa.

The traditional Tibetan yards not only reflect the indigenous knowledge of Tibetans and their customs, but are also identified as aesthetically attractive locations for tourists. The values of these sites for development as tourism attractions were well recognized. Compared with the world heritage sites and religious sites, they were regarded as significantly easier to develop, however, they were given the lowest value in terms of development desirability. The low desirability was caused by relocation cost and their attachment to the Old Town.

Daily life and customs assets were seen as valuable tourism attraction assets, but significant less so than the world heritage sites. However, they were believed to be the easiest to develop, with a medium desirability level for development.

Overall, Tibetan medicine assets were regarded as valuable assets, relatively easy to develop, but with only low desirability for development. The results for this asset were similar to the scores for the traditional Tibetan yards. Importantly, many respondents expressed their concerns about the commercial development of Tibetan medicine. The most frequent concern was not the tourists' acceptability of Tibetan medicine, but the potential price increase for locals that might result from marketing these resources to tourists.

In addition to the overall gaze on the five sets of tourism attraction assets, the four livelihoods groups' representations were also explored by adopting mixed-model factorial ANOVA and one-way ANOVA tests. Significant differences were located in their gaze of value assessment and desirability judgement. To be specific, the in-betweeners and lovers attached significantly more values to religious sites and Tibetan medicine ($P = 0.013$ and 0.005, respectively). Lovers and in-betweeners revealed significantly more desire for developing world heritage sites, religious sites and Tibetan traditional yards as tourism attractions than their counterparts (ambivalent supporters and alternative supporters). In terms of Tibetan daily life and customs, lovers showed significantly greater interest in developing these assets compared with other groups, especially more so than the alternative supporters. For the development of Tibetan medicine, alternative supporters revealed significantly less desire to turn them into tourism attractions than the other three livelihoods groups who shared a similar level.

Gaze towards the tourists

During the focus groups, images of tourists, their motivations for their travelling to Lhasa and the classification of tourist groups were examined. The generating areas of the tourists were the most recognizable grouping criteria. In the local youth's eyes, tourists to the old town of Lhasa could be divided into the following groups:

- Tourists from coastal China;
- Tourists from middle and western China;
- Residents inside Tibet regions;
- Tourists from oriental countries;
- Tourists from Western countries;
- Others (e.g. tourists from other parts of the world, like Africa, Pacific Islands).

For tourists from oriental countries, the classification included those from Hong Kong SAR, Macau SAR, Taiwan Province, Korea, Japan, India and other South Asian countries.

For tourists from Western countries, the classification was effectively Caucasians, those 'white' or light skinned people with 'big nose and blue eyes', from North America, Europe and Oceania. Respondents confessed quite frankly that, they could not tell the difference between these 'white' visitors.

Table 9.2 lists some of the Tibetan youth's overall preferences of tourist groups. Previous empirical studies of Chinese tourists showed that tourists from different regions differ in their destination preferences and behaviour (COTRI and PATA, 2010). Combing the information obtained from focus groups, it was assumed that in the questionnaire-based survey the Tibetan youth might hold different preferences for separate types of tourist groups for different tourism attraction assets.

In the questionnaire-based survey, as many as 42 respondents out of 258 chose 'others' instead of any tourist groups identified in the focus groups. According to the face-to-face conservations just after the questionnaire, most of those who chose 'others' did not care about where tourists came from. For them, all the tourists were guests and should be welcomed equally. This phenomenon is deeply rooted in both Confucian and Buddhist values (Yang, 1980; Harvey, 2000).

For the rest of the 216 young respondents who specified their preferred tourist groups, descriptive analysis was conducted. It found that the preferences pattern for the five tourist attraction assets was more or less similar. The following results were obtained.

- Tourists from Western countries were the most preferred, even though they accounted for a small share in the current tourism market (from 1.93% to 8.21% in 2005–2009).
- Overall, tourists from both coastal China and middle and western China were relatively highly preferred. Coastal Chinese were welcomed at religious sites, while middle and west Chinese were preferred more for visiting non-religious sites.
- The number of tourists from either inside Tibet or oriental countries was small at the time of research (2010–2011). Their potential as tourists was not rated highly by Tibetan 'post 80s'. Compared with tourists from other origins, they obtained the lowest preferences.

In addition to the overall preferences for tourist groups, the four livelihoods

Table 9.2. Perceptions and preferences of tourist groups.

Groups	Preferred groups (core ideas)
Focus group I	All visitors to Lhasa are guests and welcomed, no matter where they come from (4) Those who respect our culture, religious belief and rules (3) Those who will spend more and stay longer (3)
Focus group II	Those spending more are preferable, e.g. north-eastern Chinese (3) Coastal Chinese and Asians are not preferred (2) Caucasians are OK (2)
Focus group III	Those believing in Buddhism are most welcome to visit religious related sites (3) All tourists are guests and are welcomed (3) Those who respect our culture (2) Caucasians are most welcome (2) Official business visiting is not preferred (2)
Focus group IV	Tourists from coastal China are most welcomed (3) Japanese and Korean tourists are welcomed (2) Those who bring more benefits to Lhasa are more welcomed (2)

Note: The numbers in the second column indicate the frequency of these perception and preferences being mentioned during the focus group.

groups' preferences for tourist groups in the future were also explored and compared by cross-tabulation analysis with the Chi-squared test. Significant differences were only found in the preferred tourist groups of world heritages sites (F = 24.95, 2-tail P = 0.015). *Lovers* are the only group who most welcomed tourists from coastal China. *Alternative supporters* who argued for the control of tourist volume, showed significantly more preferences for Western tourists. *In-betweeners* and *ambivalent supporters'* preferences for tourists groups were relatively evenly distributed among tourists from Western countries, tourists from Coastal China and tourists from middle and west China.

Interpreting the Research Findings

This chapter examined the views of Tibetan 'post 80s', as the future major players in tourism. It adopted a forward-looking perspective. It explored the young Tibetans' gazes on tourism as a future livelihoods choice, on (potential) tourism attraction assets, as well as on preferred tourist groups. A framework of using social representations theory to provide an insightful view underpinned the study and the sustainable livelihoods framework shaped the content of the gaze and was explored using an emic approach.

The gaze on tourism as a livelihoods choice showed there are four sub-groups in the host community. They are *in-betweeners*, *ambivalent supporters*, *alternative supporters* and *lovers*. These sub-groups shared a commonality in 'seeing' tourism as a variable livelihoods choice overall, but subtle differences existed among the groups. These differences corresponded to previous studies that asserted the heterogeneous nature of tourism communities (Pearce *et al.*, 1996; Boyd and Singh, 2003; Lai and Nepal, 2006; Zhang and He, 2008; Gu and Ryan, 2009). The findings are also consistent with social representations theory in that there are competing and sometimes contradictory versions of reality existing side by side in the same

community (Howarth *et al.*, 2004; Mayers, 2005; Pearce, 2009). Tourism, is not an undifferentiated phenomenon, rather, it means many different things to different people (Wall, 1993). For *in-betweeners*, tourism seems a good livelihoods choice, and they will seize this livelihood strategy when opportunities arise. *Ambivalent supporters* noticed the benefits brought by tourism and were positive about tourism development in the future. However, they were more enthusiastic about working in other areas than the tourism industry. The third group, *alternative supporters*, advocated quality tourism and hoped to control the volume of tourists. The final sub-group, *lovers*, most of whom were current beneficiaries of tourism development, were positive about tourism in all aspects. In their eyes, tourism was a panacea for both personal and the community well-being.

On the livelihoods side, the formation of four livelihoods groups informs the role of tourism at the community level. In these young hosts' minds, tourism, though important, can only be a part of their livelihoods portfolio. Tourism acts more like a diversification, no matter whether it is measured at its current stage, or seen in the future. This kind of representation is supportive of previous studies that declared the strategic importance of livelihoods diversification (Ellis, 2000a; Barrett *et al.*, 2001; Niehof, 2004). It also links to tourism studies, which though retrospective, have argued that the appropriate role of tourism should be just a part of the livelihoods diversification (Tao, 2006; Kong *et al.*, 2008; Lee, 2008; Gurung and Seeland, 2011; Mbaiwa and Sakuze, 2009; Tao and Wall, 2009).

Concerning gazes on tourism attraction assets, Tibetan 'post 80s' respondents in this study viewed world heritage sites (e.g. Potala Palace), as well as four currently under-developed sets of resources as potential tourism attraction assets in the next 5–10 years. The specific opportunities lie in religious sites, Tibetan traditional yards, Tibetan daily life and custom, and Tibetan medicine. The identification of these under-developed or less developed tourism resources reveals the importance of local knowledge input in tourism planning and development (Wall, 2007; Moscardo, 2008). In addition to the identification of the five sets of tourism attraction assets, their values, difficulty in development and desirability of development were assessed. Significant differences were discovered in terms of value judgement and desirability perceptions.

In terms of the Tibetan youth's gaze at tourists themselves, some detailed views were established. Some previous studies have examined tourism community residents' representations of tourists. Most of these studies focused on a specific group of tourists, such as foreign backpackers in India (Maoz, 2006), Chinese tourists in Vietnam (Chan, 2006), gay tourists in a Mexican beach (Hughes and Carlos, 2010) and tourist photographers (Gillespie, 2006). There are further examples of these diverse local–tourist gazes in the present volume. A few chapters in this book focus on tourists from specific countries, such, Russian tourists in Chapter 4, and German tourists in Chapter 14. Little published research has explored residents' representations and preferences for different kinds of tourists. This chapter, however, considered the regional origins of the tourists visiting the Old Town of Lhasa.

For the young Tibetan hosts, the tourist origin was an easily recognized criterion for defining tourists. They had some clear images of tourists from different origins, such as tourists from coastal China, tourists from middle and west China (neighbouring provinces), tourists from inside Tibet, tourists from Western countries (Caucasians) and tourists from oriental countries. Overall, Western tourists and coastal Chinese were most welcomed in the future, because they were perceived as well-behaved and were seen as more generous consumers. Nevertheless, a core group of the respondents viewed all tourists as welcome. This perspective was interpreted as directly linked to the accepting and tolerant values inherent in Buddhist and Confucian culture.

It is noteworthy that in the sustainable livelihoods framework, access to other assets (e.g. economic, social and human

assets) and the contextual issues (e.g. policy, institution and process arrangement, and vulnerability issues) act as the secondary and tertiary elements affecting and mediating these Tibetan youth's gazes on tourism as a future livelihoods choice. Their perspectives are also affected by the wider contextual issues in Lhasa. These issues penetrate all the aspects and all the livelihoods choices in the society. These issues are not explored in this chapter; however, it does not mean they are not important in formulating the youth's gaze. In the future, a study focusing on how these assets and contextual issues act on and though the hosts' gaze will be reported.

This chapter has exemplified the joint power of social representations theory and livelihoods analysis in tourism community studies (Pearce and Wu, 2010). The findings in this chapter confirmed and specified relevance of the social representations theory in establishing the social and heterogeneous nature of Lhasa society (Moscovici, 1988; Howarth et al., 2004; Mayers, 2005). The work has also empirically supported tourism livelihoods studies concerning tourism's appropriate role in building a sustainable society (Tao, 2006; Kong et al., 2008; Lee, 2008; Gurung and Seeland, 2011; Mbaiwa and Sakuze, 2009; Tao and Wall, 2009).

This study has also stretched and extended the application of the concept of gaze by working with an Asian host community, focusing on perspectives about tourism oriented towards the future and assessing views from a host population that has had a dramatic surge in tourism growth. From some cynical Western perspectives, including those that lambasted the growth of tourism and were in part responsible for Urry's more sophisticated counterproposals and original work (cf. Boorstin, 1964; Mishan, 1969; Hirsch, 1978), the enthusiasm for tourism exhibited by Tibetan youth might seem misguided, even naïve. The care taken in this study to elicit local youth views rather than impose them inadvertently through researchers' practices and structured etic approaches is one part of a struggle to deal with the challenge of seeing the world through the eyes of others. In 21st-century tourism studies there can be little place for the assertions of a comfortable and privileged gaze that asserts the primacy of one gaze, which has been predominantly a romantic gaze. Instead this study along with its companions in this book has emphasized that by looking out

and looking forward there can be a more tolerant and multicultural kaleidoscope through which to gaze on the world of tourism and tourists. The metaphor of gaze has been stretched but not broken in this analysis and has helped guide the overall interpretations towards tourism of Tibetan youth who live on the 'roof of the world'.

References

Arnett, J.J. (2000) Emerging adulthood: a theory of development from the late teens through the twenties. *Amercian Psychologist* 55, 469–480.
Baerenholdt, J. O., Haldrup, M., Larsen, J. and Urry, J. (2004) *Performing Tourist Places*. Ashgate, Aldershot.
Barrett, C.B., Reardon, T. and Webb, P. (2001) nonfarm income diversification and household livelihood strategies in rural Africa: concepts, dynamics, and policy implications. *Food Policy* 26, 315–331.
Bebbington, A. (1999) Capitals and capabilities: a framework for analyzing peasant viability, rural livelihoods and poverty. *World Development* 27, 2021–2044.
Benckendorff, P.J., Moscardo, G. and Pendergast, D. (2009) *Tourism and Generation Y*. CABI, Wallingford.
Bennell, P. (2007a) Promoting liveliood opportunities for rural youth. *Knowledge and Skills for Development*. International Fund for Agriculture Development (IFAD), Rome.
Bennell, P. (2007b) Promoting liveliood opportunities for rural youth. http://www.ifad.org/events/gc/30/roundtable/youth/benell.pdf (accessed 17 December 2009).
Boorstin, D. (1964) *The Image: a Guide to Pseudo-Events in America*. Harper & Row, New York.
Bowen, D. and Clarke, J. (2009) *Contemporary Tourist Behaviour: Yourself and Others as Tourists*. CABI, Wallingford.
Boyd, S.W. and Singh, S. (2003) Destination communities: structures, resources and types. In: Singh, S., Timothy, D.J. and Dowling, R.K. (eds) *Tourism in Destination Communities*. CABI, Wallingford, pp. 19–33.
Chambers, R. and Conway, G.R. (1991) Sustainable rural livelihoods: practical concepts for the 21st century. http://community.eldis.org/.59b8bc0f (accessed 20 November 2009).
Chan, Y.W. (2006) Coming of age of the Chinese tourists: the emergence of non-western tourism and host - guest interactions in Vietnam's border tourism. *Tourist studies* 6, 187–213.
Cohen, E. (1979) Rethinking the sociology of tourism. *Annals of Tourism Research* 6, 18–35.
Collier, J. and Collier, M. (1986) *Visual Anthropology: Photography as a Research Method*. University of New Mexico Press, Winston, NM.
COTRI and PATA (2010) Are you ready? For Chinese international travellers. A practical guide for delievering superior services. China Outbound Tourism Research Institute, Heide.
Davis, D., Allen, J. and Cosenza, R.M. (1988) Segmenting local residents by their attitudes, interests, and opinions toward tourism. *Journal of Travel Research* 27, 2–8.
Deng, X., Yang, C. and Li, G. (2009) Studies on 'post 80s' youth career status and assessment: case study of Beijing region. *China Youth Studies* 20–21.
Ellis, F. (2000a) The determinants of rural livelihood diversification in developing countries. *Journal of Agricultural Economics* 51, 289–302.
Ellis, F. (2000b) *Rural Livelihoods and Diversity in Developing Countries*. Oxford University Press, Oxford.
Foucault, M. (1976) *The Birth of the Clinic*. Tavistock, London.
Fredline, E. and Faulkner, B. (2003) Host community reactions: a cluster analysis. In: Fredline, L., Jago, L. and Cooper, C. (eds) *Progressing Tourism Research – Bill Faulkner*. Channel View Publications, Clevedon, pp. 114–135.
Fu, S.T.C. (2010) A destination in transition: Lhasa after the Qinghai-Tibet railway. MSc thesis. Hong Kong Polytechnic University, Hong Kong.
Gillespie, A. (2006) Tourist photography and the reverse gaze. *ETHOS* 34, 343–366.
Graburn, N. (1977) Tourism – the sacred journey. In: Smith, V. (eds) *Hosts and Guests: the Anthropology of Tourism*. University of Philadelphia Press, Philadelphia, PA, pp. 17–32.

Gu, H. and Ryan, C. (2009) Place attachment, identity and community impacts of tourism: the case of a Brijing Hutong. In: Ryan, C. and Gu, H. (eds) *Tourism in China: Destination, Cultures and Communities*. Routledge, New York, pp. 308–325.

Gurung, D. JB. and Seeland, K. (2011) Ecotourism benefits and livelihoods improvement for sustainable development in nature conservation areas of Bhutan. *Sustainable Development*. 19(5), 348–358.

Harper, D. (2002) Talking about pictures: a case for photo elicitation. *Visual Studies* 17, 13–26.

Harvey, P. (2000) *An Introduction to Buddhist Ethics*. Cambridge University Press, Cambridge.

Hirsch, F. (1978) *Social Limits to Growth*. Routledge and Kegan Paul, London

Howarth, C., Foster, J. and Dorrer, N. (2004) Exploring the potential of the theory of social representations in community-based health research – and vice versa? *Journal of Health Psychology* 9, 229–243.

Hughes, H. and Carlos, J. (2010) 'Gay' tourists and host community attitudes. *International Journal of Tourism Research* 12, 774–786.

Janta, H., Brown, L., Lugosi, P. and Ladkin, A. (2011) Migrant relationships and tourism employment. *Annals of Tourism Research* 38(4), 1322–1343.

Jennings, G. (2010) *Tourism Research*. John Wiley & Sons, Milton.

Jentsch, B. and Shucksmith, M. (2003) *Young People in Rural Areas of Europe*. Ashgate, Aldershot.

Kong, X.Z., Zhong, Z. and Yuan, M.S. (2008) The impacts of rural tourism on farmers' livelihood: taking three tourist attractions in Shangxi for examples. *On Economic Problems* 30, 115–119.

Krueger, R.A. and Casey, M.A. (2000) *Focus Groups: a Practical Guide for Applied Research*. SAGE, London.

Lai, P.H. and Nepal, S.K. (2006) Local perspectives of ecotourism development in Tawushan Nature Reserve, Taiwan. *Tourism Management* 27, 1117–1129.

Leach, E.R. (1961) Time and false noses. In: Leach, E.R. (eds) *Rethinking Anthoropology*. Athlone Press, London, pp. 132–136.

Lee, M.H. (2008) Tourism and sustainable livelihoods: the case of Taiwan. *Third World Quarterly* 29, 961–978.

Lhasa Municipal People's Government (2009) *Master Planning for Lhasa City (2009–2020)*. Lhasa Municipal People's Government, Lhasa.

Lhasa Statistics Bureau (2010) *Lhasa Statistics Yearbook 2009*. China Statistics Press, Beijing.

Lhasa Tourism Administration and BES Consulting & Design (2010) *Master Planning for Lhasa Tourism (2010–2020)*. Lhasa Tourism Administration and BES Consulting & Design, Lhasa and Beijing.

MacCannell, D. (1973) Staged authenticity: arrangements of social space in tourist settings. *The American Journal of Sociology* 79, 589–603.

Maoz, D. (2006) The mutual gaze. *Annals of Tourism Research* 33, 221–239.

Mason, P., Augustyn, M. and Seakhoa-King, A. (2010) Exploratory study in tourism: designing an initial, qualitative phase of sequenced, mixed methods research. *International Journal of Tourism Research* 12, 432–448.

Mayers, D.G. (2005) *Social Psychology*. Posts & Telecom Press, Beijing.

Mbaiwa, J.E. and Sakuze, L.K. (2009) Cultural tourism and livelihood diversification: the case of Gcwihaha Caves and XaiXai Village in the Okavango Delta, Botswana. *Journal of Tourism and Cultural Change* 7, 61–75.

Mishan, E. (1969) *The Costs of Economic Growth*. Penguin, Harmondworth.

Moore, R.L. and College, R. (2005) Generation KU: individualism and China's millennial youth. *Ethnology* 44, 357–376.

Moscardo, G. and Pearce, P.L. (2007) The rhetorix and reality of structured tourism work experiences: a social representational analysis. *Tourism Recreation Research* 32, 21–28.

Moscardo, G. (2008) Community capacity building: an emerging challenge for tourism development. In: Moscardo, G. (eds) *Building Community Capacity for Tourism Development*. CABI, Wallingford, pp. 1–15.

Moscovici, S. (1976) Psychology of social representations. *Cahiers Vilfredo Pareto* 14, 409–416.

Moscovici, S. (1988) Notes towards a description of social representations. *European Journal of Social Psychology* 18, 211–250.

Moscovici, S. and Markov, I. (1998) Presenting social representations: a conversation. *Culture & Psychology* 4, 371–410.

Moufakkir, O. (2011) The role of cultural distance in mediating the host gaze. *Tourist studies*, 11(1), 73–89.

Muilu, T. and Rusanen, J. (2003) Rural young people in regional development – the case of Finland in 1970–2000. *Journal of Rural Studies* 19, 295–307.

Murakami, D. (2008) Tourism development and propaganda in contemporary Lhasa, Tibet Autonomous Region (TAR), China. In: Cochrane, J. (eds) *Asian Tourism: Growth and Change*. Elsevier, Oxford, pp. 55–67.

Niehof, A. (2004) The significance of diversification for rural livelihood systems. *Food Policy* 29, 321–338.

Ono, R. (2003) Learning from young people's image of the future: a case study in Taiwan and the US. *Futures* 35, 737–758.

Pearce, P.L., Moscardo, G. and Ross, G. (1996) *Tourism Community Relationships*. Elsevier Science Ltd, Oxford.

Pearce, P.L. and Lee, U.I. (2005) Developing the travel approach to tourist motivation. *Journal of Travel Research* 43, 226–237.

Pearce, P.L. (2004) Theoretical innovation in Asia Pacific Tourism Research. *Asia Pacific Journal of Tourism Research* 9, 57–70.

Pearce, P.L. (2005) *Tourist Behaviour: Themes and Conceptual Schemes*. Channel View Publications, Clevedon.

Pearce, P.L. (2009) Tourism research and the tropics: further horizons. *Tourism Recreation Research* 34, 107–121.

Pearce, P.L. (2012) Respecting the parts of preparing for the future: the rise of Australian tourism research. *Folia Touristica* (in press).

Pearce, P.L. and Wu, M.Y. (2010) The joint power of social representations theory and livelihoods analysis to assess tourism community futures. The 16th Annual Conference of Asia Pacific Tourism Association (APTA), Macau.

Pérez, E.A. and Nadal, J.R. (2005) Host community perceptions: a cluster analysis. *Annals of Tourism Research* 32, 925–941.

Pink, S. (2007) *Doing Visual Ethnography*. Sage, London.

Qin, H. (2009) The impacts of rural-to-urban labor migration on the rural environment in Chongqing Municipality, southwest China: mediating roles of rural household livelihoods and community development. PhD thesis. University of Illinois at Urbana-Champaign, Champaign, IL.

Quenza, C.J.P. (2005) On the structural approach to social representations. *Theory & Psychology* 15, 77–100.

Ralston, D.A., Egri, C.P., Stewart, S., Terpstra, R.H. and Yu, K.C. (1999) Doing business in the 21st century with the new generation of Chinese managers: a study of generational shifts in work values in China. *Journal of International Business Studies* 30, 415–427.

Scoones, I. (1998) Sustainable rural livelihoods: a framework for analysis. http://www.uvg.edu.gt/instituto/centros/cea/Scoones72.pdf (accessed 20 November 2009).

Sen, A. (1997) Editorial: human capital and human capacity. *World Development* 25, 1959–1961.

Stanat, M. (2005) *China's Generation Y, Understanding the Future Leaders of the World's Next Superpower*. Homa & Sekey Books, Paramus, NJ.

Su, M.M. and Wall, G. (2009) The Qinghai-Tibet railway and Tibetan tourism: travelers' perspective. *Tourism Management* 30, 650–657.

Tao, T.C.H. (2006) Tourism as a livelihood strategy in indigenous communities: case studies from Taiwan. PhD thesis. University of Waterloo, Ontario.

Tao, T.C.H. and Wall, G. (2009) Tourism as a sustainable livelihood strategy. *Tourism Management* 30, 90–98.

Taylor, M. (2008) Generation Y with Chinese characteristics. *China Staff* 14, 2–6.

Tienda, M. and Wilson, W.J. (2002) Comparative perspectives of urban youth: challenges for normative development. In: Tienda, M. and Wilson, W.J. (eds) *Youth in Cities: a Cross-National Perspective*. Cambridge University Press, Cambridge, pp. 3–20.

Tiley Chodag (1988) *Tibet: the Land and the People*. New World Press, Beijing.

Turner, V. and Turner, E. (1978) *Image and Pilgrimage in Christian Culture*. Basil Blackwell, Oxford.

Urry, J. (1990) *The Tourist Gaze*. Sage Publications, London.

Voelklein, C. and Howarth, C. (2005) A review of controversies about social representations theory: a British debate. *Culture & Psychology* 11, 431–453.

Wall, G. (1993) Towards a tourism typology. In: Nelson, J. G., Butler, R. W. and Wall, G. (eds) *Tourism and Sustainable Development: Monitoring, Planning, Managing*. Department of Geology, University of Waterloo, Toronto, pp. 45–58.

Wall, G. (2007) Sustainable development, sustainable tourism and sustainable livelihoods. *2007 International Tourism Biennial: Lessons From the Past. Directions for the Future*. Canakkele, Turkey.

Wall, G. and Mathieson, A. (2006) *Tourism: Change, Impacts and Opportunities*. Pearson Education Limited, Harlow.

Walter, J. (1982) Social limits to tourism. *Leisure Studies* 1, 295–304.

WECD (1987) Global Policies for Sustainbale Agriculture, a Report of the Advisory Panel on Food Security, Agriculture, Forestory and Environment to the World Commission on Environment and Development, Zed Books Ltd, London and New Jersey.

Wearing, S., Stevenson, D. and Young, T. (2010) *Tourist Cultures: Identity, Place and the Traveller.* Sage, London.

Williams, A.M. and Hall, C.M. (2000) Tourism and migration: new relationships between production and consumption. *Tourism Geographies: an International Journal of Tourism Space, Place and Environment* 2, 5–27.

World Bank (2007) *World Development Report 2007: Development and the Next Generation.* World Bank, Washington, DC

Wouterse, F. and Taylor, J.E. (2008) Migration and income diversification: evidence from Burkina Faso. *World Development* 36, 625–640.

Wu, M.-Y. (2012) Tourism gaze: a review and prospect. *Tourism Tribune* 27(3), 107–112.

Yahoo (2010) 'Post 80s' diary. http://man.cn.yahoo.com/renwu/80houriji/index.html (accessed 9 March 2010).

Yang, B. (1980) *Interpretation on Confucius.* Zhonghua Book Company, Beijing.

Zhang, W. and He, G.P. (2008) An empirical study and analysis of residents' perceptions of tourism impacts in China's tourist destinations. *Tourism Tribune* 23(6), 86–89.

Zhu, Z. (2004) *Rethinking Guo Jingming: China's One-Child Policy Generation.* Shanghai People's Publication, Shanghai.

10 Perceived Host Gaze in the Context of Short-Term Mission Trips

Yoon Jung Lee and Ulrike Gretzel

Introduction

Short-term mission (STM) travel can be considered a new version of old-aged missionary travel. Like missionaries, STM participants aim to deliver their religious messages to local residents (Klinkerman, 2002; Brown, 2003; Peterson *et al.*, 2003; Friesen, 2004). For this reason, STM travellers seek closer contact and more personal exchanges with individuals in the host community than most travellers. Local hosts are the focus of their trip. Consequently, they have to be very much aware of the host gaze and need to actively manage it. Being respected by the local hosts and being viewed as credible is central to their tourism experience.

The chapter examines Thai and Cambodian locals' gazes as perceived by US and South Korean STM travellers. It thus seeks to understand how perceptions of host gazes differ among Western and non-Western travellers. Numerous tourism studies have dealt with the topic of the host gaze (Long and Allen, 1987; Perdue *et al.* 1987; Ap, 1992; King *et al.* 1993; Pizam and Milman, 1993; Haralambopuolos and Pizam, 1996; Reisinger and Turner, 1998; Joseph and Kavoori, 2001; Enevoldsen, 2003; Gursoy and Rutherford, 2004; Kingsbury, 2005; Chan, 2006; Maoz, 2006;

Wang and Pfister, 2008; Uriely *et al.*, 2009; Chhabra, 2010; Moufakkir, 2011). Except for two studies (Chan, 2006; Maoz, 2006), however, there is little research on non-Western hosts' gazes upon non-Western tourists, and no research on identifying differences in host gaze perceptions based on the type of traveller. This chapter therefore seeks to close an important gap in the literature and points out opportunities for future research in this direction.

Host–guest relationships are especially problematic in the context of STM travel. Historically, Western Christian missionaries' work has been criticized as cultural imperialism (Comaroff and Comaroff, 1986; Dunch, 2002) because they forcefully imposed Christianity, and with it Western culture, on Indigenous people. Cohen (1990) pointed out that, because conversion to Christianity has been closely associated with Westernization in colonial times, the natives who wanted to be Christians had to change not only their religious beliefs but also their whole way of life. In recent days, however, the number of non-Western STM travellers as well as professional missionaries is expanding (Moll, 2006). Thus, the concept of cultural imperialism in colonial times cannot be simply applied to the context of contemporary STM trips. New dynamics of host–guest relationships are emerging, leading to potentially very different host gazes. This chapter tries to explain non-Western locals' gazes as perceived by American and Korean STM travellers with the theory of cultural hegemony (Gramsci, 1971) rarely applied to the tourism field.

In order to examine STM participants' perceptions of host gazes, this study used in-depth interviews as an interpretive research method. Qualitative research methods are recommended for studies that examine multidimensional human qualities such as a person's experience or culture (Creswell, 2007). Therefore, the qualitative approach is considered the most appropriate research design for understanding the multidimensional meaning of host–guest perceptions in STM contexts.

Impacts of STM Travel on Hosts

Many studies have examined the impacts of STMs on the local hosts. Fanning (2009) argued that, by focusing on the host people, the issue of STM participants' cross-cultural sensitivity becomes prominent. Thus, several studies have dealt with the negative impact of participants' cross-cultural insensitivity or ethnocentrism on the host people, which can result in dependency and cultural imperialism. On the other hand MacDonald (2006) and Gailey and Culbertson (2007) have pointed out the positive impact of STMs on the host people. They have argued that through the trips the host communities obtain what they need and experience positive cultural exchanges. According to MacDonald (2006), STM travellers help to improve the standard of living for the local people through material and non-material support. However, he also pointed out that if travellers did not prepare properly for their cross-cultural experience, their trip may do harm for the host people, change host gazes, and threaten the strong relationships established by professional missionaries with the host people over many years. MacDonald criticizes that many STM groups are not prepared for working with a foreign language in a cross-cultural context. DeHainaut (1995) also stresses the problem that participants do

not prepare enough in terms of cross-cultural knowledge.

Reese (2007) examined the dependency problem in local churches caused by American missionaries and STM travellers working in the host community. According to Reese, STM travel makes local people expect that someone else will do things for them that they could otherwise do themselves. Reese pointed out that STM travellers want to achieve something where they can see a difference over a short period, but they usually do not consider the impact that they could have on the local people in the long run. The local people can lose their initiative to work for their communities and become dependent on foreign aid from the American churches. The STM teams usually do not know the local situation they confront, and although they may be satisfied with what they have done in a foreign country, they cannot know the long-term impact of their quick-fix solutions on the host community. Reese argues that STM travellers usually think that they can solve the problems and that the local people do not have the ability to solve them by themselves. Such thoughts may unintentionally cause a feeling of powerlessness among the local people, leading to particular host gazes. Reese identified the solution of the dependency problem as lying in the improved training and awareness of cross-cultural sensitivity for STM travellers.

Like Reese (2007), other researchers (DeHainaut, 1995; Slimbach, 2000) also examined negative impact of STM travellers on host people. Slimbach (2000) mentioned that in the colonial past, many Western missionaries thought that converted local people should follow Western culture because their culture was superior to the local culture. They did not consider the feelings and opinions of the host people, and did not recognize their own ethnocentrism. By taking the example of Western missionaries' colonialism, Slimbach (2000) pointed out the reiteration of colonialism through STMs today. According to Slimbach, like colonial Western missionaries, STM travellers have a Western-centred mind and do not seriously consider the local culture. As a result, they form only superficial relationships with the local people and maintain prejudices and stereotypes of the local people. This of course in turn fosters negative host gazes.

In DeHainaut's study (1995), some local people reported their frustrations over STM travellers and their paternalistic tendencies. According to locals' descriptions, STM travellers spent a lot of time on the beach and they did not spend time with local people. DeHainaut argues that STM travellers and their evangelistic work may strengthen paternalistic tendencies by producing a false sense of partnership.

Ver Beek (2007) investigated host people's perception of STM trips through conducting interviews with Honduran locals about their views of houses built by two groups, North American STM travellers and Honduran people. Based on the interviews, whereas the work of Honduran people led to a significant and lasting impact on their communities, there was no significant impact of North American STM travellers on the Honduran local communities. Furthermore, interviewed Hondurans reported that they would like STM travellers to spend their money on making more houses for Hondurans rather than on aeroplane tickets and lodging, suggesting a rather hostile host gaze upon STM travellers.

Most international STM trips include interaction between different cultures, histories and religions. However, STM studies on local people have mainly focused on direct, tangible impacts rather than host gaze dynamics. Although more and more non-Western STM travellers go to non-Western as well as Western places to spread Christianity (Moll, 2006), the topic of host gazes on non-Western STM travellers has obtained relatively little attention from tourism researchers as well as STM researchers.

Non-Western Hosts and Guests in Tourism Studies

In the tourism literature, only a few studies (Chan 2006; Maoz, 2006; Uriely et al., 2009; Moufakkir, 2011) have dealt with the non-

Western host gaze upon non-Western tourists. Maoz (2006) has attempted to examine both non-Western tourists' gazes and non-Western locals' gazes upon each other by observing the interaction between Israeli backpackers and Indian hosts. Maoz argues that hosts are not just passive objects gazed upon by tourists but tourists are also gazed at by hosts as *Others*. So, it is better called a 'mutual gaze'. Both tourists and hosts gaze upon each other and those gazes are influenced by the media and previous experiences. When the relationships between tourists and hosts are shallow and superficial, stereotypes are reinforced. On the other hand, when hosts and tourists have close and real interactions, their previously fixed images can change.

Chan (2006) has also dealt with the non-Western hosts' gaze upon non-Western tourists by investigating the interaction between Vietnamese hosts and Chinese tourists. According to Chan, those Asian host–guest relationships are heavily influenced by specific social, cultural and historical contexts. In Chan's study, the Vietnamese working hosts were again not passive objects but very much structured the interactions based on their perceptions of Chinese tourists. In contrast, the most recent study by Moufakkir (2011) looked at the gazes of Western hosts. By focusing on hosts' and tourists' cultural backgrounds, he compared the Dutch hosts' gaze upon German tourists with their gaze upon East Asian tourists. He concludes that the Dutch–German contacts reflected the cultural and historical relationships of the two nations. Interestingly, whereas Dutch respondents described negative feelings towards German tourists, they reported positive feelings toward Asian tourists. Thus, Moufakkir (2011) argues that the host gaze is dynamic. It can be positive and negative depending on cultural and historical contexts.

On the other hand, Uriely et al. (2009) have focused on situational circumstances as a main factor affecting host–tourist interactions. They observed interactions between Israeli tourists and Egyptian service providers in the Sinai Peninsula. According to their findings, Israeli tourists and the Egyptians had peaceful encounters despite the socio-cultural and historical frictions between these two cultures. Accordingly, Uriely *et al.* argue that host–tourist relationships reflect situational circumstances. In other words, depending on the situational conditions, both hosts and tourists respond to each other differently.

This suggests that there is a great need for more research on the non-Western–Western dynamics in host–guest relationships. There is a fast growing population of non-Western tourists. According to Chan (2006), since the 1990s the numbers of non-Western tourists have been increasing dramatically at destinations throughout the world. Chan also argues that non-Western tourism conducted by non-Western tourists is completely different from what has been observed from Western tourism. In addition, STM travel provides a specific situational context that warrants particular attention due to its focus on establishing relationships with local hosts. Further, there is usually a long-term missionary present, who is of the same culture as the STM travellers and tries to facilitate interactions. This is very different from typical local mediators such as tour guides. Thus, this chapter attempts to compare Western and non-Western tourists' perceptions of gazes of their non-Western hosts in international STM trips to shed light on the host gazes that emerge in this specific context. In order to do so, cultural hegemony serves as an important theoretical framework to understand the power dynamics underlying host gazes upon STM travellers.

Cultural Hegemony Theory

Cultural hegemony theory (Gramsci, 1971) can be applied to explain the impact of the asymmetrical power relationship between STM travellers and local residents. In cultural hegemony theory, the hegemonic power of the ruling group makes subordinate people voluntarily accept the culture imposed by groups in power. In other words, subordinate people willingly take part in social practices that are not in their best interests because they can obtain some tangible benefits by taking the ideology of the ruling group (Artz and Murphy, 2000). Gramsci was more concerned with how social relations were perceived and accepted by the mass population rather than socioeconomic relations *per se.* Furthermore, Gramsci emphasized that individual activities and perceptions are heavily affected by existing social and cultural conditions.

Asad (1976) argued that in colonial times, encounters between missionaries and Indigenous people were not just the encounter of different cultures but rather 'an unequal power encounter between the West and Third World' (p. 16). He stated that those encounters provided a chance to the West to access cultural and historical sources in those societies. Such encounters strengthened the unequal relationship between the European and the non-European worlds.

Gramsci (1971) claimed that if a special vision of the future is possessed by a group of people committed to and confidently communicating that vision, such a group has a powerful influence within society. It inevitably leads to contention of or conflict with other groups committed to a different vision. Hegemony means the victory of certain socially held ideologies over others. In a hegemonic condition, an increasing number of people in a society will transform their visions to hegemonic ideology because participation in the hegemonic ideology allows people to get greater benefits from their society. Moreover, those benefits obtained from acceptance of the hegemonic ideology are attractive for those people. By contrast, less powerful people who do not accept the hegemonic ideology rarely get social approbation from their society. Therefore, people voluntarily accept the cultural hegemony to obtain social approval or to avoid being isolated from the very societies in which they live.

Nye (2008) tries to explain the contemporary world of Americanization with Gramsci's theory of cultural hegemony.

Americanization is not just about cultural diffusion across the world, but also the process by which less powerful groups, including nations or cultures, internalize the culture of the predominant hegemony. According to her, religious diffusion can also be explained with the concept of cultural hegemonic power. Widespread American power has also meant the globalization of diverse American Christian churches, as previously occurred with historical European colonialism by the British and others. America has dominant political, economic and cultural power in the world and American culture is rooted in Christianity, which is the dominant religion of America. Accordingly, Christianity has cultural hegemony in the Americanized societies. Even though other ideologies struggle against its power, Christianity is selected as a way by which individuals and groups may be involved in the hegemony.

Stutzman (1996) attempted to explain the ideological and competitive dimensions of contemporary evangelical mission activities within Eastern Europe using the concept of Gramsci's cultural hegemony. In Eastern Europe, there exists a parallel between the Marxist mission and evangelical versions of the Christian mission. Both ideologies purpose a change and a transformation of society. They make every effort to turn people's minds to the vision to which they are committed. Both the Marxist and the Christian ideologies have visions transcending nationalistic interests. According to Stutzman (1996), Gramsci's theory gives the chance to explain the competitive and ideological nature of evangelical missions. The cultural hegemony of Western missionaries in Albania today has been caused by the opening of a once-closed society's doors. The disintegration of the Marxist monopoly has produced an ideological vacuum. After the collapse of the old Communist system, Albanians were struggling to find righteousness because of the moral ambiguity and ideological chaos. Any new idea could be considered better than chaos. Therefore, the new ideas brought in by Christian Westerners were attractive enough for a chaotic Albanian society. Albanians have had favourable attitudes towards the West

because of media images. This general attractiveness of Western culture on a popular level has made the presence of Western evangelical missionaries hegemonic because they came from the powerfully attractive Western culture. The majority of evangelical missionaries in Albania have taken advantage of Albanians' longing for and attraction to Western culture.

The developed infrastructure and technology of the Western evangelical missionary community facilitated the process of modernization in the Albanian society that was recovering from the oppressive ideological control of Marxism. Western evangelicals were aware of the necessity of active participation in the struggle of ideologies in order to implement their vision of the Good News. Stutzman (1996) concluded that this struggle was a cultural war on a global scale for the hearts and minds of people. As a result, the favourable attitudes of Albanian people towards the American culture contributed to their acceptance of American Christianity. In this process, mass media played a significant role in winning Albanians' minds by making American culture desirable.

Under globalization, cross-cultural encounters continuously occur, and the West still dominates the majority of political, economic and cultural resources. This means that, in most cases, the issue of power is rooted in the cross-cultural interaction between Western and developing world countries. In recent days, however, this power dynamic has become more complicated. The Korean Wave (Jin, 2007) is an important example of non-Western cultural products, and with them language, being admired and highly sought after. In the context of tourism, the phenomenon is rooted in many tourists from non-Western countries travelling around the world. This is also true for the STM context. Although the number of Western professional missionaries is steadily decreasing, the number of non-Western missionaries is expanding at even higher rates (Moll, 2006). Moreau asserted that 'the day of western missionary dominance is over' (cited by Moll, 2006, p. 20) because non-Western missionaries are explosively increasing. Moll (2006) reported that the number of non-Western missionaries was 3,411 in 1973 and now that number adds up to almost 103,000. Therefore, the unequal relationship between Western missionaries and Indigenous people in colonial times cannot be simply applied to the present phenomenon of contemporary mission trips. Consequently, research is needed that examines issues of cultural hegemony in the context of modern STMs that include both Western and non-Western Christians.

Study Focus

The focus of this research is on Southeast Asian hosts' gazes as they are perceived by international STM participants from the USA and Korea. As indicated above, many studies dealing with the host gaze have typically involved gazes on Western tourists, rather than on Eastern tourists (Perdue *et al.*, 1987; Ap, 1992; King *et al.*, 1993; Haralambopuolos and Pizam, 1996; Reisinger and Turner, 1998; Joseph and Kavoori, 2001; Enevoldsen, 2003; Gursoy and Rutherford, 2004; Kingsbury, 2005; Wang and Pfister, 2008; Chhabra, 2010). This study attempts to compare host gazes on Korean and American mission travellers. Thus, Korean and American mission travellers visiting the same countries have been interviewed so as to be able to compare the host gazes they encountered.

Methodology

This study purports to examine locals' gazes as perceived by STM travellers throughout the trip. A rich and deep understanding of this social phenomenon can best be attained by permitting the researcher to focus on the meaning of an individual participant's responses regarding his or her relationship with local residents by asking general and open-ended questions (Guba and Lincoln, 1994). Some researchers (Blezien, 2004; Friesen, 2004) studying STMs point out that it is difficult to statistically measure the

quality of such trips. Therefore, the qualitative approach is considered the most appropriate research design for understanding the multidimensional meaning of the international mission traveller's experience.

Specifically, the study examines the gazes of Cambodian and Thai hosts as they were perceived by Korean and American mission travellers. The USA and Korea are the top two nations in terms of number of STM travellers sent, especially to Southeast Asian countries. Moreover, the USA and Korea are examples of Western and Eastern cultures, respectively. Furthermore, both cultures have produced cultural products that have been communicated widely through mass media and are seen as attractive by other cultures.

Research setting

As receiving countries, Cambodia and Thailand in Southeast Asian have been selected. Both countries have a great number of both Korean and US missionaries (Kammerer, 1990; Gifford, 1994; Veale, 2007; Pneumanaut, 2010). According to Goh (2005), Thailand is the only Southeast Asian country that has never been colonized. Although it is a very open society and allows religious freedom, Thai culture is deeply rooted in the Buddhist religion. Therefore, Buddhism is the largest religion in Thailand, and only a very small percentage of the population identifies themselves as being Christian, though there are many Protestant missionaries residing there. As in Thailand, Cambodian culture is closely associated with Buddhism. Cambodia has a history of strong resistance towards the practice of all other forms of religion, including Christianity. Since 1990, Christianity, together with other religious practices, has been allowed in Cambodia. Nevertheless, it has a very small Christian population. Furthermore, the two countries also belong to the '10/40 window'; that is, the poor and less developed, non-Christian area of special interest to evangelical Christians.

Interview process and data analysis

In-depth interviews were conducted for about 60 min per participant. Questions for interviewing were open-ended and semi-structured. Participants were interviewed after returning from their STMs and were asked about their experiences, thoughts, and feelings about locals' attitudes and behaviours towards themselves as STM travellers. If the trip was not the first instance of overseas travel for the participants, their previous travel experiences were also addressed. As background information, the researcher asked participants about their age, their personal religious history, the church that organized the trip and additional thoughts about mission trips. For Korean participants, the Korean language was used, and all the interviews with American travellers were conducted in English. Transcripts for all audio-recorded interviews were made using the services of a transcription service company. The transcripts were analysed employing a thematic analysis. Results from the Korean interview data were then translated from Korean into English by a professional translator.

Participants

This study used snowball sampling because the target of this study was STM travellers, not a random sample. Participants have been selected from US and Korean mission travellers who went to Cambodia and Thailand within the past three years. The USA and Korea are the top two nations in terms of missionaries to other countries (Moll, 2006). According to the Pneumanaut web site, the percentage of Korean missionaries working in Asian countries (Pneumanaut, 2010) was almost 50% (northeast Asian countries: 26%, Southeast Asian countries: 17.2%) of total Korean missionaries. However, there have been no statistical reports about the number of STM participants by particular destinations for both American and Korean STMs.

STM participants in the USA

The explosive popularity of STMs is the biggest transformation in Christian mission history in America (Allen, 2001). Since the 1960s, the number of US STM travellers has been growing tremendously every year (Allen, 2001). According to Allen, 29% of all 13- to 17-year-old American youths have experienced STM trips or mission services, and 10% among youth STM travellers have gone on such a trip more than three times. Study respondents were recruited among college students or church leaders organizing international STM trips from Brazos County in Texas. Texas belongs to America's Bible Belt, defined by Merriam-Webster as 'an area chiefly in the southern United States whose inhabitants are believed to hold uncritical allegiance to the literal accuracy of the Bible; broadly: an area characterized by ardent religious fundamentalism'. There are no statistics on the number of mission trip participants by states, but it is generally thought that more evangelical Christians live in the Bible Belt than in other regions of the nation. Also, college students and teenagers occupy a large percentage of STM participants (Priest, 2005).

STM participants in Korea

In the early 1990s, STMs were introduced to Christian college groups in South Korea. Since the mid-1990s, STMs organized by local churches have experienced an explosive increase every year. Now STMs seem to have become a necessary course for almost all local churches in South Korea (Go, 7 September 2007). According to CBS reports (Go, 7 September 2007), more than 50,000 Koreans annually experience international mission trips. The total travel expense is estimated at up to US$1 billion. Although members of Korean STM groups have encountered dangers, such as being kidnapped or even being killed by terrorists in Afghanistan in 2007, the number of participants is still growing. South Korea sends out more career missionaries to other countries than any country except for the USA (Moll, 2006). South Korea sends out more than 1,100 new missionaries annually and, in 2006, 14,905 Korean missionaries were serving in 168 foreign countries (Moon, 2008). That means Korea alone sends out as many new missionaries each year as all of the countries of the West (except for the USA) combined. The largest proportion (47.3%) of Korean missionaries works in Asia.

Demographic information

Twenty Korean and 19 American STM travellers joined the interviews for this study (see Tables 10.1 and 10.2). Interviewed Korean mission travellers were from four different Korean churches. Many Korean Protestant Churches organizing STMs to Southeast Asian countries were contacted, but only four churches were willing to cooperate with this study. Two participants were from Saebat Presbyterian church, five from Namseoul Presbyterian Church, six from Choongshin Methodist Church and seven from Yoido Full Gospel Church. STMs of all Korean participants were organized by their churches. All American interviewees were from A&M Church for Christ (AFC). Other American churches and Campus Christian groups that were contacted did not have a plan to send STM travellers to Southeast Asian countries. For American participants, their mission trips were also managed by their church, AFC.

Of the Korean participants, 12 people went on an STM to Cambodia and eight interviewees went to Thailand in 2010. Seven Korean interviewees had never experienced an international STM before this time, and 13 had participated in an international STM more than once. Of all Korean interviewees, 10 were male and 10 were female. Their ages ranged from 19 to 58 years. Of the American participants, five mission travellers went to Cambodia and three to both Thailand and Cambodia in 2010. Three participants had experienced STM travel to Thailand in 2009. Another five interviewees had experienced STMs to Thailand or both Thailand and Cambodia in

previous years. Only three American interviewees had never gone on an international STM before. Eight Americans were male, and 11were female. Their ages ranged from 19 to 53 years.

Results

Participants who went to Cambodia visited several, very different places. Some of them went to rural and poor areas, but others went to the largest city in the country. The same was true for STM travellers to Thailand. Many of them visited very popular tourist destinations and a few worked in a small, agricultural and poor area. Therefore, their descriptions of the destination were drastically different depending on the place they visited.

Cambodia

Three Korean groups went to Cambodia and stayed in Phnom Penh, Kampot or Kampong Speu (see Fig. 10.1). As Fig. 10.2 shows, those sites are located in southern Cambodia. Phnom Penh is the capital and the largest city in Cambodia. Phnom Penh is the commercial, cultural, historical and tourist centre of Cambodia. Moreover, it is the richest and most highly populated city in Cambodia. Phnom Penh is known as the 'Pearl of Asia' because of its beautiful and historical architecture. It has a history of French colonization. More than 90% of people in Phnom Penh identify themselves as Buddhist. Since 1975, the number of Christians has been increasing. Kampot is also a city in Cambodia. It is a riverside town and so, waterfall, boating and rafting on the river are popular attractions. In addition, this city is developing as a touristic destination. Kampong Speu is a rural area and very poor because of severe droughts faced from year to year. Two American groups visited Cambodia. One group stayed in Phnom Penh for 3 weeks; the other groups generally stayed in Thailand and visited Siem Reap in Cambodia for a week

Table 10.1. Description of American participants.

Participant[a] (interview)	Age	Gender	Job	Target destination (period/year)	Most recent trip (destination)	Previous Int'l STM (no.)	Previous destinations
A1	19	F	Student	Thailand (7 weeks/'09)	2009 (Thailand)	N	
A2	19	F	Student	Thailand (7 weeks/'09)	2009 (Thailand)	Y(1)	Brazil
A3	26	M	Probationer/ Team leader	Thailand (1 year/'08)	2009 (Dominican)	Y(5)	Thailand (4)/ Dominican Rep.
C	23	M	Student/ Team leader	Thailand (2 months/'08)	2010 (Ukraine & Russia)	Y(7)	Mexico (4)/ Thailand (2)/ Ukraine & Russia
J1	19	M	Student	Cambodia (1 month/'10)	2010 (Cambodia)	Y(1)	Honduras
J2	20	F	Student	Thailand Cambodia (3 weeks)	2010 (Thailand & Cambodia)	Y(1)	Brazil
J3	25	F	Working	Thailand (9 months/'08)	2008 (Thailand)	Y(3)	Southeast Asia/ Thailand
J4	25	M	Working	Thailand (6 months/'08)	2008 (Thailand & Cambodia)	Y(2)	Romania & Kenya/Thailand & Cambodia
J5	23	F	Teacher	Thailand (2 months/'08)	2010 (Ukraine & Russia)	Y(7)	Romania/ Thailand/ Ukraine & Russia
J6	22	M	Student/ Team leader	Thailand (3 months/'09)	2009 (Thailand)	Y(3)	Thailand
K1	53	M	Church leader	Thailand (2 weeks/'10)	2010 (Thailand)	Y Since 1978 every year	Worldwide
K2	20	F	Student	Cambodia (1 month/'10)	2010 (Cambodia)	Y(2)	Mexico
K3	22	F	Student	Cambodia (1 month/'10)	2010 (Cambodia)	N	
L	27	F	Student	Thailand (6 months/'04)	2007 (Honduras)	Y(6)	Thailand (5)/ Honduras
MI	20	F	Student	Thailand Cambodia (3 weeks/'10)	2010 (Thailand & Cambodia)	N	
N	20	M	Student	Thailand Cambodia (3 weeks/'10)	2010 (Thailand & Cambodia)	Y(4)	Honduras (4)
R	20	F	Student/ Team leader	Cambodia (1 month/'10)	2010 (Cambodia)	Y(2)	Thailand/Ukraine
S	22	M	Student	Cambodia (1 month/'10)	2010 (Cambodia)	Y(1)	Mexico
T	30	F	Church leader	Thailand (6 months/'09)	2008 (Uganda)	Y Since 2000, every year	Worldwide

Note: [a]The trips of American participants were organized by Aggies For Christ Church in College Station, TX.

Table 10.2. Description of Korean participants.

Participant (interview)	Age	Gender	Job	Target destination (1 week/'10)[a]	Church organizing the trip	Previous Int'l STM (no.)	Previous destinations
KG	28	F	Working	Cambodia	Yoido	N	
KM	33	F	No	Cambodia	Choongshin	Y(2)	Philippines/Cambodia
KS	38	M	Working	Cambodia	Choongshin	N	
KJ	32	F	No	Cambodia	Choongshin	Y(1)	Philippine
KC	28	M	Student/Team leader	Thailand	Namseoul	Y(4)	Hungary & Turkey/Egypt & Niger/Malaysia/Indonesia
KH	20	F	Student	Cambodia	Choongshin	N	
MG	22	M	Student	Thailand	Namseoul	N	
SM	42	F	No	Cambodia	Saebat	Y(3)	Mongolia (3)
SY	35	F	Working	Thailand	Yoido	Y(1)	Japan
SH	26	M	No	Cambodia	Choongshin	N	
W1	29	M	No	Cambodia	Choongshin	Y(8)	Cambodia
W2	33	M	Teacher	Cambodia	Yoido	N	
Y	31	F	Working	Cambodia	Yoido	Y(1)	Peru
L	20	F	Student	Thailand	Namseoul	N	
I	28	M	No/wTeam leader	Cambodia	Yoido	Y(2)	Cambodia
CS	59	F	No	Cambodia	Saebat	Y(3)	Cambodia (2)/Vietnam
CE	27	F	Working	Thailand	Yoido	Y(3)	India/Taiwan (2)
CJ	38	M	Working/Team leader	Thailand	Yoido	Y(10)	Taiwan (5)/China/Singapore/Hong Kong/Philippines (2)
H1	28	M	Working	Thailand	Namseoul	Y(4)	Thailand (2)/Cambodia (2)
H2	26	M	No	Thailand	Namseoul	Y(2)	Thailand

Note: [a]All Korean participants have experienced STMs in 2010 and their travel time was 1 week.

before they returned home. Siem Reap is a famous touristic destination. It is the closest city to the world-famous temples of Angkor.

Thailand

One group of Korean mission travellers stayed and worked in Bangkok and Chon Buri (see Fig. 10.2). Bangkok is the capital and the largest urban city in Thailand. Also, it is one of the nation's top tourist destinations. It ranked third in Euromonitor International's list of top city destinations in

2008. Chon Buri is the nearest beach destination to Bangkok after Pattaya, which is the most beach destination in Thailand and ranked 23rd in the Euromonitor International's list of top city destinations in 2008.

According to Korean participants, there were many tall buildings and big shopping malls in Bangkok. They said that they had a few hours of free time in Bangkok and went shopping at the mall. On the other hand, to the Korean participants, Chon Buri looked like a rural area. They explained that Chon Buri was less developed than Bangkok and

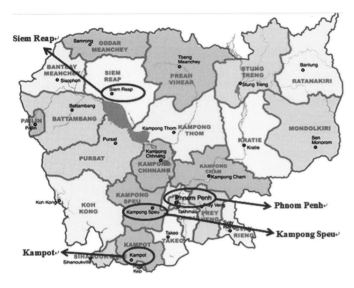

Fig. 10.1. Map of Cambodia. (Source: www. canbypublications.com.)

Fig. 10. 2. Map of Thailand. (Source: www.wordtravels .com.)

they could rarely see tall buildings. Another Korean group consisting of three people visited Chiang Mai and its suburbs. Chiang Mai is the biggest and the most culturally significant city in Northern Thailand. It is also one of the top touristic destinations in Thailand. The mission trip participants worked with children in Chiang Mai. According to their description, in the city of Chiang Mai, it seemed that children were familiar with foreigners and did not show a particular interest in the participants' work. In its suburbs, Korean participants perceived the areas to be agricultural and very poor. They described the residents of one suburb as showing hospitality and being very welcoming to them, but in another suburb people were not interested in the mission travellers and did not act very favourably towards them. The American mission travellers visited Chiang Mai and Phuket. Like Chiang Mai, Phuket is one of the most famous destinations in Thailand and ranked 31st in Euromonitor International's list of top city destinations in 2008.

Three types of local residents

There were three types of local residents interacting with STM travellers. The first type was Korean and American long-term missionaries. The second type of local residents interacting with STM travellers were local Christians. STM travellers spent most of their times with local Christians rather than local non-Christians. STM travellers reported that they did not have many opportunities to communicate with local non-Christians.

Missionaries

In all cases, there were missionaries who received STM travellers at the destination with the same cultural identity as the short-term mission travellers. From participants' reports, it is found that those missionaries had a connection with the sending churches or the individual STM travellers themselves. Peterson *et al.* (2003) have called them field facilitators. According to Peterson *et al.*, field facilitators are responsible for on-field STM arrangements because they are more familiar with the host environment than mission travellers and often speak the local language fluently. Peterson *et al.* (2003) have argued that field facilitators are essential participants of STMs along with STM travellers. Interviewed STM travellers followed the programme provided by the missionaries.

Most STM travellers stayed and acted together with missionaries because they were not familiar with the local culture and circumstances. They heavily relied on missionaries' guidance. Both American and Korean STM travellers expressed great gratitude for their missionaries' help. According to American participants, their missionaries showed favourable attitudes towards them and supported them as much as they could. Therefore, they could easily gain access to local residents and build a relationship with locals. One American traveller (C, male said:

> I think the missionary was very communicative of cultural things, and we were able to ahead of time prepare for that, I think. Most of these Thai churches have been dealing with American missionaries for a long time. They had teams in the past so they knew exactly what kinds of things to expect. So, they would say 'hey don't do this because it isn't appropriate in Thai culture' or 'this might be kind of weird for us but realize it's normal here', so they were very good with that.

Missionaries were important facilitators for STM travellers because they were familiar with both cultures. Therefore, they understood STM travellers' mistakes from not knowing a local culture and tried to teach local culture. On the other hand, according to Korean STM travellers, Korean missionaries were more concerned about locals' thoughts and feelings about STM travellers than STM travellers' feelings. Korean STM travellers of the Cambodia team reported that their missionary did not allow them to have close contact with and give their contact information to local residents because locals could be hurt by STM travellers' attitude after returning to Korea. One Korean STM traveller (KC, male) said:

> Our missionary said, 'Unless you can guarantee to keep a relationship with local people after you go back to Korea, don't give your contact information to them. Don't build a close relationship with them because local people often get hurt by STM travellers. After going back to Korea, many STM travellers forget the local people and in many cases, they do not respond to local people. For you, such a relationship may not be important but for them, a relationship with Korean people is not trivial. Some locals really want to go to Korea for getting a job or going to college. For them, a connection with Korean people is very important. So, don't think a relationship with locals is trivial.'

Some Korean STM travellers explained that their missionary scolded STM travellers for their carelessness towards local people and a lack of preparedness for their travel.

Our team members were scolded by our missionary for our lateness and unpreparedness. He said that some STM teams were not welcome because of their unpreparedness and cultural insensitivity. So, we made efforts to change our attitude and wanted to show him our assiduousness because we didn't want him to become disappointed. (H1, male, Korean)

Whereas Korean missionaries were strict about STM participants, American missionaries were flexible and generous. From participants' reports, it is considered that Korean missionaries thought of STM travellers as their students. STM travellers had to follow their guidance. On the other hand, American missionaries considered their STM members their family. According to American STM members, their missionaries were very welcoming and made them feel very comfortable.

Local Christians

A question regarding the evaluation of interactions with local residents was asked of the participants. All American, and some Korean, mission travellers replied that local residents liked them and showed hospitality towards them. Those local residents were local Christians. According to participants, they were very satisfied with the attitude and hospitality of the local Christians. Local Christians' favourable attitudes facilitated STM participants' purpose of evangelism. According to one American participant (A4, male), 'They came to us because they were our friends. They wanted to see us again. They liked us. They liked that relationship we had.' Other American mission travellers also expressed satisfaction with the local Christians' hospitality: 'I was completely satisfied with the people. They were terrific people. And I couldn't have asked for a better, more welcoming, fun group of people to have met' (N, male). Another said 'I am just blessed by the people I knew, very much so, even my frustrating students blessed me, and it was a wonderful month of my life, and they missed us a lot when we left' (K2, female). Like American mission travellers, Korean mission travellers also

described their satisfaction with the relationship with local Christian people, 'I was satisfied with the relationship with locals. We carried out everything that we had planned. The response from the locals was very good and we were all satisfied' (KG, female, Korean). Many travellers indicated that they would like to visit the same places again because of the warm and kind attitude of the locals they encountered.

Many American and some Korean participants described that they had a strong relationship with local Christians and local missionaries. They spent more time with local Christians than local non-Christians. They shared their faith, and they worked together. Local Christians provided accommodation and food, and showed hospitality towards them. Therefore, they were able to build closer relationships with local Christians than local non-Christians. They reported that local Christian people contacted them through e-mail and Facebook as soon as they had left. Some American STM travellers expressed that after they came back to the USA, some local Christians came to the USA to visit them.

Since I've been back, I still have a really close friendship with her [one of the local Christians] and I continue to kind of keep up with and chat with other friends online that I have made over there. (J6, male, American)

I've been frequently keeping in touch after returning from the trip. We talk about how they are doing there, that they are diligently studying Korean... We very often talk about these little things by online. I've registered them as my friends on Facebook and have posted photos for us to enjoy together. (KG, female, Korean)

I grew really fond of them and because they are tender-hearted, they seemed to have a hard time saying goodbye. We kept waving goodbye at the airport... I think we were able to give our love to them and receive theirs in return... We exchanged e-mail addresses ... and when I arrived, I had already received an e-mail. (W2, male, Korean)

The relationship between local Christians and STM travellers were different from host–tourist relationships found in other tourism contexts. Their relationships lasted after the STM trips had ended. Some STM travellers have visited the same place more than three times.

Local non-Christians

The last type of local residents was local non-Christians. Although STM travellers tried to have a lot of contact with local non-Christians, they had less chance to communicate with local non-Christians than expected. Many participants, mainly American STM travellers, indicated that one of their purposes was to help local Christians – including local missionaries – to meet and evangelize local non-Christians. They reported that they could encourage local Christians and missionaries by bringing local non-Christians to the church through their volunteer work. One participant (I, male, Korean) expressed, '[STM is about], first, carrying out the work of God and helping out the missionaries and local Christians there.'

For local non-Christians, STM travellers were *Others*, that is, foreigners like other travellers. However, local non-Christians followed STM travellers because STM travellers often provided material help like money, clothes, shoes or educational instruments to local people. They also represented desirable cultural values (e.g. English language skills, knowledge of Korean soap operas), which made interactions with them attractive. In order to get their services and material goods, local people would have to listen to and sometimes follow mission travellers' religious messages and do what mission travellers wanted them to do. The STM travellers perceived the gaze as generally positive but geared towards exchanges of goods and services. As a consequence, STM travellers saw their relationships with non-Christian locals as superficial and shallow.

This situation was often especially seen with the Korean STM travellers. One Korean participant reported that when she gave some gifts to local kids, she first asked them to follow what she said or to say 'Amen'.

Moreover, Thai and Cambodian people whom Korean STM travellers visited rarely had a chance to get medical treatments. Korean mission travellers provided dental and general medical services to those locals for free. Therefore, in participants' responses, the local people did not resist or reject what Korean STM travellers wanted them to do. Furthermore, there was no one who showed hostility to Korean travellers' demands. Rather, according to Korean travellers, locals were willing to follow what they asked locals to do. They put up with things to reap the desired benefits.

> Treating the sick was the apparent purpose of the trip, but what I really wanted to do was spread the Word of God and let them know that God loves them... That is why we keep telling them, 'Believe in God. God loves you.' We constantly tell the people there these two things in their language, including when they come to receive treatment. (KJ, female, Korean)

> Whenever we give them gifts or carry out an activity, we tell them, 'Believe in God. God loves you.' Then we have the children say 'Amen'. When they say 'Amen', we give them gifts and paint their faces... But they didn't seem to be saying 'Amen' because they truly felt their love for Jesus. They seemed to be saying 'Amen' because they wanted to receive the gifts and saw us handing out presents when they said 'Amen'. (KH, female, Korean)

The same situation happened to American STM travellers. They provided free English lessons. According to Pennycook (1998), English has become 'a compulsory requirement' (p. 422) by the force of globalization. Masavisut *et al.* (1986) indicated that, in Thai society, Thai people from all levels use English in order to achieve their personal goals. STM participants already knew that Thai and Cambodian people desired to learn English and to have a chance to practise talking in English: 'The educated, those who can speak English, are the ones with the nice high-paying jobs. And it amazed me that you have to be able to speak English to get a high-paying job' (K3, female, American). 'Well, I guess our students benefitted by learning some English, and that makes them more marketable for jobs. So that would help the town a lot' (A2, female, American).

From STM travellers' reports, it is considered that for local non-Christians, STM travellers are the travellers who give them something they need at a very cheap price. However, one American STM traveller (J1, male, American) reported that he received a letter from one of their non-Christian students. In the letter, she expressed her gratitude and friendship towards the mission travellers. A female American STM traveller had the same experience:

> One girl, who was one of my students, wrote me a letter that was just so beautiful when I left. Just the longest, nicest letter about everything that I meant to her and how glad she was to know me. (K3, female, American)

Nevertheless, from participants' reports, it could be found that they did not have a close relationship with local non-Christians. STM travellers explained that local non-Christians were people who they have to evangelize.

Cultural hegemony

In the context of STMs, the theme of cultural hegemony was found within the circumstances of providing volunteer work to local residents. There existed a few cases showing a conflict between Christian ideology and the local culture. One local resident resisted the exercise of cultural hegemony. According to Laitin (1986), a challenge to hegemony; that is, counter-hegemony, always happens in a society. Counter-hegemony plays a role in clarifying the existence of hegemony. A few American participants described the tension between their Christian ideology and the local culture. On the first day of free English lessons, a local resident, who was a doctor in Cambodia, came to them in order to practise English. However, after he noticed that a Bible was being used as the textbook, he never showed up again. He had a powerful position as a doctor in his country. The chance to practise English was less valuable to the doctor than to

other less powerful locals. The doctor held the power to deny what he did not want:

> Of all my students, I had one man. At the first day, we really got along he had not received the book, the Bible, yet. He's very well educated. As I remember, he was a doctor. At the second day he came back, he opened to the first page of the book. It says that the first chapter title was 'God created the Universe.' After he read, he said 'Oh, it's religious.' He kept saying, 'religious', he wanted no part of any religion, no matter what it was. He was an evolutionist and an atheist. He didn't come back the next day. (K3, female, American)

One American mission traveller (R, female) explained the relationships among development of Cambodia, the conversion to Christianity and the local culture. According to her, as the city of Phnom Penh is changing and progressing, Cambodian people are losing a part of their culture. She had lived in Cambodia for a year with her parents working as missionaries. So, this trip was the second visit to Cambodia for her. Compared with her last visit, she described that Cambodian people were more likely to act in Western ways, be more selfish, less family-based and community-based, and more independent. She also explained that Christianity is growing rapidly in Cambodia with the development of the city. From participants' reports, Christianity caused tension among family members. One American participant who went to Thailand (A4, male) emphasized the family barriers against their evangelizing work.

> Thailand is a Buddhist country. So, one thing that hinders Thai people from becoming Christian even if they want to be is their parents would disown them because they feel that if you are Buddhists, you are our family. So, if you go against Buddhism, you're going against your family. It will hinder a lot of Thai people who want to become Christian. In order to be a Christian, Thai people overcome the family barrier. (A4, male, American)

One of the Korean participants who visited Thailand also mentioned the challenges encountered when spreading Christian messages.

I visited one family because the mother asked our team to visit and pray for her family. In her family, she was the only Christian and her sons were not. When we prayed for her sons in their house, they did not want to stay with us and showed a kind of hostility toward us. Their mother said that it was due to the importance of the family union caused by a Buddhist culture. Korean missionary who took care of our team also said that it was so hard to convert Thai people to Christians because of the family barrier. He said that in Thailand, a family is everything and the family value is absolute. So, Christianity was sometimes perceived as a cultural breaker the norm of Buddhism and the Thai tradition for Thai Buddhists. (CJ, male, Korean)

The above-mentioned examples illustrate that resistance against Christianity does indeed exist. For local people, the Christian culture conveyed by STM travellers is accompanied by Christian values and therefore can create cultural conflicts.

Conclusion

This study investigated the local gazes of Southeast Asian hosts on American and Korean mission travellers by conducting qualitative research. From the reports of both American and Korean mission travellers, it was found that there are three types of host gazes. Long-term missionaries sent by US and Korean churches dealt with STM travellers like students or family members. They tried to teach them about the local culture and guide the interactions with local residents. For them, the guests were an important part of their mission. The STM travellers perceived their gaze as equal and supportive. Importantly, they were instrumental in mediating STM traveller gazes upon other locals and locals' gazes upon the foreign travellers.

For local Christians, STM travellers' visits meant encouragement and support. It is really hard to live as a Christian in Thailand and Cambodia because of conflicts with family members and their traditional values grounded in Buddhism. In this situation, cultural hegemony was very much

apparent. STM travellers embody things and values the local Christians want to adopt. Local Christians tried to change their culture as well as their faith. In this context, they had conflicts with their family and the traditional values. Therefore, STM travellers and the relationships with them have a lot of meaning for local Christians. From participants' reports, it can be seen that it was not a simple host–tourist relationship. They shared their faith and their lives with travellers. Their gazes were not superficial but geared at establishing long-term relationships. Christianity provided the common ground that facilitated exchanges and made cultural differences move to the background. Both Western and non-Western STM travellers perceived these host gazes by local Christians as warm and welcoming.

However, for local non-Christians, STM travellers were just American or Korean travellers. Local non-Christians can obtain some materials or services from them that represent cultures they admire. Like many tourists, STM travellers do not know the local culture well and they even try to evangelize the locals. However, no one rejected and resisted the STM travellers and their actions. Rather, they expressed gratitude. At the same time, the interviewed STM travellers perceived their gaze as objectifying. The locals took advantage of the STM travellers by exploiting them as cultural resources and deliverers of desirable material goods as much as possible. Consequently, their relationships with STM travellers were not close and meaningful. Hostility in the host gaze of non-Christians was only experienced indirectly and was not directed at the STM travellers but rather at the local Christians who wanted them to identify with Christian values. It is important to note that the experiences of local non-Christian gazes did not differ for Korean and American STM travellers as both groups were perceived to be *Others* like mass tourists.

The study findings indicate that in the context of STM travel, host gazes are not uniform. They also suggest that traditional notions of culture distinguishing between Western and non-Western travellers are not the only cultural values to be taken into account in this context. While cultural goods such as language were important to non-Christian locals, Christianity was the cultural framework that coloured the gazes for the local Christians. By seeking out aspects of Christian culture through interactions with STM travellers, the local Christians willingly exposed themselves to travellers' cultural as well as religious values, and the non-Christians put up with attempts aimed at cultural transformation to receive the goods and services they wanted. In this sense, this study supports that the host gaze can be a cultural gaze influenced by cultural hegemony, but what is seen as dominant and desirable differs among hosts. Both the Western and the non-Western STM travellers represented cultural values that were seen as superior by the locals. This clearly challenges the way culture has been treated in host–guest relationships. Furthermore, the host gazes and tourist gazes were mediated by long-term missionaries who are neither locals nor travellers. Therefore, the research confirms that host gazes in STM contexts are complex phenomena that need further exploration.

References

Allen, M. (2001) Mission tourism? Faithworks. http://www.faithworks.com/archives/mission_tourism.htm (accessed 4 November 2010).

Ap, J. (1992) Residents' perceptions of tourism impacts. *Annals of Tourism Research* 19, 665–690.

Artz, L. and Murphy, B.D. (2000) *Cultural Hegemony in the United States*. Sage Publications, Thousand Oaks, CA.

Asad, T. (1976) Introduction. In: Asad, T. (eds) *Anthropology and the Colonial Encounter*. Humanities Press, Atlantic Highlands, NJ, pp. 9–19.

Blezien, P. (2004) the impact of summer international short-term missions experiences on the cross-cultural sensitivity of undergraduate college student participants. *Dissertation Abstracts International* 65(1), 81.

Brown, L.E. (2003) A program for congregation-based short-term international evangelistic campaigns. Retrieved from ProQuest Digital Dissertations (AAT 3129988).

Chan, Y.W. (2006) Coming of age of the Chinese Tourists. *Tourist Studies* 6(3), 187–213.

Chhabra, D. (2010) How they see us: perceived effects of tourist gaze on the old order Amish. *Journal of Travel Research* 49(1), 93–105.

Cohen, E. (1990) The missionary as stranger: a phenomenological analysis of Christian missionaries' encounter with the folk religions of Thailand. *Review of Religious Research* 31(4), 337–349.

Comaroff, J. and Comaroff, J. (1986) Christianity and colonialism in South Africa. *American Ethnologist* 13(1), 1–22.

Creswell, J.W. (2007) *Qualitative Inquiry and Research Design: Choosing Among Five Traditions*. Sage Publications, Thousand Oaks, CA.

DeHainaut, R. (1995). Anachronism and adventurism: recent mission trends. *The Christian Century*. http://www.religion-online.org/showarticle.asp?title=144 (accessed 23 March 2010).

Dunch, R. (2002) Beyond cultural imperialism: cultural theory, Christian missions, and global modernity. *History and Theory* 41(3), 301–325.

Enevoldsen, K. (2003) See no evil, hear no evil: an 'outsider's' encounter with cultural tourism in South Africa. *Cultural Studies Critical Methodologies* 3(4), 486–502.

Fanning, D. (2009) Short-term missions: a trend that is growing exponentially. *Trends and Issues in Missions*. http://works.bepress.com/don_fanning/13 (accessed 16 September 2010).

Friesen, R.G. (2004) *The Long-term Impact of Short-Term Missions on the Beliefs, Attitudes and Behaviours of Young Adults*. University of South Africa Press, Pretoria.

Gailey, C. and Culbertson, H. (2007) *Discovering Missions*. Beacon Hill Press, Kansas City, KN.

Gifford, P. (1994) Some recent developments in African Christianity. *African Affairs* 93(373), 513–534.

Go, S.P. (2007) 개별교회 실적위주 '단기선교' 문제는 없나 [Performance-based individual churches 'mission trip' We'll hire]. http://www.cbs.co.kr/Nocut/Show.asp?IDX=611526 (accessed 17 March 2010).

Goh, R.B. (2005) *Christianity in Southeast Asia*. ISEAS Publications, Singapore.

Gramsci, A. (1971) *Selection from Prison Notebook* (Hoare, Q. and Nowell-Smith, G. trans.). Lawrence and Wishart, London.

Guba, E.G. and Lincoln, Y.S. (1994) Competing paradigms in qualitative research. In: Denzin, N.K. and Lincoln, Y.S. (eds) *Handbook of Qualitative Research*. Sage, Thousand Oaks, CA, pp. 105–117.

Gursoy, D. and Rutherford, D. (2004) Host attitudes toward tourism: an improved structural model. *Annals of Tourism Research* 31(3), 495–516.

Haralambopuolos, N. and Pizam, A. (1996) Perceived impacts of tourism: the case of Samos. *Annals of Tourism Research* 23(3), 503–526.

Jin, D.Y. (2007) Reinterpretation of cultural imperialism: emerging domestic market vs continuing US dominance. *Media, Culture & Society* 29(5), 753–771.

Joseph, C. and Kavoori, A. (2001) Mediated resistance: tourism and the host community. *Annals of Tourism Research* 28, 998–1009.

Kammerer, C.A. (1990) Customs and Christian conversion among Akha Highlanders of Burma and Thailand. *American Ethnologist* 17(2), 277–291.

King, B., Pizam, A. and Milman, A. (1993) Social impacts of tourism: host perceptions. *Annals of Tourism Research* 20, 650–665.

Kingsbury, P. (2005) Jamaican tourism and the politics of enjoyment. *Geoforum* 36, 113–132.

Klinkerman, L. (2002) Students gear up for mission trip during spring break. http://www.dailytoreador.com/archives/article_6b8e6a6d-0763-53bc-9c18-490ef6a43b62.html (accessed 31 October 2007).

Laitin, D. (1986). Hegemony and culture: politics and religious change among the Yoruba. University of Chicago Press, Chicago, IL.

MacDonald, G.J. (2006) On a mission – a short-term mission. *USA Today*. http://www.usatoday.com/news/religion/2006-06-18-mission-vacations_x.htm (accessed 18 September 2007).

Maoz, D. (2006) The mutual gaze. *Annals of Tourism Research* 33(1), 221–239.

Masavisut, N., Sukwiwat, M. and Wongmontha, S. (1986) The power of the English language in Thai media. *World Englishes,* 1/2, 197–207.

Moll, R. (2006) Missions incredible. *Christianity Today*. http://www.christianitytoday.com/ct/2006/march/16.28.html (accessed 17 March 2010).

Moon, S. (2008) The Protestant missionary movement in Korea: current growth and development. *International Bulletin of Missionary Research* 32(2), 59–64.

Moufakkir, O. (2011) The role of cultural distance in mediating the host gaze. *Tourist Studies* 11(1), 73–89.

Nye, M. (2008) *Religion: the Basics*. Routledge, New York.

Pennycook, A. (1998) *English and the Discourses of Colonialism*. Routledge, New York.

Perdue, R., Long, P. and Allen, L. (1987) Resident support for tourism development. *Annals of Tourism Research* 17(4), 586–599.

Peterson, R., Aeschiliman, G. and Sneed, R. W. (2003) *Maximum Impact Short-Term Mission: the God-Commanded, Repetitive Deployment of Swift, Temporary, Non-Professional Missionaries*. STEM Press, Minneapolis, MN.

Pneumanaut (2010) 한국 선교사 파송현황. (trans. The current state of Korean missionaries sent to foreign countries) http://www.cyworld.com/pneumanaut (accessed 1 September 2009).

Priest, R. (2005) Are short-term missions good stewardship? *Christianity Today*. http://www.christianitytoday.com/ct/2005/julyweb-only/22.0.html (accessed 17 September 2007).

Reese, R. (2007) Short-term missions and dependency. *World Mission Associates Research* 24(4), 982–984.

Reisinger, Y. and Turner, L. (1998) Cultural differences between Asian tourist markets and Australian hosts, part 1. *Journal of Travel Research* 40(3), 295–315.

Slimbach, R. (2000) First do no harm: short-term missions at the dawn of a new millennium. *Evangelical Mission Quarterly* October, 428–441.

Stutzman, L. (1996) To win the hearts and minds: evangelical mission activity in Albania as global culture war. *Journal of Ecumenical Studies* 33(1), 44–58.

Uriely, N., Maoz, D. and Reichel, A. (2009) Israeli guests and Egyptian hosts in Sinai: a bubble of serenity. *Journal of Travel Research* 47(4), 508–522.

Veale, J. (2007). Korean missionaries under fire. *Time*. http://www.time.com/time/world/article/0,8599,1647646,00.html (accessed 17 September 2009).

Ver Beek, K.A. (2007) Lessons from the sapling: review of quantitative search on short-term missions. http://www.calvin.edu/academic/sociology/faculty/verbeek/kurt/Lessonsfromasapling.pdf (accessed 17 March 2010).

Wang, Y. and Pfister, R. (2008) Residents' attitudes toward tourism and perceived personal benefits in a rural community. *Journal of Travel Research* 47, 84–93.

11 Couchsurfing through the Lens of Agential Realism: Intra-Active Constructions of Identity and Challenging the Subject–Object Dualism

Michael O'Regan

Introduction

We imagine that as soon as we are torn out of our habitual path all is over, but it is only the beginning of something new and good. (Leo Tolstoy, 1983, p. 1043)

Globalization has brought change on many levels, with metaphors of mobility increasingly used to explain a moving world with objects, dangers, people, ideas, images, knowledge, information, symbols and capital circulating through complex imaginative, physical, geographic, corporeal and virtual flows, underpinning social, material, political, economic and cultural processes. In this more globalized and interconnected world, it seems 'we are all on the move' (Bauman, 1998, p. 77), the mobilities paradigm helping to make visible circulations, flows and movements. These are born out of choice, fate, obligation or compulsion, from everyday practices of moving through public and virtual spaces, encompassing desired movement for pleasure, work and leisure to those movements generated, coerced and forced because of war, famine, failing economies and climate change. While individuals who are in control of their mobility are not simply cogs in a machine, mobility behaviours are often learned early in life

and performed almost unthinkingly as routine travel (and tourism) practices; performances based on an ability and willingness to habitually use established and increasingly efficient, speedier and more secure mobility systems. Steady, long-term trends in mobility behaviour across generations in proportion to ascending social mobility have heightened the obligations of individuals to be mobile in order to grasp the opportunities that geographic mobility is perceived to give. Tourist travel, now as much a necessity as a luxury is accelerating touristic mobilities, creating a hierarchy of mobility that is a powerful stratifying factor; the movements of second home owners to amenity migrants often seen as the result of the indulgences of an affluent Western middle class. Urry (1990) uses the metaphor of the 'tourist gaze' to refer to what he sees as the modern tourist's ability to 'seek out only the exotic, authentic "other" and experience every destination through a detached "gaze" that rarely engages the "real" (i.e. uncommodified) aspects of the place' (Williams and Kaltenborn, 1999, p. 214). The result, according to Urry (2002: 9) and MacCannell (1976: 46) is that modern tourism is 'institutionalizing' the rights of outsiders to look into its 'real lives' of others for the exclusive use of tourists, delivering access to 'back stages' while locals, even those involved in the tourism industry seek to protect those areas (Quinn, 2007). While there is no single tourist gaze, it suggests that the 'guest' is in a position of leisure, able to simply gaze upon their chosen destination and its people and culture, while 'hosts' are working and must perform their expected everyday duties (Nash, 1989; Urry, 1990; MacCannell, 2001). Smith (1977) suggests that tourism is represented largely as being complicit in the perpetuation of the exploitative relationship between the West and the rest, since tourists and an overpowering tourism–industrial complex (Salazar, 2005) attempt to enroll the other, delving deeply into cultures, peoples and places too weak to resist. It is no wonder then, that the term 'tourist' in contemporary understandings of mobility is value-laden and imbued as culturally derogative and negative (Fussell, 1980; Jacobsen, 2000), the meanings given to tourism and the 'tourist' associated with 'negative, morally suspect, activities' (McCabe, 2005, p. 103).

The Practice and Performance of Tourism

Critics argue that sedimentated tourist practices have become routine for many privileged individuals, who take 'travelling for granted' (Kaplan, 2002, p. 32); content with 'obviously inauthentic experiences' (MacCannell, 1976, p. 94) as hegemonic tourist discourses provided by the media become etched into social spaces and movements, their habits conditioned by institutionalized configurations that precede them, delimiting the options available to them while reliving the tourist of decision making. Peterson (2010) argues one develops 'predispositions to act in certain ways', where much (mobility) consumption is undertaken in the course of achieving what people count as normal social practice, signalling membership of society, conforming to convention and reproducing social order (Shove, 2002). As tourists become socialized into consuming by habitual and

unreflexive gazing, they playfully construct meanings from pseudo-events, staged authenticity, commercialism and signs; familiarity and routine often 'good enough' (Lyons and Loo, 2008). Acting out habitual tourist practices so as not to 'interfere with the carefully prepared sense of relaxation and getting-away-from-it-all that forms a basic objective of the trip' (Oakes, 2006a, p. 244), their gazing is associated with the destruction of place (O'Reilly, 2000); the resulting 'environmental bubbles' (Crick, 1989) having a disruptive impact on peoples, places and cultures (Smith, 1977). Boniface describes the way in which the tourist 'surrounded by, but not integrated in, the host society', travels in a world of their own, adhering to a formula of activity by signs, rules, scripts, codes and messages that dictates the tourist role and keeps them apart from the host community. Grateful for everything that excludes 'surprise, randomness, and change' (Boniface, 1998, p. 749), tourists are deemed largely path-dependent and on 'auto-pilot' (Boniface, 1998, p. 749), enjoying 'a certain independence and even isolation from its immediate surroundings' (McIntosh et al., 1995, p. 245). Dependent on 'distinct social spaces that orchestrate new forms of social life' (Lassen, 2006), a thick networks of shopping malls, museums, golf courses, railway stations, hotels, resorts, airports, museums and beaches are incorporated as habit, an alliance of businesses and institutions circulating (regulating) them across, and a highly 'rehearsed geography of locations, positions and routes' (Soguk, 2003, p. 32) investing deeply so habit is reproduced. Meeting the 'desire for performance' (Soguk, 2003, p. 30), tourists drawing on a 'repertoire of gestures and interactive competencies' (Gottdiener, 1995, p. 73) every time they enter a hotel, theme park or restaurant, as they seek to accumulate social, political and cultural capital.

Tourism, however, is a complex phenomenon, working more as a metaphor than a label, encompassing different activities and practices since how we move is a distinct aspect of our personal and social identity. Tourism research often fails to acknowledge how individuals confirm their identity claims around certain practices that are not linked with the accumulation of economic, social or cultural capital, identity is no longer a matter of occupying an already given subject position (Diken and Laustsen, 2001), 'individuals now seem to be more than ever prone to articulate complex affiliations, meaningful attachments and multiple allegiances to issues, people, places and traditions that lie beyond the boundaries of their resident nation-state' (Cohen, 2006, p. 189). We are only beginning to acknowledge how individuals can reposition themselves spatially, temporally and socially; building skills, knowledge and competences to achieve a mobility-related aspiration or project, which can form a stable investment of meaning and a 'deepening of the self through concerted work on the self' (Thrift, 1994, p. 330). For Hetherington (2000, p. 83) 'people want to know that they are part of something larger like that they also want to know where it is they fit in', even if that invokes a controlled disintegration or subjugation of old values as individuals induce control over their mobility to embody a 'reflexivity organized trajectory of the self' (Giddens, 1991). I argue that individuals are able to 'live 'in' the world of modernity much more comprehensively than was ever possible before the advent of modern systems of representation, transportation and communication' (Giddens, 1991, p. 211). Growing out of living at a time 'of extraordinary complexity when systems and structures that have long organized life are changing at an unprecedented rate' (Taylor, 2001), a much more fluid nomadic world (Attali, 1990; Bauman, 1996) means people enact, perform and combine mobility and stillness in new or reimagined ways, Cresswell (2006, p. 45) noting that 'not only does the world appear to be more mobile, but our ways of knowing the world have also become more fluid', which possibility might not just change the world but ways of knowing it. As individuals seek better control of their social positioning, they can invest in an identity as a reflexive project with the aid of like-minded others to transform themselves into the kinds of people they're supposed and want to be,

influencing the direction of their own moves in a fashion that is very self-aware of the rhythms they seek to gain a foothold in. Social networking sites, in particular, seem destined to become powerful tools in forms of individual subject-making as individuals, enabling individuals to explicitly act to fashion their identities by regulating their bodies, their thoughts and their conduct in new ways, assembling wider networks of relations around themselves as they use technologies to assist themselves in becoming self-transformed. This chapter, reflecting a trans-disciplinary agenda investigates one such network called couchsurfing.com, a social networking site that has attracted over three million users since 2004.

Methodology

I joined couchsurfing in 2005 and began researching how performative actions could generate intimate relations from which agency could be produced by both host and guest, exploring their distinct performances for a 2009 study (O'Regan, 2009) by identifying the interpersonal relations between them. While the idea of the original research was to get embroiled in the site and allow myself 'to be infected by the effort, investment, and craze of the particular practice or experience being investigated' (Dewsbury, 2010, p. 326), the chapter still largely relied on the clear cut entity of the host and guest and the human-based activities enabled by the site. In doing so, I gazed upon this world as a world of human movement and consumption; lacking any element of imaginative innovation on the sites material (re) configurings or research experimentalism, academics early in their careers often like tourists, experiencing the world(s) they are investigating through a detached 'academic gaze' that rarely engages the 'real'. Struggling with ambivalence, the chapter reduced or totalized the tourist (guest) and the other (host) to particular positions, the study unwilling to fully invest in the idea as to whether the classifications of host–guest should be made or the multitude of other ways in which they could be entangled. Analysed in the context of 'modernity', tourist research still remains obsessed with classification, categorizations and labelling, the preconception of the power of the gaze and the social, cultural and physical distance it is meant to create between tourist and host enforcing the idea that in host and tourist encounters, the only question is often about which of the two wins (Boniface, 1998) and the constraints that create distance between them (Huxley, 2005). In this chapter, Karen Barad's methodology of diffraction which proposes 'new ways of thinking about reflection that recognises the complexities and the relational qualities of practice' (Boud, 2010, p. 36) is adopted. The methodology is understood by Barad as 'a way of understanding the world from within and as part of it' (Barad, 2007: 88), noting how 'we do not obtain knowledge by standing outside of the world; we know because "we" are of the world. We are part of the world in its differential becoming' (Barad, 2003, p. 829). This way of diffractive thinking is used as grounds for opening new perspective about couchsurfing, so as to reveal new patterns and intra-actions; focusing on the 'study of practices of knowing in being … [as to] how specific intra-actions come to matter' (Barad, 2003, p. 829). This diffractive thinking does not build on disciplinary distinctions and separations or roles, but evokes researchers to be responsive to 'intra-active engagements with our subject matter, including attending to what gets excluded and how it matters' (Barad, 2011, p. 10). In inviting researchers to 'read through' data, diffraction – itself an entangled phenomenon (Barad, 2007) – not only brings the reality of entanglements to light, but also helps to identify all the intra-activities that emerge together in 'artful integrations' (Suchman, 1994), including the material and the discursive.

Enlisting Karen Barad's diffractive thinking draws attention to her 'agential realist' concepts of apparatus, co-emergence, materiality and intra-activity to articulate or bring to light the intra-actions making up couchsurfing's entanglements, relationalities and boundaries. While my previous

approach only offered a partial 'performative' understanding of couchsurfing based on semi-structured interviews with 15 members of the network, Barad's invitation for researchers to take responsibility for their entanglements and what they make visible drives this new analysis. From these interviews and the author's own 33 hospitality exchanges via the site, as well as participation and observations throughout the period up to August 2012; the chapter seeks to unpack from the inside, Barad's theoretical perspectives to understand the complicated, entangled nature of host–guest entanglements that emerge through couchsurfing. Viewing hospitality exchange as a phenomenon that Barad defines as 'produced through complex agential intra-actions of multiple, material-discursive practices or apparatuses of bodily production' (Barad 2007, p. 140), this chapter understands couchsurfing.com as an 'apparatus' that involve specific intra-actions that produces differences that matter. It is an apparatus engaged by humans as a material-discursive practice that offers 'possibility and performative actions' (Barad, 2011, p. 2). As such, the differences that matter are provided by the boundaries of the apparatus, since 'apparatuses are specific material reconfigurings of the world that do not merely emerge in time but iteratively reconfigure space-timematter as part of the ongoing dynamism of becoming' (Barad, 2007, p. 142). Therefore, the chapter leaves behind any binary categorization of host and guest since 'the seemingly self-evidentiary nature of bodily boundaries, including their seeming visual self-evidence, is a result of the repetition of (culturally and historically) specific bodily performance' (Barad, 2007, p. 155), specific boundaries and properties acquired through the open-ended but intertwined agential performances of intra-activity. For Barad (2007, p. ix) to be entangled is 'not simply to be intertwined with another, as in the joining of separate entities, but to lack an independent, self-contained existence'. Therefore, this methodology hopes to investigate these enacted entanglements and engagements, so as to potentially illuminate any mutually constituting agency born out of the new ways of knowing enabled by couchsurfing, and any implications for the host–guest paradigm.

The Host–Guest Paradigm

Boniface (1998, p. 748) argues that 'tourism has produced a special and distinguishing culture consisting of the behaviour of not only tourists but also those offering them hospitality services', with both tourist and host behaving very differently from the way they behave at home. While both may be performing tourism and hospitality, they are not 'completely drawn into totally inclusive group of all concerned' (Boniface, 1998, p. 748), since the tourist travels in a 'tourist culture', surrounded by, but not integrated in, the 'host society'. Grateful for familiarity so as to attain relaxation, comfort and well-being, a tourism–industrial complex has invested deeply into a tourist culture that reinforces tourist habits, preventing individuals from experimenting and risk-taking. Moreover, most tourists will not seek to 'escape' these habits of travel and tourism, since it binds them to other tourists, even while at the same time it restrains tourists from creating a friendly attitude towards the Other. Hosts, meanwhile, it is argued, either seek to financially profit from tourists' habits by orientating towards tourists or avoid or (fruitlessly) resist tourism by developing strategies of resistance that can '(re)establish local identities that are in some sense *outside* and protected against global flows' (Hardt and Negri, 2000, p. 45; original emphasis) of tourists, capital and ideas. For those who do interact with tourists, Morley (2000, p. 228) warns that the 'terms of trade of cosmopolitan exchange invariably work to favour the already powerful', their trade of the 'right proportion of genuine or pretended "otherness"' (Franklin, 2003, p. 213) means tourism it seems, is losing much of its power 'as a practice through which the everyday might be transcended via a confrontation with otherness' (Edensor, 2007, p. 201). The host–guest dichotomy is dependent on a binary categorization that ignores

overlaps or threshold spaces in which host–guest relations are played out together, any movement towards the other seen as inappropriate, rather than a form of discovery, with organizations such as Tourism Concern, institutions such as the British Foreign Office and business reducing host–guest interactions to codes of practice, contracts and rules of conduct. Businesses have made host–guest contact procedural and contractual, making 'strangers out of people who should be able to see themselves as being in relationship where discretion and moral responsibility go hand in hand' (Hugman, 2005, p. 111). Edensor (2001, pp. 78–79) warns of a 'dystopian future for tourism where every potential space becomes increasingly intensively stage-managed and regulated as part of the commodification of everything', creating what Daniel Boorstin (1961) called 'pseudo-experiences' or 'satisfaction with superficial experiences of other peoples and other places' (MacCannell, 1999, p. 10) and a 'self-perpetuating system of illusions' and spectacle disregarding the 'real' world (Urry, 2003, p. 10).

MacCannell (2001, p. 33) does refer to the 'second gaze' in an effort to return agency to the tourist, a gaze that is 'capable of recognizing the misrecognition that defines the tourist gaze', always aware that there is something concealed. Rather than dwell on the reflexive tourist, I argue that potentials of relations increasingly flow through and materialize in reflexive subjects, who can reject habitual configurations and structures; a subject who is 'conceived not so much through mobility and displacement, as through the encounters with otherness that such mobility yields' (Oakes, 2006b, p. 49). These are subjects who seek to instigate changes in lived experiences, intra-action between people and information technology, for example, creating entangled sets of material discursive practices through which both object and observer, human and non-human are connected. It means agency is no longer aligned with human intentionality, and is not 'possessed by someone or does not precede intra-action', since '*agency is a matter of intra-acting; it is an enactment, not something that someone or something has'* (Barad, 2007, p. 178; original emphasis). Barad argues that agency is a 'doing' or 'being' in its intra-activity, the *'enactment of iterative changes to particular practices'* (Barad, 2007, p. 178; original emphasis) through phenomenal configurations that allow reconfiguring boundaries, constituents and relations to take place. Boundaries only emerge through and as part of entangled intra-relating, underlining how subjects in a performative relationship are not distinct entities, but rather 'inter-twined agencies which mutually construct each other' (Birke *et al.*, 2004, p. 178), intra-action signifying *'the mutual constitution of entangled agencies'* (Barad, 2007, p. 33; original emphasis), which are not attributes of either humans or non-human, but 'ongoing reconfigurations of the world' (Barad, 2003, p. 818). While a reflexive subject may not have 'agency' to challenge the subject–object dualism, they may choose, if motivated, through mutual action to become entangled with subjects and things that merge to change the 'fundamental structure of experience' (Papadopoulos *et al.*, 2008, p. 66). 'Each extends the other, but only from the other's position' (Strathern, 2004, p. 38), since 'it is through specific agential intra-actions that the boundaries and properties of the "components" of phenomena become determinate and that particular embodied concepts become meaningful' (Barad, 2003, p. 815). Barad (2003, p. 828) states 'matter is not a fixed essence; rather matter is a substance in its intra-active becoming – not a thing but a doing; a congealing of agency', that authorizes the emergence and realization of different identities, emotions and selves. In seeking to provide a 'richer account of materiality, agency, and the nature of social practices' (Barad, 1998, p. 89) and *'how* discursive practices produce material bodies' (Barad, 2003, p. 808; original emphasis), I argue that discursive practices when adopted in our day to day life as lived experience can poses questions about the normative givenness of the differential categories of 'host and 'guest'. By examining hospitality discourse and the

emergence of discursive practices of hospitality in the material setting of the home which supports such discourses makes it necessary to re-think boundaries, particularly the practice of hospitality exchange through which these differential boundaries are stabilized and destabilized as roles and agency comes into being across bodies and materialities when in relation to one another. Barad (1999, p. 102) argues that 'we are responsible for the world within which we live not because it is an arbitrary construction of our choosing, but because it is sedimented out of particular practices that we have a role in shaping'. Therefore, subjects are engaged in 'a continuous process of passionate construction through their own interdependent activities' (Papadopoulos *et al.*, p. 64) because we enter into the process of intra-action 'not as the knowing subjects or as abstract cognisers, but as interested, careful, concerned actors' (Papadopoulos *et al.*, 2008, p. 65). I argue in this chapter that couchsurfing reconfigures habits; an individual's decision to respond to or accept the conditions (or norms of engagement) set by a design that configures and reconfigures practices and possibilities of different modes of engagement by multiple users in ways that is appropriate to each individual's knowledge and their way of knowing the world.

Emerging Phenomena in Apparatuses

Barad's notion of 'apparatus' is understood as a material-discursive practice that both enables and constrains but is neither discrete nor inert since it is constituted by and constitutive of ongoing intra-activity. Granted a high degree of agency, apparatuses are open-ended and dynamic rather than static, closed arrangements in the world. They are where human and non-human bodies and subjectivities are enacted; apparatuses not *'mere observing instruments but boundary-drawing practices'* (Barad, 2007, p. 140; original emphasis). Apparatuses are *'dynamic (re) configurings of the world, specific agential practices/intra-actions/performances through which specific exclusionary boundaries are enacted*' (Barad, 2003, p. 816; original emphasis), themselves constituted through particular practices and 'perpetually open to rearrangements, rearticulation, and other reworkings' (Barad, 2001, p. 107). While not fixed, institutional practices are often bound up with materiality that shapes and defines the contours and possibilities of life, the sociomateriality of guidebooks, for example, integrally and actively part of knowledge production, creating differences that have wide-reaching implications for the relationships between individuals. A guidebook is an ordering 'from above' and waits to serve a particular purpose when performed; its design and use resulting in some form of violence, since its users read the world through the apparatus. It is used without much thought and rather than enabling transformative practices that work outside habitual configurations, its socio-materiality does not (re)configure the normative constructions of the gaze (and is not used by the observed). When the guidebook is held loosely for navigation, it cannot be used as an instrument of observation if one is observing it. Co-emergence with 'locals' is rarely generated through the practice of guidebook use, since non-guidebook users cannot engage with its users, even if the guidebook is grasped loosely. While the line between subject and object is not fixed, 'once a cut is made (i.e. a particular practice is being enacted), the identification is not arbitrary but in fact materially specified and determinate for a given practice' (Barad, 2007, p. 155). An 'agential cut' means separate things acting on each other, guidebook design and use creating distance and a sharp divide between 'the interacting and the interacted' (Castells, 1996, p. 363), except in occasional specific intra-actions when the guidebook might be shared (Brown and Chalmers, 2003). However, emerging social networking web sites seem to offer the potential for users to develop more persistent identities (rather than habits) that can be maintained over both periods of mobility and fixity; the 'agential nature' of multiple apparatuses and intra-actions entangled in the production of boundaries inscribing new social realities as individuals construct their own relations to each other through the sites. 'Technologies of the self' (Foucault, 1988) such as social networking sites helping individuals fashion a self in connection to an outside world.

In January 2004, Casey Fenton along with other (co)founders started couchsurfing.com, a social networking site with a premise that, on the surface, seems simple: if you need a place to stay, this social networking system enables you to identify and find someone to give over sleeping space in their home for free. While couchsurfing was not the first 'hospitality exchange site' (hospex), it has become the largest, its membership over three million, its beginnings now project folklore, after Casey, a software programmer from New Hampshire (USA) hacked into the University of Iceland student directory, and spammed 1,500 students with requests for advice and guidance after finding a cheap last-minute ticket to that country. The understanding that use of the network will lead to face-to-face contact and a prolonged and intense encounter with the 'hosting' or 'surfing' member shapes the dynamics of the network, creating what Du Gay (1997, p. 15) calls a 'semantic network' – which he describes as a network of shared meanings and practices associated with its own discourse. It draws together, serves and connects a geographically dispersed network of strangers based around a shared practice, a medium by which participants draw purpose and which suggests and invites. Using an internal messaging system, individuals (called surfers) can contact potential hosts and request a 'couch'; part of a narrow code of vocabulary specific to the site. Membership is free although verification of personal details (real name and address) for a fee is increasingly encouraged. When an individual joins, they are required to build a semi-public profile, using their real name and address and fill in personal information as well as pictures and interests. The profiles, similar to those used on Facebook serve as a digital representation of one's identity, but unlike most networking sites, where you first connect to known others by 'friending' them, there is no function on couchsurfing that allows individuals to comment on other users' profiles or start 'friending', or inviting unknown others to view your profile. While Facebook are primarily designed to sustain and maintain an already known network of (former) friends, colleagues and family, couchsurfing is made up of dispersed strangers. While the profile allows users to express salient aspects of an identity, commitment to that identity can only be created and maintained through highly visible testimonials and vouches, which can only be obtained by offline participation in hospex. Once the encounter takes place (which itself relies upon technologies of synchronization such as the mobile phone); both subjects must rate the experience as positive, neutral or negative, and write personal testimonials of each other. These reputation testimonials or trust features are public to the whole community and serve to define the individual and their place within the project. They are the accumulated evidence over time as to one's character and personality; the number of vouches and reputation testimonials establishing a particular narrative of a person's status, trustworthiness, consistency, commitment and participation that's difficult to fake. Each individual helps to sustain the activities of the others through mobility and fixity, contributing to their own identity, freedom only coming in spatial, temporal and psychic relations with others, whom they approach as a stranger in the home.

The practice of hospex that forms couchsurfing, an apparatus, offers ongoing (re)configurings and serves to show that apparatuses themselves are phenomena that is actively part of knowledge production, since humans, by joining the site, become part of the apparatus; the material and the discursive 'mutually implicated in the dynamics of intra-activity' (Barad, 2007: 152). Barad argues that:

> making knowledge is not simply about making facts but about making worlds, or rather, it is about making specific worldly configurations – not in the sense of making

> them up ex nihilo, or out of language, beliefs, or ideas, but in the sense of materially engaging as part of the world in giving it specific material form. (Barad, 2007, p. 91)

Thus, through intra-action, 'bodies and technologies are mutually constituted – in and through each other' (Cooley, 2007, p. 10). While interaction presupposes the prior existence of separate entities, intra-action, by contrast, refers to the inseparability of the 'observed object' and 'agencies of observation' (Barad, 2007, p. 308), the distinction between subjects and objects as separate entities are erased. For Barad, the world is a dynamic process of intra-activity in the ongoing reconfiguring of locally determinate causal structures (boundaries), properties, bodies, technologies and meanings which 'become mutually but differentially intelligible, the particularity of their respective – matterings immanent to their intra-action' (Cooley, 2007, p. 11). Agential realism can account for the mutually constituted character of an apparatus, and how individuals enter into the process of intra-action, allowing for a greater sense of the complexity of the (re)production of host–guest, at least in the situated context of the home (that apparatus gives it a special meaning in the context of hospitality exchange and is an active participant in the world's becoming). Rather than a loosely held guidebook, the connected and interdependent nature of the intra-actions means the encounters cannot happen without the other, the performatively produced nature of hospex explaining how we 'we are not merely differently situated in the world; "each of us" is part of the intra-active ongoing articulation of the world in its differential mattering,' (Barad, 2008, p. 381), the agential intra-acting of components, conditions, situated locations, discursive practices, relations, text and context meaning 'identity formation must be understood as a (contingent and contested) material process through which different identity categories are formed and reformed through one another' (Barad, 2001, p. 99). It is only through these intra-relational entanglements that agential separability is materialized and resulting properties and boundaries become apparent and determinate, and that particular articulations become meaningful. Rather than think about the host and guest as two pre-existing and separate things acting on each other, Barad argues that phenomena/reality is sedimented out of the process of making the world intelligible through certain practices and not others. As individuals around the world construct notions of mobility in their everyday lives, mobility becomes a relation – 'an orientation to oneself, to others and to the world' (Adey, 2009, p. xvii), couchsurfing offering to elaborate alternative conceptions of self. It is a technology of the self that offers to lead them from gazing to mobility in an appreciation of the differences that occur 'when boundaries dissolve and things pass through each other' (Scott and Orlikowski, 2009, p. 6).

The Encounter

The practice and performance of guidebooks organizes encounters with the other (Urry, 2002), its design and enactment ordering the world so that particular realities are sedimented out, its inclusion as an apparatus involving boundary-making practices that reinforce the subject object dualism, the particular choice of this apparatus by humans mutually engaging them in producing a material-discursive world which the tourist understands. It is often a world that creates distance and exclusionary boundaries with the physically near but spiritually distant Other, excluding them from mattering. The gaze is a form of violence since not wanting to know is a violence against the other, a violence often 'thrown back' as the other forced to interact as tourism workers or as staging, the construct of interaction suggesting 'two entities, given in advance, that come together and engage in some kind of exchange' (Suchman, 2007, p. 267). However, each subject in hospex looks and reads through couchsurfing.com, the other inviting us to engage with them in a way that did not exist before, knowledge via direct intra-actions, a

process of co-constitutive action enabled by an apparatus that has no independent ontological authority in itself. The mutually constituting practice is a phenomenon of user-generated intra-relations, subjects and objects emerging and existing through their encounters with each other, given they are equally emergent and unsettled, both seeking out new possibilities. Resisting, subverting and accommodating each other's needs and activities, subjects become entangled in action, generating forms of human exchange that is inventive, creative and constructive, the 'complex understandings, arrange informal trade-offs, and deal with unanticipated tensions' (Boden and Molotch, 1994, p. 272) meaning each encounter produces 'material changes which cannot be avoided, negated, bypassed or simply neglected, because these bodies change the very *terms of our experience* and create new situations in which we find ourselves' (Papadopoulos *et al.*, 2008, pp. 65–66; original emphasis). The host or the guest, then do not precede their relationality as pre-existent and pre-constituted entities, mutual action, a 'kind of inter-embodiment means that people and places make themselves vulnerable to each other; vulnerable to the gaze, vulnerable to the touch, vulnerable to being consumed, and in that consumption, vulnerable to being changed for better or for worse' (Molz, 2004, p. 226). Bodies and things as part of the co-constitutive action lead to reconfigurations of materiality (the home), and the re-making of boundaries. It is a reconfiguration that carries meaning, the performatively of dynamic and lively intra-acting components and resulting agential cuts continuously configures and re-configures relations of space–time–matter (Barad, 2007). It is an apparatus sustained in people's everyday life, where '*practices of knowing are specific material engagements that participate in (re)configuring the world*' (Barad, 2007, p. 91; original emphasis). The choice of practice enacted influences the apparatus formed (and is continually being re-formed), redrawing boundaries and the nature of knowledge produced, our choices and 'intra-actions effect what's real and what's possible, as some things come to matter and others are excluded, as possibilities are opened up and others are foreclosed' (Barad, 2007, p. 393). Subjects are willing to take the risk of entering into a relationship via the site in which the social divisions and boundaries of everyday life are suspended, the dichotomy of knower and known erased, and new possibilities are given a chance to emerge through encountering and negotiating difference, unexpectedness, unpredictability and ambiguity. In far-flung housing estates, flats and squats, far from town centres, guidebooks and tourist attractions, members of couchsurfing are not performing a cultural authenticity flattened by a tourism industry, since the private sphere remains a space that cannot be disciplined in line with fantasy or performed kinds of authenticity. Providing an alternative space of encounter and where 'we can sense each other as possible companions in resistance, where company goes against the grain of sameness as it goes against the grain of power' (Lugones, 2003, pp. 18–19), the home becomes a space of encounter for their entanglements and relationalities.

Rather than staged in line with the 'tourist gaze', the home is reconfigured, becoming a liminal space of intercultural intimacy that stages encounters of dynamic relationality, enabling the coming together of bodies, and engendering new possibilities. The encounters hold bodies in proximity, conversation, small kindnesses and responsibilities (washing dishes, making up the bed, cooking dinner together), recognition, and the discovery of shared interests and concerns offering important opportunities for connection. Each encounter is dynamic and varying, each subject achieving their desired level of intra-action in spaces that lack conscious spacing and privacy, since inside homes encounters occur on bedroom floors, couches, in hallways, living rooms and gardens. Each subject cannot simply project their own sensibilities and desires onto the other in what is the other's intimate sphere without those others talking back, each subject recognizing the importance of their voice and worldviews during the encounter and through the power of the vouch or testimonial. Rather than

being enabled to gaze at every encounter or depend on professional experts for help to construct and develop a gaze, any simulation or unrealistic image projected onto each other is quickly quenched. Kristeva (1991) suggests that living with the other helps us to discover the other within our self. She writes that:

> living with the other, with the foreigner, confronts us with the possibility or not of *being an other*. It is not simply – humanistically – a matter of our being able to accept the other, but of *being in his place*, and this means to imagine and make oneself other for oneself. (Kristeva, 2012, p. 13)

Likewise, she asks 'how could one tolerate a foreigner if one did not know one was a stranger to oneself' (Kristeva, 2012, p. 182). As the other becomes visually objectified, they must be wholly separate in order for the detached gaze to be enacted, tourists conditioned to accept them as 'authentic' if they are positioned as extraordinary, separate and excerpted from the present. The intra-active experiences of hospex and the personal, situated relationships mean each subject is unable to fulfill the 'narcissistic needs of dull egos' (MacCannell, 2001, p. 26), the Other of postcards and movies, is 'on the move, diversifying, multiplying', no longer assigned to a specific place that enables them to be captured and enrolled as objects of the gaze (Augé, 1998, p. 109). The apparatus is a 'site' for agency, and the change of habits, a property not possessed by something or someone, but a component with the phenomena, subjectivity 'emergent rather than given, distributed rather than located solely in consciousness, emerging from and integrated into a chaotic world rather than occupying a position of mastery and control removed from it' (Hayles, 1999, p. 291). The different subjects' roles 'co-emerge through, and as part of, their entangled intra-relating in the ongoing performance of practices' (Keevers and Treleaven, 2008, p. 14), the co-emergence always emergent, always through complex contingent, local, temporary interrelations, specific intra-actions enacting a casual structure in the home as both subjects take an active role in relations, the apparatus requiring subjects to agentially intra-act, before properties of the phenomena become determinate. Those joining and using the site, while doing so individually accept their actions and performance must be subservient to the site's common values and norms. This requires members to engage in cultural interaction without commercialization and payment, requiring cooperation, face-to-face engagement, intimacy, tolerance, respect and reciprocity. Both are judged and evaluated through references that pertain to these overriding values, with any notion that the host ignored the guest or the guest treated the host's home as a hotel seen as major transgressions. Reputation (the perceived commitment, values, integrity of an individual) is the result of identity being continually produced; the reputation and actions both online and in the physical realm having repercussions in and on each other. These reputations can be seen as interpersonal surveillance producing a reflexive monitoring or surveillance of the self that acts as a tool for self-regulation, of one's own behaviour, in order to take up preferred subject positions. Crouch *et al.* (2001, p. 257) argue that 'performance may be something done for others as a display of identity, or for the self, in constituting and working identity'. One's reputation or performance isn't written by oneself, but by those you host, surf and intra-act with, and so taking care of one's reputation means managing the self and, in turn, to care for the self directly entails a care for those that write the references, and vice versa, entailing a sense of reciprocity that sustains the site and one's identity. Both actors perform, both having a vested interest in the performance being successful, each specific intra-action highlighting the importance of reputation as host and guest come to their own working consensus about what are appropriate and inappropriate enactions. Individuals cannot simply rely on embodied habits and synchronized enactions to establish an emotional connection, which specific practices are involved in making the agential cut. Post-encounter, via the site's voluntary feedback mechanism, each

subject in the encounter can provide feedback on the other, the entangled intra-relating continuing through the ongoing performance of the practice since boundaries are constantly re-negotiated even after one particular encounter. This public feedback, which is placed on both profiles which has their documented and assumed histories is voluntary and is indicative of a collaborative, productive, open-ended relationship that '*signifies the mutual constitution of entangled agencies*' (Barad, 207, p. 33; original emphasis) born out of intra-actional relationships. It may be months later when the cut is made (if at all), with feedback altering at any time after the encounter, acting as a testimonial as to their ethical engagement with the world.

Proximity, Accountability and Responsibility

For Urry (1990, p. 10), tourism means 'everyday obligations are suspended... There is license for permissive ... non-serious behaviour,' their touristic mobility and the encounters that their mobility yields mediated often through objects (television, guidebooks and mobile phones). However, I argue that 'mobility', when mediated through a computing and communication technology that can become an open-ended boundary-drawing practice through which intelligibility and materiality are constituted and relations of accountability and responsibility are redrawn. Each public profile picture on couchsurfing and the history of each person on the site confronts us and draws us to the other, but not as already constituted subjects who know each other, since each encounter is dependent on intense inter-personality experiences with which actors are entangled, the lively relationalities of becoming of which they are part, demanding an 'ethics of responsibility and accountability not only for what we know, how we know, and what we do but, in part, for what exists' (Barad, 2007, p. 243). The inseparability/entanglement of intraacting 'agencies' (Barad, 2007, p. 139) makes the possibilities of becoming an ethical call, 'an invitation that is written into the very matter of all being and becoming' (Barad, 2007, p. 396). Barad argues individuals need to take responsibility for the role that they play in the world's 'differential becoming' (Barad, 2007, p. 396), taking account of the entangled materializations of which we are a part, including new configurations, new subjectivities and new possibilities so as to 'intra-act respectfully in relations that are nevertheless always asymmetrical' (Keevers and Treleaven, 2008, p. 22). Drawing on Levinasan ethic of the encounter and responsibility to the other, Bauman (1992, pp. 42–43) argues that responsibility arises out of proximity of the Other, a responsibility in making the future through their choices and actions, each intra-action shaping the future and their capacity to be. 'Responsibility is silenced once proximity is eroded ... the fellow human subject is transformed into an Other' (Bauman, 1989, p. 184) by technical bureaucracy. Rouse (2004, p. 154) interprets Barad, noting that the:

> the intelligibility of anyone's participation in a practice turns on something being at stake for everyone in getting it right. That does not mean that the intelligibility of practices depends upon the possibility of ultimate agreement and conformity to what those stakes are. Rather, it depends upon an implicit mutual recognition of and by those to whom the practice matters, such that they (ought to) hold themselves responsible for their different interpretations, and accountable to one another.

Each subject in the encounter has to hold themselves accountable for the agential cut that is made by virtue of their performance, one that is made in every encounter. It assumes an active opening up on the part of one subject towards the other, to knowing, reflecting and learning from each other, entailing being open and awake to each other, each specific intra-action coming to matter. Because an encounter cannot be located in past encounters or habit, each subject must take ethical responsibility for the possibilities for what the world may become, since it is continually open to us to

recognize 'real' relations, reminding us that it is through our way of intra-acting, we bring forth the world in each moment; 'the possibilities for what the world may become call out in the pause that precedes each breath before a moment comes into being and the world is remade again' (Barad, 2007, p. 185).

Implications

The relational process of hospex blurs 'long-established and traditionally-significant boundaries between distinct spheres' (Livingstone, 2005, p. 163), a 'de-routinization' (Southerton and Tomlinson, 2005) of temporalities and spatialities 'without erasing the culturally and historically constituted differences among them' (Suchman, 2000, p. 7), agency residing neither in the individual nor in the apparatus, but in intra-actions. By incorporating the apparatus, which as a 'technology of the self' also elaborates alternative conceptions of self, reflexive subjects alter habitual structures and routines as they cultivate a reflexive awareness of their identity. A technology of the self, constituted in real practices shapes people's lives, assists individuals to become self-transformed, self-directed, self-managed, their identities produced through intra-actions with others, as mobility becomes folded into a practice. As they perform their lives together with others in homes around the world in a process of becoming, it is a performance entangled with materiality and agency, Grossberg (1999, p. 32) noting agency is more than the power to act, since it is also 'access to particular places – places at which particular kinds of actions, producing particular kinds of affects; are possible – places at which once can intercede and influence the various "forces" and vectors that are shaping the worlds'. The notion of maintained mobility can describe the ways space and place, mobility and stability, are practised or lived. As an investment and a process of belonging, individuals can 'install' themselves into a practice, while rejecting assimilation and imposition by the other in a persuasive discursive context generated by a tourism–industrial complex. Grounded in the rhetoric of mobility, they 'live in a world of journeys' (Crouch, 2010, p. 6), couchsurfing is one example of the shift from objects and subjects inter-acting to phenomena co-emerging, intra-activity highlighting how cultural identities become entangled and inseparable. If subjects continue to resist the pressure of a single or stable subject position in the genuine hope it can offer a genuine development, transformation and articulation of self, can the tourism industry continue to produce socially useful others on whom we can push undesired consequences, dictating the rhythm of their lives while inhibiting ethical thought, accountability and responsibility? Helping us to move us away from thinking of hosts and guests in terms of two separate things with very different characteristics, this chapter has asked whether individuals can effect changes in the worlds unfolding by initiating speculative ways or through unconventional spatial orientations. Barad (2007) notes that individuals can effect changes in the world's unfolding by holding themselves accountable for the agential cuts that they make, responsible to the others with whom or which they are entangled. What then for the habitual tourist, who mistakes habits for his identity, who participates in cuts that have environmental, social, cultural, political and material meanings, their individualized, distanced gaze lingering over the other? Should each tourist be held responsible and accountable for their performances, accountable for apparatuses making cuts they do not question between 'subject' and 'object'? Caldwell (2011) notes that individuals should be accountable for cuts that continue to be made and how an apparatus continues to have meaning. Rather than standing at a distance, perhaps increasing numbers will come to understand that 'knowing does not come from standing at a distance and representing but rather from *a direct material engagement with the world*' (Barad, 2007, p. 49; original emphasis); an acknowledgement that boundary-crossing, rather than ease and

comfort involves encountering and negotiating difference, unpredictability and ambiguity. No longer can the tourist or host view each other as prior existing self-contained entities performing their own 'tourist' 'or 'host' practices within their own existing, separate and identifiable boundaries, when, if they look, there is a world that is continually in the making, their agency intervening in the world's becoming. Barad (2007, p. 157) points out that 'we do not see merely with our eyes. Interacting with (or rather, intra-acting "with" and as a part of) the world is part and parcel of seeing. Objects are not already there; they emerge through specific practices.' It is important that tourists ask whose knowledge is marginalized, since 'we are responsible for the world within which we live not because it is an arbitrary construction of our choosing, but because it is sedimented out of particular practices that we have a role in shaping' (Barad, 1999, p. 102).

Conclusions

Dominant tourist discourses are etched into our social spaces, tourist movements and their inter-actions, the tourism industry helping to cement and 'set in space' certain networks that impose rhythms and habits on tourists as well as on people's places and cultures. By enabling, shaping and organizing the tourist gaze, the tourism industry is often made an oppressive rather than emancipatory project, the habitual configurations and sedimented habits it reinforces meaning few tourists or hosts unsettle the normative constructions of the gaze. This chapter questioned the traditional division between hosts and guests and the claims that there is no genuine opportunity for a fruitful encounter between tourists and hosts in a world of Hostelworld, Lonely Planet guidebooks, Hiltons and TripAdvisor. Rather than see hosts and tourists as previously formed identifies that interact 'to win', presupposing their prior existence with already pre-defined properties, Barad's framework reminds us that identities are always formed in intra-action. The meaning of host and guest are continually shifting and destabilized as subjects co-emerge and are co-shaped in and through the practices they perform, human-human encounters taking into account intra-action and entanglements of materiality and discourse. The framework offers a theoretical approach that effectively moves beyond these presumed oppositions, the emergence of social networking platforms characterized by fluid, lively, peer-to-peer off-line intra-actions meaning new patterns of becoming can emerge. Highlighting the relationship between the human and non-human, couch-surfing (re)configures the standing of hosts and guests, the relational coming-into-being changing rigid conventions of travel and the daily constitution of existence. This chapter sought to illuminate the intertwinedness of individuals, who, both in their travel and everyday activities and behaviour, create a structure of feeling and relations around themselves, moving towards the Other in appreciation and invitation. Emerging through and within intra-actions, an encounter unfolds through a material-discursive apparatus where the differences and similarities emerge within discursive phenomena, the host and guest not pre-existing, since agential enfolding occurs through one another in the home, any notion of host or guest understood as being intra-actively produced through one another after boundaries or agential cuts are established, when comparisons come to matter in different ways according to the different agential cuts that are made. Specific intra-actions produce, perform and enact a dynamic relationality that is locally determined; emphasizing the provisionally

of identifications and performances designed into the site, a site that can change how individuals encounter the world. As an apparatus in which subjects have projected concepts of freedom, independence, initiative and authenticity; their entangled relationalities blur the traditional subject–object division; since intra-actions can transform people from within, helping individuals (who are agentive participants in the world's intra-active becoming) to engage with the word in a different style. Various intertwined agencies intra-act to produce certain results, specific intra-actions mean the host–guest dichotomy is continually challenged and destabilized, subjects and objects emerging through encounters, sedimented out of individuals as 'participant parts' setting the boundaries that matter. Subjects do not constitute each other in symmetrical ways, subject–objects division not necessarily reiterated but often reconfigured. Rather than having mobility forced upon them, subjects can refashion relations in a world that is always in the process of becoming. These interventions are based on the basis of the guiding expectations of the site, performances in the environment of the home having intentional direction, holding subjects responsible and accountable to each other. As new technologies influence and give space to participatory performance-based practices (as much as individuals in turn influence how those technologies are used), the habitual, everyday configurations of tourist economies, on which much of the power of the gaze works and reinforced, is revealed and disrupted, new invitations and interventions creating a space into which to imagine and produce differences that matter.

References

Adey, P. (2010) *Mobility*. Routledge, New York.
Attali, J. (1990) *Lignes d'horizon*. Arthème Fayard, Paris.
Augé, M. (1998) *A Sense for the Other: The Timeliness and Relevance of Anthropology*. Stanford University Press, Stanford, CA.
Barad, K. (1998) Getting real: technoscientific practices and the materialization of reality. *Journal of Feminist Cultural Studies* 10(2), 87–128.
Barad, K. (1999) Agential realism-feminist interventions in understanding scientific ractices. In: Biagioli, M. (eds) *The Science Studies Reader*. Routledge, New York, pp. 1–11.

Barad, K. (2001) Re(con)figuring space, time and matter. In: Dekoven, M. (eds) *Feminist Locations: Global and Local, Theory and Practice*. Rutgers University Press, New Brunswick, NJ and London, pp. 75–109.

Barad, K. (2003) Posthumanist performativity: toward an understanding of how matter comes to matter. *Signs: Journal of Women in Culture and Society* 28(3), 801–831.

Barad, K. (2007) *Meeting the Universe Halfway: Quantum Physics and the Entanglement of Matter and Meaning*. Duke University Press, Durham, NC.

Barad, K. (2008) Queer causation and the ethics of mattering. In: Giffney, N. and Myra, J. (eds) *Queering the Non/Human*. Ashgate Publishing, Burlington, VT, pp. 311–338.

Barad, K. (2011) Erasers and erasures: Pinch's unfortunate 'uncertainty principle'. *Social Studies of Science* 41(3), 443–454.

Bauman, Z. (1989) *Modernity and the Holocaust*. Polity Press, Cambridge.

Bauman, Z. (1992) *Mortality, Immortality and Other Life Strategies*. Polity Press/Blackwell, Oxford.

Bauman, Z. (1996) From pilgrim to tourist – or a short history of identity. In: Hall, S. (ed.) *Question of Cultural Identity*. Sage, London, pp. 18–36.

Bauman, Z. (1998) *Globalization: the Human Consequences*. Polity Press, Cambridge.

Birke, L., Bryld, M. and Lykke, N. (2004) Animal performances: an exploration of intersections between feminist science studies and studies of human/animal relationships. *Feminist Theory* 5(2), 167–183.

Boden, D. and Molotch, H. (1994) The compulsion to proximity. In: Friedland, R. and Boden, D. (eds) *Nowhere: Space, Time and Modernity*. University of California Press, Berkeley, CA, pp. 157–186.

Boniface, P. (1998) Tourist culture. *Annals of Tourism Research* 25(3), 746–749.

Boorstin, D. (1961) *The Image: a Guide to Pseudo-Events in America*. Harper & Row, New York.

Boud, D (2010) Relocating reflection in the context of practice. In: Bradbury, H., Frost, N., Kilminster, S., and Zukas, M (eds) *Beyond Reflective Practice: New Approaches to Professional Lifelong Learning*. London; New York: Routledge, pp. 25–36.

Brown, B. and Chalmers, M. (2003) Tourist and mobile technology. In: Kuutti, K. and Karsten, E. H (eds) *Proceedings of the Eighth European Conference on Computer Supported Cooperative Work* (ECSCW'03), Helsinki, Finland, 14–18 September. Kluwer Academic Press, Norwell, MA.

Caldwell, E. (2011) The transformation of habit in Shannon Sullivan's transactional embodiment and Karen Barad's intra-active agency. Proceedings of the Society for the Advancement of American Philosophy's 38th Annual Meeting. Eastern Washington University, 10–12 March 2011. http://www.american-philosophy.org/events/documents/2011_Program_files/F_caldwell_saap_2011_grad_paper.doc (accessed 12 September 2011).

Castells, M. (1996) The *Rise of the Network Society*. Blackwell, Oxford.

Cohen, R. (2006) *Migration and Its Enemies. Global Capital, Migrant Labour and the Nation-State*. Ashgate, Aldershot.

Cooley, H.R (2007) The Body and its thumbnails: the work of the image in mobile-imaging. PhD thesis. University of Southern California, California.

Cresswell, T. (2006) *On the Move. New York*. Routledge, London.

Crick, M. (1989) Representations of international tourism in the social sciences: sun, sex, sights, savings, and servility. *Annual Review of Anthropology* 18, 307–344.

Crouch D. (2010) *Flirting With Space: Journeys and Creativity*. Ashgate, Farnham.

Crouch, D., Aronsson, L. and Wahlstroem, L. (2001) The tourist encounter. *Tourist Studies* 1(3), 253–270.

Dewsbury, J.-D.C. (2009) Performative, non-representational and affect-based research: seven injunctions. In: DeLyser, D., Atkin, S., Crang, M., Herbert, S., and McDowell, L. (eds) *The Sage Handbook of Qualitative Research in Human Geography*, Sage, London, pp. 321–334.

Diken, B. and Laustsen, C. B. (2001) Enjoy your fight! – fight club as a symptom of the network society. *Journal for Cultural Research* 6(4), 349–367.

Du Gay, P., Hall, S., Janes, L., MacKay, H. and Negus, K. (1997) *Doing Cultural Studies: the Story of the Sony Walkman*. Sage, London.

Edensor, T. (2001) Performing tourism, staging tourism – (re)producing tourist space and practice. *Tourist Studies* 1(1), 59–81.

Edensor, T. (2007) Mundane mobilities, performances and spaces of tourism. *Social & Cultural Geography* 8(2), 199–215.

Foucault, M. [Martin, L.H., Gutman, H. and Hutton, P.H. (eds)] (1988) *Technologies of the Self: A Seminar with Michel Foucault*. Tavistock, London.

Franklin, A. (2003) The tourist syndrome: an interview with Zygmunt Bauman. *Tourist Studies*, 3(2), 205–217.

Fussell, P. (1980) *Abroad, British Literary Travelling Between the Wars*. Oxford University Press, Oxford.

Giddens, A. (1991) *Modernity and Self-Identity: Self and Society in the Late Modern Age*. Polity Press, Cambridge.

Gottdiener, M. (1995) *Postmodern Semiotics: Material Culture and the Forms of Postmodern Life*. Blackwell, Oxford.

Grossberg, L. (1999) Speculations and articulations of globalization. *Polygraph* 11, 11–18.

Hardt, M and Negri, A. (2000) *Empire*. Harvard University Press, Cambridge, MA.

Hayles, N.K. (1999) *How We Became Posthuman: Virtual Bodies in Cybernetics, Literature, and Informatics*. Chicago University Press, Chicago, IL.

Hetherington, K. (2000) *New Age Travellers: Vanloads of Uproarious Humanity*. Cassell, London.

Hugman R. (2005) *New Approaches in Ethics for the Caring Professions*. Palgrave-Macmillan, Basingstoke.

Huxley, L. (2005) Western backpackers and the global experience: an exploration of young people's interaction with local people. *Tourism, Culture and Communication* 5(1), 37–44.

Kaplan, C. (2002) Transporting the subject: technologies of mobility and location in an era of globalization. *PMLA* 117(1), 32–42.

Keevers, L. and Treleaven, L. (2008) Feminist praxis, co-emergence and practice-based studies in organizations. Proceedings of the Fourth Organization Studies Summer Workshop Embracing Complexity: Advancing Ecological Understanding in Organization Studies, 5–7 June 2008, Pissouri, Cyprus. http://www.egosnet.org/jart/prj3/egosnet/data/uploads/OS_2008/W-075.doc (accessed 2 November 2011). Archived original to http://goo.gl/6pybD on 25 July 2012.

Kristeva, J. (2012) *Strangers to Ourselves*. Colombia University Press, New York.

Jacobsen, J. (2000) Anti-tourist attitudes: Mediterranean charter tourism. *Annals of Tourism Research* 27(2), 284–300.

Lassen, C. (2006) Work and aeromobility. *Environment and Planning* 38(2), 301–312.

Livingstone, S. (2005) *Audiences and Publics: When Cultural Engagement Matters for the Public Sphere. Changing Media – Changing Europe Series 2*. Intellect Books, Bristol, pp. 163–185.

Lyons, G. and Loo, B. (2008) Transport directions to the future. In: Knowles, R., Shaw, J. and Docherty, I. (eds) *Transport Geographies: an Introduction*. Blackwell, Oxford, pp. 215–226.

Lugones, M. (2003) *Pilgrimages/Peregrinajes: Theorizing Coalition against Multiple Oppression*. Rowan and Littlefield, New York.

MacCannell, D. (1976) *The Tourist: a New Theory of the Leisure Class*. University of California Press, Berkeley, CA.

MacCannell, D. (1999) *The Tourist: a New Theory of the Leisure Class*. University of California Press, Berkeley, CA.

MacCannell, D. (2001) Tourist agency. *Tourist Studies* 1(1), 23–37.

McCabe, S. (2005) Who is a tourist? A critical review. *Tourist Studies* 5(1), 85–106.

McIntosh, R.W., Goeldner, C.R. and Ritchie, J.R.B. (1995) *Tourism: Principles, Practices, Philosophies*. John Wiley & Sons, New York.

Molz, J. (2004) Destination world: technology, mobility and global belonging in round-the-world travel websites. Unpublished PhD thesis. Department of Sociology, Lancaster University, Lancaster.

Morley, D. (2000) *Home Territories: Media, Mobility and Identity*. Routledge, London.

Nash, D. (1989) Tourism as a form of imperialism. In: Smith, V. L. (eds) *Hosts and Guests: the Anthropology of Tourism*. University of Pennsylvania Press, Philadelphia, PA, pp. 37–54.

O'Regan, M. (2009) New technologies of the self and social networking sites: hospitality exchange clubs and the changing nature of tourism and identity. In: Abbas, Y. and Dervin, F. (eds) *Digital Technologies of the Self*. Cambridge Scholars Publishing, Newcastle, pp. 171–198.

O'Reilly, K. (2000) *The British on the Costa del Sol – Transnational Identities and Local Communities*. Routledge, London.

Oakes, T. (2006a) Get real! On being yourself and being a tourist. In: Minca, C. and Oakes, T. (eds) *Travels in Paradox: Remapping Tourism*. Rowman & Littlefield, Lanham, MD, pp. 229–250.

Oakes, T. (2006b) Tourism and the modern subject: placing the encounter between tourist and other. In: Cartier, C. and Lew, A. (eds) *Seductions of Place: Geographical Perspectives on Globalization and Touristed Landscapes*. Routledge, London, pp. 36–55.

Papadopoulos, D., Stephenson, N. and Tsianos, V. (2008) *Escape Routes. Control and Subversion in the 21st Century*. Pluto Press, London.

Peterson, M.A. (2010) But it is my habit to read the Times. Metaculture and practice in the reading of Indian newspapers. In: Bräuchler, B. and Postill, J. (eds) *Theorising Media and Practice*. Berghahn Books, Oxford and New York, pp. 127–146.

Quinn, B. (2007) Performing tourism in Venice: local residents in focus. *Annals of Tourism Research* 34(2), 458–476.

Rouse, J. (2004) Barad's feminist naturalism. *Hypatia* 19(1), 142–161.

Salazar, N.B. (2005) Tourism and glocalization: 'local' tour guiding. *Annals of Tourism Research* 32(3), 628–646.

Scott, S.V. and Orlikowski, W.J. (2009) 'Getting the truth': exploring the material grounds of institutional dynamics in social media. Proceedings of the 25th European Group for Organizational Studies Conference, Barcelona, Spain. 2–4 July. http://is2.lse.ac.uk/wp/pdf/wp177.pdf (accessed 10 November 2011).

Shove, E. (2002) Rushing around: coordination, mobility and inequality. Draft paper for the Mobile Network Meeting. Department of Sociology, Lancaster University, Lancaster.

Smith, V.L. (1977) Introduction. In: Smith, V.L. (ed.) *Hosts and Guests: The Anthropology of Tourism*. University of Pennsylvania Press, Philadelphia, PA, pp. 1–14.

Soguk, N. (2003) Incarcerating travels: travel stories, tourist orders, and the politics of the 'Hawai'ian paradise'. *Journal of Tourism and Cultural Change* 1(1), 29–53.

Southerton, D. and Tomlinson, M. (2005) 'Pressed for time' – The differential impacts of a 'time squeeze'. *The Sociological Review* 53(2), 215–239.

Strathern, M. (2004) *Partial Connections*. AltaMira Press, Walnut Creek, CA.

Suchman, L. (2000) Human/machine reconsidered. Published by the Department of Sociology, Lancaster University. http://www.comp.lancs.ac.uk/sociology/soc040ls.html (accessed 15 August 2011).

Suchman, L. (2007) *Human-Machine Reconfigurations: Plans and Situated Actions*. Cambridge University Press, Cambridge.

Taylor, M.C. (2001). *The Moment of Complexity: Emerging Network Culture*. University of Chicago Press, Chicago, IL.

Thrift, N. (1994) On the social and cultural determinants of international financial centres: the case of the city of London. In: Corbridge S., Martin, R. and Thrift, N. (eds) *Money, Power and Space*. Blackwell, Oxford and Cambridge, MA, pp. 327–355.

Tolstoy, L. (1983) *War and Peace*. The Modern Library, New York.

Urry, J. (1990) *The Tourist Gaze: Leisure and Travel in Contemporary Societies*. Sage, London.

Urry, J. (2002). *The Tourist Gaze: Leisure and Travel in Contemporary Societies*. (2nd edition). Sage, London.

Urry, J. (2002) Mobility and proximity. *Sociology* 36(2), 255–274.

Urry, J. (2003) The sociology of tourism. In: Chris, C. (eds) *Classic Reviews in Tourism*. Channel View Publications, Clevedon.

Williams, D.R. and Kaltenborn, B.P. (1999) Leisure places and modernity: the use and meaning of recreational cottages in Norway and the USA. In: Crouch, D. (eds) *Leisure/Tourism Geographies*. Routledge, London, pp. 214–230.

12 Gaze, Encounter and Philosophies of Otherness

Jo Ankor and Stephen Wearing

Introduction

This chapter begins in considering the development of the concept of 'gaze' in Western cultural and critical theory. We then examine the flâneur as a gazer and introduce the concept of the choraster, as the relationship of visitor and host in the space of the 'Other' and self. The notion of gaze is thus expanded from one of disassociation to emphasize a more engaged set of experiences that can reflect the imagined-real of both the traveller space and the host community. It draws on philosophy for an understanding of the response to gaze in the touristic encounter and leads to a framework able to deal with the complexity of contemporary tourism experiences.

This chapter contributes to an understanding of tourism that is subject-centred, dynamic and capable of dealing with the host's role in developing tourist cultures. It contributes to the building of theory that enables the gaze to be constructed from the diverse and unpredictable interactions that occur and make up the encounter – the space, the host community's values and the tourist's experience.

Concepts of Gaze

To begin to examine the gaze of the host, it is useful to consider the critical debates and theoretical concepts that have contributed to the concept of 'gaze' in Western cultural and critical theory.

The debates about 'gaze' can be traced back at least to the Renaissance. At this time, two developments were unfolding of particular importance to this concept. The first was the development of perspective in painting. Being able to put depth into a flat canvas was exciting, working through establishing a fixed point from which the view is recorded. The artist paints from a single position, displaying the chosen data from a particular viewpoint, to establish and shape the message and the meanings of the painting, such as a favourable portrayal of the artist's patron or benefactor. In this way, the viewer is provided with the position to see and 'know' the painted. They (we) are being positioned to gaze in a certain way and to see certain things.

The second development was the beginning of detailed examination of the natural physical world and its recording in written data, which provided momentum towards greater understanding of the world and the ability to manipulate aspects of that world. The belief that this gaze was neutral or objective and did not include a 'positioning' was central to its application. The 18th-century Camera Natura, a device for framing the subject to be painted and thus imposing a limit on the view, also carried connotations of objectivity – a tool cannot be held to lie, surely? When photography was developed in the 19th century, the same construction of neutrality and impersonal non-judgement was accepted as implicit in the photographs produced. The act of photographing was subordinate to the product in the faithful replication of the object, notwithstanding the choice that had been made of the particular object in that particular setting.

In this, the gaze moved from being a communication process to being a tool, it became a lens for examination. And from the paradigm of the neutral observer, alongside the proliferation of public places of pleasure in the developing cities of the 19th century, came the concept of the flâneur.

For Baudelaire, writing in that century, the flâneur epitomized the idler on the streets, filled with curiosity but without goal or interests, and fashioned out of the emerging commodity culture of the time (Leith, 2001). The concept of the flâneur was that of a new kind of public (male) person with the leisure to wander, watch and browse, and set in opposition to femininity's domestic emplacement.

The flâneur spends most of his day simply looking at the urban spectacle; he observes new inventions and passes the hours by shopping or window-shopping, looking at books, new fashions, hats, combs, jewellery and novelties of all kinds. He is a gentleman, he has some private wealth and he stands wholly outside the productive process (Wilson, 1995, p. 61).

He was also away from home and in search of the unfamiliar (Lechte, 1995), a lone traveller wandering through the cities searching for private experiences, aiming at discovering the deep and real nature of objects, especially objects of art (Benjamin, 1973). But these 'private experiences' were solo activities. The flâneur's gaze was one-sided, seated in the supremacy of the eye and appropriating all power from the surrounding company, the host. The flâneur could be taken to be the archetypal tourist, Bauman (1996) suggests: disengaged and specifically not interested.

The Chora

In the 20th century, such embedded assumptions of neutrality in the production of gaze have been the subject of new critical debate. Postmodern theorists argue that, rather than being an interpretive structure that flows out of the subject who is observing from a central position, the gaze impacts on and shapes the subject (Fuerty and Mansfield, 2000). We take in information as we gaze and this information must be considered in some form, from being acted upon to being ignored.

All of the characteristics of the flâneur do fit the tourist, or rather male perceptions of the tourist. As Wolff points out, 'There is no question of inventing the flaneuse: the essential point is that such a character was rendered impossible by the sexual divisions of the nineteenth century' (1985, p. 45). Women could not wander alone in public places:

> It is this flâneur, the flâneur as a man of pleasure, as a man who takes visual possession of the city, who has emerged in postmodern feminism discourse as the embodiment of the 'male gaze'. He represents men's visual and voyeuristic mastery over women. According to this view, the flâneur's freedom to wander at will through the city is essentially a masculine freedom. Thus the very idea of the flâneur reveals it to be a masculine concept. (Wilson, 1995, p. 65).

However, while the flâneur could be taken as 'the icon of freedom, of the autonomy of movement and thoughts, of the intellectual capacity of originally reading the city', he is very different from the modern tourist 'with a time-constrained journey, forced to follow default circuits and codified behaviour' (Nuvolati, 2009, p. 49).

The flâneur's selective gaze seeks disengagement but its assumption of authority is challenged constantly. He has no one to share with, no interested audience or reader in front of whom to play out his freedom. What defeats the flâneur is, in fact, this remainder – the group, the mob, the community, that talks, argues, shares, walks, sits and makes the public space/place 'vibrant' (MacCannell, 1992). These crowd the flâneur out of mind, out of place, out of relevance, in their varying and dynamic engagements with the place and people of the moment, including gaze.

And where we stand, how we stand and where we have come from all affect what we see when we gaze:

> A simple exercise – take a small but varied group [to a vantage point] and have each describe the landscape, what it is composed of and something of the 'meaning' of what can be seen. It will soon be apparent that even though we gather together and look in the same direction at the same instant, we will not – we cannot – see the same landscape.

> Thus we confront the central problem: any landscape is composed not only of what lies before our eyes but what lies within our heads ... not with the elements but with the essence, with the organising ideas we use to make sense out of what we see. (Meinig, 1979, p. 33)

Let us go back to the Renaissance struggle with bringing perspective into visual representations of places. The painter selects a viewpoint and thereby creates a position of preferred reading of the object or scene. Without necessarily a conscious decision to influence, this locates the position from which the text is supposed to be viewed, and so aims to control the gaze whether it was to tell a particular story or simply to show what pleased the sense of beauty and wonderment of the artist's eye. Even in this structuring of gaze, the establishing of a viewpoint (and a vanishing point) comes from an encounter (a meeting, or a coming together in a setting) that demanded a response. This encounter is the critical moment of the gaze, when acknowledgement and response become imperative. In this, the gaze is not a neutral stance – it is emplaced and interactive.

Wearing and Wearing (1996) and Wearing *et al.* (2010) introduce the idea of the *choraster* as a theoretical model to move beyond the flâneur. The 'chora' is any place given meaning by those using it, taking it

from simply a place to a special context of engagement and response. 'Space is practiced place' says de Certeau, 'place becomes transformed into space by the people who use it' (de Certeau, 1988, p. 117). Chora is space whose meaning can be constantly redefined by its inhabitants and users. It is 'the space that engenders without possessing' (Grosz, 1995, p. 51); the chora gives life to and is given life by, the chorasters who use it. Chorasters can be tourists who bring meaning to the chora from their own culture and who creatively incorporate into their sense of self the experiences of interaction in the tourist space. Chorasters are also the everyday users of the space.

However, in the space where tourist and host encounter each other, understanding and interpretation of what is seen becomes uncertain, positions collide. In theoretical terms, the encounter is the nexus of a range of social and cultural readings, where the knowledge informing the gaze is challenged by the presence of the Other and the new context. Grosz considers that space 'evades ... the disconcerting logic of identity, of hierarchy of being, the regulation of order' (Grosz, 1995, p. 51). The new space denies the self access to familiar frames of reference and becomes a site of destabilization of the subject. Space and subject form a dynamic relationship, and the subjectivity of those who use the chora will change and develop within that use, for the possible encounters with the space are almost infinitely variable (Soja, 1996, p. 260). And in the space, gaze as directional and one-way is refuted and the inclusivity from which gaze cannot be isolated is revealed; the place, the people, the response are inseparable within the act of gaze.

Engagement

Postmodern discussion, in establishing that subjectivity and the gaze are inseparable, also reinserts the emplaced body into understanding subjectivity. The Cartesian separation of the (pure) mind and the (uncontrollable) body allowed the notion of an objective gaze to be sustainable. Admitting the body is inseparable to identity and hence subjectivity, forces a relationship of body and gaze. This is highly relevant for tourism studies as it is the body that is transported to the new space where the Other will be encountered. It is noted that most often, characterizing a person or group as 'the Other' is to place them outside the system of normality or convention of one's own society or culture, and that this is often done as a binary opposition within a Western cultural perspective; the term is used here as a respectful term of recognition of the absolute alterity of individual difference. In travel, it is the individual body that is interposed into an-Other's space. What is also occurring is the situating of the body into an emplaced viewing position. Thus the space confuses the gaze's supposed objectivity through the response demanded by the interactive nature of space and gaze. It therefore becomes evident that:

> gaze cannot be taken as simply a physical mechanism of perception but is a fundamental structure in the subject's relationship with the physical, cultural and social order in which they live. It is tied up with formations and operations of subjectivity. (Fuerty and Mansfield, 2000, p. 71)

MacCannell writes that spaces are 'meeting grounds ... vibrant with people and potential' (MacCannell, 1992, p. 2). If we accept that tourist and host are each chorasters within the given space, then we accept that interaction is inevitable. The range of responses that could be implemented is wide, establishing a dynamic potential of unknown possibilities. Importantly, the tourist 'cannot evade their condition of outsider' (Feifer, 1985, p. 271) and their position in the engagement with the host, due to this being located outside and only able to gaze in from there, contributes to the uncertainty of an encounter. However, Huggan suggests the postmodern traveller is more aware of the transferability of the 'tourist gaze' as directed towards their self and of becoming the exotic object within the space they are visiting (Huggan, 2001, p. 201),

with an associated ironical acceptance of outsider status that offers greater respect for the agency of the host within touristic interactions.

Lefebvre (1991) considers that the experience of place works at perceived, conceived and lived levels, a constantly changing array of noticed, considered and bodily experienced meanings. 'Experience' is a complex term within postmodern discourse, but at a fundamental level it is the meeting of person and form that is a moment of invention through a reflexive interaction (Leith, 2001). For the tourist, certainly, it is their actual experience that is the reality. For example, in spite of the globalization of the five star hotel in which the affluent tourist may stay, and the inauthenticity of its attempts to copy local decor, the interaction of the tourist with the representatives of the host community in the form of the receptionist, the bell boy, the waiter/waitress, the hotel manager/ess and the taxi driver is real and will colour the tourists' subjective construction of the host culture and the values of that culture. The host's difference is not an external product that we pass or buy, it is an essential part of the experience of encounter; it becomes a part of who we are through our response. The gaze of the host occurs simultaneously with that of the visitor; place is viewed as 'spectacular' simultaneously with being seen as 'everyday' – realizing these multiple positions confounds both viewers.

Are there limits in our responses? Lacan holds that the gaze begins in self-knowledge and uses the presence of the other as a reflective apparatus to reassure the self; the Other's difference as something in and of itself is not considered and no response towards the Other is offered. If, as Lacan suggests, we define ourselves in relation to others, this forces or positions the Other as a passive necessity for our identity. Yet the Other can be an unsettling presence: 'the perceived ambiguity of the other ... lies in its appearance of both similarity and difference simultaneously' (Shapiro, 1996, p. 42). The gaze of the Other confounds our established perceptions and knowledge. The gaze, then, is not merely perception but informs us about who we are. The interaction of the encounter may not always be pleasant, but it does offer opportunities for self-awareness and self-enhancement. Tourism cannot always be defined as enjoyment, as some would suggest (see MacCannell, 1989), but it does offer the space for expansion of the sense of self.

What exactly in the encounter is unsettling? Suvantola explains 'things are there as objects we contemplate but whose meanings in their local context we cannot grasp' (Suvantola, 2002, p. 44). We know but also realize we don't know as well as we may have thought we did. The challenge of the encounter with elements known and unknown extends to the host, who has a set of socially and culturally prescribed perceptions of the places within which they live, move and have their being. The tourist likewise comes with a set of perceptions for the place being visited and, to varying extents, of the society of that place, often provided through tourism literature and various media. However, the encounter with both place and host gaze can crumble the visitor's certainty, while the host for whom the place is already constructed through familiarity, is similarly affected. The tourist, then, is a point of disruption of the host's regular gaze. Each subject is challenged in their understanding of self and place. Foucault refers to the 'self' as that individual who exists apart from the relation with institutions of culture and knowledge that constitute our discourses of identity; this resistance is the site for development of the self through an aesthetic project of self-authoring. Practices of subjectivity are not something that the individual invents, Foucault (1988) asserts, they are patterns that are proposed, suggested and imposed on us by our culture, our society and our social group. However, in his later work Foucault acknowledged that some individuals resist beliefs dictated by institutionalized knowledge–power structures. He began to consider that the individual constitutes her/himself in an active fashion through the practices of the self, that practices of self-formation of the subject form 'an exercise of self upon self by which one

tries to work out, to transform one's self and to attain a certain mode of being' (in Starkey and Hatchuel, 2002, p. 644). 'Since ... the self is not given to us' Foucault surmised, 'I think there is only one practical consequence: we have to create ourselves' (1997, p. 262).

For some tourists this may come as an increasing awareness of the transferability of the 'tourist gaze' as directed towards their self; they are aware of becoming the exotic object within the space they are visiting (Huggan, 2001). Indeed, travel can be understood as 'encounters with otherness that fracture both a boundary and an apparatus of representation'; it 'impels one to come face-to-face with the other' (Islam, 1996, p. vii).

The gaze, then, is not merely perception but informs us about who we are.

Response

To further examine this, we turn to philosophy, where gaze and the response to difference have formed a focus for debate, and which offers an analysis that applies to both guest and host.

The other is 'the most profound of what our human, ethical and imaginative faculties must confront and are confronted by' (Shapiro, 1996, p. 42). It is the relationship between the subject (the self) and the person who faces me (the other about whom I know nothing and can know nothing) that is implicated in how we see ourselves and how we see those who are outside our self, and establishes our relationship with the world around us.

In Western philosophy, different orientations to analyses of the relationship of subject and other continue to raise energetic debate over whether internal (self-) knowledge is pre-existent and how much is learned from outside; whether one is present before the other; how much of either is present in order to recognize the alternative. Returning to the Renaissance, scholars initially sought to break away from the deo-centred ideologies imposed by religion and began instead to place the subject (humankind) as central in our relationship to the world and our sense of being. This raised notions of the perception of self and Other in this relationship. Metaphysics, for example, brought a big-picture approach to bear on the relationship of self, Other and difference; the Other and the unknown are identified as a 'problem', something to be investigated and known – 'solved', as it were. What grew into discourse was an ontological framework of the belief that, by assembling all the 'rights', 'truths' and 'facts' of any object, subject or situation, the single, final explanation would be available: its fundamental, universal truth would be revealed. The whole story would be known and could be verified, told and recorded. However, the attempt to identify fact, truth and right establishes, by default, the existence of opposites: 'fiction', 'untruth' and 'wrong'. This sets knowledge as a process of choices for the 'correct' answer and limits our learning because, once taken, the choice is immutable – once established, the 'fact' is unassailable. All decisions pertaining to and associated with that fact can be taken to be reliable and not requiring further debate or attention. This applies to gazing at the visited site with perceptions established prior to engagement – if the knowledge that the visitor has brought along is considered to be the 'truth' then interaction with difference is impossible. It has already been identified and established.

Any discourse that is based in metaphysics will always select one (concept, situation, object, subject) as the preferred ('correct') and privilege that one over whatever is taken as its opposite – take the history of male/female, white/black, West/East, civilized/uncivilized oppositions of Western ideologies as examples. This oppositional dualism permeates Western thinking, including establishing the self as opposing the other in an adversarial discourse of dichotomous relations. Through an assumption that there is a preferential way of knowing the world and that difference can be dissected and re-arranged according to this accepted known, what is taken to be 'other' is reduced, absorbed or appropriated into being something the 'same' (something already known about).

This denies difference its entity and autonomy as well as its pre-existence and its originality. In relation to subjectivity, this is a process of taking the other as serving the selfhood of the subject that subtly subjugates the other into a satellite/centre relationship.

Husserl, through his phenomenological enquiry into consciousness, proposed that the subject can only understand itself by transferral from the experience of meeting separate animated bodies; that is, the realization that other separate bodies exist (Simms, 1997). The introduction of the Other is necessary in order for intuition to proceed from the purely internal to exteriority, Husserl considered (Simms, 1997). This meant that the Other was not simply a resource to the introspective knowledge of self, supporting the self's pre-existing egoistic knowledge; instead, through recognizing the Other's external existence, an extrospective relation of identity and subjectivity is needed. For Levinas, this relation takes place in the face-to-face encounter.

Levinas examines the human experience to build on Husserl's challenge to metaphysics as a way of understanding our being in the world. Levinas considers that the egocentric view does not do justice to our original experience of the other person. This is enacted, according to Levinas, in the face-to-face encounter, through acknowledging the absolute difference, the radical alterity, of the Other.

Human interaction, Levinas believes, begins with an ethical position, a response in relation to the other. 'The other is not the simple reversal of identity and is not formed out of resistance but is prior to every initiative,' he writes (Levinas, 1969, p. 38). While all the body expresses feelings, the face is the most expressive and it is in the face that we display thoughts, emotions and responses, both openly and inadvertently. 'The imperative of responsibility is articulated in the locus of the other who faces, the face of the other,' Levinas considers (1998, p. xix). Levinas uses the metaphor of the face, as the most expressive and personal element of meeting another person, to represent the immediacy of engagement with difference. The face confronts us, it disrupts by 'coming as a meaning which signifies *by itself*' (Davies, 1993, p. 263) [emphasis in original]. The encounter is an experience of immediacy, the other is realized but the question becomes one of how do I then relate to this other?

The face-to-face meeting demands a meaningful response – the self is responsible to offer something, Levinas contends. The ethical position in this relation is to assume the responsibility 'to listen carefully, to use our linguistic, emotional and cognitive imagination to grasp what is being expressed – and we must do this in a way where we resist the dual temptations of either facilely assimilating ... or dismissing' (Bernstein, 1991, p. 65). This respect for the separate alterity of the Other occurs before any cognizant categorization or limiting explanation is put onto the difference of the other. It is:

> the respect for the other as what it is; other. Without this acknowledgment, which is not a knowledge, without this 'letting be' of an existent other as something existing outside me in the essence of what is (first in its alterity), no ethics would be possible. (Bernstein, 1991, p. 184)

To say this another way, any understanding I may have had about myself is brought sharply into relativity against someone else's knowledge of their own self, which is inaccessible to me. I am not able to comprehend the radical alterity of the other, their autonomous difference. But I am able to choose my response. I can choose to reject any engagement with this Other whose difference frightens me, to retreat to suspicion or even label this Other as a threat, for 'the other is viewed as hostile, whose autonomous being is inherently a threat to the self's interests' (Woods, 1997). If the response is one of opening to the Other, however, the possibility of engagement is presented. The ethical response, then, 'consists not in comprehending but in relating' (Simms, 1997, p. 9). Indeed, 'the basic condition for all understanding requires one to test and risk one's convictions and prejudgements in and through an encounter with what is radically

"other" and alien ... only by seeking to learn from the other, only by fully grasping its claims upon one, can it be critically encountered' (Bernstein, 1991, p. 4).

For Levinas, the face-to-face relationship is where one can escape the Western binary to an ethical relationship 'which subtends discourse and is not a species of consciousness whose ray emanates from the I, [but] puts the I in question ... [and] this putting in question emanates from the other.' (1969, p. 195) The response to the act of facing is 'a responsibility which is a relationship with the other and his alterity, and this relationship is constitutive of our subjectivity' (Levinas, 1998, p. xix).

But for host and guest who are open to the difference of the Other in the gaze of the face-to-face encounter, vision tells of the other's alterity and discourse that 'opens divergence ... and contests the meaning I ascribe' is made possible (Levinas, 1969, p. 195). Levinas thus turns the Cartesian dialectic on its head – it is not through knowing myself that I know the Other, but rather that I am indebted to the Other for knowledge of myself (Simms, 1997, p. 11). The self must accept that this Other exists in complete separateness and thus absolute difference, and the only way to connect to the Other is to reach out.

Generosity

Levinas names the openness to give, the handing away of individual ownership (of knowledge or understanding), 'generosity'. The response that is ethical in its respect for the integrity of that Other, is one that begins in generosity (Levinas, 1969). Levinas proposes that the encounter with the face of the Other is the point where generosity is enacted, for the self must respond to the need for the Other's alterity to be recognized and respected for the immutable dignity of its difference.

Levinas locates radical generosity as outside ontological discourse, rather, generosity precedes, bypasses or crosses the boundaries of established discourse. It is unpredictable, for who knows when it may be enacted? Levinas uses the openness of the face and the reach of the hand as metaphors for the invitation to engage. Responsible communication that allows difference depends on an initial act of generosity; by speaking to the Other, I come into a relation with the individual while my autonomy remains intact, as does theirs (Levinas, 1969, p. 14). This allows the possibility of connection, of learning. The hand may reach out to touch the Other's hand. Voice may employ language to articulate response. In engagement that does not demand, expect or dismiss, lies the opening to communication wherein ethical responsibility becomes the basis for interaction. In this response, we realize and enact our responsibility. The generosity in the ethical response, Levinas writes, offers 'powers of welcome, of gift, of full hands, of hospitality' (1969, p. 205); it is both a sensibility and a condition of subjectivity (1998, p. 51). Deleuze and Guattari assert that we need to acknowledge the truly complex nature of subjectivity as an open-ended process of becoming, in which multiple contradictory positions and roles coexist and clash, but which form a highly energized, dynamic, open-ended series of interconnected possibilities (in Leith, 2001, p. 17). Our picture of the tourist and host in the space of the encounter shows the potential for change generated through each one's gaze. The host gaze, through the exchange, here becomes a part of the experience and, in the manner of dynamic energy of change, the other becomes a part of the self.

Gaze and Self

So where does this lead us? Do the tourist gaze and host gaze enact a generosity? Do they eventually meet 'in the self'? Travel, according to Islam, is a 'performative enactment of becoming-other' (1996, p. vii) and aligns with Butler's (1990) concept of performative acts as being the process for the self to grow and enlarge. The individual who travels opens the opportunity to absorb things outside their established frameworks.

Following Wearing and Wearing (2001), we are thus able to emphasize each individual's construction and reconstruction of the self in the light of experiences of interaction with significant others. 'Experience itself, or becoming ... confers meaning [and] the narration of experience is what will allow it to be ordered and codified for understanding' (Simms, 1997, p. 12). We have also demonstrated that the Other is necessary in the process of the individual's construction of self. Significant reference groups influence the conceptualization of the generalized Other through established cultural values, symbols and language. The social process and practices through which meanings are produced, circulated and exchanged (that we name 'culture') can precipitate responses. The host, then, may also exhibit a generalized reduction of the visitor's difference in the individual encounter in the tourist space.

However, experience, in the meeting of person and form, holds the potential to reach beyond the limitations of culture. It follows that there is a need to move beyond simplistic typologies of tourism experiences, towards a more flexible conceptualization that allows for the complex development of ideas and concepts of the self that occurs. This will further allow a critical analysis of the dominant ideas, values and constructions implicit in concepts of the gaze discussed earlier. A deconstruction of the assumptions of truth and validity in concepts of the gaze undertakes to reveal the subjectivity of both culture and experience as concepts and, indeed, the subjectivity of how different cultures are experienced by host and visitor. In addition, critical analysis of gaze requires a flexible conceptualization to better account for the significant range and diversity of experience and encounter in the practice of tourism.

Wearing and Wearing (2001) have urged for a conceptualization of tourism as an experience that involves 'complex and often subtle interactions between the tourist, the site and the host community' and in which the 'psychic space' of interactants (Craib, 1998), and thus their mutual understanding, can be realized. Craib's psychic space is another way of describing the individual internal space that allows acceptance and change. Psychology, along with philosophy, offers something to the development of conceptualizations of the tourist–host interaction; they approach this area of the meeting of self and other, difference and displaced familiarity, which has been under examination in this chapter. The space to allow the difference of the other and to value what that alterity can offer to the self is a vital factor in the tourism experience to which a flexible conceptualization can bring greater understanding. As Rojek notes, there is the opportunity for an individual to 'find oneself' in the context of unknown territory:

> Travel, it was thought, led to the accumulation of experience and wisdom. One began with nothing, but through guidance, diligence and commonsense one gained knowledge and achieved self-realisation. (Rojek, 1993, p. 114)

While there is great insight and value to be gained from questioning what we are told we are, there is some danger of deconstructing 'self' to the point of risking losing sight of human agency and being fully determined by discursive construction. Craib (1998, p. 9) has been concerned with the over-emphasis on the discursive to the exclusion of individual experience. In the postmodern present, people still choose to travel for extended periods of time. Many use this time to consider where their life is heading and what they want from it. As we have demonstrated, coming face to face with other people and cultures, through visiting, staying with and learning from them, develops and transforms the self. Acknowledging the radical alterity of the Other allows us to step aside from a position of surety and accept alternative ways of seeing and being in the world. It is the host gaze, because of its situated individualism, that holds the tourist as the radical Other and can open a transformation of self.

While this cannot be formulated as a reciprocal encounter – experiences are absolutely individual – the host and visitor, at separate times, in separate ways, are formed by each other through encounter. We each take on something of that Other from the experience of difference. The Other does not become me, nor I the Other, but the encounter changes us both in separate ways. Within post-structuralist analyses, it is held that 'the subject is not a rational whole but a changing contradictory site' making possible a new identity 'without a hierarchy of causation' (Wearing and Wearing, 2001, p. 145). Post-structuralist approaches have critiqued established structuralist models that place meaning, and therefore the self, in relations of binary opposition. Rather, post-structuralist thought holds that meaning is generated through the processes of social relationships, which are constituted through interactions in the daily ideological activities of social life (Bahktin, in Leith, 2001), and that these are formative of the self through constructions of identity.

Individuals are, and not necessarily passively, sites of discursive struggles. Some appear to have the ability to critique their own positions and discern positive and negative change, avoiding performative acts that are merely a repetition. However, Jagtenberg and McKie (1997, p. 149), have argued for a 'postmodern interactionism' in which the reflexive self is able to move beyond prior definitions. An adopted postmodern stance has encouraged individual travellers, for example, to question the role of significant others and reference groups (Sherif and Sherif, 1964, p. 6) in relation to their own self and identity, and so the tourist can discern the other and the host can set aside the cultural imperialism of the tourist. A flexible conceptual framing then assists our understanding of an individual's broader questioning of the relative 'merits' of particular facets of a different culture or environment. They might either engage with or reject/avoid them, in keeping with an internal belief and value system, partially exposing the degree of adherence they have to their own cultural 'centre' (Cohen, 1979).

By the host's choice, the Other of the visitor becomes a part of their self, incorporated through their experience of encounter.

For the visitor, what they experience within the conscious and unconscious register of identity (Lacan's 'imagined-real') at the destination relates to an authenticity within the experience (in Heidegger's meaning of 'authentic' as being the condition of acquiring identity from social and cultural contexts through a critical reflection). In this way, we begin to understand that 'one's sense of self derives from turning to another, and the self is thus always finding its source elsewhere, rather than being located in some form of Being separate from and prior to any consciousness-of-other' (Woods, 1997, p. 53).

Conclusion

In many tourism practices, the other does not exist except in relation to a discourse dictated by a dominant Western culture of dualistic opposition. We began our examination with the concept of the disengaged gaze of the flâneur, which supported discourses of observational neutrality. However, the concept of the choraster challenges the validity of a dichotomous stance of the self–Other relationship through establishing the role of context and the indivisibility of gaze, embodiment and emplacement. The tourist space inheres interactions between tourist, the host's culture and values and the destabilizing of preconceived understanding. The gaze is confounded by the alterity of the other and it is necessary to understand that gaze is much more than a tool of observation but is fundamental to concepts of being and existence.

If travelling is an activity that enables the individual negotiation of identity and subjectivity through a non-reductive relation with the other, then the return of the gaze is an invitation for simultaneous generosity. In acknowledging the host's separateness, the tourist takes the host gaze into their own, in a response of opening to difference. We offer this conception to a subject-centred understanding of tourism that allows for the host's role in tourist cultures.

References

Bauman, Z. (1996) From pilgrim to tourist – or a short history of identity. In: Hall, S. (eds) *Questions of Cultural Identity*. Sage, London.

Benjamin, W. (1973) *Charles Baudelaire: a Lyric Poet in the Era of High Capitalism*. Zohn, H. (trans.) New Left Books, London.

Bernstein, R. (1991) *The New Constellation: The Ethical/Political Horizons of Modernity/Postmodernity*. MIT Press, Cambridge, MA.

Butler, J. (1990) *Gender Trouble: Feminism and the Subversion of Identity*. Routledge, New York.

Cohen, E. (1979) A phenomenology of tourist experiences. *Sociology* 13, 179–201.

Craib, I. (1998) *Experiencing Identity*. Sage, London.

Davies, P. (1993) The face and the caress. In: Levin, D. M. (eds) *Modernity and the Hegemony of Vision*. University of California Press, Berkeley, CA.

De Certeau, M. (1988) *The Practice of Everyday Life*. Rendell, S. (trans.) University of California Press, Berkeley, CA.

Feifer, M. (1985) *Going Places*. Macmillan, London.

Foucault, M. (1988) *The Care of the Self*. Hurley, R. (trans.) Vintage Books, New York.

Foucault, M. (1997) On the geneaology of ethics: an overview of work in progress. In: Rabinow, P. (eds) *Ethics: Subjectivity and Truth*. The New Press, New York.

Fuerty, P. and Mansfield, N. (2000) *Cultural Studies and Critical Theory*. Oxford University Press, Melbourne.

Grosz, E. (1995) Women, *chora*, dwelling. In: Watson, S. and Gibson, K. (eds) *Postmodern Cities and Spaces*. Blackwell Publishers, Cambridge, MA.

Huggan, G. (2001) *The Postcolonial Exotic: Marketing the Margins*. Routledge, London.

Islam, S.M. (1996) *The Ethics of Travel: from Marco Polo to Kafka*. Manchester University Press, Manchester.

Jagtenberg, T. and McKie, D. (1997) *Eco-Impacts and the Greening of Postmodernity*. Sage, Thousand Oaks, CA.

Lefebvre, H. (1991) *The Production of Space*. Blackwell, Oxford.

Lechte, J. (1995). (Not) belonging in postmodern space. In Watson, S. and Gibson, K. (eds), *Postmodern Cities and Spaces*. Blackwell Publishers, Cambridge, MA, pp. 99–111.

Leith, V. B. (2001) *The Norton Anthology of Theory and Criticism*. W W Norton & Company Inc., New York.

Levinas, E. (1969) *Totality and Infinity: an Essay on Exteriority*. Lingis, A. (trans.) Duquesne University Press, Pittsburgh, PA.

Levinas, E. (1998) *Otherwise Than Being, or Beyond Essence*. Lingis, A. (trans.) Duquesne University Press, Pittsburgh, PA.

MacCannell, D. (1989). Semiotics of Tourism. *Annals of Tourism Research*, 16, 1–6.

MacCannell, D. (1992) *Empty Meeting Grounds, the Tourist Papers*. Routledge, London.

Meinig, D.W. (1979) *The Beholding Eye: Ten Versions of the Same Scene*. In: Meinig, D.W. (eds) *The Interpretation of Ordinary Landscapes*. Oxford University Press, Oxford.

Nuvolati, G. (2009) The gaze of the flâneur. *Ri-Vista ricerche per la progettazione del paesaggio* (gennaio-giugno), 46–52.

Rojek, C. (1993) *Ways of Escape: Modern Transformations in Leisure and Travel*. Rowman and Littlefield Publishers, Lanham, MD.

Shapiro, R. (1996) Ethics, the literary imagination and the other. *Journal of Australian Studies* 50/51, Fabrications.

Sherif, M. and Sherif, C. (1964) *Reference Groups: Exploration into Conformity and Deviation of Adolescents*. Harper and Row, New York.

Simms, K. (1997) *Ethics and the Subject*. Rodopi, Amsterdam, Atlanta.

Soja, E.W. (1996) *Thirdspace: Journeys to Los Angeles and Other Real-and-Imagined Places*. Blackwell, Cambridge, MA.

Starkey, K. and Hatchuel, A. (2002) The long detour: Foucault's history of desire and pleasure. *Organization* 9(4), 641–657.

Suvantola, J. (2002) *Tourist's Experience of Place*. Ashgate, Aldershot.

Wearing, B. and Wearing, S. (1996) Refocussing the tourist experience: the flâneur and the chorister. *Leisure Studies* 15, 229–243.

Wearing, S. and Wearing, B. (2001) Conceptualizing the selves of tourism. *Leisure Studies* 20(2), 143–159.

Wearing, S., Stevenson, D. and Young, T. (2010) *Tourist Cultures: Identity, Place and the Traveller*. Sage, London UK.

Wilson, E. (1995) The invisible *flâneur*. In: Watson, S. and Gibson, K. (eds) *Postmodern Cities and Spaces*. Blackwell, Oxford.

Wolff, J. (1985) The invisible *flâneuse*: women and the literature of modernity. *Theory, Culture and Society* 2, 37–45.

Woods, T. (1997) The ethical subject: the philosophy of Emmanuel Levinas. In Simms, K. (eds) *Ethics and the Subject*. Rodopi, Amsterdam, Atlanta.

13 The Bellman and the Prison Officer: Customer Care in Imperfect Panopticons

Thomas Ugelvik

Introduction

Standing next to or close to the main entrance, the hotel bellman is often the guests' first impression of the hotel. Consequently, he is also often the first member of the hotel staff who gets an impression of the guest. The vigilant bellman's gaze is a discriminating one. As he stands there in his red uniform, gold buttons and all, he is, as one might expect, constantly sorting guests according to two different schemas: the possible needs they may have, and their potential for tipping. However, and perhaps less often acknowledged, the bellman gaze will also focus on a third kind of issue: that of security and control. Hotel employees regularly see people on less than their best behaviour. Hayner (1936) describes how the hotel experience may lead guests to take a 'moral holiday', leaving their manners and morals at home. The bellman gaze is explicitly considered to be the first line of defence against unwanted or difficult guests. Is the guest carrying plastic bags heavy with bottles? Is he trying to sneak prostitutes into his room? Often the bellman will know, and if he knows, the room in question will soon be on list of 'difficult rooms'. His duty, then, is to relay any relevant information to the hotel security department, whose more inconspicuously dressed agents will take the necessary actions.

In fact, this control mode of the bellman gaze might be said to have a lot in common with the powerful panoptic gaze characteristic of modern prisons as described by Foucault (1995). The purpose of this chapter is to compare and contrast these two different kinds of professional gazes; that of the hotel bellman and that of the prison officer. The point of comparison is often to be able to show something new about the things compared. Introducing a new contrast agent may make something already known appear in a new light. By comparing the two, I am not saying that hotel employees are in every way very similar to prison officers, nor that hotels and prisons generally have very much in common. What I want to do, rather, is to put the professional prison guard gaze analytically to use in order to say something new about the host gaze employed in hotel lobbies around the world. At the same time, and equally interesting, the bellman gaze thus analysed cannot help but return the favour and reflect back on and comment on the prison officers and their optics and practices of power. The two different kinds of gazes compared will thus be put to work as each others' mirrors, hopefully giving novel insights on both sides as a result.

(eds O. Moufakkir and Y. Reisinger)

More precisely, I am going to show that both professions, although radically different in many ways, have in common a way of seeing that tries to balance professional customer care with specific control duties. I want to show that these different kinds of gazes have in common a dual optic partly focused on the needs of others, partly on the potential problems and dangers these others represent.

Research Methods and Context

It is important to recognize that the two different kinds of gazes analysed in this chapter have been made observable to me through very different kinds of experiences. In the following, the two main parts of the chapter will be based on different forms of data, which must be given different empirical status.

The hotel parts of the chapter are based on a retrospective autoethnographic account (see Cotanda, 2006; Freitas and Pathon, 2009; Neumann, 2010) of my five years as a part-time bellman in one of Norway's largest hotels. The hotel in question is part of a large international chain. With its 676 guest rooms and 1,500 beds on offer, it would be considered industrial by any standard. There is absolutely nothing understated about the huge glass and steel phallic structure with its polished brass and shining marble; it is the kind of hotel that seems to appeal to TV celebrities and the nouveau riche.

As is true with all research methods, authoethnography has strengths and weaknesses. I never took any kind of field notes after work in the hotel lobby.[1] In fact, I was not in the field to observe at all, but to smile, carry suitcases and put my professional bellman gaze to work. The fact that writing about it years later has come quite easy has probably partly to do with my later training and experience as an ethnographer, partly with the fact that I spent enough time as a bellman to be able to say that it is one of the few things I really know how to do (whereas as a prison researcher, I would be hard pressed to work as a prison officer for even a day). The embodied knowledge of the little but all-important things, like how to safely load a luggage trolley to its maximum capacity and how the luggage room should be properly organized, as well as the pleasant and promising feeling of a trouser pocket filled with Norwegian change and dollar bills on a hot summer day, are still fresh in my mind. To aid my memory work, I also met with a former bellman colleague as part of the writing process. Our meeting did not change the overall direction of the chapter, but it did provide me with new, illustrative anecdotes as well as an important arena for validation of my analyses.

In contrast to this research strategy, the prison parts are based on systematic ethnographic fieldwork over a period of 1 year (May 2007 to May 2008) in two connected prison wings for remand prisoners in Oslo prison, Norway's largest prison. I was given free access to the two wings, could come and go as I pleased, and talk to any prisoner I wanted to without going through the officers first. Conversations mainly took place in the small common area shared by the two wings, or in the privacy of a cell together with one or two prisoners. I wore civilian clothes, an ID card identifying me as a university employee, a single visible key to get me between wings and an alarm on my belt. Having no official role in the prison and no cell keys, I spent most of my time hanging around the wings, drinking coffee, playing pool and talking with anyone interested about whatever they would want to talk about. What Geertz has called *deep hanging out* – 'localized long-term close-in vernacular field research' (1998, p. 69) – worked well as a research strategy in an environment where people have a lot of time on their hands and not a lot to do with it, although it did provoke a lot of jokes about my seemingly endless break from 'real work'. The fact that I resemble the prisoner (and officer) average both in terms of gender and age (male, early 30s), probably also played a part in making this a fruitful strategy (Phillips and Earle, 2010). I never took notes in the prison. Observation notes were written on the same or following day, with an effort to reflect meaning, language tone and style, as well as the relevant context.

According to Alison Liebling, the most essential tool for ethnographers is 'the *full use of yourself*' (1999, p. 475). In contrast to many other research traditions, it is commonly argued by ethnographers that the researcher is him- or herself vital to the research result. One cannot have ethnography without the ethnographer. This is why many researchers choose to go against the many academic genre conventions in writing up their research (e.g. those demanding that one should avoid the use of personal pronouns and remove the researcher from the finished text). For many ethnographers, keeping the researcher-author visible in the text is not only a matter of academic style; it is a question of epistemology. Given ethnography's grounding in real social interaction between actual people, something that the particular researcher necessarily is a vital part of, suspending yourself from the finished paper could actually be considered to be a bit dishonest. This is why I have chosen to use a more personal style than is common in many academic texts throughout the chapter.

The Bellman Gaze

When comparing two different classes of things, it is often tempting to give priority to differences between the classes, ignoring or at least downplaying the differences between units belonging to the same class (Nelken, 2010). I must start off, then, by saying that all hotels are not the same. Some radiate the sort of subtle and classic elegance associated with old wealth. Others are like worn down and tarnished signs of greatness lost; others still are neutered and streamlined plastic chain hotels, devoid of any individuality. Some hotels communicate to the world that they offer a decent room for an affordable price, others scream flamboyantly that whoever enters better have their platinum card ready to back it up. Hotels are sometimes tiny family-owned neighbourhood stores with a handful of beds, sometimes sleep supermarkets with hundreds of rooms and thousands of new arrivals every week.[2]

But there are also many things that all hotels have in common. One is that all hotels will continuously sort and evaluate their guests, both prospective and actual. From the hotel's perspective, one is always a specific type of guest. Once you enter the building, you are always already part of a guest category with specific features, placed in a typology with categories that are meaningful for hotel workers in specific ways. You may, for instance, be a domestic or a foreign guest, a good or bad tipper, a professional conference guest or part of a family of four on holiday. And you may be a nice, polite and respectful guest or a somewhat difficult and demanding one. Or you may, certainly less frequently, even be a complete bastard.

A bellman is part of the hotel's public image, its 'face' towards the world. They are chosen for their appropriate behaviour (stand up straight, no hands in pockets) and respectable looks (no tattoos showing, short hair, no sideburns), their gender (no women allowed, not because women are not strong enough, many certainly would be, but because gender roles and stereotypes prohibit male guests from surrendering their heavy suitcases to a woman) and their interpersonal skills and service mindedness (service with a smile, 'can do' attitude). Accomplished bellmen are able to 'perform bellman', they 'speak hotel' fluently and can exhibit a bellman persona at will if required. Bellmen carry your bags and walk you to your room, but they do much more: they often do concierge-type things like make dinner reservations and confirm aeroplane tickets, they show people where to find all kinds of things in the city, they act like couriers, guides and the hotel's jack-of-all-trades.

What is the fundamental sorting principle of the bellman gaze? As stated above, guests are scanned searching for the needs they may have and their potential as a source of tips. For bellmen, needs are all about the type, weight and numbers of suitcases, as well as other special cases like guests with impaired mobility. Spotting this is relatively easy, even for the beginner. The skill of singling out and targeting heavy tippers is what defines an accomplished bellman. This has been described by Hayner:

> Front office employees can usually pick out the guest who will tip more liberally than average. The 'rounder' is said to be a bellboy's best friend. General appearance, manners, clothes, speech, facial expressions, signature and 'hotel attitude' ... tell the experienced employee what type of person the guest is... It is difficult to describe the exact psychology of the process, but it is sufficient to say that when a bellhop carries your bags he knows whether or not you will tip him. (Hayner, 1936, p. 157)

In my experience, this is mostly based on the (perceived) nationality of guests. Norwegian guests, for instance, are not used to bellmen, and are uncomfortable in tipping situations, while US guests feel right at home. Japanese guests are also good tippers, yet also uncomfortable with the face-to-face tipping situation. They often prefer to leave dollar bills on the suitcases for you to collect when they are not around. These are the hard-and-fast rules, but it is certainly also true that one develops a feel for the situation, a certain *je ne sais quoi* part of a bellman *habitus* (Bourdieu, 1990), which makes tips flow more steadily as time goes by.

I will, however, concentrate on the control part of the bellman gaze, the part of the optic that first and foremost focuses on guests as potentially bad customers and security problems. This is fundamental for understanding the relationship between host and guest/customer: it is only through the use of his wallet that the guest may receive the room key as a material sign of the fact that he has been acknowledged as a legitimate guest. The key signifies the fact that the room with the lock that fits it has been surrendered to the guest for the duration that has been or will be paid for. As the entire relationship is based on a transaction, the worst kind of guest is he who is unable or unwilling to pay for services rendered. So the ability to pay is a major concern for all front office staff. In this day and age, the hotel's services will often be paid online in advance. When this is not the case, getting guests to actually pay before they leave is a perpetual concern. Most of the time, a hotel will sort this out by freezing a deposit on the guest's credit card account on arrival. Guests insisting on the somewhat outdated practice of paying in cash need to put up a considerable cash deposit in its stead, raising suspicion in the process. Nevertheless, some guests manage to sneak past the hotel's defences and make their way, from the lobby to their room and back into the world outside without ever having had the intention of paying. Because any guest may turn out to be a fraud, the hotel needs continuously to be on watch for guests who are not real guests after all. The back room of a hotel reception will often have a reasonably updated list of known swindlers, complete with CCTV still pictures and different known aliases.

The hotel staff's gaze upon the guests is thus a discriminating and controlling one. From the bellman's point of view, ethnic minority youths parking their pimped-out BMWs on the pavement and parading through the lobby, motor still running, to see if there are any suites available, raise one kind of suspicion. Middle aged men without any luggage arriving late with a scantily clad woman half their age on their arm, another. Hayner (1936) describes how a stay in a hotel temporarily pries a guest loose from many of the ties to the common moral and social community of 'normal' and 'decent' people, making a 'moral holiday' possible. A hotel room is in a way a kind of room that makes the transgression of norms possible and even probable. Anyone with experience of working in the service industry during the Norwegian office Christmas party (or *julebord*) season will know instantly what I am talking about. The guest in his hotel room feels disconnected from the normal ties of social control; morals and manners temporarily made irrelevant. It is in this perspective that guests arriving without luggage seem suspicious, as well as guests carrying too many bottles. These guests are put on the security department's list of rooms to keep an extra eye on.

The same happens when small children come down to eat breakfast by themselves, when the maid reports that a non-smoking room reeks of cigarettes, and when other guests, properly behaving ones, complain about loud music or screaming. As a rule, such control practices go unnoticed by the guests. This is just what the hotel wants; the ideal is a form of control that is efficient enough, but that also is masked as and feels like hospitality. It is a form of power that should be hidden at all costs, a power that should not stand in the way of consumption, a softer, more indirect power, designed to look like something else. Guests must continue to feel like guests at a hotel, even when they are being scrutinized. Appearance is, as always, key, the division between front stage and back stage paramount (Goffman, 1971).

The bellman gaze needs to detect potential problem guests, alert the security department, and also observe these guests as closely as possible throughout their stay, both from their vantage point in the lobby, and, in more extreme cases, whenever they are on hotel premises. The job description may not include such practices, but I have, on direct orders from superiors, listened outside guest room doors, walked through corridors smelling for cigarette smoke and even, on more than one occasion, locked myself into guest rooms to look around for any general signs of unwanted behaviour.

These control efforts notwithstanding, it is well known by hotel employees that guests will steal anything not bolted down. Unless they bring bolt cutters, that is. They drink too much, they ruin or smash furniture and they make amateur (or not so amateur) pornographic movies and post them online with the hotel's name in the title. The cleaning staff will find vomit in the staircase, blood on the lobby lounge leather sofa and faeces on the elevator floor. Simply put, hotel workers regularly see people behaving badly. If one finds a reason good enough, such guests are simply put out on the street, but most of the time, hotel staff must simply deal with these transgressions as best they can. Experienced hotel workers are able to make difficult guests behave

better, yet still be happy and pleased with their stay. Such staff members have advanced diplomatic skills, because a customer is of course always right, at least until he definitely and without any kind of doubt is wrong. Given this, it may come as no surprise that in addition to the tales about known swindlers, more light-hearted anecdotes and 'war stories' about encounters with difficult guests circulate among staff, often in friendly contests of one-upmanship over a tip-bought beer after work. These stories more often revolve around indecent behaviour, questionable sexual morals or terrible personal hygiene, rather than outright fraud. Behind the harmless release offered by a shared laughter at the guests' expense is a shred of sombre seriousness, however: the bottom line is that the hotel's reputation (or maybe rather its status as a brand) is always put on the line when a new guest arrives.

To sum up so far, one might say that the bellman gaze focuses on the hotel guests as a configuration of needs (those needs bellmen are able to meet), wallet (which must be opened for the bellman to do anything) and potential problems hopefully to be avoided. When focusing on the problems, the bellman gaze has certain things in common with the gaze described by Foucault (1995) as the fundamental engine of discipline in the model panoptic prison invented by Bentham, where the fundamental mechanism of power rests on the fact that the observable many (prisoners) are unable to tell when the observing few (prison officers) are watching them. They thus have to act as if they are being watched all the time. Ideally located on the sprawling lobby floor, bellmen also direct a trained gaze at the observable many (in many cases, at least, unaware of the fact that they are being observed) searching for the minority of problem guests.

The Prison Officer Gaze

Just as there are differences between hotels, there are also between prisons. Oslo prison for instance, the prison where I conducted my fieldwork, is as Norwegian prisons go industrial in size with about 400 prisoners, even though it would hardly be considered mid-sized in an international perspective. As many prisons are in many jurisdictions, it is materially dated and undergoing constant ad-hoc renovation to make the best out of a less than perfect situation. The facility has two major units. The oldest part, built as a Philadelphia-style penitentiary[3] and opened in 1851, houses prisoners with sentences of up to 2 years. The newest part, an old brewery made part of the prison in 1939, is predominantly for prisoners held on remand. On remand wings, you will mostly find prisoners suspected of violent crimes, drug crimes and sexual offences. The cells are small and gloomy, still reminiscent of the 1930s rebuilding process. They all have had sanitation facilities installed at a later date, however, and a small TV. The cramped conditions are considered acceptable only because the wings are supposed to be temporary stops for prisoners awaiting their sentence.[4]

The newly opened (2010) Halden prison, Norway's second largest with a capacity of 248 prisoners, is another story. At the opening, the new facility was described as the world's most modern prison, the state-of-the-art for criminal justice everywhere, a triumph for the social-democratic welfare state. According to *Time* magazine:

> The cells rival well-appointed college dorm rooms, with their flat-screen TVs and minifridges. Designers chose long vertical windows for the rooms because they let in more sunlight. There are no bars. Every 10 to 12 cells share a living room and kitchen. With their stainless-steel countertops, wraparound sofas and birch-colored coffee tables, they resemble Ikea showrooms.[5]

Oslo and Halden prisons are both giants compared with the smallest Norwegian institutions: we have Sandefjord prison with 14 prisoners, Mosjøen prison with 15 and Horten prison with 16. All five are completely dwarfed, however, by the behemoth prison at Fleury-Mérogis, just south of Paris.

At the time of my 1-day visit in 2005, it was booked to 150% of capacity (3,000 capacity, 4,500 prisoners). The two giant concrete structures look from the air like dark shadows of the Pentagon, from the ground like something from out of a dystopic science fiction movie, complete with condensation running down mildewed walls in damp and dimly lit cells. Over the period of a year, its high turnover rate makes it the short-term home of a dizzying number of remand prisoners and illegal immigrants awaiting deportation.

Yet there are things also all prisons have in common. For instance, all prisons, like all hotels, will direct a professional gaze at new arrivals. If the bellman gaze has panoptic qualities, how does it compare to that of prison officers, the archetypal workers in the original panoptic machine? Made famous by Foucault (1995), Bentham's idea was that the prison's architecture should be thought of as a mechanism of power: if you light cells in a certain way, and place them all opposite a central guard tower in a certain way, all prisoners can be observed at once by one or just a few officers. Further refinements made it possible for prisoners to be unable to see when the officers actually were looking; they thus had to behave like they were being watched at all times.

It has been argued that Bentham's vision is not a good description of real prisons, neither historical nor present ones (Alford, 2000). Certainly, present day Norwegian prisons are not panoptical in this sense. What happens behind a closed cell door is invisible to the officers unless they open the small control hatch. In Norway, prisoners are even accorded a legal right to privacy. This does not mean, however, that prison officers do not direct a controlling gaze upon the prisoners out in their care, only that the point of focus has changed.

Like the bellman gaze, the prison officer gaze is a discriminatory one, sorting prisoners into various formal and informal categories: big or small, Norwegian citizens or foreigners, killers or drug traffickers, nice guys or dangerous and risky individuals, run-down or resourceful. Like the bellman gaze, the prison officer gaze has a dual optic, focusing simultaneously on control issues and the care for prisoners' needs. Behind the concrete walls of Halden prison, for instance, you find, like stations around a conveyor belt, all the various welfare state agencies responsible for meeting different kinds of (Norwegian citizen) prisoners' needs: the public employment agency, public health care, public school system, and so on, all have their own facilities inside the prison. Taken as a whole, they are the welfare state team of rehabilitation workers put there to influence, control and improve the prisoner population. The fundamental purpose of the whole system is that prisoners arrive with an assortment of needs and lacks the institution needs to identify, prioritize and correct. The prison officers know that prisoners in general score badly on every sort of standard of living variable: they are undereducated and underemployed, have large debts, they are more often physically and mentally ill, more often homeless with drug problems, and so on (Skarðhamar, 2002; Friestad and Hansen, 2004; Thorsen, 2004). The challenge for the prison officer gaze when faced with a new arrival is to find out where an individual prisoner is positioned in all this, and what can be done about it in the time the prison has at its disposal. The prison officer gaze thus also, like the bellman equivalent, tries to identify 'customer' needs.[6] Of course, this does not mean that the prison is no longer also a place where powerful technologies of control and discipline are important. The gaze is interested in locating and identifying prisoners' needs, but only to the extent that these needs have been shown to be relevant for the overall goal of prisoner rehabilitation and risk management, creating a safer society and decreased levels of crime on the macro level of society as a whole (Ugelvik, 2011).

The prison officer, then, directs a gaze that is simultaneously diagnostic, care-oriented and control-oriented towards the prisoners. This gaze must have multiple foci, it must both generalize and individualize at the same time. On the one hand, all prisoners are the same; that is, they are

potential escape risks and must be treated as such. On the other hand, they are all different; Robert, for instance might want to finish his secondary education, while Adil has no income and nowhere to live when released. Both the generalizing knowledge about all prisoners and the individualizing knowledge about each and every prisoner are on different levels of detail than the types of knowledge the hotel gathers about its guests. To attain its goals (less crime in a safer society), the prison must get to know a lot about both Robert and Adil, and with their different needs, the goal of successful rehabilitation dictates that they must be approached in different ways. Neither must be allowed to just walk out of the door though; again, care and control are intertwined. That is the point where the different aspects of the present day prison officer gaze overlap: where prisoner needs and the risks they pose cross paths (cf. Hannah-Moffat, 2005; Giertsen, 2006; Strand [Ugelvik], 2006).

While a legitimate hotel guest can be known by the key he temporarily carries in his pocket, a prisoner is defined by the lack of keys. Every time a prisoner in a high-security prison crosses a threshold, in principle he needs to have been authorized by a prison officer to do so. This, of course, is why a prison spell, unlike a weekend in a nice hotel room, is no moral holiday. On the contrary, the everyday life in a prison puts prisoners under high moral pressure; prisoners are painfully aware of the fact that they are being watched, and that this almost constant observation is put into work because they are prisoners. Where hotel guests are made to feel society's social control efforts ease, prisoners are continuously positioned as morally deficient, with personal autonomy and agency understandably removed or at least heavily curtailed because of past wrongs committed. Prisoner status thus carries with it a moral stigma (Goffman, 1963); the status is in itself one of the principal pains of imprisonment (Sykes, 1958).

Prisoners, however, are not only the objects of the prison officer gaze. Prisoners also watch each other all the time. Here, the difference between hotels and prisons become even more pronounced. Hotel guests may be physically close to each other, but they seldom fraternize much, at least not in the kind of hotel where I have worked. A nod at the breakfast buffet, perhaps, or a polite yet often uninspired 'How do you do?' in the elevator, but that's about it. In a prison, prisoners are made socially responsible to and for the community of prisoners over a period of time, they are thus aware of each other in a different way. A hotel guest is always on the move, always going elsewhere, away from maids and receptionists he has an exclusively professional relationship with (even though the professional smile of the receptionist aims to professionally familiarize it) and who he will most likely never meet again (an important part of the foundation for the moral holiday). Prisoners will meet each other and their counterparts, the officers, over a longer period. The common areas of a prison are thus spaces where one has to be responsible for one's actions to a stronger degree, a forced community where one cannot choose one's neighbours nor how much one has to socialize with them. Wacquant describes it as a:

> total subjection to the permanent and pervasive gaze of others who are themselves subjected to the same ongoing visual and sensory penetration... One of the most degrading aspects of penal confinement is this denial of any 'backstage', of any 'territory of intimacy', to speak like Goffman. (Wacquant, 2002, p. 378)

It is part of the prison's (and the hotel's) nature that inhabitants cannot fully close their assigned spaces off from the people working there. The ownership of and control over the various spaces in a prison must be administered and negotiated. Prison researchers often write about the uncomfortable feeling of invading other people's spaces when they enter occupied cells (Wacquant, 2002). Prison officers will seldom share this experience (nor will bellmen entering hotel rooms), they are professionals working in other people's private spheres. The pronoun 'my' in 'my cell' and

'my hotel room' obviously does not reflect any true ownership, that much is clear. But in a hotel, the borders between public and private spaces are at least supposed to be strictly regulated; hotel guests may put out a 'please do not disturb' sign that hotel staff at least need some sort of reason to ignore. The seemingly private sphere of a prison cell may at any time and without notice be invaded by uniformed personnel. Officers may decide that prisoners are to be moved to another cell, or another prison, with only minutes' notice. Or they can decide that they need to go through the cell and its contents searching for weapons or contraband.

Given this, it may come as no surprise that prisoners invest a great amount of energy to create the illusion of ownership, a feeling of privacy, albeit a fragile one. Like a hotel guest arriving at his room, the new arrival in a prison wing will work hard at individualizing and privatizing his assigned space. Both a prison cell and a hotel room are empty spaces, made for whoever and everyone. Prisoners and hotel guests alike are like numbers in a series of similar units who for a time occupy the generalized space. Van Lennep (1987) describes how the anonymous and pristine hotel room positions the new arrival as a stranger, someone who does not feel responsible for the choice of furniture or colour of the wallpaper. This 'strangeness' makes it difficult to feel comfortable; so the hotel guest starts taking possession of the space to make it his own. He starts using the room; he leaves traces, thus materializing his presence and making the room his (temporary) property. Hotel guests and prisoners are similar in this respect: they actively place and position material items in the empty space they temporary occupy to make it into *their* space.

Looking for the Needs/Risks of Others

Notwithstanding the current pan-European trend of converting old prisons into hotels, prisons and hotels are not the same. Stating the obvious, Hayner puts it like this:

The best American prisons with their short length of stay, wholesome food, recreational programs and radio in every cell approach the standards of a second-class hotel; but the guests are not free to check out when they wish. (Hayner, 1936, p. 47)

Prisons and hotels are solutions to very different problems on very different levels. The hotel offers a service to its guests for a limited period, including privacy, safety and a roof over their head. There are often add-ons: expensive hotels in addition sell a specific identity by distinguishing (Bourdieu, 1995) its guests from non-guests in a flattering way as to contribute to their self-esteem as guests of a particular kind (rich ones with good taste). Buildings and objects cannot be totally separated from the symbolic values and meanings they are ascribed. Symbolically speaking, a fancy hotel and a high-security prison refer to their inhabitants in very different ways. A prison cell positions its occupant as a prisoner the same way that an expensive hotel room refer to its guest's economic status (van Lennep, 1987). But the fact remains that the two professional gazes detailed in this chapter also have a lot in common.

Urry describes tourists as people consumed by the need to generate pleasurable experiences which are different than their everyday life: 'The tourist gaze is directed to features of landscape and townscape which separate them off from everyday experience' (2002, p. 3). These landscapes and townscapes have inhabitants who live and work in these places, however, and the question is what happens when these people look back. The tourist gaze is socially organized and systematized; it is intertwined with optics and relations of power according to Urry. The host gaze equally so. If Urry is right that the tourist gaze constitutes the tourist attraction (it is hardly an attraction if no one bothers to look), it might be said that it is the host gaze which makes the tourist into a tourist: a special kind of guest who is not received in the spirit of a true relationship between equals (e.g. one where gifts would be exchanged reciprocally), but as the result of a transaction where one party buys the services of

another. The transaction part of the relationship is problematic, however. Hotel 'guests' (who really are consumers) should be made to feel like they are home, like they are in a home away from home (Urry, 2002, p. 12). Hotels must cultivate in their guests the illusion of entering and taking possession of a pristine space specially made just for them, as the first human beings ever to occupy it. Every guest should feel unique even though the creation of this individual uniqueness is (and must be) perfectly routine from the point of view of the service worker (Urry, 2002, p. 62). Many hotel rooms do a poor job at it, but that is the ideal, at least; in expensive hotels, this is a major part of what the guests are paying for.

The host–guest relationship is one of mutual interdependence, certainly on the practical and pecuniary levels, but also on the more abstract level of everyday life identity work. The tourist becomes a tourist also through encountering the host gaze, in the same moment as the host becomes a host because he is seen as a host and is able to act as one. He can be a poor host or a fantastic one, but without guests around with needs to be met, he is no host, the way a prison officer with no one to look after is not a prison officer after all. When tired bellmen, sweat running down their backs as they empty the bowels of yet another bus of its multicoloured Samsonite cargo, remark that *this would be a really good gig if it wasn't for all these guests arriving all the time*, it should not be taken too literally. In my experience, the reason people stay in the job is the feeling of helping someone, of solving some problem, perhaps of showing someone how to get to a part of the city they would not otherwise explore, or helping someone more unfortunate to get to the closest hospital. It is through the eyes of the guests, as they gaze back and acknowledge a job well done, that the work is given meaning. That and the pleasure of lifting the odd extraordinarily heavy suitcase, of course: *you should come over and feel this one – we have another rock collector!* Bellmen are not bellmen because they enjoy catching guests in the act of misbehaving, as most prison officers are not prison officers because they enjoy locking doors. Prison officers may, of course, have thought more about these various parts of their gaze more explicitly. Unlike bellman, prison officers are, in Norway at least, part of a specialized profession based on a formal educational training with a specific and definable common knowledge base, a trade union, a code and a strong professional identity.

It must be made perfectly clear: as laid out above, these practices and potential problems are not the sole focus of the bellman's gaze. He is of course concerned with guest needs and the guest's happiness for most of the time. A hotel will often go a long way to fulfil guest need, although there are obvious exceptions (Guerrier and Adib, 2000). My point is simply that alongside these more common services, the issues of control and security always run parallel; there is perhaps no form of care, professional or other, which is not also a form of control and power (Basberg, 1999; Neumann, 2009). In both prison and hotels, the professional gaze is preoccupied with the well-being of the guests/prisoners. Both kinds of places, however, also have other interests in mind. When bellmen employ the controlling gaze of a host made responsible for the guests' behaviour because they need to be kept in line with formal and informal norms related to appropriate guest behaviour, they are not-so-distant cousins of prison officers. When the hotel collects knowledge about its guest to better distinguish between ordinary guests and the respectful ones, they are employing an optic of power, a dividing practice, not unlike the ones prison officers are trained to use. And, equally important, when prison officers seek out prisoners' needs and make strategies for how they may effectively be met, one could also say that they are being good hosts. The fact that the guests may not always appreciate the service is another matter. So, even though obviously not a panoptic gaze in a strict Benthamite/Foucauldian sense, where the invisible few may observe and control the visible many (at the very least, being invisible to the guests would make for a really bad tip day), the bellman gaze nevertheless is a controlling gaze where the few observe the many – the many probably not being aware that they are being observed in this way. The problem, of course, is that hotel guests, to stay hotel guests, cannot be made aware of the fact that the hotel is watching. Hotel guests are, unlike prisoners, mostly unaware of the fact that they are being watched, effectively cancelling out most of the disciplinary effect. And thus the moral holiday continues. The conclusion, then, for prison research and hospitality research alike, is that the bellman gaze and the prison officer gaze both have, at their very foundations, a dual optic in common, focusing partly on the needs of others, partly on the risks these others represent.

References

Alford, C.F. (2000) What would it matter if everything Foucault said about prison were wrong?: Discipline and punish after twenty years. *Theory and Society* 29(1), 125–146.

Basberg, C.E. (1999) *Omsorg i fengsel?* Pax, Oslo.

Bosworth, M. (2007) Creating the responsible prisoner. *Punishment & Society* 9(1), 67–85.

Bourdieu, P. (1990) *The Logic of Practice*. Polity Press, Oxford.

Bourdieu, P. (1995) *Distinksjonen: En sosiologisk kritikk av dømmekraften*. Pax, Oslo.

Cotanda, D. (2006) Voices at mother's kitchen: an autoethnographic account of exile. *Qualitative Inquiry* 12(3), 562–588.

Foucault, M. (1995) *Discipline and Punish: The Birth of the Prison*. Vintage Books, New York.

Freitas, E.D. and Pathon, J. (2009) (De)facing the self: poststructualist disruptions of the autoethnographic text. *Qualitative Inquiry* 15(3), 483–498.

Friestad, C. and Hansen, I.L.S. (2004) *Levekår blant innsatte*. Fafo, Oslo.

Geertz, C. (1998) Deep hanging out. *The New York Review of Books* 45, 69.

Giertsen, H. (2006) Oppdelt i småbiter og satt sammen på nytt: Oasys 'Offender Assessment and Management System' – et lovbrytermålesystem. *Materialisten* 34(1), 23–46.

Goffman, E. (1963) *Stigma: Notes on the Management of Spoiled Identity*. Prentice-Hall, Englewood Cliffs, CA.

Goffman, E. (1971) *The Presentation of Self in Everyday Life*. Harmondsworth, Penguin.

Guerrier, Y. and Adib, A.S. (2000) No, we don't provide that service: the harassment of hotel employees by customers. *Work, Employment & Society* 14(4), 689–705.

Hannah-Moffat, K (2005) Criminogenic needs and the transformative risk subject. *Punishment & Society* 7(1), 29–51.

Hayner, N.S. (1936) *Hotel Life*. College Park, McGrath.

Lennep, D.J.V. (1987) The hotel room. In: Kockelmans, J. J. (ed.) *Phenomenological Psychology: the Dutch School*. Martinus Nijhoff, Dordrecht.

Liebling, A. (1999) Doing research in prison: Breaking the silence? *Theoretical Criminology* 3(2), 27.

Nelken, D. (2010) *Comparative Criminal Justice: Making Sense of Difference*. Sage, Thousand Oaks, CA.

Neumann, C.B. (2009) *Det bekymrede blikket*. Novus, Oslo.

Neumann, I.B. (2010) Autobiography, ontology, autoethnology. *Review of International Studies* 36(4), 1051–1055.

Phillips, C. and Earle, R. (2010) Reading difference differently?: Identity, epistemology and prison ethnography. *British Journal of Criminology* 50(2), 360–378.

Rose, N. (1998) Governing risky individuals: the role of psychiatry in new regimes of control. *Psychiatry, Psychology and Law* 5(2), 177–195.

Rose, N. (2000) Government and control. In: Garland, D. and Sparks, R. (eds) *Criminology and Social Theory*. Oxford University Press, Oxford.

Skarðhamar, T. (2002) *Levekår og livssituasjon blant innsatte i norske fengsler*. Institutt for Kriminologi og Rettssosiologi, Oslo.

Smith, P.S. (2011) A critical look at Scandinavian exceptionalism: welfare state theories, penal populism, and prison conditions in Denmark and Scandinavia. In: Ugelvik, T. and Dullum, J. (eds) *Penal Exceptionalism?: Nordic Prison Policy and Practice*. Routledge, Abingdon.

Sollund, R. (2006) Mechanic versus organic organisations' impact on immigrant women's work satisfaction and occupational mobility. *Scandinavian Journal of Hospitality and Tourism* 6(4), 287–307.

Strand [Ugelvik], T. W. (2006) Mot en senmoderne kriminalomsorg?. *Materialisten* 34(1), 55–76.

Sykes, G.M. (1958) *The Society of Captives: a Study of a Maximum Security Prison*. Princeton University Press, Princeton, NJ.

Thorsen, L.R. (2004) *For mye av ingenting ... Straffedes levekår og sosiale bakgrunn*. IKRS, UiO, Oslo.

Ugelvik, T. (2011) Hva er et fengsel?: En analyse av manualen til en sosial teknologi. *Retfærd* 34(1), 85–100.

Urry, J. (2002) *The Tourist Gaze*. Sage, Thousand Oaks, CA.

Wacquant, L.J.D. (2002) The curious eclipse of prison ethnography in the age of mass incarceration. *Ethnography* 3(4), 371–397.

Endnotes

[1]As Neumann (2010) notes, this kind of retrospective research should therefore perhaps be called something else entirely, given that the Greek *graphein* means 'to write'.

[2]For a more systematic attempt at categorizing hotels, see Sollund (2006).

[3]Characterized by a system of separate confinement where prisoners are denied any form of contact with each other.

[4]In practice, remand prisoners in Norway may spend a long time incarcerated here, in some cases several years, before they get to start doing 'real time' (Smith, 2011).

[5]*Time* reported on Norwegian prisons in general and the opening of Halden prison in particular in a series of three articles, published on 10 May, 1 July and 12 July 2010. The quote can be found at http://www.time.com/time/magazine/article/0,9171,1986002,00.html.

[6]In fact, in present day criminal justice, the so-called Risk-Needs-Responsivity principle (or RNR) is regarded as fundamental in many jurisdictions (Bosworth, 2007). The idea is that levels of prisoner *risks* are connected with certain prisoner *needs* (lack of education, vocational training, lack of housing, etc.), that these needs are *criminogenic* (Rose, 1998, 2000; Hannah-Moffat, 2005). Successfully filling such needs is considered a vital part of successful rehabilitation.

14 The Third Gaze: De-constructing the Host Gaze in the Psychoanalysis of Tourism

Omar Moufakkir

Introduction

The second gaze is always aware that something is being concealed from it; that there is something missing from every picture, from every look or glance. This is no less true on tour than it is in everyday life. The second gaze knows that seeing is not believing. Some things will remain hidden from it. Even things with which it is intimately familiar... It looks for openings and gaps in the cultural unconscious. It looks for the unexpected, not the extraordinary, objects and events that may open a window in structure, a chance to glimpse the real. (MacCannell, 2001, p. 36)

Foucault has revolutionized the gaze in the humanities, Urry (1990) has tamed it in tourism, and MacCannell has envisioned its future. Urry's notion of the tourist gaze is not much different from that of MacCannell's (2001) 'second tourist gaze'. While Urry's tourists are free to gaze upon touristic objects, MacCannell's tourists are freer; they are conscious of the hidden or the invisible, and see beyond the postcards. MacCannell's proposed gaze, however, goes beyond the notion of the 'what you see is what you get' (p. 35) a little more. This type of gaze, he explains, is conscious that there is something hidden from it. As such, 'it is always aware that something is being

concealed from it; that there is something missing from every picture, from every look or glance... The second gaze knows that seeing is not believing ... the second gaze may be [more] interested in the ways attractions are presented than in the attractions themselves' (p. 36). Although MacCannell's proposed second gaze as an alternative to Urry's remains preoccupied with authenticity–inauthenticity and the front stage–back stage regions of touristic objects, and tourist agency, it has nevertheless been able to 'open some doors and windows in the prison house of tourism' (p. 24). He comments: 'if we go to Sartre, Merleau-Ponty and/or Lacan we will get a very different version of the gaze' (p. 28). It is this version of the gaze that this chapter is trying to plunge into. As such, the chapter is advancing a third gaze, a gaze that offers a deeper look into the gaze, and this time goes truly beyond the visible to reach the invisible in the unconscious of the gaze.

That is, this third gaze is ingrained in psychoanalysis and psychoanalytical concepts and theories advanced by Freud and Lacan. While both Urry's and MacCannell's gazes are concerned with an elaboration of the construction and doing of tourism, the third gaze is interested in and is engaged with the interpretation of the second gaze, which ostensibly is also not dissimilar from

Foucault's gaze of the medic. The third gaze is the gaze of the tourism academic upon the gaze of the tourism gaze. Defined as the gaze of the gazer upon the gaze of the gazer gazing upon the object of the gaze, this gaze tries to understand the *whys* of the host gaze. It is not different from the Freudian gaze or the gaze of psychoanalysis in that it engages with the invisible which is located in the human mind, and which is there for the academic to uncover and thereafter to decipher, to the extent possible, for the gazer and gazed upon to understand and digest. To Freud, there is no discovery when we deal with the unconscious; what is hidden is already there but remains to be uncovered. Similarly, to Lacan, while the surface is the level of the superficial the unconscious is always presented on the surface.

In his seminal work *The Birth of the Clinic* Foucault (2003) calls upon us to look critically at societal events in order to uncover new layers of meaning and significance. By visiting Freud and Lacan, passing through psychoanalytical theories and concepts of the unconscious, I am venturing into the unknown in tourism, and will venture even further to unlock and interpret the meaning of the host gaze in tourism from a psychoanalytical perspective. As Freud has said, psychoanalysis has long been 'of interest to others than psychiatrists' (2010, p. 2802). However, its implications for and application to tourist studies remain unchartered, with the exception of a few tips here and there from MacCannell (especially 2001) and one, if not perhaps the only, serious elaboration undertaken by Kingsbury (2005). (Interestingly, Kingsbury's article was received in 20 May 2002, received in revised form in 2 February 2004 and published in 2005. Surprising? Not at all; considering that only 800 copies of *Studies in Hysteria* were printed in the original edition, 13 years later, 626 copies had been sold.)

While plunging into the dark territory of the human mind, or more precisely the mind of the tourism host, this chapter supports that a theoretical conceptualization of gaze with psychoanalytical theory is necessary for an understanding of the host gaze and any analysis of tourism to be sufficiently critical and rigorous (e.g. Kingsbury, 2005). Like Kingsbury whose hope has been 'to alert scholars who routinely use psychoanalytic theory to the relevance of international tourism as an object of study' (p. 115), my hope, too, is to re/orient psychoanalytical theory (MacCannell has done it albeit briefly) to the attention of tourism academics. Hayes (2008) explains:

> Increasingly psychoanalysis is being taken seriously as *part* of social theory, and yet the promise of a *psychoanalytic social theory* requires theoretical work that is prepared to interrogate the social applicability of current psychoanalytic concepts, and a willingness to transform these concepts for the social domain, and this might even mean inventing or developing 'new' concepts. (Hayes, 2008, pp. 111–212)

A splendid invitation it is indeed to travel beyond and through Goffman's 'front' or the collective representation of the visible in the host gaze. Using the third gaze in this chapter, I gaze upon the gaze of Dutch hosts upon German tourists (and thereby gaze upon my previous gaze upon the host gaze). In my previous study of the host gaze (Moufakkir, 2011), to *my surprise*, I found this gaze to be overwhelmingly negative in tourism. I thought that cultural proximity would mediate this gaze. The paper was, in fact, rejected by one of the lead tourism journals because of the argument that 'Yes, we know the source of the Germanophobic attitudes: it's the war stupid!' It is needless to say that this type of argument makes anything that is German predictable. Initially, *it's the war* would then be the only *skeletal* book about Germany to be found on the shelves of public libraries. It suffices here to argue that several studies have found similar negative sentiments towards Germans in Switzerland although Switzerland was not occupied during the Second World War (e.g. Helbing, 2010). Helbing points out that 'Minor difference can be instrumentalized to draw group boundaries' (p. 14) and may result in rejection of the *Other* (Lacan himself was not sure which one was more appropriate *Other* or *other*, and he would use both). Nor does the absence of war preclude the possibility of tensions between groups.

Furthermore, that is not to say that my previous paper is without merit, however, though its conclusions are interesting, they nevertheless remain, like other tourism gaze studies, if not somewhat shallow, only preoccupied with the surface of the gaze. By visiting with Freudian and Lacanian subjects there is a possibility to understand the *whys* of this gaze, or at least try to shed more light on its darker side. Now that we know the symptoms or *signifiers* of this negativity – stereotypes, cultural distance and the Second World War, I wanted to go beyond the visible to dig out what lies beneath and understand those negativities. To Freud, symptoms are but the tip of the iceberg. Taking account of unconscious psychic process in this chapter may offer a critical addition to the host gaze hypotheses. Accordingly, I made use of a research technique known to psychoanalysis as 'free associations' to begin uncovering the hidden in the host gaze. Before getting to the gaze, first I will *unpretentiously* re/introduce psychoanalysis.

Psychoanalysis

Freudian psychoanalysis is the study of the mind, a specific type of treatment in which the 'analysand' (analytic patient) verbalizes thoughts, including fantasies and dreams, from which the analyst deduces the unconscious conflicts causing the patient's troubles, and interprets them for the patient to create insight for resolution of the problems. Freud defines it as a 'technical method of discovering the unconscious' (Freud, 2010, p. 2220). Using Breuer's word, he also calls it 'the talking cure' (p. 2202). Freud expresses it as the 'task of learning from the patient something that I did not know and he did not know himself' (p. 2211). This is not to say that the patient did not know consciously about the experience, but that experience was hidden in the realm of the unconscious waiting to become visible. The

task of Freud was to 'dig out' whatever feelings the patient has but is not able to decipher himself. It is an endeavour to bring into consciousness the forgotten or hidden ideas of the patient's unconscious. As Freud put it, in psychoanalysis 'one tried to introduce the unconscious memories into the patient's consciousness' (p. 2212). Through psychoanalysis Freud uncovers the latent answers that lie hidden, and the repressed and unconscious wishes that in turn explain the malady of the patient. Once the sources of this malady are uncovered, they become the conscious treatment itself. A representative illustration given by Freud himself is his treatment of a young girl who suffered from a severe and complicated hysteria which had developed into a tic. He writes:

> The mother of a very sick child, which had at last fallen asleep, concentrated her whole will-power on keeping still so as not to waken it. Precisely on account of her intention she made a 'clacking' noise with her tongue. (An instance of 'hysterical counter-will'.) This noise was repeated on a subsequent occasion on which she wished to keep perfectly still; and from it there developed a tic which, in the form of a clacking with the tongue, occurred over a period of many years whenever she felt excited. (Freud, 2010, p. 7)

The symptom of her hysteria was visible and the visible conscious was a repeated tic. The source of this tic, while existent, was however hidden in her unconscious, which through psychoanalysis was deduced from her past experience with her sick child. Certainly, no other method or science brings out the subjective and individual motives behind maladies of the mind like psychoanalysis does. Psychoanalysis has been applied to dreams, myths, fairy tales, jokes, arts, education, infantile development, formation of character, yet its theories have yet to be applied to tourism. Despite its applicability and resourcefulness, psychoanalysis has received less credit than it deserves, as Freud put it:

> It has not been the fate of psycho-analysis to be greeted (like other young sciences) with the sympathetic encouragement of those who are interested in the advance of

knowledge. For a long time it was disregarded, and when at last it could no longer be neglected it became, for emotional reasons, the object of the most violent attack from people who had not taken the trouble to become acquainted with it. (Freud, 2010, p. 2816)

Resistance to psychoanalysis is rooted in its restricted concept of sexuality. Psychoanalysis has been subject to criticism and many manifestations of the resistance to its use have been amply discussed and relate among others to issues of validity, fabrication and denial. For example, psychoanalysts have been accused of 'transcendental stupidity' (Derrida, 2007, p. 35). Derrida (2007), joining Deleuze's criticism of psychoanalysis, ironically remarks:

> So psychoanalysts are not stupid when they say stupidities because they know and they understand what they try not to understand, what they want not to understand. They have the intelligence of what they want not to understand. (Derrida, 2007, p. 41)

Nevertheless, it remains that a 'similar application of its [psychoanalytical theory] point of view, its hypotheses and its findings has enabled psycho-analysis to throw light on the origins of our great cultural institutions – on religion, morality, justice and philosophy' (Freud, 2010, p. 2821). Following Zizek's (1998) analysis of critical approaches to society and racism, where he argued that 'We must give psychoanalysis another chance,' Kingsbury declares that in 'tourism research, however, psychoanalysis cannot be given another chance because it has yet to be given any chance'. He goes on to say that 'Researchers' terse and sweeping criticisms of psychoanalysis have resulted in widespread rejection, denigration, and misconception' (Kingsbury, 2005, p. 117). It is not only the misconceptions that restrict the use of psychoanalysis in tourism, but it is also the failure of tourism academics to take the time to devote to 'reading over a century's worth of primary psychoanalytic text and interdisciplinary commentary' (p. 117). In addition to misconceptions and lack of immersion in, or even basic knowledge of, psychoanalysis, there is also a

'dogged belief in the epistemology and methodology of existing psychological approaches' (p. 117). The agreed upon conclusion is that the material published in most of the leisure and tourism literature typically relies upon quantitative methodology and focuses on questions of observable practice (Rojek, 2010). Moreover, the editorial policy of some academic journals remains discriminatory and subsequently discourages creativity in research. Discriminatory practices work in tandem with tourism education boards to pressurize academics to publish in tier journals, thereby perpetuating academic stagnation. It is also the case that books and book chapters have become less valued than journal articles. Less valued, however, does not necessarily make them less valuable. The only article that seriously considers psychoanalysis in tourism (Kingsbury, 2005) has been published in a non-tourism journal.

Research in tourism is predominantly consumer behaviour-driven. 'Since the early 1970s, research on the psychology of tourism has mainly examined pleasure, motivation, consumer behaviour, image-perception, decision-making and identity creation' (Kingsbury, 2005, p. 17). There is no study, however, on the psychology of tourism that provides a critically informed and sustained evaluation of psychoanalytic theories. Kingsbury's (2005) article 'Jamaican tourism and the politics of enjoyment', published in *Geoforum*, is the first account of a serious use of psychoanalytic concepts in tourism. By drawing on the psychoanalytic theories of Freud and Lacan, Kingsbury elaborated a 'politic of enjoyment' in the context of Jamaican tourism. His critical psychoanalysis of tourism fits into a research agenda that goes beyond impact studies and modelling of tourism flows. Psychoanalysis is not restricted to psychoanalytic clinical practice, and thus 'There seems to be too little discussion about questioning the idea of psychoanalysis' (Hayes, 2008, p. 210). Perhaps, psychoanalysis has something interesting and useful to contribute to tourism. Hayes points out that the 'question is not so much about why, or why not, psychoanalysis, but rather what psychoanalysis might look like in its social application [to tourism]' (p. 210). Focusing on individuals and individual cases, psychoanalysis need not be seen as only offering individual solutions. Freud explains:

> Our knowledge of the neurotic illnesses of individuals has been of much assistance to our understanding of the great social institutions. For the neuroses themselves have turned out to be attempts to find individual solutions for the problem of compensating for unsatisfied wishes, while the institutions seek to provide social solutions for the same problem. (Freud, 2010, p. 2822)

Similarly, to Lacan (1970), psychoanalytic theory would throw some light on the shadows of social construction by advancing our understanding of some of the unconscious dimensions that underlie the disorganized aspects of social life. To MacCannell (1999, p. 173), psychoanalysis appeared to offer 'some ingenious ways' to explain alienation of individuals in the industrial society (for the legitimacy of psychoanalysis in understanding culture and society, see, example.g. Frosh and Baraister, 2008). One might ask what has the host gaze got to do with it? The incorporation of the 'psycho in the social assumes immediately the presence of a certain kind of psychoanalytic subject' (Hollway, 2006). In her usage of the psychosocial and drawing on psychoanalysis for this purpose, she writes:

> We are psycho-social because we are products of a unique life history of anxiety- and desire-provoking life events and the manner in which they have been transformed in internal reality. We are psychosocial because such defensive activities affect and are affected by material conditions and discourses (systems of meaning which pre-exist any given individual), because unconscious defences are intersubjective processes (i.e. they affect and are affected by others with whom we are in communication), and because of the real events in the external, social world which are discursively, desirously and defensively appropriated. (Hollway, 2006, pp. 467–468)

The gaze is both social and psychological. It is granted agency but it is also manipulated (MacCannell, 2001). Although MacCannell's second gaze is not psychoanalytical, it has some psychoanalytical elements in it, the subject of the upcoming discussion. Whereas one might think that dealing with the unconscious is discovery, Freud reminds us there is no discovery when we deal with the unconscious; rather, what is hidden is already there but remains to be uncovered. In other words, as supported by Lacan, the surface is the level of the superficial and the unconscious is always presented on the surface. While some psychoanalytical concepts may be strong tools of social and political analysis in some contexts (Hayes, 2008), the call is then what psychoanalytical concepts are useful to tourism (gaze) and in which socio-historical circumstances? I have made use of free associations to find out.

Method

Projected free association

I have selected the 'talking cure' –*without the element of the sofa, the phallic or the child* – as a technique to uncover the unconscious mental state of the gaze. To investigate what lies beneath the mundane explanation of gaze, I have made use of the technique of free association that is used in psychoanalysis, and adapted it to suit the purpose of this study. Freud adopted the method of free association during 1892–1898. To Freud, free association was the first instrument for the scientific examination of the human mind. He departed from hypnosis as a psychoanalytical technique to later embrace the technique of free associations because some patients resisted hypnosis and/or hypnosis did not always produce the material that the analyst was hoping for. With free association, the patient speaks freely of anything that may cross his mind without being interrupted by the analyst. In a search for the repressed complex in the patients, Freud explains: 'we allow the patient to say whatever he likes, and hold fast to the postulate that nothing can occur to him which is not in an indirect fashion dependent on the complex we are in search of' (2010, p. 2219). Guarding against emergent ideas to repress other emerging ideas, the patient is asked to follow the flow of his ideas regardless of whether they appear to him as 'incorrect or irrelevant or nonsensical' (p. 2219). The patient, then, transfers his feelings and meanings onto the analyst (Hollway, 2006, p. 545). The flow of thoughts permits the analyst to connect events and experiences to the affect of the patient and unravel the mystery of apparent symptoms. According to Hollway, 'There is still some way to go in incorporating psychoanalytic ideas into research methods' (Hollway, 2006, p. 545). We have found Freudian *projection* to have value for researching the host gaze from a psychological perspective. Projection is defined in orthodox psychology texts as a 'defense mechanism in which the individual attributes to other people impulses and traits that he himself has but cannot accept. It is especially likely to occur when the person lacks insight into his own impulses and traits'.

To talk openly about sensitive issues, and in our case how we gaze upon people, is not always easy or simple, and may produce the feeling of being condescending, naive, shallow, cognitively unsophisticated, narrow-minded or even prejudiced. This feeling of *manufactured consent*, (see Walter Lippmann's (1922) *Public Opinion*; and his chapter VI on stereotypes) may result in reservation and therefore in a brief encounter and unfruitful discussion with the participants. People are reluctant to talk about sensitive and personal matters to strangers, and perhaps they are even more so when the stranger is also the researcher. And this is a fortunate misfortune, because *at least* the majority of people (or at least my respondents) were conscious that, in their formation, stereotypes could be a dis-formation of reality, and that as Walter Lippmann (1921, p. 3) puts it:

> each man is only a small part of the world, that his intelligence catches at best only phases and aspects in a coarse net of ideas, then, when we use our stereotypes, we tend

to know that they are only stereotypes, to hold them lightly, to modify them gladly. We tend, also, to realize more and more clearly when our ideas started, where they started, how they came to us, why we accepted them. All useful history is antiseptic in this fashion. It enables us to know what fairy tale, what school book, what tradition, what novel, play, picture, phrase, planted one preconception in this mind, another in that mind.

This consciousness discouraged my respondents from being part of the construction of those solid impressions that characterize Germans. Talking about stereotypes openly and especially those that bear negative connotations and that are stigmatizing, is not always easy. For example, Sniderman and Carmines' (1997) study found that some people are very much inclined to give socially desirable answers in surveys on xenophobia. To overcome reluctance to participate, repression of ideas and sensitivity in researching the host gaze from a psychoanalytical perspective, instead of asking respondents why they hold particular stereotypes about Germans they were asked to freely comment on those stereotypes. Specifically, respondents were asked the following open narrative question to comment on: 'Why do you think Dutch people think this way … about German people?' In this case, the respondents become informants telling their story about why they think people think the way they think about a certain group. This process of inquiry I called 'projected' free association of ideas. The respondent understood that the research is not about him/her but about the 'Other' and their state of mind, perceptions and stereotypes. For example, when I asked Rob (male lecturer aged 56, two children, divorcing) why do you think Dutch people *perceive* German people as arrogant? His first reaction was 'I don't think they are. I have always had a good experience with German people and also when I travel to Germany.' Although we know that perceptions are constructed and fabricated, that stereotypes are exaggerations, and that in perceptions generalities and certitude are and should be minimized, the question inflicted in the interviewee an uneasy feeling, doubt, and thus not only deviated the discussion away from the primary concern of the research, but the interviewer became the interviewee.

Subjectivity

Although there is a growing tradition of using psychoanalysis to critically inform empirical qualitative research, both theoretically and methodologically, psychoanalysis was also criticized for its subjectivity (Hollway, 2008). Holloway supports that psychoanalysis was re-embraced 'because it provided a resource for understanding the role of the subject and subjectivity in social change where positivist psychology had largely failed'. She further explains that the 'concept of transference (the unconscious projection of our feelings and meanings onto the other person) is an example. It enables researchers to become more aware of the difference between what belongs to the participant and what belongs to the researcher' (Hollway, 2006, p. 545). In our case, what belongs to the participants is their ideas and subsequent meaning making of why they think people think the way they do; what belongs to the analyst is the psychoanalytic interpretation of this baggage of meaning making. The constructed psychoanalytic interpretation of ideas was shared with the respondents who were also asked to comment on this construction.

Three main psychoanalytical theories have emerged as candidates to inform what lies behind the meaning and explanation of our informants, namely Freud's narcissism, Lacan's mirror stage and Derrida's territoriality. While these are intertwined, it is also evident that parallel hypotheses from the discursive repertoire (and the centring questions of power) can be drawn. There is much to discover and uncover within the complexity of psychoanalysis, and there is no guarantee against the conceptual difficulties that have beset this field, but it is at least useful to establish its relevance to the task in hand indicatively (Hollway, 2008).

The third gaze

There are several gazes. In Foucault we can find the careful gaze, patient gaze, fixed gaze, attentive gaze, dilated gaze, pure gaze, observing gaze, classifactory gaze, meticulous gaze, pure gaze, happy gaze, insistent gaze and penetrating gaze. To Foucault, the gaze is 'an operation which, beyond first appearance, scrutinizes the body and discovers at the autopsy a visible invisible' (2003, p. 114). Foucault calls us to gaze critically upon what we are looking at in order to uncover new layers of significance.

> we map out the visible where "the signifier (sign and symptom) would be entirely transparent for the signified, which would appear, without concealment or residue in its most pristine reality, and that the essence of the signified – the heart of the disease –would be entirely exhausted in the intelligible syntax of the signifier". (Foucault, 2003, p. 111)

What is visible to us is the symptoms of the gaze; that the gaze may be sympathetic, empathic, irritated, apathetic, timid or harsh. These visible gazes can betray the invisible or what lies beneath. The third gaze tends to go beyond the appearance and naivety of the first gaze and the discovery and sophistication of the second gaze. The first gaze is what you see is what is, the second gaze is what you see is more than what you think is. The third gaze is interested in the decoding of those gazes, to reach their significance beyond the obvious through the uncovering of the unconscious of the gaze or in the gaze. This gaze is suggested in Foucault's gaze which is 'no longer the gaze of any observer, but that of a doctor ... that could and should grasp colours, variations, tiny anomalies' (Foucault, 2003, p. 109). It is the gaze of the professional (or academic) upon the gaze of the gaze and gazed upon. In this sense, it is the professional – like the medic – who helps us to de-construct and re-construct the gaze by uncovering and interpreting the hidden reasons behind a specific gaze. The third gaze is a psychoanalytical gaze – the gaze that goes beyond the obvious of seeing, whether objective, back-staged or authentic, romantic or collective –to concentrate not on the object of the gaze but on the gazes themselves. Thus, the interpretation of the gaze of the gazee becomes the third gaze. Like Freud's interpretation of dreams, the tourism gaze can lend itself to psychoanalysis and its link to other spheres of knowledge. Treating Fraulein Elisabeth who was suffering from hysteria, Freud argues:

> These, incidentally were not the kind of questions that physicians were in the habit of raising. We were usually content with statements that the patient was constitutionally a hysteric, liable to develop hysterical symptoms under the pressure of intense excitations *of whatever kind*"(Freud, 2010, p. 130).

Similarly, in the third gaze, we are no longer content with discovering the gaze, but ask questions to uncover the causes of the gaze. In Andre Green's words, 'psychoanalysis takes as its object the unobservable and the repressed' (1981, p. 319). Psychoanalysis is not reduced to the sofa and to clinical analysis, neither does it offer only individual solutions, nor does it have to necessarily relate back to suppressed sexuality. As such, 'Psychoanalysis does not deserve to capture our imagination if it continues to remain so silent on questions of social transformation, and only speak for personal and individual transformation' (Hayes, 2008, p. 212). We do understand that the 'road for aspiring analysts from nonmental health fields is quite arduous' (Malone, 2008, p. 180), and we are up to the journey, its challenges and the many *imagined or expected* smirks.

A Psychoanalytical Interpretation of the Host Gaze

> With racism being officially blacked, it is surprising that the Dutch express an almost unilateral hatred for their nearest neighbours –the Germans. Yes, we all know about the Nazi atrocities committed over half a century ago, but much of today's venom is spat by a generation that was then largely unborn. So what is the root cause of

> this rampant rejection; why do the Dutch doubt Duitsers? (White and Boucke, 2006, p. 164)

This is a passage from *The UnDutchables*, a famous book about Dutch culture and people. It is 'not a dry, scholarly offering. Rather, it is offered as a pro-Dutch, fun yet irreverent expose' (White and Boucke, 2006, p. xi). Certainly, no generalization should be made, and similarly in this chapter we are *only* concerned with the whys of the negative perceptions, and therefore our intention is not to expose those negativities but to locate their source and remedy them through our gaze of the host gaze.

'Mirror, mirror on the wall, Who is the fairest of them all?'

Lacan (1970) affirms that psychoanalytic social theory can contribute to the understanding of 'the unconscious dimensions that underlie the disorganizing aspects of social life'. Freud maintained that psychoanalysis can throw some light on broader social formations. So then how can psychoanalysis contribute to the study of tourism, and in particular interest to the study of host gaze? MacCannell (2001) demonstrated that 'if we go to Sartre, Merleau-Ponty and/ or Lacan we will get a very different version of the gaze' (p. 28), a gaze that goes beyond the obvious or conventional gaze. A comprehensive analysis with this respect is far beyond the scope of this chapter. Therefore, I have concentrated on narcissism and the mirror-stage as two concepts that have emerged directly from our interviews and that have complimentarily informed our understanding of the host gaze from a psychoanalytical perspective.

Narcissism in the host gaze

Freud explains that 'Narcissus, according to the Greek legend, was a youth who preferred his own reflection to everything else' (Freud, 2010, p. 2274). Generally, narcissism can be defined as 'an inflated sense of self, reflected in feelings of superiority, arrogant behaviour, and a need for constant attention and admiration' (Bogart *et al.*, 2004, p. 36), envy and lack of empathy (*DSM-IV-TR*; American Psychiatric Association, 2000). Brown *et al.* (2009, p. 951) explain that narcissism theories are now used by analysts and social scientists outside the fields of psychology and psychoanalysis to explain societal phenomena and patterns of cultural and social change. Cultural studies use narcissism to study, for example mass consumption, mass media, lifestyles, racism, politics, culture and more recently terrorism (Tyler, 2007). Modern analysis uses psychoanalysis mostly to explain job motivation and personal development. Tyler reports:

> While the mythical figure of Narcissus has a long history in literature and the fine arts, before the 1970s the term narcissism was still confined to the disciplines of psychology and psychoanalysis and had no currency or meaning outside this 'expert' literature (p. 254)

According to Freud no one is free from narcissism. And so it will appear that neither is the host gaze.

When the host gaze in tourism is considered from this perspective, one finds out that this gaze can be narcissistic as is supported by our interviews. For example, Adriaan explains: 'the Germans are high spenders. The Dutch are more frugal, also because of the polder system that we used to have in the Netherlands. They [Dutch] like to say that they are "neuchter" or as you would say in English down to earth people, but in fact they are just jealous of the Germans.' Theo (male, retired, empty nester, aged 65), pointing to the roots of this jealousy opines: 'yes, these Germans, they like to show off with their big cars, big cameras, big boats. They like it big. Everything with them is big.' These quotes are examples of many other statements that exemplify *cancelled* jealousy. Like a narcissistic person, this gaze seems to put more emphasis on what the other has than on what the person who is criticizing does not have or does not value. Compared with Germany, the Netherlands

is, in fact, a small country, and this has an influence on the Dutch culture and values. This feature resonates in the Dutch saying: 'wij leven in een kelin kikkerlandje (we live in a little froggie-land)' (White and Boucke, 2006, p. 218). In their witty and funny analysis of the Dutch language, these authors explain how the character of Dutch people is reflected in their language with a particular attention to the suffix, je: 'They will tell you that they use a lot of diminutive because they live in a small land', and that '*Everything has to bear the stamp of the small-scale complacency, which personally I consider to be one of our most typical features* [quoting a Dutch physician]' (p. 214).

A look at the European Values Survey suggests existing difference in values between Dutch and German people. Those differences and group personality traits could be the source of the narcissistic gaze. Whereas the Dutch are reported to be straightforward, less competitive, tolerant, sober and Calvinistic, valuing privacy and team work; the German are reported to be sincere, loyal, cold, argumentative, thorough, orderly and stubborn. Certainly, personality traits have negative as well as positive connotations, depending on who is the gazer and who is the object of the gaze. Helbing (2010) for example explains that in a US study Asians are positively perceived by Americans as highly competent in their professions but at the same time since they are in competition with US Americans they are also perceived as cold. Similarly, reviewing the literature Helbing found Bulgarians and Czechs to be often described as:

> moral/social, but incompetent whereas other groups such as Germans and Jews are seen as immoral/unsocial, but competent ... Germans [in the Netherlands] are perceived as very hard-working, very reliable, and progressive, but also as very power hungry ... less generous, less jovial and more aggressive (p. 18)

Helbing (2010) reports two reasons why Swiss Germans dislike Germans: they are jealous of the cultural, political, scientific and other achievements of Germans and feel inferior, as most Swiss Germans do not speak High German as eloquently as Germans (p. 14). Similarly in our interviews, Rob (lecturer, male, aged 56 with two children) comments: 'I think we do have an inferiority complex towards the Germans'. He goes on: 'They are rigid compared to the Dutch, like when you hear them say, for example [laughs] *heer dokter*, we hear them behaving arrogantly. The Dutch will be irritated. The Dutch icon of Germans is Hitler, which connotes thinking of superiority. This is still in the Dutch psyche.' The Dutch like the expression: 'doe maar gewoon, dan doe je al gek genoeg (just act normal, that's weird enough)' (White and Boucke, 2006, p. 214).

This projection of 'normalcy' is also sarcastic and ironically denotes a feeling of superiority. However, this feeling of superiority is rejected, yet internalized to yet again codify the superiority of one group over another. This attitude could be referred to as covert narcissism. Researchers have made a distinction between overt and covert narcissism (Foster and Trimm, 2008). While both overt and covert narcissists are found to be 'extraordinarily self-absorbed and arrogant'. Rose (2002) points out that covert narcissists 'feel profoundly inferior to others, are hypersensitive to others' evaluations, and are generally dissatisfied' (p. 380). By announcing inferiority and rejecting superiority a latent desire of superiority is covertly pronounced. Underlying covert narcissism, Rowena (female, psychologist, aged 45, married, two children) explains: 'when Dutch people say they don't like the German people it is because they are jealous of them. They say that the German are arrogant, but in fact it is the Dutch who are arrogant. Dutch people think that they are better than other people and that they know it all'. This covert narcissism is benign as will be explained further, but before that it appears that the host gaze is also culturally narcissistic.

Gaze, cultural narcissism and territoriality

The problem of narcissism is by no means an exclusively masculine or individual one (Whitford, 2003). Narcissism can also be cultural. The concept of cultural narcissism (for a comprehensive and authentic account see Lasch's 1982 *The Culture of Narcissism*) has been defined by Eissler (1975) "as the internal force, which pushes us to overestimate our religion, our nation and our political camp" (cited in Biran, 2003, p. 494). Cultural narcissism is also manifested in countries that share similar religion and who have high culture proximity. Commenting on the whys of the Dutch negative gaze upon the Germans, Rowena bluntly opines that:

> Dutch people are negative about German people because they are satisfied with their own life and they pretend to be tolerant, but in fact they are intolerant... They think that they have a better culture. They think they are better than the German. It seems like they are kind of protecting their own culture. They build their own world and exclude the others... They build a wall around them because it feels safe. I think a lot of Dutch people are not satisfied with their life, job, and family life.

Ylse (39 year old female, unemployed, married, two children) comments: 'They [Germans] think of themselves that they are the best and their language is also like that. They think that they are better people. Their language is what we call "beschaafd Duits", translated to "civilized German". The Swiss have also something like that they call it "Hochdeutsch".' Similar comments have been empirically supported by Helbling's (2010) study. 'The Die Hochdeutschen kommen (The High-Germans are coming) with their High German language (compared to Swiss German the Swiss speak High-German only in formal situations) and High skills, represents a perceived economic and cultural threat to educated and skilled Swiss workers' (p. 6). White and Boucke (2006) say that 'the character of a people is reflected in its language' (p. 214). Despite cultural and geographic proximity and similarity of language and religion German immigrants in Zurich are the least favoured by the Swiss. Helbling reports: 'It will appear, unsurprisingly, that attitudes towards people from West European countries are much more positive than those towards people from other regions. Among the West Europeans, however, Germans have by far the most negative image [in Zirich]' (Helbing, 2010, p. 5). Theiler (2004) uses Freud's 'narcissism of minor difference' to explain the attitudes that the Swiss have to the Germans in Switzerland. Freud explains: 'it is precisely communities with adjoining territories, and related to each other in other ways as well, who are engaged in constant feuds and ridiculing each other – like the Spaniards and Portuguese, for instance, the North Germans and South Germans, the English and Scotch, as so on' (p. 4506).

According to White and Boucke (2006, p. 5), Dutch people also:

> seem to be caught up in a cycle of endless envy. They cannot free themselves from feelings such as, 'If you are sitting, then I should be sitting too!' They are extremely jealous of each other's possessions and keep a constant updated mental inventory of what their neighbours, relatives and colleagues have and have not. (White and Boucke, 2006, p. 5)

Similarly, Ron (lecturer, male 47 years old, married, two children) clarifies his opinion by saying: 'what can I add, the Germans are better. Look at BMW, Siemens and Mercedes. We have Philips.' Rob continues:

> [laughing] yes I am not surprised that you say that Dutch people have negative feelings towards the German. I think it is because of the war. The younger generation are strongly influenced by their parents. I think this feeling will disappear one day with passing generations. The feeling comes from the war. Even right after the war this feeling was stronger in the southern part of the Netherlands, but less in the north. Why it is still today? It's soccer stupid [laughs]. When it comes to football, the German are our deepest enemy. We lost to the German in the world championship in 1974. They are four times world champion. Here is the thing, they are four times champion but we the Dutch we think that we play better [laughs].

Rob goes on: 'We do have an inferiority complex. We realize that Germany is superior over the Netherlands in many things.

They win in football and have superior products for example.'

Cultural boundaries, although small, can lead to tension between groups because there is always the perceived danger of cultural contamination. Zürn (1998) argues 'that the "narcissism of minor difference" is the result of increasing transnationalism which makes minor cultural differences arguably more visible and renders them very important' (Helbing, 2010). The phenomenon of narcissism of minor differences provides a framework within which to understand a negative host gaze. For example, Adriaan one of our informants (English teacher, male aged 54, married, no children) thinks that:

> this negative sentiment is related to the increasing number of Germans in the Netherlands… I mean this was not like this after the war. I used to go on holidays to Germany with my parents. We enjoyed it very much. Now, I think it is always the case when you see too many Germans or foreigners you get somehow negatively excited.

It is this negative excitement that explains the link to aspects of territory. It is an unconscious way of defending one's feeling of violation of territory. All types of territory – physical, social and psychic – seem to be endangered by incoming visitors. While territoriality is positively associated with individuality, personality, heritage and power, it also negatively connotes invasion, destruction, appropriation of goods and property. Territoriality is defined as a behaviour pattern in animals consisting of the occupation and defence of territory. If personal territory is violated frequently it can cause severe stress. In psychoanalytical terms territoriality has a libidinal aspect (a matter for another discussion). What is important here is that territoriality is hidden in the mundane gaze. In the unconscious side of the gaze the informants seem to be preoccupied with their deterioration, an invasion that is destabilizing and works against the preservation of their species. What is also significant is that cultural superiority also manifests in the 'White

World', within 'White Cultures'. While this argument is evident in society, it has not been apparent in the tourism host gaze because most host gaze studies have been limited to Western tourists visiting Eastern countries.

The mirror stage and the host gaze

How can the mirror-phase shed some light on our understanding of the host gaze in tourism? It shall appear that the gaze that is focused on the Other is nothing less than the gaze upon oneself reflected in the gaze upon oneself and the Other. In this sense, the host gaze is a dual gaze, that of the gaze of the host upon the tourist and also that of the host upon himself. It is not a passive gaze but an interacting one. Merleau-Ponty (1968, p. 139) put it this way: 'since the seer is caught up in what he sees, it is still himself he sees: there is a fundamental narcissism of all vision' (quoted in Fullagar, 2001, p. 175). We could cite the whole text of Lacan for an extended illustration, but perhaps Lacan's title could be most revealing: *The Mirror Stage as Formative of the Function of the I as Revealed in Psychoanalysis*. Discussing narcissism in the mirror stage Lacan (1977) opens his speech by invoking and refuting Descartes' Cogito:

> The conception of the mirror-phase which I introduced at our last congress, thirteen years ago, has since become more or less established in the practice of the French group; I think it nevertheless worthwhile to bring it again to your attention, especially today, for the light that it sheds on the formation of the I as we experience it in psychoanalysis. It is an experience which leads us to oppose any philosophy directly issuing from the *Cogito*. (Lacan, 1994, p. 93)

The mirror stage is related to the mirror image, where in Lacan's description the child goes through stages of dialectic discovery of self when he looks in the mirror (Lacan, 1977). Lacan starts his paper with the above paragraph. It is also important to start with *a* reading of this first paragraph, because by rejecting Descartes Cogito

'I think therefore I am' Lacan also rejects the idea of the self knowing itself outside of the Other. Perhaps, it is sufficient to quote Foucault (1984, p. 63) also saying: 'Nothing in man – not even his body – is sufficiently stable to serve as a basis for self-recognition or for understanding other men.' The self does not exist separated from its entourage. The entourage is what the gazer sees when looking at himself in a mirror. Lacan argues, the 'total form of the body by which the subject anticipates in a mirage the maturation of his power is given to him only as a *Gestalt*, that is to say, in an exteriority in which this form is certainly more constituent than constituted'. It is this totality that forms the self. What one sees when looking in a mirror is not only himself but an image constituted of signs that reflect his reflection upon himself, upon the Other and the background environment that feeds those images and garnishes the construction of the self. It is this, real, imagined and reflected ensemble that constitutes one's own reality. It is this compelled gaze that situates the self and locates it in his constructed and real world. This *psycho*analysis of the self is important to the host gaze in that the focus of the gaze shifts *le regard* from focusing on oneself to a focus on the Other; for the self cannot exist without the Other. By focusing on the Other to locate the self, one can find the self, accept it or reject it. Rejection is important to the gaze because it embodies doubts, doubt about who we are as hosts (and people), who we are not, who we want to be, who we do not want to be, who we want to become and who we do not want to become. This inspirational wishful thinking is negotiable through locating the self in comparison to the other.

When this negotiation is positive it is a developmental vision towards becoming the best (universally accepted) host or *ego ideal host* we can be (and ego ideal humans we aspire to). First, who I am does not exist separate from who the Other is. This dialectic discovery of the self occurs in stages. The self is confronted with its own image. This image reflects who he is; but the gaze brings the self to an understanding of its formation beyond what is directly seen and in relation to the mirror setting and its reflected background environment. Suggested in this view is a healthy auto-criticism represented in the projection of the rejection of a narcissistic attitude towards the self and the other. What is implied here is the confession of the host that a narcissistic gaze exists. What is also projected is a rejection of this narcissism by denouncing cultural superiority.

Heinz Kohut (1971) argued that narcissism is developmental from archaic in the first stage to a healthy maturation stage. Symington (1993) supported that: 'positive and negative narcissism always go together – one does not exist without the other' (p. 8). The narcissistic Dutch gaze upon German tourists, though negative, is not unhealthy, in that its acknowledgment negates its acceptance and therefore supports its maturation. According to Symington, the importance of recognizing 'narcissistic currents' is a mature way to self-knowledge, acceptance of self and acceptance of the other. In other words, by acknowledging that the Dutch gaze upon the German tourist is affected by jealousy, envy and self-serving bias, that gaze becomes consciously critical and positively developmental. The developmental aspect of the gaze is also addressed by Lacan (1977) in his mirror stage analysis. Our existence and also development thus depend on how the Other sees us, and this translates into 'I am because I am not', or even more so 'I am because he is'. This may sound like a game. It is, and it is a serious conscious game of existence. Indeed, in the French origin of Lacan's text, the *I* or *le je* also phonetically pronounced as *je* is also heard as the French word *jeux*, which translates into *game* in English. Looking in the mirror is like a child consciously playing hide and seek, but who, unconsciously, is looking for himself. In the host gaze, this game unconsciousness is represented in a host–guest love–hate relationship or what Rob intuitively describes as:

> The feelings of the Dutch towards the Germans is something like big brother– young brother. We like them but we don't like them. We admire them but we criticize them. They seem to be all what we are not

and what we don't want to be, but we like them... I mean they are amazing, but they are not like us so they [Dutch people] don't like them.

The complexity of Rob's analysis of the Dutch gaze upon the Germans also represents this ambiguity between attraction and repulsion. Ylse argues 'we don't hate them but we don't like them too. They seem to be our opposite; we are more relaxed they are not, they are very much work oriented, we are more flexible, you see what I mean?' Embodied in the gaze is fantasy, illusion, lack, discovery, conflict, distance, acceptance, rejection, identification or regression or the reluctance to accept 'the Otherness of the Other'. Referring to the Works of Irigaray, Whitford (2003, p. 34) explains that 'What he cannot possess, the narcissistic subject will denigrate, devalue, hold in contempt and even destroy'.

Conclusion

Host gaze and positive and negative narcissism

The purpose of this chapter was to discuss the host gaze in relation to psychoanalysis in order to uncover the roots of its imperfectness in terms of becoming a better gaze and a better host. What we know of the host gaze is but its 'little realities', while ignoring the interrelationship between the fragmented self, the whole self, imaginary self and the ideal self. The mirror is the mediator between these selves, the internal world, the external world and the real world (Lacan, 1949). The *Other* that we see through our gaze reflects our successes and pitfalls as hosts and human beings. Every gaze has some degree of narcissism. The great sin of the gaze is its narcissism; the great virtue of the gaze is its narcissism. Narcissism does not always denote a pejorative connotation (e.g. Green, 1983; Kernberg, 1994; Symington, 1996). There are different types of narcissism and these can be found on a narcissism spectrum as indicated by Lyon *et al.* (2010):

narcissism runs along a continuum from healthy to unhealthy. A healthy state of narcissism indicates a stable ego, whereas unhealthy narcissism is exhibited in people with a grandiose sense of self and entitlement and may be demonstrated by behaviour that can be violent, antisocial, exploitative, and lacking in empathy. (Lyon *et al.*, 2010, p. 1268)

Although the examples of statements given by our informants similar to, for example, those by Ylse and Rowena seem alike, they nevertheless differ in their critique approach. While the latter attributes the negative perceptions that Dutch people have about the Germans to the perceived shortcomings of the Dutch, the former attributes those perceptions to the perceived shortcomings of the Germans. The self-serving bias (Miller and Ross, 1975) is manifested in statements similar to that by Ylse, whereby the individual blames failure, or in this case negative stereotyping, on the behaviour or attitudes of the other (e.g. Kaplan and Ruffle, 2002). Statements similar to this one by Rob: 'in reality I never had problems with German people. I visited Germany many times with my parents as a kid. My experience has always very positive and friendly people;' 'personally I never had problems with German people, but I understand why Dutch people have a negative image' suggest that the type of narcissism discussed is benign narcissism; a narcissism that is oriented towards *Le devenir or the coming-into-being*.

The quest for an ideal self is nothing more than a quest for love (Freud) – explicitly and also implicitly – crafted in psychoanalytical jargon, for psychoanalysis is nothing less than 'the cure by love'.

The gaze and the cure by love

Relating back to the role of the medic, the objective of the study of host gaze is to understand the nature of the gaze and identify the need for specific procedure with a view to correcting the lenses of this gaze when they are myopic, hyperopic or simply blind. Various cultural orientation and

training programmes have been identified and employed in different contexts for this purpose. These are well summarized in Furnham and Bockner (1986):

cognitive training or providing information about the new culture, usually about its social rules; the raising of self-awareness, where the assumptions of one's own culture are made explicit and the sojourner is exhorted to become a cultural relativist; attribution training, where participants are taught to explain behaviour from the perspective of another culture; learning theory-based approach where participants are taught to seek reinforcement or to reinforce themselves for culturally appropriate behaviour; and behavioural training, where participants role-play life in simulated environments. (Furnham and Bockner, 1986, p. 6)

Some of these remedies are effective; others are not even when the cultural differences are small. As Freud pointed out: 'It is precisely the minor differences in people who are otherwise alike that form the basis of feelings of strangeness and hostility between them... This "narcissism of minor differences" the hostility which in every human relation we see fighting successfully against feelings of fellowship and overpowering the commandment that all men should love one another' (Freud, 2010, p. 2355). So what then after all is the cure? It is 'the cure by love' (Freud, 2010, p. 2954). To love is not dissociated from the question of *how one ought to live*. People will recover their capacity to love when they forfeit a part of their narcissism. 'A strong egoism is a protection against falling ill, but in the last resort we must begin to love in order not to fall ill, and we are bound to fall ill if, in consequence of frustration, we are unable to love' (Freud, 2010, p. 85). Like a mirror, the gaze functions as a medium for becoming, becoming a loving and loved gaze. Critique, extrapolation and illumination, illusion, denial, attraction, repulsion, hope, fear, danger, identification, jealousy, envy, sympathy, empathy, spectator, change, fantasy, friend, enemy, maturation, maturity, ambivalence, rivalry, aggressiveness, desire, mimicry, perfection, ideal, malformation,

confusion and entrapment are all manifested in the host gaze. Thus, the host gaze is
value-laden and is governed by its own
voice and that of its semblables and imaginary rivals. "A person who loves has, so to
speak, forfeited a part of his narcissism, and
it can only be replaced by his being loved"
(Freud, 2010, p. 2951). The word *love* is
mentioned 1,430 times by Freud in his work.

To this end, we would just like to comment
that after all the sex talk on the sofa, the cure
of psychoanalysis is love and so is its ultimate end – a thesis that has been widely
overlooked. Finally, the Germans might see
their being stigmatized and negatively stereotyped as insulting, unjustified or even
unacceptable. It is also time for the Germans
to gaze upon their gaze upon the Other(s).

References

American Psychiatric Association (2000) *Diagnostic and Statistical Manual of Mental Disorders*. American Psychiatric Association, Washington, DC.
Biran, H. (2003) The difficulty of transforming terror into dialogue. *Group Analysis* 36(4), 490–502.
Bogart, L.M., Benotsch, E.G. and Pavlovic, J.D. (2004) Feeling superior but threatened: the relation of narcis-sism to social comparison. *Basic and Applied Social Psychology* 26(1), 35–44.
Brown, R.P., Budzek, K. and Tamborski, M. (2009) On the meaning and measure of narcissism. *Personality and Social Psychology Bulletin* 35(7), 951–964.
Derrida, J. (2007) The transcendental "stupidity" ("betise") of man and the becoming – animal according to Deleuze. In: Shwab, G. (ed.) *Derrida, Deleuze, Psychoanalysis*. Columbia University Press, New York, pp. 35–60.
Foucault, M. (2003) *The Birth of the Clinic*. Tavistock, London.
Foster, J.D. and Trimm, R.F. (2008) On being eager and uninhibited: narcissism and approach-avoidance motivation. *Personality and Social Psychology Bulletin* 34, 1004–1017.
Freud, S. (1914) *On Narcissism*. The Standard Edition of the Complete Psychological Works of Sigmund Freud, Volume XIV (1914–1916): On the History of the Psycho-Analytic Movement, Papers on Metapsychology and Other Works, pp. 67–102.
Freud, S. (2010) *Complete Works*. Ivan Smith 2000, 2007, 2010. http://www.valas.fr/IMG/pdf/Freud_Complete_Works.pdf (accessed 10 July 2012).
Freud, S. (1910) The origin and development of psychoanalysis. First published in *American Journal of Psy-chology* 21, 181–218. http://psychclassics.yorku.ca/Freud/Origin/origin5.htm#ftnt1 (accessed 26 June 2012).
Freud, S. (2000, 2007, 2010) *Complete Works*. Ivan Smith. http://users.iafrica.com/m/mw/mwivansm/freud.htm (accessed 25 June 2012).
Frosh, S. and Baraitser, L. (2008) Psychoanalysis and psychosocial studies. *Psychoanalysis, Culture and Soci-ety* 13, 346–365.
Fullagar, S. (2001) Encountering otherness: embodied affect in Alphonso Lingis' travel writing. *Tourist Studies* 1(2), 171–183.
Furnham, A. and Bochner, S. (1986) *Culture Shock*. Methuen, London.
Green, A. (1981) Negation and contradiction. In: Grotstein, J. S. (eds) *Do I Dare Disturb the Universe?: a Memorial to Wilfred R. Bion*. Caesura Press, London.
Green, A. (1983) *Narcissisme de Vie, Narcissisme de Mort*. Gallimard, Paris.
Hayes, W. (2008) Psychoanalysis in the shadow of post-apartheid reconstruction. *Theory and Psychology* 18(2), 209–222.
Helbing, M. (2010) Why Swiss Germans dislike Germans. On negative attitudes towards a culturally and socially similar group. Paper prepared for presentation at the Annual Meeting of the Swiss Political Science Association, University of Geneva, Geneva.
Hollway, W. (2006) Paradox in the pursuit of a critical theorization of the development of self in family relationships. *Theory & Psychology* 16(4), 465–482.
Hollway, W. (2008) Psychoanalytically informed observation. In: Given, L.M. (ed.) *SAGE Encyclopedia of Qualitative Research Methods*. SAGE, Thousand Oaks, CA.
Kaplan, T.R. and Ruffle, B.J. (2002) *The Self-Serving Bias and Beliefs about Rationality*. Mimeo, Ben Gurion University, Beer-sheva.

Kernberg, O. F. (1994) The psychotherapeutic management of psychopathic, narcissistic, and paranoid transferences. In Millon, T., Simonsen, E., Birket-Smith, M. and Davis, R.D. (eds) *Psychopathy: Antisocial, Criminal, and Violent Behavior*. Guilford, New York.

Kingsbury, P. (2005) Jamaican tourism and the politics of enjoyment. *Geoforum* 36, 113–132.

Kohut, H. (1971) *The Analysis of the Self: a Systematic Approach to the Psychoanalytic Treatment of Narcissistic Personality Disorders*. International Universities Press, New York.

Lacan, J. (1949) The mirror stage as formative of the function of the I. In: Sheridan, A. S. (trans.) *Lacan, J. Écrits: a Selection*. Tavistock, London.

Lacan, J. (1970) Of structure as an inmixing of an otherness prerequisite to any subject whatever. In: Macksey, R. and Donato, E. (eds) *The Structuralist Controversy*. Johns Hopkins University Press, Baltimore, MD, pp. 186–200.

Lacan, J. (1977) *Ecrits: a Selection*. Routledge, London.

Lacan, J. (1994) The mirror-phase as formative of the function of the I. In: Zizek, S. (ed.) *Mapping Ideology*, Verso, London, pp. 93–99.

Lasch, C. (1982) *The Culture of Narcissism*. Abacus, London.

Lippman, W. (1921) *Public Opinion*, http://www.faculty.english.vt.edu/Collier/5314/lippmannpublicop.pdf (accessed 10 July 2012).Lyon, P.A., Kenworthy, J.B. and Popan, J.R. (2010) Ingroup identification and group level narcissism as predictors of US citizens' attitudes and behavior toward Arab immigrants. *Personality and Social Psychology Bulletin* 36(9), 1267–1280.

MacCannell, D. (1999) The tourist: a new theory of the leisure class. University of California, Berkeley, CA.

MacCannell, D. (2001) Tourist agency. *Tourist Studies* 1(1), 23–37.

Malone, K.R. (2008) Psychoanalysis: formalization and logic and the question of speaking and affect. *Theory and Psychology* 18(2), 179–193.

Merleau-Ponty, M. (1968) *The Visible and the Invisible*. Northwestern University, Evanston, IL.

Miller, D.T. and Ross, M. (1975) Self-serving biases in the attribution of causality: fact or fictions. *Psychological Bulletin* 82, 213–225.

Moufakkir, O. (2011) Diaspora tourism: using a mixed-mode survey design to document tourism behavior and constraints of people of Turkish extraction resident in Germany. *Journal of Vacation Marketing* 17(3), 209–223.

Rojek, C. (2010) *Leisure Studies. Origins: Classic and Contemporary Theories*. Sage, London.

Rose, P. (2002) The happy and unhappy faces of narcissism. *Personality and Individual Differences* 33, 379–392.

Sniderman, P. and Carmines, E. (1997) *Reaching Beyond Race*. Harvard University Press, Cambridge, MA.

Symington, N. (1993) *Narcissism: a New Theory*. Karnac Classics, London.

Symington, J.S. (1996) *The Clinical Thinking of Wilfred Bion*. Routledge, London.

Theiler, T. (2004) The origins of Euroscepticism in German-Speaking Switzerland. *European Journal of Political Research* 43, 635–656.

Tyler, I. (2007) From 'the me decade' to 'the me millennium': the cultural history of narcissism. *International Journal of Cultural Studies* 10(3), 343–363.

White, C. and Boucke, L. (2006) *The UnDutchables*. White Boucke Publishing, US.

Whitford, M. (2003) Irigaray and the culture of narcissism. *Theory, Culture & Society* 20(3), 27–41.

Urry, J. (1990) *The Tourist Gaze: Leisure and Travel in Contemporary Societies*. Sage, London.

Zizek, S. (1998) Love thy neighbor? No, thanks! In: Lane, C. (ed.) *The Psychoanalysis of Race*. University of Colombia Press, New York, pp. 154–175.

Zürn, M. (1998) *Regieren Jenseits des Nationalstaates*. Frankfurt am Main, Suhrkamp.

15 Real-and-Imagined Women: Goddess America Meets the World

Petri Hottola

Introduction

Stereotyping is a way of categorizing the world and creating a private or collective illusion of knowledge and understanding. It defines most of our perceptual functions in situations of inadequate or contradictory information and saves cognitive energy in a significant way, protecting the mental well-being (MacRae *et al.*, 1994). The knowledge that we have of the world is far from complete, and imagination is needed to fill the gaps in most cases. Categorization by stereotypic imagery is a practical way to negotiate with other objects and subjects in existence, including the people we meet.

The stereotypic images are societally produced and they affect our situational evaluations of others, such as in the mutual gaze between tourists and their hosts. They are, however, seldom empirically studied. This is regrettable because we do not only see but we also imagine. The exploration of tourism is, following Edward Soja (1996), a journey to 'real-and-imagined' spaces, the Thirdspace. In other words, the lived worlds that postmodern human geography studies do not consist only of the dimension of space that is directly observed but also of the dimension of space that is extrasensory. It is not possible for observations to be definite because the gaze of an observer always has a number of societally constructed filters between the target and its interpretation.

These evolving perceptions of the mind are important for tourism but may also reflect larger societal developments (e.g. Pritchard, 2000; Santos and Buzinde, 2006; Caton and Santos, 2009). In fact, national, regional and gender stereotypes become of scientific interest mainly in connection with social groups (Pickering, 2001; Schneider, 2004). Groups observe one another and adjust their gaze according to what they expect, fear or desire to see. Categorizations of foreign people may consequently become caricatures (see Dann, 1996; MacCannell, 1999) rather than realistic. They nevertheless manage to provide a reassuring sense of being in control, which ultimately encourages us to travel (Hottola, 1999, p. 306). Occasionally, these perceptions may be deceptive, guiding people to mistreat one another (e.g. Goings, 2001; Garrick, 2005). In those situations, attempts to understand the process become a moral obligation for a researcher.

The following two interlinked case studies have explored one such perception, that of a typically Western/American woman. First, as seen through the eyes of Indian men, and to a lesser extent Sri Lankan men (Hottola, 1999, 2002a, b, 2008), with the 'local gaze' of Darya Maoz (2006). Second, in the light of a sociotypic perception, a consensus between seven nations of Europe, North America, Africa and Asia (Hottola, 2012a, c). The focus will be on the female gender, even though similar analysis was also completed on the typically Western/American man. It was the former perception that created almost all the intergender visitor–host conflicts in the sSouth Asian travel scene and was therefore deemed to be in primary need of analysis. The gendered aspects of intercultural encounters have received relatively wide interest in tourism geography, more so than is often assumed (see Tivers, 2012).

an obnoxious manner and were encouraged by the local power relations. Blatant sexual violence towards foreigners is rare in South Asia. Interestingly, the women also reported that a number of men had been genuinely surprised when their amorous attempts were rejected.

Consequently, the local perceptions of Western women were charted by interviews, topical discussions and an analysis of the locally available information sources: education, television programmes, South Asian and imported movies, newspapers, magazines and advertising. Additionally, earlier research findings on the topic were collected for analysis.

Sexual Advances in South Asia

The first phase of the research was completed in Bharatpur, Rajasthan, in 1993–1994, with additional field work in the Sri Lankan highlands in 1996–1997. As a side result of a project on the aspects of intercultural adaptation as a learning process (Hottola, 2004, 2005; see also Berno and Ward, 2005), no less than 97% of the 36 Western women interviewed in Bharatpur were found to have been sexually harassed by Indian men, many of them on a frequent basis (Hottola, 1999, pp. 263–293; 2002). Numerous others confirmed the situation. In Sri Lanka, 31% of 16 women had had similar experiences. The common forms included continuous staring (up to 8 h on a train), leering and ogling, indecent comments, touching and groping. The foreign women had arrived in a societal environment that generated a profusion of sexual advances, and they had to find ways of coping with the situation, without fully understanding what was going on.

The relationship between stereotyping and sexual harassment has oftentimes been discussed almost in terms of racism and violence (e.g. Fiske, 1998). Many of the incidents in South Asia could, however, be labelled as unwanted attraction-based advances and not so much as misuse of power, even though several men behaved in

Amoral and Available

In South Asia, the Occident has for ages been the epitome of amorality, a place where sexual urges have become rampant. One explanation for this lies in the uncontrolled status of Western women. Amorality in general is commonly connected with breaking of the codes of intergender behaviour, especially in public spaces where such behaviour can be judged by the social gaze prevalent in each society (Goffman, 1963). According to Hindu philosophy, the sexuality of women should be strictly controlled and women should live as dependants (Conlon, 1994, p. 53). Otherwise, their and others' lives will be ruined by excessive spread of immorality and eventually the whole universe will spin out of control. Women themselves are not considered to be able to control their desires (e.g. Rampal, 1978). Therefore, they need to be guarded and protected by men.

In rural towns such as Bharatpur, the custom of *purdah* means that women will not leave home without being escorted by the men of the clan (Jeffery, 1984; Mandelbaum, 1988). If something should happen to jeopardize the honour of a woman, the negative consequences would be felt in the whole family line. A young woman whose reputation is lost becomes a burden to her family and is unlikely to attract a proper marriage arrangement (Ahuja, 1993). There-fore, the local women should not, among other things, have direct eye contact with men or speak with unrelated males. Cus-toms such as these have been developed in a long historical process, in which the Aryan and Mogul invasions to the Indian subcontinent and introduced practices such as *niyoga*, marriage by kidnap, have played a significant role (see Upadhyay, 1991; Ahuja, 1993; Jayakar, 1996).

In many societies, the forms of human communication such as speech, bodily appearance, personal acts, dress, move-ment, position and emotional expressions are institutionalized in the public (Goffman, 1963). In other words, there are more or less strict rules of personal appearance and behaviour. The rules regarding the expres-sion of the body are the most salient ones. The bodyscape of embodied social space requires certain conformity (Hottola, 1999, 2002a). In India, the social control of women manifests itself in the form of open disap-proval from both men and women if a woman for example dares to run in public (Harasym, 1990). In Sri Lanka, the situation is slightly more relaxed.

According to *Kama Sutra*, the type of women who can easily be won over are those who loiter around the house gazing along the highway, those who continuously stare, give a sideways glance when noticed, display passionate tendencies, are proud of their cleverness and have common qualities with men (Burton and Arbuthnot, 1995, pp. 110–111). The views are relevant also today. The tourist women fit the description; they have left their home and travel by them-selves, socialize freely with men, address and challenge them, and make eye contact, perceived to be a call for intimacy according to the local norms. They behave and dress in ways which add to the picture. Born in individualistic cultures, the women do not understand the importance of paralinguistic signs in a collectivist culture (Triandis, 1994). South Asian people communicate with their clothes and behaviour as an act of loyalty to the social order.

While in India and Sri Lanka, I made notes on the dress and styles of each

interviewed backpacker, men and women, and also some of the ones observed (Hottola, 2008). The majority of the women travellers tried to follow the local dress code, voluntarily, or after the first incidents with local men, by dressing in a modest way. On the other hand, there were also travellers who made mistakes that were all too obvious and attracted attention on the streets, thereby confirming the reputation of Western women. The provocative clothing increased the frequency of sexual advances. The style of the dress was, however, not crucial. Many were harassed despite con-formist clothing.

Simplification, exaggeration, general-ization and denial of individuality are all integral parts of a stereotyping process (e.g. Pieterse 1992; MacRae *et al.*, 1994; Krebs and Denton, 1997; Moufakkir, 2008). As Robert Stewart, Graham Powell and Jane Chetwynd (1979, p. 2) have written, stereo-typing can be conceived to be a 'form of cat-egorising behaviour, in which a single characteristic or label serves to elicit a set of expectations or attributions which are too simple to describe accurately the class of person in question and, at the same time, are too broadly generalised to individuals to have more than occasional validity'.

Overall, we have a tendency to perceive outgroup people as being more homogenous in their traits and behaviour than ingroup members (e.g. Rudman *et al.*, 2001). There-fore the target persons who show similar qualities are perceived to belong to one category irrespective of their obvious or not so obvious secondary differences. On the streets of South Asia, a white woman is a woman of the West/USA and is conse-quently supposed to share all the inherent qualities of that particular stereotype, irre-spective of her individual behaviour or attire.

Bollywood Vamp Meets Hollywood Babe

In the 1990s, watching domestic popular movies was the favourite pastime of Indian men (Hottola, 1999, 2002a). In the forefront of advancing globalization, posters of Samantha Fox and other buxom blondes were already adopted to increase the eroticism of the movies, before the current fashion of employing exotic dancers from the post-Soviet Eastern Europe. On the other hand, one of the five central characters of a Bollywood *masala* movie was the 'vamp', an Indian woman with Western life-styles and code-breaking behaviour. A lesson was taught to the audiences by pitting her against the pure and submissive heroine. Additionally, she was there to answer to an increasing demand for titillation on the screen, which could not be fulfilled otherwise. This aspect could not be as much attached to an Indian woman without offending the audiences. The 'amorality' had to be Westernized.

The small number of imported Hollywood movies also confirmed the stereotypic assumptions. As concluded by 5 months of daily reading of the *Indian Express* and *Daily News*, practically all Western films shown in the theatres of South Asia were of the soft porn action quality, the B-movies. Day after day, advertisements of the movies brought the images of scantily clad Western 'bombshells' to the readers of local newspapers. More explicit materials were, according to interviews, widely and readily available under the counter, also in rural towns.

As Indian censorship authorities had much earlier predicted, uncensored foreign films indeed had a major effect on the reputation of Western women (Barnouw and Krishnaswamy, 1980). There was, after all, next to zero information on Western societies and their values to be found in education, newspapers and magazines. In addition, the public television network, Doordarshan, passively participated in the process by not broadcasting documentary material on gender relations in the West, not to mention general information on Western societies. Consequently, the available fantasy presentations could be taken as documentary. In Sri Lanka, Rupavahini had three imported series in its programming – 'Baywatch', 'Acapulco Heat' and 'The Bold and the Beautiful' – each one strengthening

the prevalent host gaze. Unlike the Indian audiences, the well-educated Sri Lankans had, however, been exposed to global media already for decades and were therefore more capable of enjoying them as fantasy entertainment (Hottola, 1999, p. 383).

From Victorian Liberalism to Present Day Tourism

During the history of the subcontinent, Western visitors have contributed to the local prejudices (Hottola, 1999, 2002b, 2004). The arrival of British colonial women in India challenged local gender relations (Bhatia, 1979). Although the Victorian era certainly did not have a reputation of loose morals in Europe, people living under the Mogul regime found its norms too permissive. Not only 'liberal' gender relations but various other breaks against the traditions of purity and prestige, such as a meat diet, defined the foreigners as morally inferior. According to H. S. Bhatia, the locals initially disliked the European women's dress, demeanour, habits, customs and open-air lifestyle. Later, when the Raj had been established, some Indians began admiring the British, including the 'odd ways' their women behaved. Nevertheless, for the majority the Western woman was a breaker of social codes and remained so.

Then, tourists started to arrive in South Asia by their tens of thousands. In the 1960s, the hippie movement formed a counterculture to conservatism in the West and was often considered morally doubtful even in its originating cultures (e.g. Hall, 1968; Zicklin, 1983). The hippie invasion and especially the 'wild days' of the 1960s and 1970s in Goa are still remembered. Orgies on the beaches created conflicts with local people, and articles about them were widely published in newspapers (Turner and Ash, 1975; Mehta, 1979). Later, the presence of hippies, ravers and others in beach tourism enclaves has continued to produce scandalous news in the media. The start and expansion of conventional beach tourism in Goa and in the south of Sri Lanka added to the stereotype of a 'culture of nakedness' (e.g. Seneviratne *et al.*, 1988; Wilson, 1997).

Transitory Encounters and Sexual Frustrations

In a situation of relative power equality – wealthy but less than omnipotent minority among the multitude of local people – a common relationship was turned around. It was not the native woman who was there to seduce the tourist gaze (e.g. McClintock, 1995; Opperman and McKinley, 1997; Saarinen and Niskala, 2008) but the white tourist woman who seduced host gaze, because of her Other embodiment and reputation of sexual prowess. In India, the interest in tourist women has actually developed to a special form of tourism (Davies *et al.*, 1987, p. 267; Wilson, 1997; Hottola, 1999, p. 282; 2002b). Busloads of men are transported to beach tourism locations to observe and photograph Western women in bikinis. The domestic women swim in saris. This brings to mind another peculiar dualism of women on the beach, in South African tourism marketing (Hottola, 2006). In both the apartheid and post-apartheid era national tourism brochures, the role of a bikini-clad seducer was reserved solely for white women, with a glaring absence of the black majority and other ethnicities.

Much of the described situation is in line with John Lea's (1988, pp. 62–64) classical analysis of tourist–host encounters in the developing world. The transitory nature of the encounters between local men and traveller women opens the door for code-breaking behaviour – the foreign women appear and disappear. The time and space restraints press for immediate gratification. There is an imbalance in the satisfaction gained in the encounter, even though the satisfaction of the men is also oftentimes questionable. On the other hand, unlike in Lea's thinking, there is a relative balance of wealth (and power) between the men and women (see also Frohlick, 2007); the men tend to be educated and middle-class. The situations also arrive as unplanned and require spontaneous action. The men have to improvise with less than smooth action and, as a rule, fail in the end. Moreover, there are cultural constraints, with mutually limited understanding of the other's behaviour.

On the host side of the conflict, there is an unfulfilled need. The men are bound by the custom of no sex out of wedlock, for largely the same reasons as women (e.g. Rampal, 1978). Boys are prevented from having premarital sex, which could lead to unwanted romantic relationships and ruin their reputation in the marriage market, not to mention creating serious conflicts between families. Additionally, young people who have practically no experience of sex before marriage see sex gratification as an important motivation to accept their arranged spouse (e.g. Ahuja, 1993).

Nevertheless, because of the regional excess of men and the cost of dowry, numerous men are never able to marry and satisfy themselves (Ahuja, 1993; Government of India, 2011). Consequently, there are many sexually frustrated males on the streets of India. As a male travel writer commented his travels with a sexy Austrian girlfriend: 'Her yellow hair was a candle for over two hundred million sexually repressed male moths. Beating them off would be an exhausting task' (Ward, 1996, in Belliveau, 2006, p. 211). For them, the arrival of tourist women is a chance to find their repressed sexual identity with women who are thought to be consenting. Therefore, a minority of boys and men try to realize their fantasies in mostly misguided ways (Hottola, 2002a, b). The majority of Indian men are, however, respectful towards foreign women despite their commitment to the leading role of men in the society.

Being sexually suppressed and spatially segregated from women, and therefore only able to observe them from a distance, the men of Bharatpur had a habit of categorizing and rating them according to the level of visual titillation (Hottola, 1999, pp. 263–281). Consequently, they tended to see the foreigners primarily as unknown and unrelated bodies of women, as objects to be gazed at, rather than subjects or personalities.

This is a good example of a transitory situation where the observers on both sides are biased towards simplistic dispositional attributions because they have less information about the actors than the actors have about themselves (Krebs and Denton, 1997).

Opposite Desires

The concept of 'amoral' becomes complicated in this context. What is lacking in Our society or individual lives is often perceived to be found beyond the horizon, in an Other society or in its individual members. Consequently, the Other may become idealized and compelling (e.g. Said, 1995). From the viewpoint of the local men, the Western women were not seen to be amoral in a negative way. On the contrary, according to discussions in Bharatpur, there was a kind of glorified aura around the women (Hottola, 1999). In the fantasies of the men, these foreigners were considered to be sex goddesses of the West: powerful, experienced, ready and equal to men in sexual relations, while the local unmarried women are unreachable and wives too passive and submissive. What is more, a white Western girlfriend could be seen as a 'trophy'.

To the disappointment of the men, India is not on the list of popular destinations for travelling Westerners who look for sex and romance on the road (Belliveau, 2006, pp. 210–213). Men who expect immediate sexual gratification, but are not able to communicate on the same level, are seldom attractive to traveller women. Among the women interviewed in South Asia, there was only one who had experienced a romance with a local man during her visit. She was the 'kernel of truth' that is necessary for a stereotype to remain convincing (Bond, 1986; Bhabha, 1994). However misguided a stereotype may be, it has a chance of surviving if empirical evidence supporting it can be found and used to justify its continuous existence. The rest of the women expressed their desire to avoid the indigenous men, and field observations confirmed this.

There were genuine and irreconcilable differences in the goals and aspirations of the groups in contact. The approaches of local men had become a problem to these women. They had been sexually harassed and the harassment had become an important source of gender mistrust between the local men and visiting women.

Nevertheless, the majority of women showed mental strength and were able to manage the situation, and continued to enjoy travelling in South Asia. A minority of women, mostly North Europeans, became depressed, spending most of their time in their accommodation and barely tolerating the presence of any local men. And then there were the few who said that they enjoyed being so popular, unlike at home, and found enjoyment in the ample interest, as long as they perceived themselves to be able to harness it.

The Israeli Woman Incident

Conflicts between local men and tourist women may occasionally cause significant disturbances in South Asian communities. One such incident, which I directly witnessed in part, occurred in Bharatpur on 16-18 January 1994 (Hottola, 1999, pp. 292–293). The missing details were collected from several travellers, rickshaw drivers and tourism entrepreneurs who had been involved in the process. One particular rickshaw-wallah, who was a friend of mine and had personally observed the early stages, could cast light to the viewpoints of the misbehaved men, now without employment.

For me, it all started on the morning of 17 January when something extraordinary was seen to happen to privately run guesthouses by the Keoladeo Bird Sanctuary, on the road to Jaipur. A truckload of policemen and a number of rather stern-looking officials had arrived from the state capital and were giving orders to the managers. Government roadside regulations would be enforced on this 500-m stretch. Consequently, all illegally constructed structures in a 30-m buffer zone by the trunk road had to be demolished within 30 h, with immediate effect. The structures included brick walls, gardens, guesthouse gates and restaurant facilities. I also learned that two guesthouses, Flamingo and Bambino's, and tea-stalls opposite Saras Lodge, a government-run hotel, had been closed for the time being.

I wondered what had happened to trigger this exceptionally forceful reaction by the state officials, while noting that an attractive Israeli traveller was attempting to go and argue with the police about the demolition. Her travel companions prevented this by pulling her back on her chair. Next to them, the young manager of the Pelican guesthouse was weeping as he observed the destruction of structures completed just days ago. In the process, several people and their families had suddenly lost their livelihood. All the guesthouses lost valuable facilities, and also customers, because the rubble unsurprisingly did not increase their appeal. Furthermore, there was the emotional stress. Careful attempts to influence the authorities to minimize the damage had not initially been effective.

The incident had begun when the above-mentioned Israeli woman arrived in Bharatpur and rented accommodation at the Pelican. She was like the dream woman of the men working on the Jaipur road, with a beautiful face, long dark hair, slender but curvaceous and fit body with a large bust, and she immediately gained fame through the grapevine. Not only was she built like Bollywood goddesses or US B-film heroines (the ideals coincide), with somewhat Oriental features, but she was also Western and therefore potentially available, behaving like only men locally did. The sight of her walking on the road caused admirers to hurry to get a view. There was plenty of talking and fantasizing, and the men went slightly crazy over her. A 'bombshell' like her, obviously not married and without the protection of the men of her kin... Why would she place herself in such a vulnerable position if she were not looking for action with men?

On the evening of 16 January, the Israeli traveller visited Saras Lodge for some reason. Her movements did not go unnoticed.

Eager to get a close look, or more, some men from the later closed establishments followed her in. Eventually, at least two of them groped her breasts. Naturally, the woman defended herself and started to beat the assailants. This was probably not expected by them because Indian women do not express anger as readily, especially publicly, as Israeli women do (Gannon and Pillai 2010, pp. 331–350). The traveller had recently finished her military service, just like many other Israeli visitors in India who treat these two 'journeys' as a rite of passage into adulthood (Maoz, 2004). Some of the lodge staff hurried to help her. The fight escalated, and the manager got a bleeding wound on his head.

A single case of groping would probably not have developed into a situation that involved half of the tourism services in Bharatpur if the financial pressures of competition between the private and the public sectors had not been there. The following morning, the wounded and irritated manager of the lodge complained to high authorities in Jaipur and swift action was taken. The borders of power and ownership were re-established on the land where the private guesthouses were located. The state-owned lodge could not, however, gain much in the end. Known for its average facilities, noisiness and indifferent service, the place did not become any more popular. The excess of accommodation in Bharatpur could easily cover the temporary closure of two guesthouses, which were reopened later.

The original offenders, now criticized by fellow unfortunates, were probably more than sorry that they did not resist the temptation. The local community put the blame solely on them. I did not hear a single hint that the foreign woman would have been accused at all. She had not provoked the men in any way, unless behaving like a normal Western woman is considered being provocative, which should in principle not be the case among men who work with tourists and are therefore used to foreigners. These situations are, however, not based on rationality.

Although somewhat exceptional, the incident illustrates well the unpredictable nature of consequences even a relatively minor intercultural conflict may in some cases trigger. The outcomes of these situations can seldom be fully controlled or anticipated by the initiators, who may also end up in trouble. It is important to notice that even though the male dominance in public space provides the unscrupulous offenders considerable freedom of action, the tourist women also have power in their ethnicity and wealth, not to mention the ability to react in a code-breaking way. The majority of the women travellers interviewed in South Asia were confident in their ability to keep the men at bay; by force, if necessary.

Seven-Nation Survey: the Sociotype of an American Woman

Years after discovering the challenging realities of visitor–host interaction in South Asia, I started to ponder the intriguing lack of stereotype and sociotype surveys, not only in tourism studies, but in general. The main problem was found to be a methodological one. Because of the plenitude of possible attributes (thousands), no quantitative survey on the topic could have been created without manipulation of the result. If categories are given, the results may easily reflect the individual stereotypes of the researcher. An experimental methodological tool, the collage method (Hottola, 2012a, c) was consequently designed to overcome the dilemma, to enable the discovery of unbiased approximations of perceptions of ethnicity. The image to be studied in the experiment was that of a typically American (the USA) place and its typically US inhabitants: a typically American woman and man.

The reason for the choice was double-edged. It is the white Westerners who form the bulk of the world's international tourists and are gazed on in tourism destinations. In India and Sri Lanka, the concept of Western woman had frequently been equated with an American woman, apparently as a consequence of popular media imagery, just like the perceptions of a Western man tended to

have features of popular US action movie and wrestling heroes (see Iyer, 1988). There are 400,000 US tourist arrivals in India (Government of India 2004) every year, but the authentic Americans are a rare sight for the majority of local people.

On the other hand, the role of the USA is unique in globalization. Only US media entertainment has been able to cross cultural and ideological borderlines with such extent and volume, consequently creating a hegemonic group stereotype (Schneider, 2004; Caton and Santos, 2009, p.n191; Hottola, 2012a), and providing billions of people liminal experiences of touristic nature. The worlds of entertainment are real-and-imagined, with an emphasis on fiction (e.g. Ryan and Martin, 2001). The spaces of tourism share the same qualities (e.g. MacCannell, 1999; Hottola, 2012b). It was therefore interesting to do a comparative study to find out how the Americans were seen by the host gaze in a variety of tourism destinations.

Seven nations – Finland, Spain, the USA, South Africa, Zambia, Sri Lanka and Japan – were chosen for the study, with samples of 22–40 students (total 201) surveyed in lecturer exchange situations, or with the help of trusted colleagues. Finland and Zambia are less involved with international tourism, but the rest belong to the category of major tourism destinations. Spain, in particular, is a favourite destination, consistently among the global top five in terms of international arrivals (e.g. UNWTO, 2011). One million US tourists visit the nation annually (IET, 2011).

The perceptions and interpretations of the USA, in particular the American woman, would certainly not be as unique as in India, I presumed. The Indians had, after all, very different norms and traditions combined with limited understanding of life in the West, whereas the nations of Europe, for example, shared many cultural concepts with the Americans. Moreover, their people had access to more accurate information on the USA. The Japanese and South Africans also had strong ties to the Western world. The Americans themselves, on the other hand, had the benefit of self-observation. The Zambian perceptions were difficult to predict, but the understandings of the Sri Lankans, part of the original analysis, were expected to have deepened in the decade between studies.

To my surprise, the perceptions of typically American people not only indicated a strong sociotypic consensus – views of those who stereotype and those who are stereotyped agreed (e.g. Triandis, 1995, p. 21) – but were also remarkably close to the South Asian host gaze of the 1990s. Even the Spanish gaze coincided with many of the views prevalent in Bharatpur, despite the close cultural proximity (Hottola, 2012b). A sociotype, or a social stereotype, is an especially powerful perception that may develop into an archetype, an image thought to truthfully reflect the inherent characteristics of a group of people (e.g. Pieterse, 1992). It therefore may have a defining effect on more than one host gaze, across cultural borderlines.

The Collage Method

In the collage approach, respondents filled out an open questionnaire with written descriptions. They were asked to describe the physical and other qualities of a typically US place and its typically US inhabitants, including the attire, lifestyles and character traits of the latter. The samples combined, the questionnaires produced a total of 2,430 attributes to be categorized and organized. In the present text, the focus is on the 1,298 attributes of a typically American woman. The attributes were first categorized and then ranked according to their frequency. The construction of the collage, a conclusive textual synthesis, was started with the most dominant attributes with highest frequency and the dominant attributes on top of each category (e.g. 'blue' under 'eyes'). Lower ranking dominant features were added to the text as long as they did not disagree with the previously selected ones. The numerous scattered attributes at the bottom of the ranking order were left out.

In other words, according to survey material, a typically American woman had blonde hair (dominant colour choice, voluntarily brought by 53% of the respondents), which was long (dominant length choice) and abundant (dominant volume choice). The hair was mostly straight (dominant hair style choice) but in places it had been styled and there are also some curls (two less dominant but significant hair style choices not in exclusive contradiction with the more dominant ones). Mrs America's hair was well cared for and important to her (two significant other hair qualities not in contradiction with the previous ones). In a similar manner, the chains of attributes accumulated to a full textual description of the qualities of the US woman, as agreed by the international observers of the seven samples.

The sociotypic collage produced the following description of the American woman (Hottola, 2012a). The core of the collage was formed by the seven (out of 1,298!) most dominant attributes, which were written down by at least one-third of the respondents. As the female American starts to emerge from the cognitive mist, we can see that she is (i) white-skinned; (ii) blonde, and wearing a pair of (iii) jeans. She has (iv) blue eyes; (v) extra-large breasts; (vi) a slender body; and (vii) long hair. This is the 'skeleton' of the social stereotype, around which the rest of the attributes are accumulated in the ranking process of inclusion and exclusion.

The most dominant attributes are also the most salient features of the sociotype collage, the ones in a lower ranking position being increasingly more random in a relatively small sample. The less dominant characterizations are not there by accident, either. They reflect the tone and direction of the perceptions, whatever the minor details produced by the sample happen to be at that particular point in history. This is also the nature of stereotypic perceptions; they tend to be relatively solid at the core but hazy and evolving predominantly on the fringes. That is why the approximate nature of the understandings produced by the collage method, with its qualitative epistemology, may be acceptable in this type of research, the handicap being compensated by practicality and ability to collect unbiased responses.

Mrs Pamela America

The iconic American woman was named Mrs Pamela America in homage to the popular US actress Pamela Anderson of Baywatch, because her name was mentioned most often when the respondents were asked, towards the end of the survey: Could you name a real-life US person who fits in with the description of a typically American woman you just created? Guided by the information they consumed, the students named a real-and-imagined person of the entertainment media. The selection tells volumes on the nature of the host gaze and its tendency to prefer fiction to reality, even when factual information is available.

The 27-year-old gorgeous blonde has a rounded, small face with soft, delicate features, and blue eyes that are large and round. Her white complexion is good, with freckles and suntan. She has long eyelashes and perfectly shaped, plucked eyebrows. There is a friendly expression and quite a lot of make-up on her face. She is always smiling and showing off her perfect, straight and shiny teeth. The luscious, shapely lips of her small mouth have been painted pink. She has high cheekbones and a relatively large, sharp nose. There is usually a rosy flush on her full cheeks. Her neck is long and ears small, and the dyed hair covers the ears. The long and abundant hair is mostly straight, but in places it has been styled and there are also some curls. Her hair is important to Mrs America and she takes good care of it.

The tall (around 170 cm) woman has an attractive, slim but at the same time rather curvaceous body, considered sexually appealing especially by heterosexual male observers. She is fit and healthy, and has good posture although there is little grace in her movements. Pamela America is very conscious of her body; she is on a permanent diet and ready to have liposuction in order to attain the perfect shape. Her extra-large breasts have obviously been enlarged by implants, which explain their youthful firmness and round shape. Her skin is flawless and soft to touch; she has shaved all her body hair. She has balanced shoulders, narrow waist and flat belly, and rounded, eye-catching hips of average size. Her behind is ample but shapely, with round buttocks and full, trim thighs. Her legs and arms are long and slender, well-toned and beautifully formed, and her feet small. Her hands are delicate and well formed. The long nails of her long fingers have been painted and manicured, just like her toenails.

Pamela America prefers casual and simple but stylish clothes with brand-name designs such as GAP, Calvin Klein and Levi's. Everything has to be new and trendy, and preferably of bright colour. She likes to show her body in public and therefore normally dresses in revealing clothes of skintight fit. She does not mind if her nipples show. At the moment, she is wearing a very tight and short white T-shirt with a wide cleavage and bare midriff, and a pair of tight blue jeans, her second skin. Underneath, she wears a tiny G-string bikini and a push-up bra.

On her feet, she has white socks and a pair of white high heels. There is a purse in her hand and a watch around her wrist. She also often wears some gold jewellery; a necklace, rings or earrings. Mrs America never leaves home without sunglasses, although she does not wear them all the time. If we could take a peek in her wardrobe at home, we would see her other favourites: a tank top, a long-sleeved blouse, a dress, khaki shorts, a short skirt of black colour, a baseball cap and a scarf, a black overcoat, a business suit and sports shoes.

The character of the typical American woman is friendly and outgoing, cheerful and talkative. She is quite independent and extrovert, and also has some caring qualities. Unfortunately, she is also self-centred and pompous. Quite a few observers consider her to be shallow, aggressive towards fellow human beings, ignorant, and too loud mouthed. At the end of the day, 47% of the observers like her, 29% do not, and the rest do not really know what to think. Those who admire her, underline her pleasant character, pretty face and sexy body. According to them, she is helpful and easy to communicate with. Some also underline her open and confident character. Those who dislike her, point out her arrogant, superficial and pretentious qualities, and the blunt behaviour of Western women in general. She is also considered to be egoistic and lacking substance.

It was not, after all, only the South Asian host gaze that had eroticized the Western woman tourist. Also the US women students in the survey supported the widespread perceptions. The USA is a nation of many ethnicities and traditions, but women of the entertainment industry are more uniform and can be adopted as the type specimen for the nation. Moreover, the Western women on screen are more familiar to the local gaze than the visiting women, with their transitory existence. Consequently, the unknown tourist women become attached to the attribute schemes of their acquainted 'digital sisters', not only in India but other tourism destinations of the world.

The collage portrays the 'Goddess America' of the South Asian host gaze in detail: Pamela America is attractive with sex appeal and likes to show her body in public, being dressed in revealing clothes. She is outgoing and independent, and therefore easy to approach. On the other hand, her values can be considered to be somewhat shallow and she apparently is not submissive enough for a number of respondents, for those who come from more patriarchal societies than the USA. They added the slight critique of amorality in the collage. She also does not know how to behave properly in social situations and is too self-serving. In conclusion, the typically US/Western woman elicits admiration but is also defined as code-breaking, just the way she was perceived to be in the South Asian travel scene.

Conclusions

Morality is a situational issue. We foreign tourists are amoral if measured by the scale of traditional sSouth Asian customs and values, although probably not more so than the South Asians themselves are if measured by the scale of our values (Hottola,

2002a, b). Western tourist women certainly seem loose from the viewpoint of a society where the women's role is restricted and sexuality in general is strictly controlled by extended families and the common public. The foreign women do occasionally dress in clothes that enhance the beauty of their body in ways unusual in India and Sri Lanka, they mix freely with non-relative men in public space, and undoubtedly are more promiscuous on average than South Asian women (see Ahuja, 1993; Kolanad, 1994). 'No religion, no family, no responsibilities, no limits in sex life' as one Muslim man summed up us Westerners in Bharatpur (Hottola, 1999, p. 312).

As we have seen, the West has recently been eroticized in the East from the Occidentalist point of view (see also Buruma and Margalit, 2004), much the same way the East was earlier eroticized in the West, in the spirit of Orientalism (Said, 1995). The US has also globally eroticized itself by the worldwide entertainment media. This would have been a shrewd way of spreading influence and seducing other cultures to share the American dream, if there had actually been a conspiracy behind it. I do not believe there was. It is, however, not an accident that 'Baywatch' has had wider global audiences than any other television series so far, or that X-rated materials so easily cross borders otherwise closed to Western capitalism (see also Featherstone, 1995). Even in the most traditional and ideologically anti-Western societies there is a demand for eroticism, based on one of the basic needs of human beings who perhaps live, in this regard, in repressive societal environments. With the imported entertainment, the local audiences may visit the West in their imagination.

It is the markets that spread the imagery, and since the introduction of the internet their task has become easy. The world has indeed become culturally more homogenous, partly because of the global media, which is for the time being controlled by relatively few producers and distributors (Herman and McChesney, 2001; Bose, 2006). The gaze of the Indian men and the seven other nationalities in the sociotype survey – including Sri Lanka – were remarkably similar. In other words, the South Asian host gaze was not as uneducated as has sometimes been assumed (cf. Maoz, 2006), but informed by imported imageries.

At times, also a self-created stereotype may become a problem in an unexpected way when nations meet in tourism. The case of the Israeli traveller woman portrays one extreme, but there are many less direct consequences of the host gaze. In India, it restricts the spaces available for tourists and affects the image of the nation as a travel destination, to name but two examples (see also Tasci, 2009). Some consequences may actualize only after the visit, with new or confirmed prejudices against South Asians who travel to the West (see Milman *et al.*, 1990; Pizam *et al.*, 1991) – another problematic host gaze.

In Bharatpur, the perceptually perceived and the extrasensory were intertwined and guided the interpretative gaze. A combination of locally prevalent views of women and their sexuality, biased interpretation of tourist behaviour, the dominant stereotypes of the West, low levels of factual information and a flow of one-sided information in the form of visual entertainment had contributed to the situation. The stereotype born in the process should not, however, be automatically labelled as a misconception, even though such an approach has been a common practice in stereotype studies. In order to define a misconception, one would to need to be able define 'accurate understanding', which does not exist in the strict sense. There is a multitude of understandings, each of them simultaneously 'accurate' and 'mistaken', depending on which standpoint the evaluation is made from.

The local societal structures turned the unescorted women into transitory targets of code-breaking advances and induced men

to behave in a regressive manner. As Michel Foucault (1980, p. 55) has said: 'The phenomenon of the social body is the effect not of a consensus but the materiality of power operating on the bodies of individuals.' The way the body of women travellers became exploited in south Asian public space speaks volumes about power relations in that space. The gaze of the tourists, a tiny minority, did next to nothing to change the local realities. It was the gaze of the locals that changed things on the tourist side.

There appears to be one powerful lens and filter through which the host gaze adjusts itself to the arrival of the US/Western tourist woman, on the streets and screens of the eight nations in this study, but the interpretations of the sojan real-and-imagined space vary depending on cultural proximity or distance, particularly in regard to gender relations and perceptions of a female as a human being. Both the gaze and the interpretations are negotiable and evolve through time.

Most importantly, for the women 'on the road', the consequences vary according to a number of variables in the local societal space, even though the perceptions themselves are relatively similar, and the women themselves also have negotiating power. In some places such as Northern India, the Western women stood out in the bodyscape of the streets, not only because of their observable qualities – their individual sex appeal, code-breaking behaviour and appearance – but also because of the demeaned and idealized stereotype of a Western woman. For women travellers, the public space was consequently not Goffman's (1963) 'realm of unfocused attention' but a realm of attention focused on them. Somewhere else they may be noticed and observed with a relatively similar gaze, without instantly becoming magnets of interest.

References

Ahuja, R. (1993) *Indian Social System*. Rawat, Jaipur.
Barnouw, E. and Krishnaswamy, S. (1980) *Indian Film*. Oxford University Press, New York.
Belliveau, J. (2006) *Romance on the Road: Traveling Women Who Love Foreign Men*. Beau Monde, Baltimore, MD.

Berno, T. and Ward, C. (2005) Innocence abroad: a pocket guide to psychological research on tourism. *American Psychologist* 60(6), 593–600.

Bhabha, H.K. (1994) *The Location of Culture*. Routledge, London.

Bhatia, H.S. (1979) *European Women in India – Their Life and Adventures*. Deep and Deep, New Delhi.

Bond, M.H. (1986) Mutual stereotypes and the facilitation of interaction across cultural lines. *International Journal of Intercultural Relations* 10(3), 259–276.

Bose, D. (2006) *Brand Bollywood: a New Global Entertainment Order*. CABI, Wallingford.

Burton, R. and Arbuthnot, F.F. (1995) *The Kama Sutra of Vatsyayana*. Granada, London.

Buruma, I. and Margalit, A. (2004) *Occidentalism: the West in the Eyes of Its Enemies*. Penguin, New York.

Caton, K. and Santos, C. A. (2009) Images of the other: selling study abroad in a postcolonial world. *Journal of Travel Research* 48(2), 191–204.

Conlon, F.E. (1994) Hindu revival and Indian womanhood: The image and status of women in the writings of Vishnubawa Brahamachari. *South Asia* 17(2), 43–61.

Dann, G. (1996) The people of tourist brochures. In: Selwyn, T. (eds) *The Tourist Image: Myths and Myth Making in Tourism*. John Wiley, Chichester, pp. 61–82.

Davies, M., Longrigg, L., Montefiore, L. and Jansz, N. (eds) (1987) *Half the Earth – Women's Experiences of Travel Worldwide*. Pandora Rough Guides, London.

Featherstone, M. (1995) *Undoing Culture: Globalization, Postmodernism and Identity*. Sage, London.

Fiske, S. (1998) Stereotyping, prejudice, and discrimination. In: Gilbert, D. G., Fiske, S. T. and Lindzey, G. (eds) *The Handbook of Social Psychology*, Vol IV. Oxford University Press, New York.

Foucault, M. (1980) *Power/Knowledge: Selected Interviews and Other Writings, 1972–1977*. Gordon, C. (ed. snd trans.) The Harvester Press, Brighton.

Frohlick, S. (2007) Fluid exchanges: the negotiation of intimacy between tourist women and local men in a translational town in Caribbean Costa Rica. *City & Society* 19(1), 139–168.

Gannon, M.J. and Pillai, R. (2010) *Understanding Global Cultures: Metaphorical Journeys Through 29 Nations, Clusters of Nations, Continents, and Diversity*. Sage, Thousand Oaks, CA.

Garrick, D. (2005) Excuses, excuses: rationalization of western sex tourists in Thailand. *Current Issues in Tourism* 8(6), 497–509.

Goffman, E. (1963) *Behavior in Public Places: Notes on the Social Organization of Gatherings*. Free Press, London.

Goings, K. (2001) Aunt Jemima and Uncle Mose travel the USA. *International Journal of Hospitality & Tourism* 2(3–4), 131–161.

Government of India (2004) *India Tourism Statistics 2003*. Ministry of Tourism, Market Research Division, New Delhi.

Government of India (2011) Provisional population totals. In: Government of India, *Census of India*. Government of India, New Delhi, pp. 160–177.

Hall, S. (1968) *The Hippies: an American 'Moment'*. University of Birmingham Sub and Popular Culture Series No. 16, Birmingham.

Harasym, S. (1990) *Gayatri Chakravorty Spivak: the Post-Colonial Critic – Interviews, Strategies, Dialogues*. Routledge, London.

Herman, E.S. and McChesney, R.W. (2001) *The Global Media: the New Missionaries of Corporate Capitalism*. Continuum, New York.

Hottola, P. (1999) *The Intercultural Body: Western Woman, Culture Confusion and Control of Space in the South Asian Travel Scene*. Publications of the Department of Geography nr. 7, University of Joensuu, Joensuu.

Hottola, P. (2002a) Touristic encounters with the exotic west: blondes on the screens and streets of India. *Tourism Recreation Research* 27(1), 83–90.

Hottola, P. (2002b) Amoral and available? Western women travelers in South Asia. In: Swain, M. B. and Momsen, J. H. (eds) *Gender/Tourism/Fun?* Cognizant, Emsford, pp. 164–171.

Hottola, P. (2004) Culture confusion – intercultural adaptation in tourism. *Annals of Tourism Research* 31(2), 447–466.

Hottola, P. (2005) The metaspatialities of control management in tourism: backpacking in India. *Tourism Geographies* 7(1), 1–22.

Hottola, P. (2006) Paradise confused? Marketing South Africa for tourism in 1985 and 2002. *Aurora* 1, 91–111.

Hottola, P. (2008) Farewell, countercultural wanderer? Backpacker dress and styles in south Asia. *Tourism, Culture and Communication* 8(1), 45–52.

Hottola P. (2012a) The sociotype of United States and the Americans: Mr. Brad America and Mrs. Pamela America from California. *Tourism Geographies* 2012, 1–15.

Hottola, P. (2012b) Tourist spaces, behaviours and cultures – The metaspatialities of tourism. In: Wilson, J. (eds) *Routledge Handbook of Tourism Geographies: New Perspectives on Space, Place and Tourism.* Routledge, London, pp. 139–146.

Hottola, P. (2012c) Perceptions of the United States and the Americans: The Collage Approach. *Finisterra* 47. Accepted for publication in 2012.

IET (2011) *Movimientos Turísticos en Fronteras: Entradas de Turistas Según País de Residencia.* Instituto de Estudios Turisticos (IET), Madrid.

Iyer, P. (1988) *Video Night in Kathmandu and Other Reports from the Not-So-Far-East.* Alfred A. Knopf, New York.

Jayakar, P. (1996) *The Earth Mother.* Penguin, New Delhi.

Jeffery, P. (1984) *Frogs in a Well – Indian Women in Purdah.* Zed Books, London.

Kolanad, G. (1994) *Culture Shock! – India: a Guide to Customs and Etiquette.* Times Books International, Singapore.

Krebs, D.L. and Denton, K. (1997) Social illusions and self-deception: the evolution of biases in person perception. In: Simpson, J. A. and Kenrick, D. T. (eds) *Evolutionary Social Psychology.* Lawrence Erlbaum, Mahwah, NJ, pp. 21–48.

Lea, J.P. (1988) *Tourism and Development in the Third World.* Routledge, London.

MacCannell, D. (1999) *The Tourist: a New Theory of the Leisure Class.* University of California Press, Berkeley, CA.

MacIntyre, C. (2012) *Tourism and Retail: the Psychogeography of Liminal Consumption.* Routledge, Abingdon.

MacRae, C.N., Milne, A.B. and Bodenhousen, G.V. (1994) Stereotypes as energy-saving devices: a peek inside the cognitive toolbox. *Journal of Personality and Social Psychology* 66(1), 37–47.

Mandelbaum, D.C. (1988) *Women's, Seclusion and Men's Honor: Sex Roles in North India, Bangladesh and Pakistan.* University of Arizona Press, Tucson, AZ.

Maoz, D. (2004) The conquerors and the settlers: two groups of Young Israeli backpackers in India. In: Richards, G. and Wilson, J. (eds) *The Global Nomad: Backpacker Travel in Theory and Practice.* Channel View, Clevedon, pp. 109–122.

Maoz, D. (2006) The mutual gaze. *Annals of Tourism Research* 33(1), 221–239.

McClintock, A. (1995) *Imperial Leather: Race, Gender and Sexuality in the Colonial Contest.* Routledge, New York.

Mehta, G. (1979) *Karma Cola: Marketing the Mystic East.* Jonathan Cape, London.

Milman, A., Reichtel, A. and Pizam, A. (1990) The impact of tourism on ethnic attitudes: the Israeli-Egyptian case. *Journal of Travel Research* 29(2), 45–49.

Moufakkir, O. (2008) Destination image revisited: the Dutch market perceptions of Morocco as a tourism destination. In: Burns, P. and Novelli, M. (eds) *Tourism Development: Growth, Myths and Inequalities.* CABI, Wallingford, pp. 85–112.

Oppermann, M. and McKinley, S. (1997) Sexual imagery in the marketing of pacific tourism destinations. In: Oppermann, M. (eds) *Pacific Rim Tourism.* CABI, Wallingford, pp. 117–127.

Pickering, M. (2001) *Stereotyping – the Politics of Representation.* Palgrave, Basingstoke.

Pieterse, J.N. (1992) *White on Black: Images of Africa and Blacks in Western Popular Culture.* Yale University Press, New Haven, CT.

Pizam, A., Jafari, J. and Milman, A. (1991) Influence of tourism on attitudes: US students visiting USSR. *Tourism Management* 12(2), 47–64.

Pritchard, A. (2000) Ways of seeing 'them' and 'us': tourism representation, race and identity. In: Robinson, M., Long, P., Vans, N., Sharpley, R. and Swarbrooke, J. (eds) *Expressions of Culture, Identity and Meaning in Tourism.* Business Education Publishers, Sunderland, pp. 245–262.

Rampal, S.N. (1978) *Indian Women and Sex.* Printox, New Delhi.

Rudman, L.A., Greenwald, A.G. and McGhee, D.E. (2001) Implicit self-concept and evaluative implicit gender stereotypes: self and ingroup share desirable traits. *Personality and Social Psychology Bulletin* 27 (9), 1164–1178.

Ryan, C. and Martin, A. (2001) Tourists and strippers: liminal theater. *Annals of Tourism Research* 28(1), 140–163.

Saarinen, J. and Niskala, M. (2008) Selling places and constructing local cultures in tourism: the role of the Ovahimba in Namibian tourism promotion. In: Hottola, P. (eds) *Tourism Strategies and Local Responses in Southern Africa.* CABI, Wallingford, pp. 61–72.

Santos, C.A. and Buzinde, C. (2006) Politics of identity and space: representational dynamics. *Journal of Travel Research* 45(3), 322–332.

Said, E.W. (1995) *Orientalism.* Penguin, Harmondsworth.

Schneider, D.J. (2004) *The Psychology of Stereotyping.* Guilford, New York.

Seneviratne, M., Candappa, E. and Haas, H. (1988) *Sri Lanka and You: a Traveller's Guide.* Inter Cult, Bandarawela.

Stewart, R.A., Powell, G.E. and Chetwynd, S.J. (1979) *Person Perception and Stereotyping.* Saxon House, London.

Soja, E.W. (1996) *Thirdspace: Journeys to Los Angeles and Other Real-and-Imagined Places.* Blackwell, Cambridge.

Tasci, A.D.A. (2009) Social distance: the missing link in the loop of movies, destination image, and tourist behavior? *Journal of Travel Research* 47(4), 494–507.

Tivers, J. (2012) Tourism, space and gender. In: Wilson, J. (eds) *The Routledge Handbook of Tourism Geographies.* Routledge, London, pp. 90–96.

Triandis, H. (1994) *Culture and Social Behavior.* McGraw-Hill, New York.

Triandis, H. (1995) A theoretical framework for the study of diversity. In: Chemers, M. M., Oskamp, S. and Costanzo, M. A. (eds) *Diversity in Organizations: New Perspectives fora Changing Workplace.* Sage, Thousand Oaks, CA, pp. 11–36.

Turner, L. and Ash, J. (1975) *The Golden Hordes – International Tourism and the Pleasure Periphery.* Constable, London.

UNWTO (2011) *UNWTO Tourism Highlights.* 2011 Edition. World Tourism Organization (UNWTO), Madrid.

Upadhyay, H.C. (1991) *Status of Women in India.* Vols I–II. Anmol, New Delhi.

Ward, T. (1996) *Arousing the Goddess: Sex and Love in the Buddhist Ruins of India.* Somerville, Toronto.

Wilson, P. (1997) Paradoxes of tourism in Goa. *Annals of Tourism Research* 24(1), 52–75.

Zicklin, G. (1983) *Countercultural Communes – a Sociological Perspective.* Contributions in Sociology nr. 44. Greenwood Press, Westport, CT.

16 Synthesis – the Eye of Power in and Through Tourism: the Banal Ubiquity of Agents of Naturalization

Keith Hollinshead and Chunxiao Hou

Introduction

The scopic drive of tourism revisited

The function of this chapter is to distill what has been learnt about the tourist gaze in the chapters offered by the contributors to this book. This distillation will be carried out via the following seven steps: first, the meaning of the umbrella term 'the scopic drive of tourism' will be revisited; second, the opening observations of Hollinshead and Kuon from Chapter 1 will be revisited in terms of how Urry and others have sought to contextualize the French litero-philosophical concept of *le regard* in tourism and travel, and the meaning of 'eye dialectics' will be brought into play in that respect; third, the catalysing thought of Foucault will be revisited in terms of how all sorts of things are 'seen' (or rather 'known') in all sorts of institutional, industrial and insular settings, and the meaning of the introduced Foucauldian concept of 'juridical space' will be touched upon once again in terms of its relevance for the declarative authority(ies) of tourism and travel; fourth, further coverage will be given as to what Urry appears to have explicitly and implicitly stated in terms of his (perhaps) fast and loose mining of *le regard* and his

application of 'the gaze' to tourism; fifth, an inspection will be given as to what each of the contributors in this 2012 book now offers in terms of their various case studies and commentaries of the tourist gaze in their selected host gaze/host–visitor/host–locale settings, and particular critique will be given as to what they individually and collectively say about Foucauldian practices of governmentality and Urryan consequences of gazing; sixth, some summary statements will be put forward as to how the contributors in this volume have seemingly elevated or neutralized aspects of our received wisdom as to what the tourist gaze conceivably is as a general eye-of-power, and thereby as to what operationally the host gaze may particularly constitute in that light; seventh, some prospective statements will be generated as to how what managers, administrators and planners in tourism and travel do and say matters, and as to how what researchers in Tourism Management and Tourism Studies think and identify matters – with a view to throwing further light on the required research agendas of our time on the normalization of peoples, places and pasts in tourism and travel, and thus into the ubiquitous (we-all-engage-in-it-everywhere) ordinary and therefore banal naturalization of the heritages, the spaces and the drawcards of tourism.

© CAB International 2013. *The Host Gaze in Global Tourism*
(eds O. Moufakkir and Y. Reisinger)

Hence this summary chapter comprises a synthesis of *the completely commonplace repertoires and reaches* of those who work in tourism and travel and of those who investigate tourism and travel quantitatively or qualitatively: it stands as an early 21st century assessment of what we know today about the human and ahuman role of agents of naturalization (agents of normalization) that characterize each place and every space.

Recap One: the Meaning of 'Eye Dialectics'

In the opening chapter of this book Hollinshead and Kuon provided a useful examination of the French litero-philosophical term *le regard* contextualized for Tourism Management and Tourism Studies as they sought to provide a scene-setting introduction to Foucault's insights into the eye-of-authority, which acts through the institutions, the organizations and the agencies that act powerfully in tourism and also in research into tourism. In probing Foucault's observations on 'surveillance', on 'power/knowledge' and on 'will-to-power', within the *dispostif* (i.e. the governing apparatus) of such institutions, organizations and agencies, Hollinshead and Kuon's treatment of eye dialectics attempted to show how 'quiet' and seemingly 'smalltime' but ultimately significant and essentializing powers of judgement and governance may so frequently be caught up within the authoritative mix that constitutes the totalizing discourse and the objectifying praxis of those institutions as certain preferred visions of heritage, of society and of the world are normalized and made universal through Tourism Management and/or research into tourism and travel. Through this distillation of the Foucauldian concept of surveillance, Hollinshead and Kuon attempted to extend Urry's (1990) earlier adroit translation of the French humanistic construction of *le regard* by revealing how an individual who works in Tourism Management (and, importantly, also the individual who travels) may be seen to some degree to be *homo docilis*; that is, someone who not

only engages in the petty and the quotidian governance of the world and in the related objectification of its social, cultural, natural and geographical milieux, but becomes an individual who administrates herself, and thereby disciplines herself through the scopic drive (i.e. the outlooks of surveillance) which she supports in her everyday work in and across tourism. Thus, this opening chapter on the eye dialectics of tourism was an endeavour to sharpen up what could be seen to be the somewhat blunt and unelaborate Foucauldian insights that Urry (1990) had provided in his best-selling text.

One may argue, however, that the observations of Hollinshead and Kuon were also insufficiently translative for the maturing field of Tourism Studies, and the dictates of available journal space in an opening chapter of a book reduced the degree to which they were able to provide penetrative transcriptions of Foucauldian ideas on normalization of and through universalized vision and on the objectification of and through totalized talk and practice for Tourism Studies. Such matters of the everyday dominance and subjugation of peoples, places and pasts warrants much fuller scrutiny, and much more pointed ferriage of Foucault's constructions into Tourism Studies. One could argue that many of the subsequent contributions to this book have richly added to our understanding of 'eye dialectics' at play and in performance through tourism. Individually and cumulatively, these subsequent chapters have significantly coloured in that conceptual conveyability: they variously (if unevenly) elaborate further upon Foucault's ideas on the way the scopic drive of institutions in tourism additively (over time) totalizes the world (a field-force of subjectivity that indeed occurs in all other domains and demesnes of human endeavour, according to Foucault's theses on the *governmentality* of things) as the so called agents-of-normalcy of those institutions in tourism and travel – or wherever – suspectingly (but more powerfully, *unsuspectingly*) indulge in their petty games of truth and participate in their micro-power projections of privilege.

This elaboration providing a follow-up chapter to Hollinshead and Kuon now seeks to synthesize what has been learnt in terms of the appreciation of *le regard* and 'the gaze'. It constitutes an attempt to show how and where Foucauldian critique has been and can be brought more concertedly into Tourism Studies, not so much as a fresh bureau of investigative approaches, but more as a re-tooling or a re-empowering of the existing conceptual work of the work of Shames and Glover (1989), of Fjellman (1992), of Richter (1994), of Edwards (1996), of Hall (1996), of Kirshenblatt-Gimblett (1998), of Meethan (2001), of Franklin (2009) and of others on matters of the normalization and naturalization of things in Tourism Management and in research into tourism and travel. The purpose of this synthesis – as built on the various offerings of the contributors to Moufakkir and Reisinger here – is to show that Foucauldian insight into the surveillance of organizations and agencies is not merely some vague, esoteric and acutely philosophical pursuit of little operational value to tourism management and operation, but it is a highly luminous and richly productive way in which the day-to-day governance of tourism and travel can be made understandable and traceable. It stands as an attempt to show that there are all kinds of readily observable thoughts and conscious and subconscious intentions behind and within the *governmentality* (or, rather, within the governmentalities) of tourism, where that which governs 'is not just a [removed] power needing to be tamed or a [supreme] authority needing to be legitimized. It is an [everyday] activity and [ubiquitous] art which concerns all [who manage, develop and research] and which touches each [who manage, develop and research]' (Burchell *et al.*, 1991). The concluding realization from this chapter (and thereby from the work of the pool of contributors to the book) is thereby that 'there is a parcel of [governing] thought in even the crassest and most obtuse parts of the social reality' (Burchell *et al.*, 1991) whether it be located in managed tourism, in developed travel or in the researched trade of either.

Thus, taken in tandem with the opening chapter, this summary chapter comprises the endeavour to inspect how much of Foucault's insight into 'governmental rationality' was indeed captured by Urry (1990) in his highly praised work *The Tourist Gaze* according to the mixed bag of commentators assembled by Moufakkir and Reisinger. To that end, it is crucial to closely outline what Urry himself meant when he adapted Foucault's construction of the magisterial or clinical gaze of organizations specifically for tourism and travel: namely, what did Urry mean by the take-home term 'the tourist gaze', *per se*? It is important to scrutinize the ways in which Urry delineated *the tourist gaze* as that set of disciplinary techniques by which the nature and the practice of the governance of tourism and travel is carried out. Hence, this summary chapter seeks to clarify just what Urry proffered as the principal characteristics of the microphysics of the power that is *the tourist gaze* – something that Urry did not himself do at length or accessibly, perhaps. Rather, it is something that can instead be painstakingly reconstructed from the various ways in which the contributors to this book have taken further the ideas cryptically posited by Urry in his landmark 1990 work.

Recap Two: The Meaning of Tourism as 'Juridical Space'

Just over a decade ago, at a millennial moment conference on tourism and travel, and within an assessment of how a Foucauldian approach in Tourism Studies could conceivably compare with the research agendas of various contemporary investigators of tourism and travel, Hollinshead (1999) examined Foucault's work from the point of view of the following 12 illustrative and suggestive (rather than comprehensive) outlooks: namely, in terms of:

1. The relations of power;
2. The normalizing consequences of the exercise of power;
3. The ubiquitous illusory projections of tourism;
4. The closed fields of knowledge of tourism;

5. The political apparatus of tourism;

6. The rhetoric of tradition in tourism;

7. Individual action in the management and administration of tourism;

8. The seductive properties of the semiotics of tourism;

9. Invisible sites of mediated coercion;

10. Transformative political events;

11. The disjunctive temporalities of dominant or suppressed populations;

12. The creation or invention of 'totalized' objects.

These twelve outlooks, or commonly defined Foucauldian issue arenas, are still useful for deployment in Tourism Management and Tourism Studies. In that millennial presentation at Sheffield in the UK, Hollinshead (1999) examined the work of a sample of established Tourism Studies researchers who were already conducting research in that issue arena as cited, and then the evidential relevance of Foucault's own line of attack (as translated for Tourism Studies) was given for it. Thereby, the Sheffield presentation table suggested that Foucauldian forms of critique of governmentality could fruitfully be deployed in Tourism Studies to pry into:

- For issue arena 1: relations of power
- The making visible of the privilege – bestowing networks of various management and development practices in tourism (which are all too frequently hidden or unsuspected).
- For issue arena 2: normalizing consequences
- The making visible of the invented nature of notions of society that are exhibited in tourism (whereby those promoted notions of societal place or societal identity are not so much 'given' as 'made' in discourse and praxis).
- For issue arena 3: ubiquitous illusory projections
- The making visible of the everyday essentializing power of tourism articulations of people, places and pasts (where so much of the industry's powers of representation and objectification is illusory).
- For issue arena 4: closed fields of knowledge
- The making visible of the huge potential for the projection of culturally violent storylines through the discursive suppressions and in-service subjugations of tourism and travel (particularly where only narrow pre-selected ranges of storylines are articulated through the entrepreneurial talk or through the commodifed deeds of industry practitioners).
- For issue arena 5: political apparatus
- The making visible of the opaque apparatuses of administration and of pre-judgement or pre-suppression by which means tourism narratives and tourism services are normalized (and on which the promotions and actions of the industry are regularly platformed);
- For issue arena 6: rhetoric of tradition
- The making visible of the potential role of tourism as an important source of transformative knowledge – production about peoples, places and pasts (not just as a channel of externally derived narrative about things);
- For issue arena 7: individual action
- The making visible of the need for institutions to regularly critique the games of truth they may be indulging in (and of the need for individuals within those agencies or organizations to more concertedly self-examine the character of their own will-to-power);
- For issue arena 8: seductive properties of semiotics
- The making visible of the infinite number of alternative styles of interpretation and contested articulations of difference or interest that invisibly lie within the language(s) of tourism (and that variously relate to rise or fall of different 'doxa' ['doxa' – holding populations] in a given territory);
- For issue arena 9: mediated coercion
- The making visible of tourism and travel as an important site of juridical space where all sorts of judgements and pre-judgements are made or exercised that render some populations dominant and others suppressed (and where all sorts of privileges are bestowed upon the same constructions of culture, history, geography and nature vis-à-visother

conceptualizations of culture, history, geography and nature);

- For issue arena 10: transformative political events
- The making visible of subtle changes in rationality across different economic, different cultural, different political and different other contexts across the world of tourism and travel (particularly where seemingly imperceptible transformations of meaning are involved);
- For issue arena 11: disjunctive temporalities
- The making visible of the incohesive affiliations of local, mobilizing and diffuse populations within states (and the mapping of those changes in the profile and juxtaposition of those disjunctive temporalities overtime, as occasioned through developments in or of tourism);
- For issue arena 12: 'totalized' objects
- The making visible of the manner in which things have been inappropriately essentialized or indecently subjectified through tourism (and of the way in which certain natural or cultural phenomenon have become appropriated via false totalizations or false naturalizations).

Hollinshead and Hou now seek to redeploy the above 12 issue arenas, for they were never formally published despite being presented at the University of Northumbria's well-attended international conference in Sheffield. Later in this summary chapter, they will each be used to gauge what the various contributors to Moufakkir and Reisinger have freshly and specifically unearthed to elucidate on *le regard*, the tourist gaze and eye dialectics.

The deployment of such conceptual constructions (as encapsulated in the Sheffield set) in and across the micro-physics and macro-physics of power as exercised in and through the eye dialectics of tourism, may be expected to unearth a litany of previously unsuspected (or, at least, underinspected) instances of how certain usages of power – that is, of power/knowledge formations – held an almost absolute capacity

to muzzle and regulate individuals. Such constructions of the order of things in tourism and travel would constitute an examination of the games of truth that inevitably lie here and there within the tourism industry and that inevitably crop up round and across the travel trade (as they conceivably appear to do in all other domains (Danaher *et al.*, 2000). It should be realized, though, that such Foucauldian manifestations of truth (i.e. such encountered power relations) are always to some extent potentially reversible (Morris and Patton, 1979). Consonantly, under Foucauldian thought, the suppressed need not always be suppressed, particularly if they learn to appreciate the degree to which they may have been blindly participating in discourse and praxis that sustains their own very suppression.

Caveat: the Dimension of the Tourist Gaze – Urry's Translation of Foucault's Scopic Drive

Having attempted to clarify how Foucauldian lines of critique into practical philosophy can readily and productively be deployed in tourism and travel to probe the held rationalities that determine the order of things in and across the industry, it is now propitious to examine in closer detail the degree to which Urry (1990) faithfully built Foucauldian outlooks into his own construction of 'the tourist gaze'. Now clearly, since Foucault did not himself pass judgement on the nature or profile of any industry as globally tentacular as the tourism industry, Urry's effort ought not so much be sincerely transcribed Foucauldian ideas *exactly* or *literally* to the industry, but rather in terms of the degree to which his concept of 'the tourist gaze' perhaps does creditable service as an extension of Foucauldian *logique* into the domain of tourism and travel in the spirit of Foucault's clinical gaze and magisterial gaze (Merquior, 1989). In this respect, Urry's endeavour to relocate Foucauldian discursive model of knowledge and of power across service settings (from the conglomerate profiles of the medical service and the prison service to the disparate-*cum*-linear profiles of the tourism industry) conceivably matches in kind Lindstrom's (1990) thoughtful and earnest attempt to relocate Foucauldian thought away from Foucault's own visual theoretical targets in open cosmopolitan Western Europe to the removed apography and closely contained island culture of the South Pacific.

In Hollinshead (1999), a brief critique was given of Urry's deployment of the term 'the tourist gaze' via the use of six broad questions:

- What is the fundamental nature of the tourist gaze?
- What do 'gazers' principally do in tourism and travel?
- What do 'gazers' also do in tourism and tourism and travel?
- Why (else) is the tourist gaze important?
- What are the consequences of the tourist gaze?
- What other features or tangential trends of the tourist gaze are significant?

In light of the absence of a clean, clear and comprehensive explanation (from Urry himself) of what indeed constitutes 'the tourist gaze', Hollinshead's presentation at Sheffield in 2000 comprised an interpretation of what Urry appears to have built into his composite concept. That Sheffield Millennium delivery has consisted of a refinement of the points previously registered in Hollinshead (1999), and it details pointed references to both Urry (1990) and to his valuable follow-up piece of work in the *American Behavioral Scientist* journal some 2 years later (Urry, 1992).

So, indeed, what does Urry conceivably imply 'the tourist gaze' consists of or otherwise activates? A close reading of Urry (1990) and of Urry (1992) suggests that 'the tourist gaze' is a theoretical construction which embraces the following 38 interacting imperatives – registered here as A to Z and AA to LL:

(A) An institutional way of perceiving things (i.e. a highly scopic regime).
(B) A spectacle producing force (i.e. a highly ocularcentric marvel-making regime).
(C) A pungently contemporary mood (i.e. a voguish regime).
(D) A cool, anonymous, liminal, unengaged but empowering outlook on the world (i.e. a superficial, uninvolving regime).
(E) A revelatory power of or about culture and inheritance (i.e. an admixed regime that exposes interestingly yet highly selectively as it recombines with other forces in and of culture).
(F) A highly dramatic and reproductive performative force (i.e. a regime that 'makes' and 'manufactures' as it 'makes manifest').
(G) A self-celebratory mood of unification (i.e. a self-congratulatory/rallying regime).
(H) A normalizing, universalizing, mainstreaming power (i.e. a concretizing and privilege-bestowing regime).
(I) An unconscious will-to-truth (i.e. an unsuspected or under-suspected regime of compilation to 'place' and 'position' things in relation to one's own felt world-order)
(J) An impulse to self-actualize and see, know, and talk of and about the world and also 'be' therein (i.e. a regime of inquiry and articulation).
(K) An impulse to be supreme or superior in and across the world (i.e. a regime of heightened and comparative pride).
(L) An ethos of difference and celebrated 'specialness' (i.e. a regime of imagined distinctness and exhibited uniqueness).
(M) A celebration of pleasure and fun (i.e. a hedonistic regime of self-indulged immersion in that which is desired – of animated *joie de vivre* and play).
(N) A spirit of freedom and mobility (i.e. a regime of liberation to be, to travel, to see).
(O) A spirit of escape from responsibilities and care (i.e. a regime of liberation from domesticity).
(P) A celebration of choice in/of life (i.e. a regime of profusion).
(Q) An experiential mood of novelty-seeking encounters (i.e. a regime of infective (but generally superficial) sensation).
(R) A compulsion to consume (i.e. a regime of owned experience/possessed object/marketplace-captured-entity).
(S) An impulse to appropriate 'the other' (i.e. a regime of cultural conquest).

(T) An industrializing outlook on or over the world (i.e. a regime predicated upon productivist/developmentalist/progressivist notions).

(U) A utilitarian re-evaluation of the natural/inherited world (i.e. a regime that harnesses that which is serviceable).

(V) A professionalized outlook (i.e. a regime of conspiracist, banausic profanities).

(W) A falsifying order generally shorn of traditional value or embedded worth (i.e. a regime of decorous, expedient 'value' and mediated 'myth' ... a regime of 'fantasque').

(X) A highly inventive and hyper-real projectivity (i.e. a regime of heightened creativity and inflationary fanciful fecundity).

(Y) An essentializing framework (i.e. a regime that invents and bestows imagined pedigrees on peoples, places, and/or pasts).

(Z) A portrayal of the 'elevated' ordinary (i.e. a regime that triumphalizes the assumed 'simple', 'customary' or 'prosaic').

(AA) An anti-auratic temper (i.e. a de-differentiating regime that can disarticulate received differences in and of things).

(BB) A mediated world of massified consciousness (i.e. a regime of mechanized or electronic kinematics).

(CC) A potently postmodern and implosive spirit (i.e. a regime of accelerating abandonment that casually replaces the received, the foundational and the established with the new, the ephemeral and the hybrid).

(DD) A fleeting, transitional re-envisionment of culture and community (i.e. a regime of reduced and decontextualized understanding).

(EE) A compulsively semiotic world order (i.e. a regime of constant signification and directive representation).

(FF) A place-making power (i.e. a regime that manufactures local identity, and that generally engenders a highly inventive sense of place).

(GG) A romantic affectation about self and of quaint nostalgia about the world (i.e. a regime of whimsical allure and sentimental attachment towards the seemingly 'pastoral' world).

(HH) A sentiment that selectively sacralizes nature as being bounteous and wonderful (i.e. a regime of mild (but generally not informed) awe of and about nature that anthropomorphizes and reculturalizes it, or otherwise that denaturalizes it).

(II) A submissive temper (i.e. a regime that promotes ease and passivity in the getting of experience and the gain of sensation).

(JJ) A democratizing or popularizing power (i.e. a regime that reflects an egalitarian spirit, or that otherwise conjures one up ubiquitously across the world).

(KK) An internationalizing mood (i.e. a regime that privileges the global connectivity and ecumenical reach of things).

(LL) An aestheticization of life (i.e. a regime that accentuates the creative, artistic, atmospheric and sumptuous merit in and of objects, ideas and places – though not necessarily in terms of received, orthodox or conventional differentiations).

Clearly then, Urry does not envision the gaze as being one single or constant thing! The close scrutiny of *The Tourist Gaze* which led to the interpretive production of the above 38 different imperatives or characterizations suggests that within Urry:

- The plurality of tourist gazes
- There are many sometimes distinct and sometimes interfusive 'sub–gazes' rather than one all-purpose magisterial *le regard* in tourism and travel.
- The historicity of tourist gazes
- The gaze (or other, these gazes) may change considerably over time.
- The complexities and counter-complexities of the imperatives behind tourist gazes
- There may sometimes be internal disjunction between the imperatives behind any such sub-gazes (where for instance (AA) 'the pressure through the tourist gaze to build up an anti-auratic temper', may lie in tension with (LL) 'the pressure to aestheticize life', and where (I) 'the highly activated drive towards an unconscious will-to-truth' may work with some disaccord against other 'passive' or submissive tempers [such as II]).

Such is the complexity of human outlooks on life being and identity: such is merely reflective of the richer rational, irrational or arational make-up of the dance (or rather, the dances) of our depolarizing and yet repolarizing lives. No one should expect that the realm of life we label 'tourism' or 'travel' should be any more fathomable or any more classifiable than the intricacies of 'life' itself. This crude external deconstruction of Urry's tourist gaze therefore seems to tell us that in tourism and travel, tourists, travel programmers and leisure managers *are all driven* by a litany of different (sometimes conflictive) impulses, and that they also coterminously *drive* a litany of different (sometimes conflictive) impulses, themselves.

And obviously, the deconstruction embedded within the above long list of potential/actual is only one individual's (Hollinshead's) fast interpretation of what Urry inferred, implied or was indicative about in his undefined term 'the tourist gaze'! No doubt some readers of this book may find that the deconstruction offered is not sufficiently 'vision-based' vis-á-vis being 'imaginatio-based', *per se*. No doubt some astute social economists will insist that the above lengthy deconstruction does not reflect the degree to which Urry views 'the tourist gaze' as being largely a middle class imposition on and over the world. No doubt there are other readers of Urry elsewhere (especially those well versed in the Urry within Lash and Urry 1994) who would insist that the deconstruction offered via the medium of the protracted list (of imperatives A to Z and AA to LL) is insufficiently reflective of Urry's strongly held views about the accelerating mobility of organized capitalism and citizenship whereby the tourist gaze is conceivably seen to be a highly representative cultural, geographic, economic, political and psychic sense of 'social flow' across space, place and territory. No doubt others would state that the above hasty outsider's deconstruction makes an insufficient effort to distinguish what Urry was stating about the nature of 'the tourist gaze' in his post-industrializing hinterland of northern England (namely, which is perhaps the strong and contained econo-geographical space *cum* psycho-structural axis of *The Tourist Gaze*) as

compared with what Urry was attempting to uncover in terms of the character of the tourist gaze *in a more generalized form* elsewhere around the globe. And no doubt there are specialists in 'time' out there who would maintain that the loose deconstruction provided here does not adequately capture what Urry was stating (or implying) about the subtle ways in which 'the tourist gaze' mirrors rich recent changes in social temporality.

The Critique: Fresh Scrutiny of the Governmentality of Foucault and Urry

In examining the chapters that comprise this book on the host gaze and its supposed ramifications, many different sorts of 'gaze' have been covered. For some of the contributors, understanding the gaze in action is almost the straightforward matter of comparing resident attitudes against visitor attitudes (Gelbman), and Moufakkir is confident that a sound psychoanalyst is the required and sufficient analytical beast-of-burden to do that sort of job. Other contributors are adamant that there is little merit in working with singular concepts as to what the gaze might indeed be (Canziani and Francioni, O'Regan), and Pattison condemns 'host gaze' and 'guest gaze/visitor gaze' assessments as being poor in capturing the panoply of impulses and aspirations that drive *tourism* (as opposed to 'tourists', *per se*). Sadly, none of the contributors provided a rich explanation of the steps by which they conducted their respective critiques of the host gaze, the tourist gaze or whatever, at work, and (for instance) it was frustrating not to be able to assess how 'grounded' the claimed grounded theory findings of Gelbman and Collins-Kreiner actually were. But Hottola's work on grounded collage approaches deserves to be repeated and experimented with in a litany of other contexts.

While some of the contributors have worked with a contained classification as to what *the tourist gaze* (it really belongs just to tourists! (Bunten) or *the host gaze* is, and tend to operate with positivist notions that there is a singular reality out there that can be densely known (where the host gaze or local gaze is seen to be 'closer to [that] reality' (Gelbman and Collins-Kreiner), other contributors have adopted much more flexible constructionist *cum* constructivist understandings that draw upon social theorists of mobility such as Edensor to interpret the various overlaps and the highly contextualized threshold places and spaces of tourism (e.g. O'Regan). Accordingly, Bunten still appears to be satisfied exploring the definitive (and almost 'fixed') character of front stage locales (the supposed realm of tourists) and back stage locales (the supposed realm of hosts). O'Regan would no doubt insist that such watertight MacCannellian inspections miss the highly varied and highly unpredictable dynamics of not only 'being' but also of 'becoming'. But Hottola's work on grounded collage approaches deserves to be repeated and experimented with in a litany of other contexts.

While several of the contributors to this book clearly salute Urry as being the originator of tourist gaze and host gaze thinking (Gelbman and Collins-Kreiner) and even the 'tamer' of it (Moufakkir), others (as will be discussed later in this chapter) give indirect credit to Foucault, and even to a longer continental literophilosophical origin emanating back to the Renaissance (Ankor and Wearing). But even though Foucault and other continental theorists may be acknowledged as primary conceptualists, it does not mean that the Foucauldian or the originating literophilosophical position has been faithfully adhered to. For instance, Canziani and Francioni see the tourist gaze as an external entity and as something that the host has to respond to, rather than being something that they have helped compose *relationally* as Foucault's notion of power/knowledge subjectivity would demand. Thus, to Canziani and Francioni, the tourist gaze is a distinct externality, which hosts can learn to not only internalize, but also consciously manage. Perhaps that view of the gaze diminishes the force of the Foucauldian

concept of the gaze, for Foucault deems it to be more virulent, important, and potentially 'violent' or 'positively productive' when it works institutionally in capillary fashion below the level of conscious and regular 'management'.

No doubt on account of such imponderables about relationality and consciousness, almost all of the contributors bemoan the general poverty of theory about the so called host–gaze encounter. Reisinger is keen to play with cultural relativist thought to throw light on the impacts and consequences of tourism, but recognizes that such relativist theory tends to unduly exaggerate cultural difference, *ipso facto*, and is not robust in its capacity to assess the fit of absolute vis-à-vis universal standards cross-culturally (Reisinger). Such relativisms are conceivably a blind alley to the heavily contextualized scrutiny of O'Regan, who is accordingly keen to break down adamantine boundaries between who indeed constitutes a 'host' and who a 'guest'. In a similar vein, Savener finds the moniker 'host' to be particularly misleading, and finds that too much assessment in Tourism Management/Tourism Studies is based on kneejerk understandings that routinely position 'the tourist' as the power-player and that routinely only inspect who the host is and what the host does through the medium of the lens of the tourist (Savener).

Although most of the contributors to this book supply useful conceptual coloration on the host–guest encounter, there is a regular and potent call amongst them for much more critical and perhaps less crudely empiricist forms of inspection (Gelbman and Collins-Kreiner). To this end, Bunten makes the case for a much richer critique of that which is supposedly inauthentic and that which is supposedly exploitative in the host–guest encounter – notably in terms of the different or contesting intergenerational responses that appear to exist in cross-cultural settings (Bunten). She records the often difficult-to-decipher sense of ambivalence that Indigenous 'hosts' she has studied in Alaska actually hold towards their clients (namely, to tourists, and by implication to tourism, itself). Ankor and Wearing are also decided that much more penetrative critical assessment is required to probe the tourist encounter, and weigh up the potential contributions of Lefebvre and of Lacan to help scaffold such future investigations. Perhaps O'Regan has advanced rather more pointedly along the trajectory to bring in deep-seated explanatory theory to matters of contemporary display and contemporary visitation, though, and the case he makes for the fast import of Borad's intelligent work on *agental realism* will hopefully be heard in many different encounter sites and settings and for many different lifestyle and lifecourse scenarios over the coming decades.

The call for richer or more fulsome critique of the host–guest encounter in fact has a number of noted refrains to it among the work of the contributors. While Bunten condemns analyses of the encounter that are based on overly static classifications of 'host' and 'visitor', Pattison maintains the gaze itself ought not be seen so much as a singular *event*, but as a *process*, of acquaintance, of learning and of adaptive disposition. Such an insight tallies closely with Canziani and Francioni's view that existing typologies of hosts and guests are much too restrictively scripted at present. And Pattison's refreshed thinking certainly accords well with O'Regan's judgement that all individuals involved in the tourism encounter are inevitably involved in an evolving process of 'passionate construction' with regard to the manner and fashions in which they *interdependently* respond to and *interdependently* activate and reactivate the who, the what, the where and the when of tourism encounter 'engagement'. Hence, Bunten, Pattison, Canziani and Francioni and O'Regan (and also Ankor and Wearing), all reject standardized classifications of and about the tourism encounter and tight 'binary models' of what a 'host' and a 'guest' conceivably are. In their respective ways, Bunten, Pattison, Canziani and Francioni, O'Regan and Ankor and Wearing all call for new sorts of critical mapping and monitoring of the subject positions that crop up in tourism locations,

where critical interpretation must be responsive to the very varied interactivities involved and to the very potent dynamisms generated there. And though so much of the promotion of projection of tourism focuses upon 'bodies' or 'bodily display', Hottola implicitly suggests that we are still immoderate in our understanding of how the dynamisms of the gaze translate into a or the materiality of power on or onto the bodies of individuals. Inherently, there is so much still to analyse about the ways in which (for instance) women travellers are contextually and/or situationally exploited in all sorts of tourism settings.

So what does this demand for richer criticality mean? To Canziani and Francioni it means Tourism Studies scholars must learn to situate the so-called tourism encounter in a wider range of facets of human life to be able to detect the plurality of roles that all individuals in a found 'encounter' may indulge in and the many entanglements that particular hosts may have with particular guests. To Canziani and Francioni, this consequentially involves a reduction of emphasis on 'the professional role' of hosts at these encounters, and the enriched cognizance of the extra-occupational relationships those tourism industry, travel trade or related field 'professionals' actually support. To O'Regan and to Pattison and to Canziani and Francioni such enriched critique would put less emphasis upon the significance of 'the encounter' itself, thereby minimizing the artificiality of the ruling dichotomy that currently is believed to exist between defined 'hosts' and defined 'guests'. And to Ankor and Wearing and O'Regan, it would help break the strict demarcation between 'self' and 'Other' that governs contemporary thought in Tourism Studies, and might help managers and researchers in tourism more clearly identify the presence of 'the Other' within all of us, and the fact that we are all (hosts, guests, bystanders) all on the move in some significant way or other. And perhaps O'Regan registers the call for added criticality best when he concludes that studies of the host–guest encounter really need to shift towards the view that each host, each guest, each bystander mutually constitutes each other: they (we) are not so much distinctly separate subjects but much-entangled objects. We have spent too much time in Tourism Management and Tourism Studies essentializing hosts and guests as fixed bodies thereby turning them into stereotypical 'things': we need to pay much more attention to what they each 'do', differentially, vis-à-vis their own repertoire of roles, purposes and meanings. While O'Regan implores that transdisciplinary stances are crucially needed to carry out more informed and relevant differentiation, other commentators (such as Coles *et al.*, 2006) will insist that in many neo-colonial, globalizing, postcolonial or decolonial settings in international tourism, discernment must be postdisciplinary in temper if uncertain or difficult identificatory matters of being, becoming and aspiration are to be effectively probed. Coles *et al.* will no doubt not concur with Moufakkir when he states that the within-discipline genius of 'improved psychoanalysis will be enough to do the deciphering of the cultural, social, political, and symbolic entwinement and interactivities of our ever-mobile time'.

A synthesis of what the contributors to this book have proffered in terms of our received understandings of the host gaze or tourist gaze 'at work', and thus of the possibilities of Foucauldian dialectics 'in action' is presented, followed by a matching interpretation of how the coverage of the host gaze and the tourist gaze by the motley crew of contributors further informs or challenges what Hollinshead and Kuon generated in the opening chapter in their 'takeaawy glossary on the (Foucauldian) scopic drive of Tourism'.

The aim here is not to yield close and definitive 'answers' as to what 'normalcy' is in terms of tourism encounters, or as to how 'the political apparatus of tourism' should be explored, for such matters are highly interpretive and distinctly contextual. After all, as Foucault himself once famously stated, as soon as one has reached an interpretation, there and then the art and craft of interpretation dies.

Nuanced Understandings on the Eye Dialectics of Foucault: Re-Regarding 'Le Regard'

Observations on the Foucauldian Scopic Drive, Vis-à-Vis Hollinshead's (2000) 12 Dimensions of and About the Tourism Gaze

Dimension 1: Relations of power

Many of the contributors to this volume bemoan the fact that too many practitioners and researchers of tourism and travel see *le regard* (the Foucauldian gaze) as a mere aspect of vision, not a broader matter of governing relationships (e.g. Ankor and Wearing). O'Regan – in fine Foucauldian hue – calls for more penetrative and robust understandings of not so much the relationships and allegiances that promote this or that in tourism, but the multiple and fast-changing character of those allegiances. Pattison – also in Foucauldian spirit – makes it clear that supposedly suppressed or subjugated populations always have 'resistance' options in the working of those power relationships. And though so much of the promotion of projection of tourism focuses upon 'bodies' or 'bodily display', Hottola implicitly suggests that we are still immoderate in our understanding of how the dynamisms of the gaze translate into a or the materiality of power on or onto the bodies of individuals. Inherently, there is so much still to analyse about the ways in which (for instance) women travellers are contextually and/or situationally exploited in all sorts of tourism settings.

Dimension 2: the normalizing consequences of the exercise of power

All of the contributors address the Foucauldian normalizing/naturalizing consequences of tourism directly or indirectly. Reisinger maintains that insufficient attention has been paid in Tourism Management and Tourism Studies to the longstanding culture-based biases of the media. Bunten supports the view that such normalizing effects may become transparent (and unnoticed) because of their sheer longevity.

O'Regan warns, however, that these days there is more merit in looking for co-constituted and dynamic forms of action rather than for forms of naturalization of things which are longstanding and almost unchanging.

Dimension 3: the ubiquitous illusory projections of tourism

Savener believes that many of the world's Indigenous (and suppressed/silenced) populations indeed suffer from the illusory projections of tourism, where the tourist gaze persistently projects them as a 'pure' folk. And though so much of the promotion of projection of tourism focuses upon 'bodies' or 'bodily display', Hottola implicitly suggests that we are still immoderate in our understanding of how the dynamisms of the gaze translate into a or the materiality of power on or onto the bodies of individuals. Inherently, there is so much still to analyse about the ways in which (for instance) women travellers are contextually and/or situationally exploited in all sorts of tourism settings. Other contributors (e.g. Gelbman and Collins-Kreiner) suggest that the initial gaze that tourists have of such populations is often brief and superficial, yet highly determinant in how these people and their places are subsequently seen to be: the tourist gaze is routinely not an enquiring one, according to such analyses. Ankor and Wearing demand much more thorough scrutiny, however, of how tourists and travellers indeed differentially engage with visited populations, places and spaces, and put forward the concept of the choraster to account for these sorts of rather particular engagement. This concept (the choraster) envisions travellers as having diverse and individuated rather than being uncommonly 'docile', as Foucauldian thought on the normalizing authority of force-field institutions would have it.

Dimension 4: the closed fields of knowledge of tourism

While Bunten adopts the strong Foucauldian stance that (in order to succeed in tourism), culture producers for Indigenous and subjugated populations have to learn fast how to think and operate in closed forms of non-Indigenous knowhow and procedure, Reisinger, Kozak and Visser warn that so limited may such ruling fields of knowledge be, that 'hosts' and 'guests' frequently provide and/or participate in tourism in a realm of considerable mutual misunderstanding. Wu and Pearce caution, however, that the views of few host communities are rarely ever 'uniform': the eye dialectics of local or resident populations is always much more diverse and unpredictable than surface understandings of the Foucauldian gaze would have us believe.

Dimension 5: the political apparatus of tourism

In writing about tourism development in The Gambia, Pattison adopts a strong Foucauldian line concerning the force of relational power (power/knowledge) as a productive machinery. O'Regan is also keen to apply Foucault's 'post-Althusserian notions' of the governing apparatuses of tourism management and development as technologies of subjectivation, though he is keen to punctuate that Foucauldian understanding about productive power (power/knowledge) with Borad's notion of governing apparatuses as 'physical-conceptual devices' that are much more open-ended in what they productively allow and productively help fertilize. To O'Regan, it is important to see the work of the governing apparatuses of tourism as material-discursive practices (again, after Borad), which are not so much fixed and static (as Foucauldian apparatuses of power/knowledge would normally be seen to be), but are much more responsive to dynamic 'rearrangements, rearticulations, and other reworking'.

Dimension 6: the rhetoric of tradition in tourism

To Bunten, the unenquiring presence and leverage of all sorts of middle-men in the tourism marketplace indeed enables old, stale and uninformed outlooks on and over 'the Other' to perpetuate. All too axiomatically, this rhetoric of tradition and primitivity tends to cultivate the hope or desire amongst tourists that they can indeed see and access 'the native world' in its 'true' primal state. O'Regan tends to concur with Bunten about the limited character of the generalized scopic drive of tourism, a drive that merely deals in terms of its own held awarenesses in a rehearsed (and contained) geography of locations, positions and routes.

Dimension 7: individual action in the management/administration of tourism

A number of the contributors to this book implicitly tend to suggest that Foucault's verdict that individuals (who work in closely regulated institutions or purblind organizations) have little scope for individual action is not entirely supportable. In covering 'the Indigenous host gaze' present in Alaska, Bunten notes that Indigenous guides become very skilled at 'deep acting' in self-inducing 'real feelings' to consciously manage and manipulate the host gaze: they are not Foucauldian dupes to it. In analyzing the orientation of the tourism industry in Israel to Russian and other tourists, Canziani and Francioni register the point that individuals who work in the travel trade are not only subject to the governing normalizations of their own home institution or home organization, they are also subject to the standards and assumptions of third party bodies (be they governmental, media, professional or whatever), which tends to dissipate the authority of singular scopic drives. But how controlled are those individuals who work for Tourism Studies research institutions rather than for Tourism Management operational bodies? Moufakkir is on the case (via his concept of the bystanding third gaze): watch this space in the second edition of this book, perhaps!

Dimension 8: the seductive properties of the semiotics of tourism

Clearly, the majority of the contributors to this book believe that the seductive authority of promotion and projection in tourism is over-stated: while (at face value) such representational agency is hugely influential (enn grossly determinant), individual tourists are actually very skilled at translating those supposedly seductive messages to their own aspirations and interests. Again, tourists are not axiomatically 'unthinking dupes' in the strong Foucauldian sense, it seems. To Gelbman and Collins-Kreiner, it is only early days in terms of the analysis of visitor minscapes vis-à-vis semiotic encoding and decoding. To O'Regan, much more deep critique is required to understand how particular tourists act 'in the world' and personally translate the symbols and significations they receive about destinations.

Dimension 9: invisible sited of mediated coercion

Evidently, it is (was) the force of invisible (i.e. Foucauldian code for unrecognized or under-recognized) structures and sites of mediated coercion that inspired this book. To Reisinger, Kozak and Visser, it is the industry's unwritten codes that have to be more deeply probed. To Moufakkir, the visible gazes clearly betray what lies imaginately beneath. But O'Regan warns that what is under-recognized in Tourism Studies is not only what is unsuspectingly normalized and hidden within the dominant capillary discourse and praxis of the tourism industry, but how what is normalized and hidden can meaningfully be read and interpreted. All too frequently, host–guest interactions are assessed economically, socially and culturally (i.e. inter-culturally) but they are not inspected affiliatively (i.e. psychically) in terms of the deep meanings that places and spaces have for visitors (or, for that matter, for hosts. Much more and much deeper understanding of 'invisible' non-economic, non-social and non-cultural ways in which places are reflexively imagined is called for. And though so much of the promotion of projection of tourism focuses upon 'bodies' or 'bodily display', Hottola implicitly suggests that we are still immoderate in our understanding of how the dynamisms of the gaze translate into a or the materiality of power on or onto the bodies of individuals. Inherently, there is so much still to analyse about the ways in which (for instance) women travellers are contextually and/or situationally exploited in all sorts of tourism settings.

Dimension 10: transformative political events

To Foucault, power was not something possessed by anyone or by any institution; it was a productive potential or productive relationality that existed between broader organizations and interest groups. Thus, 'power' was (is) the tension that exists between dominant and suppressed agencies. Savener has clearly taken such an understanding on board, and in her coverage of Indigenous agency in Panama, she draws attention to the options of aggressive resistance that the Kuna Yala people have themselves recognized to help themselves deal with the field of discourse and praxis that confronts them in and through tourism. Such matters of contingent and contextual reaction are also central to Borad's insights on agental realism. Borrowing heavily from Borad, O'Regan calls upon Tourism Studies researchers to inspect the dynamic intra-activities of the host–guest encounter to explore how identities are mutually constituted and formed and reformed transformatively. To O'Regan, both host and guest are not just highly 'mobile' today physically and geographically, they are highly mobile politically and affiliatively. And though so much of the promotion of projection of tourism focuses upon 'bodies' or 'bodily display', Hottola implicitly suggests that we are still immoderate in our understanding of how the dynamisms of the gaze translate into a or the materiality of power on or onto the bodies of individuals. Inherently, there is so much still to analyse about the ways in which (for instance) women travellers are contextually and/or situationally exploited in all sorts of tourism settings.

Dimension 11: the disjunctive temporalities of dominant and suppressed population

Foucault is often condemned for over-accentuating the degree to which suppressed, silenced or subjugated populations are governed through and contained by ruling epistemes of thought (and governing modes of 'unthinking'). Diehard supporters of Foucault insist that such an interpretation is unfair because Foucault regularly championed the possibilities of resistance to normalizing discourse and praxis (and to naturalizing scopic drives) as has been registered in several of the other dozen points within this chapter. At face value, the projections embodied in the discourse and the praxis of tourism can fast impose a disjunctive temporality over populations (where, typically, gazing tourists are modern and 'with it', and visiting populations are premodern and 'without'. But once more, Savener notes that there are always Foucauldian options of resistance for the seemingly disempowered or marginalized. Pattison concurs: in Africa, the widespread presence of the ubuntu philosophy enables African groups, communities and individuals to constantly forge new identities in relation to other populations. To Pattison, such acts of creative subjectivity are not just the preserve of (stereotypically) the well-heeled, mobile tourist, they are also part of the imaginative dialogue of supposedly suppressed local/Indigenous populations. Identity dialectics, like eye dialectics, are rather protean.

Dimension 12: the creation/invention of 'totalized' objects

The observations being made for this 12th and last dimension compose something of a recap for much of what has been stated under the previous 11 dimensions of interpretation about the Foucauldian scopic drive of institutions. An over-hasty application of *le regard* might suggest that (in tourism) the agency and authority of normalizing discourse and naturalizing praxis regularly produces totalized objects that are difficult to escape from under. But perhaps, again, such an assessment does injustice to both the capacity of the subjugated to reposition themselves through the operating discourse and modes of practice – and to supposedly institutionalized individuals to reflexively reconstitute themselves 'ethically' (in the Foucauldian sense of life and being as 'a work of art'). At least two of the contributors to Moufakkir and Reisinger get close to the creative possibilities. To Ankor and Wearing, the impositions of culture, of society and social groups (and, implicitly of institutions) may constitute governing practices of subjectivity, but they can always be resisted through inventive/creative action. And to Ankor and Wearing, tourism is a very potent field in which the totalization of received identities can be resisted: it is a strong realm where the self can become 'Other'. O'Regan takes the issue further. To him – again informed by Borad – researchers in Tourism Studies have too readily tended to link notions of agency with fixed notions of subjectivity and intentionality. Thus identities can be formed and reformed relationally and dynamically. They can quickly and performatively cross boundaries of perceived understanding. And where subjects can be recreated or invented, so can the objects of place or the objects of destinations. Such is the intra-active potential of the host–guest gaze, and of the other gazes of tourism.

Reflections on the Scopic Drive Glossary: Illustrative Coverage of the Contributors to the 10 Foucauldian Concepts from Chapter 1 (Hollinshead and Kuon)

Glossary term 1: agents of normalcy

O'Regan supports further work on Foucauldian technologies of the self, which clearly have a bearing on the role and function of the self as an agent-of-normalcy. Bunten supports deeper scrutiny of the alienated positions that Indigenous people find themselves in when their products are used for capitalist purposes not necessarily related to their own engagement at the tourism 'site' or 'project' in question. Wu and Pearce – in seeking to use social reproduction theory – note the commonplace ways in which the work of individuals and institutions in tourism can have profound world-making

effects, but seem to be oblivious to the strongly developing in-field literature in Tourism Studies, *per se.*

Glossary term 2: carceral society

O'Regan is implicitly dubious that tourism indeed contributes a carceral society these days in which the options of hosts and guests are heavily regulated: he maintains that opportunities for display and visitation are much more fluid and nomadic for all parties. Pattison is of a like mind to O'Regan, and thinks the arena of tourism nowadays provides ample scope for Indigenous or entrant populations (removed from received seats of mediation) to continuously negotiate their involvement as 'hosts'. And though so much of the promotion of projection of tourism focuses upon 'bodies' or 'bodily display', Hottola implicitly suggests that we are still immoderate in our understanding of how the dynamisms of the gaze translate into a or the materiality of power on or onto the bodies of individuals. Inherently, there is so much still to analyse about the ways in which (for instance) women travellers are contextually and/or situationally exploited in all sorts of tourism settings.

Glossary term 3: discourse

Moufakkir (2006) is keen to promote much more work on the discourse and praxis of tourism to particularly map the social and psychological relevances of that discourse. Ugelvik has set up an imaginative comparison of the gaze of hotel staff (in tourism) with that of correctional staff (in prisons), thereby aiming to get close to Foucault's original insights on *le regard*. And his 'deep hanging out' approaches deserve to be expanded to futher realms of application elsewhere in tourism and travel. Sadly, for the present, like a good number of researchers in Tourism Management/Tourism Studies he does not present a 'demonstrable critique' of found discourse or provide a telling rich-in-evidence scrutiny of encountered praxis.

Glossary term 4: dominance

Pattison readily acknowledges that large dominances (and large suppressions!) come freighted with the tourist gaze, but is adamant that the host gaze (and implicitly the visitor's gaze) is not as rigid as Foucauldian thought might suggest – in his own experience in Africa. Savener (writing about Panama) echoes Pattison, and reminds that while there may be clear dominances (and suppressions) in a given place at a given time through the working (for instance) of processes of commodification, that battle over the commodified form is not (never?) the only gazing game in town!

Glossary term 5: the clinical gaze

In writing about tourism development in Gambia, Pattison adopts a strong Foucauldian line concerning the force of relational power (power/knowledge) as a productive machinery. O'Regan is also keen to apply Foucault's 'post-Althusserian notions' of the governing apparatuses of tourism management and development as technologies of subjectivation, though he is keen to punctuate that Foucauldian understanding about productive power (power/knowledge) with Borad's notion of governing apparatuses as 'physical-conceptual devices' which are much more open-ended in what they productively allow and productively help fertilize. To O'Regan, it is important to see the work of the governing apparatuses of tourism as material-discursive practices (again, after Borad), which are not so much fixed and static (as Foucauldian apparatuses of power/knowledge would normally be seen to be), but are much more responsive to dynamic 'rearrangements, rearticulations and other reworking'.

Glossary term 6: historical meaning

To Bunten, the unenquiring presence and leverage of all sorts of middle-men in the tourism marketplace indeed enables old, stale and uninformed outlooks on and over 'the other' to perpetuate. All too axiomatically, this rhetoric of tradition and primitivity tends to cultivate the hope or desire amongst tourists that they can indeed see and access 'the native world' in its 'true' primal state (Bunten). O'Regan tends to concur with Bunten about the limited character of the generalized scopic drive of tourism, a drive which, following Sugrue, merely deals in terms of its own held awarenesses in a rehearsed (and contained) geography of locations, positions and routes. And though so much of the promotion of projection of tourism focuses upon 'bodies' or 'bodily display', Hottola implicitly suggests that we are still immoderate in our understanding of how the dynamisms of the gaze translate into a or the materiality of power on or onto the bodies of individuals. Inherently, there is so much still to analyse about the ways in which (for instance) women travellers are contextually and/or situationally exploited in all sorts of tourism settings.

Glossary term 7: micro-power

A number of the contributors to this book implicitly tend to suggest that Foucault's verdict that individuals (who work in closely regulated institutions or purblind organizations) have little scope for individual action is not entirely supportable. In covering 'the Indigenous host gaze' present in Alaska, Bunten notes that Indigenous guides become very skilled at 'deep acting' in self-inducing 'real feelings' to consciously manage and manipulate the host gaze: they are not Foucauldian dupes to it. In analysing the orientation of the tourism industry in Israel to Russian and other tourists, Canziani and Francioni register the point that individuals who work in the travel trade are not only subject to the governing normalizations of their own home institution or home organization, they are also subject to the standards and assumptions of third party bodies (be they governmental, media, professional or whatever), which tends to dissipate the authority of singular scopic drives. But how controlled are those individuals who work for Tourism Studies research institutions rather than for Tourism Management operational bodies? Moufakkir is on the case (via his concept of the bystanding third gaze): watch this space in the second edition of this book, perhaps!

Glossary Term 8: panopticism

Clearly, the bodyweight of contributors to Moufakkir and Reisinger believe that the seductive authority of promotion and projection in tourism is over-stated: while (at face value) such representational agency is hugely influential (and grossly determinant), individual tourists are actually very skilled at translating those supposedly seductive messages to their own aspirations and interests. Again, tourists are not axiomatically 'unthinking dupes' in the strong Foucauldian sense, it seems. To Gelbman and Collins-Kreiner, it is only early days in terms of the analysis of visitor minscapes vis-à-vis semiotic encoding and decoding. To O'Regan, much more deep critique is required to understand how particular tourists act 'in the world' and personally translate the symbols and significations they receive about destinations. The travel trade and the Tourism Studies research field is raw in its appreciation of the ways manifest and potential tourists use the knowledge they receive about place and space to differentially become (O'Regan). And though so much of the promotion of projection of tourism focuses upon 'bodies' or 'bodily display', Hottola implicitly suggests that we are still immoderate in our understanding of how the dynamisms of the gaze translate into a or the materiality of power on or onto the bodies of individuals. Inherently, there is so much still to analyse about the ways in which (for instance) women travellers are contextually and/or situationally exploited in all sorts of tourism settings.

References

Burchell, G., Gordon, C. and Miller, P. (1991) *The Foucault Effect: Studies in Governmentality*. University of Chicago Press, Chicago, IL.
Edwards, E. (1996) Postcards: greetings from another world. In: Selwyn, T. (ed.) *The Tourist Image: Myths and Myth Making in Tourism*. John Wiley, Chichester, pp. 197–222.
Fjellman, S.M. (1992) *Vinyl Leaves: Walt Disney World and America*. Westview Press, Boulder, CO.
Hall, C.M. (1996) *Tourism and Politics: Policy, Power and Place*. John Wiley, Chichester.
Hollinshead, K. (1999) Surveillance of the worlds of tourism: Foucault and the eye-of-power. *Tourism Management* 20, 7–23.
Lash, S. and Urry, J. (1994) *Economics of Signs and Space*. Sage, London.
Lindstrom, L. (1990) *Knowledge and Power in a South Pacific Society*. Smithsonian Institution Press, Washington, DC.
Richter, L.K. (1994) The political dimensions of tourism. In: Ritchie J. R. B. and Goeldner, C.R. (eds) *Travel, Tourism, and Hospitality Research: a Handbook for Managers and Researchers*. John Wiley, New York.
Shames, G.W. and Glover, W.G. (1989) *World Class Service*. Intercultural Press, Inc, Yarmouth, MN.
Urry, J. (1990) *The Tourist Gaze: Leisure and Travel in Contemporary Society*. Sage, London.
Urry, J. (1992) The tourist gaze 'revisited'. *American Behavioral Scientist* 36(2), 172–186.

Conclusion

Yvette Reisinger and Omar Moufakkir

There is no doubt that tourism has expanded significantly in recent years. The question arises as to whether the current tourism research adequately explores, theorizes or conceptualizes the complexity inherent in tourism. The argument is that tourism research has not sufficiently embraced the concept of the gaze, particularly from the host perspective. Although numerous researchers have analysed the tourist gaze and the tourist–host relationship these are no longer sufficient to understand the complexity of the tourism experience, which is affected by both the tourist gaze and the host gaze. The experiences of the host and their impact on the tourist and tourist–host relationship become equally important to understanding the whole phenomenon of tourism.

Since the contemporary literature does not go far enough in conceptualizing and explaining the gaze of the host, this volume aimed at deepening its analysis and understanding. Thus, the significance of this book lies in contributing to our understanding of the gaze and its numerous aspects from the perspective of the host. The book identifies the aspects of the host gaze that distinguish it from the tourist gaze and from the conventional gaze encountered. The book identifies different types of host gazes and roles associated with them, as well as various categories of visitor that are recognized in the host gaze. The book analyses important religious, communal, cultural as well as psychological and emotional aspects of the host gaze. It shows how host communities construct, organize and systemize their gaze upon different tourists in different socio-economic, political and cultural environments. The pre-existing cultural images of the host gaze and the differences in the host gaze across various geographical regions and nations are presented. The consequences of the host gaze for the tourists who are its object and for the places that are its object are presented. The host gazes on tourism and tourists on the future are described. It is recognized that the host gaze is a process; it is dynamic, continuously negotiated and adjusted for different audiences to better accommodate guests and themselves. The standardized host–guest dichotomy is destabilized and the hegemonic Western assumptions of the host gaze and representations of 'Other' people and places are challenged. Summaries of the previous chapters are presented below.

Chapter Summaries

In Chapter 1, Hollingshead and Kuon focused upon the foundational concept of

the tourist gaze and explained it in the Foucauldian context as the institutionalized
form of power through which specific
subjects are ruled and regulated. They
explained that the gaze is not so much an
act of seeing, but an act of knowing. The
chapter helped to gain a richer understanding of Foucault's concept of the gaze. However, it also warned readers about the
difficulties that various schools of critical
thought have with the application of Foucauldian analysis.

In Chapter 2, Canziani and Francioni
used role theory to analyse the hosts'
expected performances in terms of hospitable and cultural behaviours, associated with
their occupational and resident roles in destinations. The roles associated with their
destination-contextualized behaviour permits hosts to engage in self-inspection of the
role they engage in. Role-taking and role
behavioural compliance are seen as a form
of internalization of the tourist gaze that, as
in any other social domain, carry the considerable affective baggage of resentment,
guilt, disappointment, or relief associated
with human decisions and can lead to
various emotional outcomes, such as host
defensive tactics, and shifts in host
self-concept.

In Chapter 3, Morrison argued that the
tourist seen as a potential stranger appears
disturbing within the host gaze. The recent
interventions of the Thai state into tourism
policy, efforts to govern visitors and change
the image of Thailand are the responses to
the perceived risks posed by strangers and
a manifestation of particular discourses of
travel and of otherness and governance,
within which desirable and undesirable
visitors emerge. Within the host gaze, each
category of the visitors (desirable and undesirable) is characterized by particular costs
and benefits and risks. This categorization
of visitors allows the host to maximize the
benefits of the desirable and minimize the
costs of the undesirable.

In Chapter 4, Reisinger, Kozak and
Visser showed that cultural errors in the
host interpretations of Russian tourist
behaviour create misperceptions of and dissatisfaction of Turkish hosts. Although it

was implied that only an adequate knowledge of tourists' societal rules can facilitate
hosts' understanding of tourists across cultural boundaries, the cultural relativism
theory doesn't provide a clear answer as to
whether hosts should accept the cultural
norms of tourists and tolerate the behaviour
that is perceived by hosts as inappropriate
and/or unacceptable.

In Chapter 5, Savener analysed tourist–
Indigene interactions in Kuna Yala from a
human and cultural geography perspective.
The historic events contributed to a sense of
communal Kuna dignity and autonomous
independence. The Kuna saw themselves
reflected in tourist's eyes and thus dramatized and brought the elements that interested tourists to the forefront of tourist
consciousness. The Kuna lacked the interest or financial need to serve tourists. The
Kuna gazed upon tourists as a dehumanized
group of people that appeared the same to
them as other tourists. The Kuna reminded
tourists that they were not at home; they
were not necessarily welcome. The tourist
was a visitor and the power balance created
by mass tourism was inverted. Kuna resisted
cultural diffusion and communicated only
in ways that served them.

In Chapter 6, Gelbman and Collins-
Kreiner analysed the manner in which tour
guides in Israel gazed upon the Christian
pilgrim groups. Tour guides' gaze was influenced by religious characteristics and affiliation of the tourists arriving in Israel. The
host gaze indicated the existence of clear
stereotypes among hosts as they gazed on
tourists. Four main types of host gazes were
distinguished that is the initial, distinguishing, overall, and differentiating and analysing gaze. Guides used the initial gaze
(tourists' external appearance) to differentiate between religious and non-religious
tourists and identify their religious affiliations. Guides also used a deeper gaze to treat
tourists according to their religious affiliation. The non-religious tourists were perceived as easier to work with. Since religious
tourists required the hosts to adapt to their
religious rituals and beliefs tour guides felt
that they were more limited in transmitting
intercultural messages to religious tourists

than to secular tourists. Non-religious tourists were preferred because they were open to broader and more varied cultural messages. Guides also developed specialization for members of a particular Christian sect.

In Chapter 7, Pattison proposed for the hosts to use cameras as a tool for recording and reflecting upon the host gaze in rural Gambia. By using cameras the Gambian hosts captured and made visible their own feelings, experiences and understanding of tourists and tourism. The villagers perceived and experienced tourism by communal values and a philosophy of communalism, a collective pursuit of ends shared by members of a community that guided the action of the self and the self's interaction with others. The photographs captured cooperation, social relationships and community cohesiveness. The villagers placed importance on tourism rather than tourists and they understood tourism holistically, as part of the process integrated into the daily functioning of the community. The hosts were not static; they continuously negotiated and worked on relations of power and adjusted their identities to benefit from tourism. The host gaze was a process. The hegemonic Western assumptions of the host gaze and representations of 'Other' people and places were challenged.

In Chapter 8, Bunten argued that the host gaze can change to better accommodate guests and protect them from alienation. While Indigenous tourism workers in Sitka, Alaska felt a sense of pride in sharing their lives and cultural experiences with admiring visitors, they also felt pressure to provide services to visitors compiled with negative stereotypes of the 'Other' and psychological pain associated with the after effects of colonization. By serving visitors who twisted the social outcomes of colonization, Indigenous workers became emotionally drained and exposed to negative stereotypes to justify the inhumane acts of colonization. Although Tribal Tours' workers had negative feelings towards non-native visitors they had to develop sensitivity to the tourist gaze at hosts as colonized 'Other'. To shape the host gaze and develop ideas about tourists, Indigenous workers went

through training to learn about the emotional style of offering the service and the importance of public distancing which require self-deception and deep acting.

In Chapter 9, Wu and Pearce examined the gazes of young Tibetan 'post 80s' on tourism and tourists in the future, as a future livelihood choice, on tourism attraction assets and on preferred tourist groups. Social representation theory (how people see the world) and the sustainable livelihoods framework (defines perceptions and preferences) was used for this purpose. The gaze on tourism as a livelihoods choice identified four subgroups in the host community, such as 'in-betweeners', 'ambivalent supporters', 'alternative supporters' and 'lovers' supporting the notion of the heterogenous nature of tourism community. The young hosts recognized the role of tourism as a part of their livelihoods.

In Chapter 10, Lee and Gretzel examined Thai and Cambodian locals' gazes on the US and South Korean short-term mission travellers. Three types of host gazes were identified. The long-term missionaries (LTM) sent by US and Korean churches treated short-term missionaries (STM) like students or family members who needed to learn about the local culture and be guided in their interactions with local residents. The host gazes were mediated by LTM missionaries who were neither locals nor travellers.

In Chapter 11, O'Regan questioned the traditional division between hosts and guests and the claims that there is no genuine opportunity for a fruitful encounter between tourists and hosts. The chapter illuminated the intertwinedness of individuals, who, both in their travel and everyday activities and behaviour, created a structure of feeling and relations around themselves moving towards the other in appreciation and invitation. The standardized host–guest dichotomy was challenged and destabilized.

In Chapter 12, Ankor and Wearing argued that the gaze is more than a tool of observation but it is fundamental to concepts of being and existence. The tourist–host reciprocal encounter is formed separately and it changes both in different ways through each one's gaze. It creates meaning through the process of social relationships and generates identities from social and cultural contexts. The 'Other' is a part of the self developed through experiences of encounter. Tourism thus offers an opportunity for discovery of the self through accepting alternative ways of seeing and being in the world.

In Chapter 13, Ugelvik, who compared the hotel bellman and the prison officer gaze, argued that although both gazes are different, they also have a common way of seeing that balances professional customer care with specific control duties. The hotel bellman sorts and evaluates their guests searching for the needs they may have and their potential as a source of tips, as well as the security issues. This 'hospitality' gaze is, nevertheless, discriminating and controlling. Although in both the prison and the hotel the professional gaze is concerned with the well-being of the guests/prisoners, both gazes are controlling and employing power. Both gazes focus on the needs of Others, partly on the risks these Others represent.

In Chapter 14, Moufakkir proposed a third gaze to understand the *whys* of the host gaze from a psychoanalytical perspective. The third gaze is the gaze of the tourism academic upon the gaze of the tourism gaze. It is the gaze of the gazer upon the gaze of the gazer gazing upon the object of the gaze. This gaze is characterized by cultural narcissism and territoriality and is value-laden and governed by its own voice.

In Chapter 15, Hottola discussed the effect of stereotyping on the gaze of the male host in India and Ski Lanka, and documented the extent to which culture and values have on the production and perpetuation of the 'sexualized' gaze. He also maintained that the gaze can be interpreted and negotiated by the gazed upon in different ways, thereby suggesting that the object of the gaze (the female Western traveller) can, in some situations, become an active subject responding to the gaze.

In Chapter 16, Hollinshead and Chunxiao Hou offered a comprehensive and powerful synthesis, not only of the book, but also, and more importantly, of the Foucauldian gaze and its use in tourism. This chapter builds on Chapter 1. In this chapter, the authors revisit the tourist gaze and the host gaze in relation to Foucault's gaze to offer an insightful and 'practical' analysis of the meaning of the gaze in general and its meaning in and to tourism. The authors' fresh security of the gaze and their treatment of the chapters in this book shed more light on the different gazes that have been covered in the preceding chapters. Their observations on the Foucauldian scopic drive vis-á-vis Hollinshead's (2000) 12 dimensions of and about the tourism gaze is groundbreaking.

To conclude, following the themes discussed in this book, more work is required to support the findings proposed here, and to develop new theoretical perspectives that can explain societal phenomena in our increasingly globalized world. New *gazed* host gaze studies can help us to move on from the conventional gaze towards a deconstruction of the gaze in tourism and in society.

Index